The Business of Tourism

The Business of Tourism

J Christopher Holloway

Third edition

Pitman

PITMAN PUBLISHING
128 Long Acre, London WC2E 9AN

A Division of Longman Group UK Limited

© J C Holloway 1989

Third edition first published in Great Britain 1989
Reprinted 1990

British Library Cataloguing in Publication Data
Holloway, J. Christopher
    The business of tourism. – 3rd ed.
    1. Tourism
    I. Title
    338.4′791

ISBN 0 273 03026 4

Typeset by C. R. Barber & Partners (Highlands) Ltd,
Fort William, Scotland.
Printed and bound in Great Britain.

Contents

Preface to the third edition

Britain has a well-deserved international reputation for its success in marketing tourism, both as a destination for incoming tourism and as a country generating tourism to overseas destinations. Indeed, both the original concept of the package tour, introduced by Thomas Cook in the middle of the nineteenth century, and its modern equivalent using air charters, introduced in the middle of the twentieth century, were British in origin. The inclusive tour concept has since been emulated by the developed nations to a point where international tourism has become one of the strongest growth industries in the world. The potential for growth in this field, however, has hardly been tapped. Even in Britain, only 35 per cent of the population travels abroad in any one year, and the number of international tourists from the developing nations represents only a tiny minority of their populations.

Yet increases in leisure time, cheaper travel and rising curiosity about other lands, peoples and ways of life promise a bright future for the tourism industry in the twenty-first century.

This rosy picture is not without its blacker side, however. The phenomenon of mass tourism in the second half of the twentieth century, with its accompanying pollution, congestion and human relations problems, is increasingly criticised by observers.

Whether tourism is to be seen as a force for good or evil in the world is a subject of endless debate. What is unquestionable, though, is that nations will have to come to terms with international tourism, and its effects must be taken into account in the planning of their economies. The needs of tourists and residents alike must be satisfied and their often conflicting interests reconciled. In this sense an understanding of tourism is essential for those involved in central or local government planning.

But tourism is also a business, like any other business, and one which has become increasingly multinational in structure and organisation over the past 20 years. Tourism has also become a highly competitive industry, both within and between the generating countries.

The importance of travel and tourism as a field of study is emphasised by the decision of the Business and Technician Education Council (BTEC) in 1989 to validate the first National Diploma in Travel and Tourism, as distinct from the business and finance courses with travel and tourism options which had until then been the principal formal educational qualification in this field. The new course, designed in consultation with the industry and ABTA's National Training Board, reflects changing views which now favour the study of travel and tourism as a stand-alone discipline. At higher education level, too, the subject has finally achieved recognition as a field worthy of study in its own right, with the introduction of first degrees in tourism validated by the Council for National Academic Awards (CNAA).

At the same time, a more instrumental approach to the study of tourism is noticeable in recent years, with emphasis moving away from the broad educational perspective in favour of the acquisition of job specific skills and competences, under the influence of bodies like the NCVQ (National Council for Vocational Qualifications). The ITT's (Institute of Travel and Tourism) imposition of membership through examinations has failed to stem an increasing flow of experienced practitioners willing to put their knowledge to a formal test, while the larger travel companies are showing, if not enthusiasm, then guarded support for formal educational qualifications in their recruitment.

Against this background, the purpose of this book remains that of providing a sound foundation in the principles of business operations in travel and tourism. It offers a framework for problem solving and analysis in business, while encouraging those who seek to make their career in tourism to be mindful of their social responsibility towards its development.

The book will appeal particularly to those students following the new BTEC National Diploma in Travel and Tourism, and to those following BTEC business and finance courses with options in travel and tourism at both National and Higher National level. It can be recommended to those following college diploma courses in tourism, and tourism options on BTEC Leisure Studies and Hotel and Catering courses, as well as professional courses such as HCIMA; as an introductory text for students on degree and postgraduate tourism courses; and as a useful adjunct to study for professional City and Guilds skills courses, for those seeking to widen their perspective of the industry. The content will also be helpful for others already employed in tourism, who wish to broaden their knowledge of the industry as a whole and appreciate the relationship between their sector of the industry and others.

The book's perspective is essentially British, but the international character of tourism requires also that a wider perspective be adopted at times and there are frequent references to, and comparisons with, tourism in other countries. The tourism business itself is constantly changing and for this reason the training element in tourism work – that is, aspects of the business such as the travel agency skills of airline fare construction, ticket issuing and sales returns – are not dealt with in this

7

book. It is the author's belief that this need is best met by specialist publications which can be continuously amended and updated, complementing the work of skilled teachers in the classroom. The author also takes the view that certain specialist subjects applicable to tourism are best treated in separate texts, or again they run the risk of superficiality. For example, tourism marketing embraces knowledge and skills such as salesmanship, promotion, advertising and public relations, and this knowledge is best acquired through specialist texts; the author has written a companion text for this purpose, *Marketing for Tourism* (J C Holloway and R V Plant, Pitman) to which the interested reader is directed. The same may be said for tourism planning, a subject essential for those planning to work in the public sector of tourism, and for travel geography, which will provide students with a more comprehensive background to the factors leading to the development of tourist resorts and attractions.

The structure of the book has been designed to help students in the systematic study of tourism as a business. The introductory chapters deal with the nature and significance of tourism and its historical development, with particular reference to the growth of mass tourism in the present century. This is followed in Chapter 4 by an examination of the business of tourism by reference to the general structure and organisation of the industry, and in the subsequent seven chapters by detailed examination of each sector of the industry in turn. The final two chapters are concerned with the role of public sector tourism and the impact of tourism in economic and social terms, with a look ahead to tourism in the twenty-first century.

It will be apparent to readers that a certain amount of repetition occurs throughout the chapters. This is intentional. Compartmentalising knowledge facilitates learning, so a sectoral approach has been taken in examining the industry and the way it operates. However, these sectors are interdependent and one cannot examine them entirely discretely. Rather than to cross-reference the material, which would require students to skim backwards and forwards through the book, wherever possible the issues are examined in their entirety as they arise.

Many earlier works have gone to influence the structure and content of this book. In particular, one must cite the important contribution to tourism education made by A J Burkart and S Medlik in their *Tourism: Past, Present and Future* (Heinemann, 1981) which has become a standard text for tourism students over the past decade. My views and knowledge have also been shaped by my work in the tourism industry – in shipping, tour operating and retail travel – and in my subsequent teaching of tourism, and I owe a debt of gratitude to former employers and students, all of whom have in their own way helped to make this book possible.

Many individuals working in the travel industry have helped in the preparation of this edition, and my thanks go to them collectively for their contribution. I am particularly grateful to Ron Plant of Profit From Travel, who took the trouble to scour the text and identify points of change that have occurred since the previous edition, as well as picking up the occasional error or omission. Those that remain are, of course, all my own.

1 An introduction to tourism

Chapter objectives: After studying this chapter, you should be able to:

- define what is meant by tourism, both conceptually and technically;
- explain the characteristics of the tourist product;
- list the various types of tourist destination, and identify the attractions of each;
- explain why tourist destinations are subject to
- changing fortunes;
- understand the purpose of statistical measurement of tourism and outline the main methods of gathering such data; and
- demonstrate the importance of tourism to a nation's economy.

DEFINING TOURISM

In a book dealing with tourism, it is sensible to begin by defining exactly what is meant by the term before we go on to examine the different forms which tourism can take. In fact, the task of defining tourism is not nearly so easy as it may appear.

While it is relatively easy to agree on technical definitions of particular categories of tourism or tourist, the wider concept is ill-defined. Firstly, it is important to recognise that tourism is just one form of recreation, along with sports activities, hobbies and pastimes, and all of these are discretionary uses of our leisure time. Tourism usually incurs expenditure, although not *necessarily* so; a cyclist or hiker out for a camping weekend and carrying his own food may contribute nothing to the tourism revenue of a region. Many other examples could be cited where tourism expenditure is minimal. We can say, then, that tourism is one aspect of leisure usually, but not always, incurring expense on the part of the participant.

Tourism is further defined as the movement of people away from their normal place of residence. Here we find our first problem. Should shoppers travelling from, say, Bristol to Bath, a distance of 12 miles, be considered tourists? And is it the *purpose* or the *distance* which is the determining factor? Just how far must people be expected to travel before they can be counted as tourists for the purposes of official records? Clearly, our definition should be specific.

One of the first attempts to define tourism was that of Professors Hunziker and Krapf of Berne University. They held that tourism should be defined as 'the sum of the phenomena and relationships arising from the travel and stay of non-residents, in so far as they do not lead to permanent residence and are not connected to any earning activity'. This definition helps to distinguish tourism from migration, but it makes the assumption that it must necessarily include both *travel* and *stay*, thus precluding day tours. It would also appear to exclude business travel, which *is* connected with an earning activity, even if that income is not earned in the destination country. Moreover, it is difficult to distinguish between business and pleasure travel since so many business trips combine the two.

In 1937 the League of Nations recommended a definition be adopted of a 'tourist' as one who travels for a period of 24 hours or more in a country other than that in which he usually resides. This was held to include persons travelling for pleasure, domestic reasons or health, persons travelling to meetings or on business, and persons visiting a country on a cruise vessel (even if for less than 24 hours). The principal weakness here is that it ignores the movement of domestic tourists. Later the United Nations Conference on International Travel and Tourism, held in Rome in 1963, considered recommendations put forward by the IUOTO (now the World Tourism Organisation) and agreed to the term 'visitors' to describe 'any person visiting a country other than that in which he has his usual place of residence, for any reason other than following an occupation, remunerated from within the country visited'.

This definition was to cover two classes of visitors:

(*a*) *Tourists*, who were classed as temporary visitors staying at least 24 hours, whose purpose could be classified as leisure (whether for recreation, health, sport, holiday, study or religion), or business, family, mission or meeting;

(*b*) *Excursionists*, who were classed as temporary visitors staying less than 24 hours, including cruise travellers but excluding travellers in transit.

Once again the definition becomes overly restrictive in failing to take domestic tourism into account. The inclusion of 'study' in this definition is an interesting one since it is often excluded in later definitions, as are courses of education.

A working party for the proposed Institute of Tourism in Britain (now the Tourism Society) attempted to clarify the concept, and reported in 1976: 'Tourism is the temporary short-term movement of people to

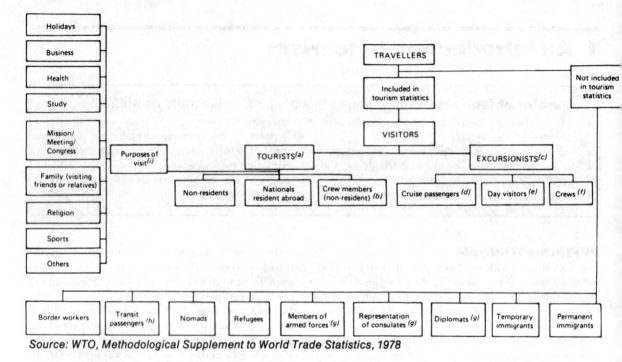

Source: WTO, Methodological Supplement to World Trade Statistics, 1978

Fig 1.1 Classification of travellers (a) Visitors who spend at least one night in the country visited. (b) Foreign air or ship crews docked or in lay over and who used the accommodation establishments of the country visited. (c) Visitors who do not spend at least one night in the country visited although they might visit the country during one day or more and return to their ship or train to sleep. (d) Normally included in excursionists. Separate classification of these visitors is nevertheless preferable. (e) Visitors who come and leave the same day. (f) Crews who are not residents of the country visited and who stay in the country for the day. (g) When they travel from their country of origin to the duty station and vice versa. (h) Who do not leave the transit area of the airport or the port in certain countries, transit may involve a stay of one day or more. In this case they should be included in the visitor statistics. (i) Main purposes of visit as defined by the Rome Conference (1963).

destinations outside the places where they normally live and work, and activities during their stay at these destinations; it includes movement for all purposes, as well as day visits or excursions.'

This broader definition was reformulated slightly without losing any of its simplicity at the International Conference on Leisure–Recreation–Tourism, held by the AIEST and the Tourism Society in Cardiff in 1981: 'Tourism may be defined in terms of particular activities selected by choice and undertaken outside the home environment. Tourism may or may not involve overnight stays away from home.'

The above definitions have been quoted at length because they reveal how broadly the concept of tourism must be defined in order to embrace all forms of the phenomenon. Indeed, the final definition could be criticised on the grounds that, unless the activities involved are more clearly specified, it could be applied equally to burglary or any of a hundred other activities! Here, no guidance on the particular activities is offered, nor does it get us any nearer the solution as to how far away a tourist must travel from his home base before he

can be termed as such. Indeed, with the growth of second home owners, who in some cases spend considerable periods of time away from their main homes, and timeshare owners, a tourist is no longer necessarily 'outside the home environment'.

Figure 1.1 illustrates the guidelines produced by the WTO to categorise travellers for statistical purposes. The loopholes in the definitions remain, however. Even attempts to classify tourists as those travelling for purposes unconnected with employment can be misleading if one looks at the social consequences of tourism. Ruth Pape has drawn attention to the case of nurses in the United States who, after qualifying, gravitate to California for their first jobs, since employment is easily found and they can enjoy the benefits of the leisure facilities which California offers. They may spend a year or more in this job before moving on, but the important point is that they have been motivated to come to that area not because of the work but because of the area's attraction to tourists. Many similar examples could be given, of young working people working their way around the world (a kind of twentieth century Grand Tour?), or workers who seek summer jobs in the seaside resorts of the English South Coast or the French campsites.

Finally, there is a growing group of those who retire abroad in order to benefit from the lower costs of living in the foreign country. Britons moving to the south of Spain, or Americans moving into Mexico on retirement, will often retain their main homes in their country of origin while spending a large part of their year abroad. Once again, their motivation is not simply lower costs of living but the enjoyment of climate and all those facilities which attract tourists to the same resorts.

Conceptually, then, to define tourism precisely is a difficult if not impossible task. To produce a technical definition for statistical purposes is less problematic. As long as it is clear what the data comprises, and one compares like with like, whether inter-regionally or internationally, we can leave the conceptual discussion to academics. With the advent of twentieth century mass tourism, perhaps the most accurate definition of a tourist is 'someone who travels to see something different, and then complains when he finds things are not the same'!

THE TOURIST PRODUCT

Having attempted to define tourism, we can now look at the tourist product itself. The first characteristic of the product to note is that it is a service rather than a tangible good. Its intangibility poses problems for those concerned in marketing tourism. It cannot, for example, be inspected by prospective purchasers before they buy, as can a washing machine, a hi-fi or other consumer durable. The purchase of a package tour is a speculative investment involving a high degree of trust on the part of the purchaser.

It has often been said that selling holidays is 'selling dreams', and this is to a great extent true. When a tourist buys a package tour abroad, he is buying more than a simple collection of services, i.e. aircraft seat, hotel room, three meals a day and the opportunity to sit on a sunny beach; he is also buying the temporary use of a strange environment, incorporating novel geographical features – old world towns, tropical landscapes – plus the culture and heritage of the region and other intangible benefits such as service, atmosphere, hospitality. The planning and anticipation of the holiday may be as much a part of its enjoyment as is the trip itself, and the later recalling of the experience and the reviewing of slides or photos is an added bonus. The product is therefore largely psychological in its attractions.

The challenge for the marketer of tourism is to make the dream equal the reality. The difficulty in achieving this is that tourism is not a homogeneous product; that is, it tends to vary in standard and quality over time,

unlike, say, the production of a television set. A package tour, or even a flight on an aircraft, cannot be consistently of equal standard. A bumpy flight can change an enjoyable travel experience into a nightmare, and a holiday at the seaside can be ruined by a prolonged rainy spell. Because a tour comprises a compendium of different products, an added difficulty in maintaining standards is that each element of the product should be of broadly similar quality; a good room and service at a hotel may be spoiled by poor food, or the experience of an excellent hotel may be marred by a disappointing flight to the destination. An element of chance is always present in the purchase of any service, and where the purchase must precede the actual consumption of the product, as is the case with tourism, the risk for the consumer is heightened.

Another characteristic of tourism is that it cannot be brought to the consumer; rather, the consumer must be taken to his product. In the short term, at least, the supply of this product is fixed; the number of hotel bedrooms available at a particular resort cannot be varied to meet the changing demands of holidaymakers during a particular season. The unsold hotel room or aircraft seat cannot be stored for later sale, as is the case with tangible products; hence great efforts are made to fill hotel rooms and aircraft by, for example, heavily discounting the prices of these products at the last minute. If the market demand changes, as it does frequently in the field of tourism, the supply of tourism products may take time to adapt – a hotel is built to last for many years and must remain profitable over that period. These problems, unique to tourism, call for considerable ingenuity on the part of those responsible for marketing it.

THE NATURE OF A TOUR

To analyse the topic of tourism systematically, it will be helpful at this point to examine more closely the characteristics of a tour under five broad categories.

The motivation for touring

Motivation identifies first the purposes of the visit. There are a number of recognised categories of purpose, the most common of these being:

(a) holiday (including visits to friends and relatives, known as VFR travel);
(b) business (including meetings, conferences, etc.); and
(c) other (including study, religious pilgrimages, health, etc.).

It is important to distinguish between each purpose of visit because the characteristics of each will differ. Business travel will differ from holiday travel in that the businessman has little discretion in his choice of destination or the timing of his trip. Business trips frequently have to be arranged at short notice to offices and dealers overseas, and for brief periods of time. Businesspeople need the convenience of frequent, regular transport, efficient service and good facilities at their destination. Because their company will be paying for the tour, they are less concerned about the price for these facilities; higher prices will not seriously impair their travel plans nor would lower prices encourage them to travel more frequently – we can say, therefore, that business travel is relatively *price inelastic*. Holiday travel, however, is highly *price elastic*: lower prices *will* encourage an increase in the number of holidaymakers generally and will encourage other holidaymakers to switch their destinations. Holiday travellers will be prepared to delay their travel, or will book well in advance of their travel dates, if this means that they can substantially reduce their costs.

We therefore need to identify the reasons why a specific type of holiday or resort is chosen. Different markets look for different qualities in the same resort; a ski resort, for example, may be selected because of its excellent slopes and sporting facilities, because of its healthy mountain air, or because of the social life which it offers to skiers and non-skiers alike.

The characteristics of the tour

These define what kind of visit is made and to where. First, one can distinguish between *domestic* tourism and *international* tourism. The former refers to travel taken exclusively within the national boundaries of the traveller's country. The decision to take one's holiday within the borders of one's own country is an important economic one since it will affect the balance of payments and reduce the outflow of money from that country.

Next, the kind of visit should be determined. Is it to be to a seaside resort, mountain resort, country town, health spa, or major city? Is it to be a single centre visit, multicentre visit (involving a stopover at two or more places) or a touring visit involving extensive travel with brief overnight stays along the route? Or it could mean a sea cruise, in which case a decision has to be made as to whether to count this as international travel if the vessel visits foreign ports.

The length of time spent on the visit needs to be identified next. A trip that does not involve an overnight stay is termed a day trip or excursion. Expenditure by day trippers is generally less than that of overnight visitors and the statistical measurement of these forms of tourism is often collected separately. A visitor who stops at least one night at a destination is termed a tourist, as opposed to an excursionist, but he can, of course, in turn make day trips to other destinations from his base; indeed, a domestic tourist to, say, Eastbourne, may make a day excursion to France and in doing so becomes an international visitor for the purposes of the records of that country.

Again, for the purposes of statistical measurement we shall need to define some maximum length of stay, beyond which a visitor should no longer be considered a tourist for the records but take on the role of 'resident'. This maximum figure must of necessity be an arbitrary one, but is generally accepted as one year.

Mode of tour organisation

This further qualifies the form which the tour takes. A tour may be *independent* or *packaged*. A package tour (more correctly called an 'inclusive tour') is an arrangement in which transport and accommodation is purchased by the tourist at an all-inclusive price and the price of the individual elements cannot be determined by the purchaser himself. The tour operator who organises the package tour programme purchases transport and hotel accommodation in advance, generally obtaining these at a lower price because he is buying them in bulk, and he then sells his tours individually to holidaymakers, direct or through travel agents. By contrast, an independent tour is one in which the tourist purchases these facilities separately, either making reservations in advance through a travel agent or *ad hoc* on route during his tour.

Tourists purchasing inclusive tours may do so on the basis of either individual or group travel. An independent inclusive tour is one in which the tourist travels to his destination individually, while on a group inclusive tour he will travel in company with other tourists who have purchased the same programme. The abbreviations IIT and GIT are used respectively to describe these two forms of package tour where scheduled airline flights are used.

The composition of the tour

This consists of the elements comprising the visit. All tourism involves travel away from one's usual place of residence, as we have seen, and in the case of 'tourists' as opposed to 'excursionists' it will also include food and accommodation. So we must here identify the form of travel – air, sea, road or rail – that will be used. If air transport is involved, is it charter or scheduled service? If an overnight stay, will this be in a hotel, guest house, campsite or self-catering facility? How will the passenger travel between airport and hotel – by coach, private taxi or airport limousine? A package tour will normally comprise transport, accommodation and transfers, but in some cases additional services may be provided in the programme, such as car hire at the destination, excursions by coach or theatre entertainment.

Fig 1.2 Traditional tourism: sun, sea and sand
(*Courtesy Thomson Holidays*)

The characteristics of the tourist

An analysis of tourism must also include an analysis of the tourist himself. We have already distinguished between holidaymakers and businesspeople. Now we need to identify the tourist by nationality, by socioeconomic background (social class and life-style), by sex and age. What stage of their life-cycle are they in? What are their personality characteristics?

Such information is valuable not only for the purpose of record keeping. It will also help to shed light on the reasons why people travel and how patterns of travel differ between different markets. The more that is known about these factors, the more effectively will those in the industry be able to meet the needs of their customers and develop appropriate strategies to promote their products in different markets.

THE TOURIST DESTINATION

We can now examine the tourist destination itself. The success of a tourist destination depends upon the interrelationship of three basic factors: its attractions; its amenities (or facilities); and its accessibility for tourists.

Attractions

The principal appeal of a destination is the attraction or aggregate of attractions which the destination offers. Cataloguing and analysing these attractions is no easy matter, especially when one recognises that what appeals to one tourist may actually deter another.

We can start by distinguishing between site and event attractions. A site attraction is one in which the destination itself exercises appeal, while an event attraction is one in which tourists are drawn to the destination largely or solely because of what is taking place there. A site attraction may be a country, a geographical region such as the Alps or the Lake District, a city, resort, or even a specific building. Examples of event attractions include exhibitions and festivals such as the Edinburgh Festival, sports events such as the Olympic Games, or an international conference. The success of event attractions is often multiplied if the site is an attraction in its own right.

We must now distinguish between natural and man-made (or purpose-built) attractions. Natural attractions include beaches, mountains, open countryside or game parks; climatic features such as sunshine and pure air; unusual flora and fauna; and 'spectacles' such as Niagara Falls or the Grand Canyon. Man-made attractions include buildings of historical or architectural interest; holiday camps; or 'theme parks' such as Disneyworld in the USA or Thorpe Park in England.

Obviously, the success of many tourist destinations will depend upon the combination of man-made and natural attractions which they have to offer; a rural manor house may be as much an attraction because of its setting as its architecture, and of course a holiday camp must be sited in an area which is also attractive for its climate and location. The success of the early spas rested on their ability to combine man-made attractions with the supposed medical benefits of the natural springs, and a ski resort requires both the good geographical features of weather and mountain slopes and the construction of adequate ski-runs, ski-lifts and 'après-ski' entertainment.

Site attractions may be *nodal* or *linear* in character. A nodal destination is one in which the attractions of the area are closely grouped geographically; although tourists may make day excursions out of the region, their holiday is centred on a particular resort or area which provides most of the attractions and amenities they

Fig 1.3 New tourism: history and heritage –
Edinburgh Military Tattoo
(*Courtesy Scottish Tourist Board*)

require. Seaside resorts and cities are examples of nodal attractions, this making them ideal as destinations to be packaged by the tour operators. This has led to the concept of 'honeypot' tourism development, in which tourism planners concentrate the development of tourism resources, whether in the construction of new resorts or the embellishment of existing ones. Aviemore in Scotland is an example of recent nodal tourism development – a purpose-built winter and summer holiday resort with all its attractions and amenities closely grouped. This development helps to preserve the natural beauty of the unexploited countryside.

Linear tourism is that in which the attractions are spread over a wide geographical area, with no obvious centres of interest. Examples include the Shenandoah Valley in the USA, and the natural beauty of the Highlands of Scotland or the Scandinavian countryside. Such destinations lend themselves best to touring holidays by coach or private car with accommodation in motels or private bed-and-breakfast facilities, since such mobile tourists are likely to stay only one or two nights at each stopover point.

Readers are reminded that much of the attraction of a destination is intangible, depending upon the image which the potential tourist has of it. India will be seen by one group of travellers as an outstanding attraction because of its unusual scenery and buildings, its strange culture and traditions, but others will reject the country as a potential destination because of its poverty or its alien culture. The image of a destination, whether favourable or unfavourable, tends to be built up over the course of many years. Thus for many continental Europeans, Britain is still seen as a fog-engulfed, rain-battered island noted for the reserve of its inhabitants, an image frequently stereotyped in the media, which increases the National Tourist Office's difficulty in selling the country.

Amenities

However attractive a destination, its potential for tourism will be limited unless the basic amenities which a tourist requires are provided. Essentially this means accommodation and food, but will include local transport and entertainment at the site. Amenities will differ according to the attraction of the site; at the Grand Canyon, for example, it would clearly detract from the beauty of the attraction to over-develop the rim with tourist hotels similar to those built in beach resorts. It should also be recognised that sometimes the amenity is itself the principal attraction, as is the case when a resort hotel is built to offer every conceivable on-site entertainment in a previously unexploited region. An area famed for its regional food may also attract gourmets to its restaurants, which then become not just amenities but the attraction themselves.

Accessibility

A third factor which must be present to attract tourists is ease of access to the destination. While the more intrepid explorers may be prepared to put themselves to great inconvenience to see some of the great scenic attractions of the world, a destination will not attract mass tourists until it is readily accessible, regardless of the amenities it may have to offer. In this sense 'readily accessible' means having regular and convenient forms of transport, in terms of time/distance, to the country from the generating country, and all at a reasonable price. If private transport is to be the means of access, tourism flow will depend upon adequate roads, petrol stations, etc. Here, the importance of amenities designed to facilitate accessibility becomes apparent – good railways and coach services, airports and sea ports.

On the other hand, if access becomes too easy this may result in over-demand and congestion, making the destination less attractive to tourists. The introduction of new motorways in Britain has opened up the Lake District and the West Country to motorists in a way not possible before, leading to increasing numbers of day trippers and severe congestion at resorts which are in high demand. It should be noted that the *perception* of accessibility on the part of the traveller is often as important as actual accessibility: many tourists perceive Corfu as being more accessible than Cornwall, in terms of travelling time. Such perceptions undoubtedly affect travel decision-making.

Now that we have looked at the factors motivating tourists to visit certain sites, let us look at two very different examples of resort destinations and explore what it is that makes them successful.

Bath, England

This city firmly established its reputation as a spa over 200 years ago. Its attraction lay initially in the supposed healing properties of its mineral springs, and it became fashionable to 'take the waters' for the sake of one's health at this and other contemporary spas in Britain. Over time it gradually passed from fashionable resort to fashionable place of residence as its social amenities increased. The fine buildings erected in the eighteenth and early nineteenth centuries in turn attracted the attention of the mass tourists of the twentieth century, making the town a popular venue for domestic and foreign tourists alike. Mass tourism has been aided by the provision of good hotels, guest houses and restaurants, a growing number of unique museums and cultural events such as the Bath Festival. Specialist shops and boutiques have added to the town's attraction. Its location close to the M4 and M5 motorways, on British Rail's Inter-city service only an hour from London and close to Bristol, have all heightened its attraction. It is close enough to London to make it an ideal destination for one day tours, and as a centre for the Cotswolds to

Fig 1.4 Royal Crescent, Bath
(*Courtesy Bath City Council*)

the north and the Mendips to the south it is within easy access of some of Britain's best scenery, using private car or coach.

Oberammergau, West Germany

This village resort in Bavaria manages to combine both site and event attractions. As a mountain resort in the Alps it lies at the heart of Europe, accessible through Munich by air from all over the world and with good road connections from north (Germany) and south (Austria). It is both a winter and summer resort, offering summer guests peace and tranquillity, healthy mountain air, outstanding alpine scenery and opportunities for hiking and mountaineering, with skiing in the winter. It offers unique wood-carving shops and the outstanding shopping centres of nearby Garmisch-Partenkirchen and Munich (less than an hour's drive away). A good range of accommodation is available at all prices and a recently-installed indoor and outdoor swimming pool complex has added to the amenities. But once every ten years, Oberammergau becomes the focus for hundreds of thousands of international tourists

who wish to see the famous passion play which has been staged here since the middle ages. In other years the theatre where the play is staged still attracts countless day trippers.

These examples highlight another important point in relation to tourist destinations; the chances of their long-term success will be considerably enhanced if the attractions they offer are unique. Uniqueness is relative, however. There is only one Oberammergau passion play in the world, just as there is only one Grand Canyon, Eiffel Tower or Big Ben. But to draw tourists from the developed nations of Northern Europe and North America, mass tourism is based largely upon the attractions of sand, sea and sun, which the Mediterranean and Caribbean countries provide. Such attractions are seldom unique, nor do their customers require them to be so. These tourists will be satisfied so long as the amenities are adequate, the resort remains accessible and prices are competitive. If prices rise, however, or competing countries can offer similar facilities at lower prices, holidaymakers will switch their allegiance. Because of the singular properties of 'heritage'

Fig 1.5 The Passion Play at Oberammergau
(*Courtesy Verkehrs- und Reisebüro Gemeinde Oberammergau OHG*)

tourism against those of seaside tourism, the former will retain its attractions for tourists to a far greater extent should prices rise, providing this increase is not exorbitant compared to those of other countries.

Tourist destinations have life cycles, as have all products; that is to say, they will enjoy periods of growth expansion, but will invariably suffer periods of decline or decay. If we examine the history of any well-known resort or destination we can see the truth of this. Along the French Riviera, Nice, Cannes, Antibes, Juan les Pins, St Tropez, all have in turn enjoyed their period as fashionable resorts, but ultimately the early tourists have moved on to more fashionable resorts, often to be replaced by a new less fashion-conscious, less free-spending, market. In time this decline may become irreversible unless the resort can be regenerated by successful marketing. This may mean updating facilities as tourists become more demanding. In Britain's seaside resorts, failure to update many of the older hotels built in the Victorian era has meant that tourists who have experienced the improved facilities offered by foreign package holiday hotels are no longer attracted to British resorts. It may mean adding new attractions, such as indoor leisure complexes which cater for all-weather demand.

In recent years, Brighton, Torbay, Bournemouth and Blackpool have invested considerable sums of money to retain their tourist markets, with the construction of such facilities as the Bournemouth International Centre and Blackpool's Sandcastle Centre (a £16 millon all-weather investment designed to provide a wide range of entertainment under one roof).

STATISTICAL MEASUREMENT IN TOURISM

Gathering data on tourism is a vital task for the government of a country, for its national tourist offices and for the providers of tourism services. Governments need to know the impact which tourism makes on the economy in terms of income, employment, investment and contribution to the country's balance of payments. Concern with regional development requires that these statistics be sufficiently refined to allow them to be broken down by region. Governments will also wish to compare their tourism performance with that of other countries and to compare performances over a period of time.

Tourism organisations, whether in the public or private sector, require such data to enable them to make projections about what will happen in the future. This means identifying trends in the market, patterns of growth and changing demand for destinations, facilities or types of holiday. On the basis of this knowledge future planning can be undertaken; the public sector will make recommendations on the expansion or addition of tourist airports, road improvements or other services, while the private sector will recognise and react to changes in demand for hotel accommodation and develop new destinations or facilities. National tourist offices will plan their promotional strategies on the basis of these data, deciding where to advertise, to whom and with what theme. We can summarise the chief methods of research undertaken under the categories of international and national surveys.

International surveys

Although statistics of intra-European and transatlantic tourism flows were being collected before World War II, the systematic collection of tourism data on a world-wide scale developed in the early post-war years. This has intensified in recent years, particularly among the developing nations who have seen the introduction and rapid expansion of tourism to their shores. Global tourism statistics, dealing with tourism traffic flows, expenditure and trends over time, are produced and collated annually by the World Tourism Organisation (WTO) and the Organisation for Economic Co-operation and Development (OECD), and are published in the WTO's *World Tourism Statistics Annual Report and Tourism Compendium*, and in the OECD's annual *Tourism Policy and International Tourism*. Statistics, however, are not always strictly comparable, as data gathering methods vary and differences in definition of terms remain.

In Britain, information on travel into and out of the country is obtained in a variety of ways. Until the early 1960s most basic data on incoming tourism were obtained from Home Office immigration statistics, but as the purpose of gathering such data was to control immigration rather than to measure tourism, the data have major weaknesses, including failure to distinguish the purpose of travel – obviously a vital factor in measuring incoming tourism. The Government therefore decided to introduce a regular survey of visitors entering and leaving the country. The International Passenger Survey has enabled data to be collected since 1964, including the number of visitors, purpose of visit, geographical region visited, expenditure, mode of travel, transport used and duration of stay. This information is published quarterly, and compounded annually, in the Government's *Business Monitor* series (MQ6/M6 *Overseas Travel and Tourism*).

Numerous other surveys, both public and private, are undertaken, and these provide additional data on tourism volume and expenditure in Britain. The English Tourist Board carries out an annual Holiday Intentions Survey before Easter, which helps to forecast the anticipated level of tourism by British residents within Britain and overseas in the coming year. The same board also carries out regular hotel occupancy surveys. Private research organisations such as the BMRB (British Market Research Bureau) carry out interviews with consumers which include details of expenditure and volume of tourism consumption, although the details of such research are usually available only to subscribers.

National surveys

In Britain, as in other European countries, surveys producing broadly comparable statistics on tourism flows within the country are undertaken annually. Here, the most important is the British Tourism Survey Yearly (BTSY), administered jointly by the British Tourist Authority (BTA) and the three National Tourist Boards of England, Scotland and Wales. This is a development of the former British National Travel Survey, which collected data on British holidaymakers abroad between 1951 and 1985. The survey is based on research conducted at home on some 3500 British residents, and although full results are available only to subscribers, a summary of key data based on the survey is available publicly. The former British Home Tourism Survey (BHTS), which produced statistics on all forms of travel within the UK between 1971 and 1985, is based on a much larger sample and is now published by the Boards as 'The British Tourism Market'.

While some information is available on regional tourism from these surveys, more sophisticated measurement of regional tourism is obtained through destination surveys which are carried out by the regional tourist boards, or in some cases by public bodies at county or local resort level. These are designed to produce a more accurate picture of tourism patterns, and will generally involve a combination of district accommodation surveys and a random visitor survey, designed to measure the contribution of both day excursionists and staying visitors within the region.

Techniques and problems of tourism measurement

From the foregoing it can be seen that tourism data

collection has been largely quantitative in the past; that is, it has been designed to measure the volume of tourism traffic to different destinations, tourism expenditure en route and at those destinations, and certain other characteristics such as length of stay, time of visit, purpose of visit or mode of travel. These are questions which deal with the 'how', 'when', and 'where' aspects of travel, and over time they have been refined so that additional data have been obtained. Expenditure, for example, can now be broken down by sector (shopping, food, accommodation, etc.), by nationality or by some other common variable. But recently the emphasis on travel research has shifted, and the aim has been to examine more qualitative aspects of tourism – questions as to *why* people behave as they do. Studies have been undertaken which are designed to reveal how and when holidays were planned and why a particular destination, time or mode of travel was selected.

Such data are less easily obtained through the medium of structured questionnaires and require the use of techniques such as motivation research, involving depth interviews, panel interviews and other qualitative methods which are time consuming to undertake and expensive. Nor can the results be subjected to tests of statistical probability, as can quantitative methods, in order to 'prove their accuracy'. Nonetheless, they do offer a valuable insight into the psychology of tourism behaviour which can advance our understanding of tourism as a phenomenon. Some researchers have argued, too, that quantitative methods may be too simplistic to be valuable, and it is often difficult to gauge the honesty and accuracy of answers elicited by the use of mailed questionnaires.

There are numerous other problems connected with the use of questionnaires for data gathering. Asking questions of arriving passengers at a destination is in reality an 'intention survey' rather than an accurate picture of what a tourist will do or spend while at that destination, while surveys carried out on departing travellers involve problems of recall.

Using the results of such surveys for the purposes of comparison can be very misleading. An international journey requires an American resident to make a trip of many hundreds of kilometres, while in Europe day trips for the purposes of shopping or leisure are common experiences for those living near international borders. In some cases it is difficult to think of border crossings as international; no border control exists, for example, between Holland, Belgium and Luxembourg, nor are records available of crossings between these countries. Some countries still use hotel records to estimate visitors, these being notoriously inadequate; visitors travelling from one hotel to another are double counted while those visiting friends and relations will be omitted entirely. The author has experience of one hotel where

records of nationality were based entirely upon the front office clerk guessing the origin of visitors' surnames! Accurate measures of tourist expenditure are equally difficult to make. Shopping surveys have problems in distinguishing between residents and tourists when shopkeepers are questioned, and tourists themselves will frequently under- or over-estimate their expenditure.

While international standards for methods of data collection and definition of terms have become widely accepted, variations still make comparisons difficult, not only between countries but within a country over a period of time, as a result of changes in methods of estimating data.

Some observers have argued that data should be collected not only to provide the economic impact of tourism on a country or region but also the social impact. Statistics on the ratio of tourists to residents, for example, or the number of tourists per square kilometre would provide some guidance on the degree of congestion experienced by a region. However, the social impact of tourism is also the outcome of many other variables, and statistical measurement is still a comparatively recent art which will require further refinement in the future for the purposes of both economic and social planning.

THE INTERNATIONAL TOURIST MARKET

We can end this chapter by looking at the business of international tourism today. Tourism is very big business indeed. Over 2500 million tourists (approaching half the population of the world) travel away from home on a trip lasting four days or more in their own countries, and a further 355 million travel abroad. Direct expenditure on international tourism alone amounts to more than $150 000 million per annum, and accounts for over five per cent of all world exports. Although one of the fastest growing industries in the world, its potential for growth remains enormous; only one in fifty of the world's population actually travel across international borders in any one year (many of those who do travel, of course, make more than one such trip each year), and international travel is restricted largely to a handful of countries, with Europe responsible for some two-thirds of the traffic and North America accounting for most of the rest. The number of international travellers from the developing nations is minute, yet if one were to project increased living standards for these countries to a level equivalent to our present standard of living in the next century, the international tourism market would achieve staggering proportions. If only five per cent of the Chinese population were to travel abroad, this would inject a further 50 million travellers into the market! Such progression in living standards among the lesser developed nations is no longer certain, and indeed the strains that this development would impose upon the

Table I A Profile of International Tourism 1950–1987

Year	International Arrivals (millions)	International Expenditure ($ billions)
1950	25.3	2.1
1960	69.3	6.9
1970	159.7	17.9
1980	284.8	102.4
1985	333.8	108.6
1986	341.4	129.1
1987	355.0 (p)	150.0 (p)

p = provisional (Source: WTO)

tourism industry and its impact upon the destination countries would be appalling. Nevertheless, although the increase in international tourism has slowed recently, the underlying expansion continues (see Table I).

Analysing the international tourism market, we must begin by distinguishing the countries which generate tourists, known as 'generating countries', and countries receiving tourists, known as 'destination', 'receiving' or 'host' countries. A few countries, of which Britain is one, play an equally important role in both generating and receiving tourists. For the most part it is the wealthier industrial nations, with their high per capita disposable income, which generate the tourists and the lesser developed nations, offering low living costs, good climates and fine beaches, which receive tourists. The leading tourism generating countries include West Germany, USA, France, Canada, Holland, Belgium, Japan, Luxembourg and the United Kingdom; other countries with significant numbers of residents travelling abroad include Sweden, Switzerland, Denmark, Italy and Norway.

Within all these countries there are marked differences in the actual proportion of residents taking holidays abroad. For example, the proportion of Swedish residents taking a holiday of four nights or more is far greater than the proportion of Italians doing so, and the proportion of Swedes travelling abroad also far exceeds that of Italians taking a foreign trip. We can say then that the *propensity* to take holidays is much higher among the Swedes, who live in a comparatively wealthy country, than among the Italians, although a significant number of the latter still do travel abroad.

We measure the *gross travel propensity* of a nation by taking the total number of tourist trips per annum (or some other appropriate period of time) as a percentage of the population, while *net travel propensity* reflects the percentage of the population taking at least one tourist trip. The *travel frequency* of a population is therefore defined as

$$Tf = \frac{Gtp}{Ntp}$$

where Tf = travel frequency; Gtp = Gross travel propensity; and Ntp = Net travel propensity.

In Britain, 20 million residents were estimated to have had a holiday abroad of four nights or longer in 1987 (of which nearly 12 million were travelling on package holidays), representing nearly 36 per cent of the population. This figure excludes business travel, which would substantially add to the total. Expenditure on holidays abroad amounted to £7800 million (including fares paid to British carriers operating on international routes). In return, Britain welcomed some 15½ million foreign visitors in the same year, who brought over £6200 million into the country.

Thus we begin to recognise the importance of international tourism for the economy of a country. Countries aim for a favourable balance of trade. They need to sell products abroad in order to obtain the foreign currencies with which to pay for their imports. Britain's visible trade balance has often been in the red in recent years – that is, we have brought goods abroad of a greater value than the goods we have sold abroad – but this situation can be rectified if we have a favourable surplus on our 'invisible' trade, which includes services such as banking and insurance and also tourism. Britain has a good reputation for these services abroad and the balance of trade on invisible earnings has often been sufficient to make up for the deficit in the visible terms of trade.

Although there is no logical economic reason why the outflow of funds spent by British tourists abroad should be balanced by the inflow of foreign tourist expenditure (as long as other invisibles make up the deficit), successive governments have shown concern when the gap between incoming and outgoing tourist revenue becomes too marked. If the general terms of trade become too unfavourable this can lead to governments imposing a limit on the amount of foreign currency which residents are permitted to take abroad with them – the so-called 'travel allowance'. In the UK this has ranged, since World War II, from a low of £25 in 1952 to a maximum of £1000 in 1979 (immediately prior to the lifting of all exchange controls in that year). While restricting the travel allowance does have some effect in reducing the demand for foreign travel, there is always the danger of retaliation by other countries. Such controls are also questioned on moral grounds, since they have the effect of restricting the freedom of movement of individuals which is regarded as a basic right in a democratic country. Fortunately, Britain has also been very effective in selling itself as a destination, increasing the number of foreign tourists from just over a million in 1955 to a high of 15½ million in 1987.

The role played by tourism in the economic

development of the lesser developed nations is equally important. Many of these countries are turning to tourism as a means of improving their balance of payments deficits, attracting foreign investment and solving their unemployment problems. Because tourists are generally attracted to rural and comparatively undeveloped areas of these countries, where few alternative prospects exist for employment other than agriculture, tourism is seen as a viable industry. The fact that it is also labour-intensive, requiring only limited skills for most of its workforce, provides an additional attraction. However, substantial capital has to be invested initially to develop the infrastructure – roads, airports and other services – before capital can be attracted for the construction of hotels and other amenities.

In addition to direct income and employment generated by tourism, there is also an indirect effect on the economy of a region. To measure the total impact of tourism on a region one must take account not only of the direct beneficiaries of tourists' money but also of the many indirect beneficiaries: farmers and wholesalers who supply food and drink to restaurants and hotels where tourists eat; the suppliers of hotel equipment and furniture; and the many other organisations and individuals who benefit to some extent by tourists visiting their area. Retail stores, banks, laundries, all derive some advantages from tourism in their area. Furthermore, since money spent by tourists is helping to pay the salaries of workers in these enterprises, these workers in turn are buying goods and services which they would not otherwise be purchasing. In this way money coming into the region is re-circulated and the total amount of tourist income generated is considerably greater than that spent by tourists alone. This phenomenon, known as the *multiplier effect*, will be discussed at greater length in Chapter 13.

The annual holiday represents a major expenditure in the year for most people, something to be saved for or to take out a loan for, but once on holiday people like to forget the normal financial restraints of daily life and they tend to spend more freely. In an earlier age, workers from the Lancashire mills would 'blue' their annual savings in a glorious fortnight in Blackpool and this pattern is still prevalent among working-class holidaymakers in the popular resorts of the Mediterranean. However, the propensity to spend on holiday will differ not only according to socioeconomic background but also according to nationality. Tourists from certain countries are more prone to stay at self-catering apartments or campsites than are those from other countries, for example. In planning for tourism growth, therefore, tourist authorities must consider more than just how many tourists they can attract; they must also consider which types of tourists they can best attract, which are most desirable in terms of expenditure and acceptability to local residents, which will have least impact upon the environment, and they must then develop appropriate strategies to attract the markets for which they have targeted.

QUESTIONS AND DISCUSSION POINTS

1 What are the main purposes behind the collection of tourism statistics?

2 What potential problems can you see in lesser developed countries turning to tourism in order to boost their economies?

3 Identify two tourism destinations known to you, one of which is attracting a growing number of tourists, the other facing a decrease in its tourist demand. Account for the changing fortunes of each. Is either likely to experience a change in demand in the foreseeable future? What would need to be done by the destination facing a decline in demand in order to increase its attractiveness?

4 Explain the differing requirements of business and leisure travellers for (a) air transport and (b) hotel accommodation. Do the growing numbers of businesswomen have needs distinct from businessmen that should be catered for by the airlines or hotels?

ASSIGNMENT TOPICS

1 You have recently taken up the position of Assistant Tourist Officer in a county of your choice. The county has only recently created a tourism department, and your immediate superior is preparing a new plan of action to increase the number of visitors during the next five years. He asks you to produce a brief report for him which:

(a) looks at trends in domestic and in-coming tourism over the past decade,

(b) identifies significant trends and forecasts for the future flow of tourism within Britain, and

(c) suggests the relative advantages and disadvantages the county has to offer in attracting more visitors.

Your report should specifically indicate the shortcomings you find in the amount and quality of the statistical data you seek, and what further research you think might be needed to guide the Department in its activities.

2 As an in-coming ground handling agent serving the needs of the US market, you have been approached by a specialist tour operator, Ralph Quackenbusch of Quackenbusch Tours, Sacramento, California. He is interested in bringing groups to your area of the country, and has written to you asking for your assessment of local towns which might be attractive to older Californian residents. Select one town you consider might be suitable in your area, and subject this to an evaluation of its attractions, amenities and accessibility for the overseas market, bearing in mind that some groups will be wanting to spend time in London, while others will prefer to come more directly to your part of the world.

Write him a short business letter spelling out the attractiveness of the destination as you see it.

2 The history of tourism

Chapter objectives: After studying this chapter, you should be able to:

- explain the historical changes which have affected the growth and development of the tourism industry, and the forms of travel and destinations selected by tourists;
- identify and distinguish between the enabling conditions and motivating factors encouraging the
- pursuit of travel;
- appreciate the historical and present-day role of tour operators in generating tourism;
- understand the major present-day trends affecting tourism in the UK and abroad.

EARLY ORIGINS

The term tourism dates from the early years of the nineteenth century, but this should not obscure the fact that what we would today describe as tourism was taking place much earlier in history. If one excludes travel for the purpose of waging war, early tourism can be said to have taken two forms: travel for the purpose of business (either for trading, or for business of state), and religious travel. Throughout history merchants have travelled extensively in order to trade with other nations or tribes. Such travel was often hazardous as well as arduous, relying on inadequate roads and uncomfortable transport, but the potential rewards were substantial. Both the Greeks and Romans were noted traders and as their respective empires increased, travel, often over great distances for the time, became necessary. There is also evidence of some travel for private purposes at this time; as an example, the Greeks hosted international visitors during the first Olympic Games, held in 776 BC,

Fig 2.1 The first Olympic Games held in Greece, 776 BC.
(*Courtesy National Tourist Organisation of Greece*)

and wealthy Romans travelled on holiday not only to their own coast but as far afield as Egypt for enjoyment and, in some cases, to visit friends and relatives, thus setting the precedent for the substantial VFR market of the twentieth century. The Roman traveller in particular was greatly aided by the improvement in communications which resulted from the expansion of the Empire: first class roads coupled with staging inns (precursors of the modern motels) led to comparatively safe, fast and convenient travel unsurpassed until modern times.

Holidays, of course, have their origin in 'holy days', and from earliest times religion provided the framework within which leisure time was spent. For most this implied a break from work rather than movement from one place to another. The village wakes of the Middle Ages, held on the eve of patronal festivals, provide an example of such 'religious relaxation'. However, by the time of the Middle Ages travel for religious reasons was also in evidence, taking the form of pilgrimages to places of worship (Chaucer's tale of the pilgrimage to Canterbury has popularised knowledge of such travel). Here, dedication or obligation were the motivating factors; travel occurred in spite of, rather than owing to, the prevailing conditions.

This generalisation can be made about most, if not all, forms of travel during the Middle Ages. Limited but varied travel did take place; adventurers seeking fame and fortune, merchants seeking new trade opportunities, strolling players, all moved freely around or between countries. All these, however, are identified as business travellers. There are certain preconditions to the development of travel for personal pleasure, and travel – certainly up to the time of the Middle Ages, if not until the nineteenth century – was something to be endured rather than enjoyed.

CONDITIONS FAVOURING THE EXPANSION OF TRAVEL

One can identify two categories of condition that have to be present before private travel is encouraged; *enabling* conditions (*travel facilitators*) and travel *motivators*. Of the former, two key conditions are time and disposable income (or better, *discretionary* income – that which is available after paying for essentials such as housing, food and clothing); throughout history, until very recent times, both have been the prerogative of a small elite in societies. Leisure involving the travel and stay of the vast majority of the population was out of the question in a world where workers laboured from morning to night, six days a week, in order to earn sufficient to stay alive. Sunday was expected to be treated as a religious holiday and was, of necessity, a day of rest from the week's toil.

Equally important, the development of pleasure travel depends upon the provision of suitable travel facilities. The growth of travel and the growth of transport are interdependent; travellers require transport that is priced within their budget and that is fast, safe, comfortable and convenient. Until the nineteenth century transport fulfilled none of these requirements. Prior to the arrival of the stagecoach (itself not noted for its comfort), the only form of transport other than the private carriages of the wealthy was the carrier's wagon, and this vehicle took two days to cover the distance between London and Brighton. Road conditions were appalling – ill-made, potholed and in winter deeply rutted by the wagon wheels which turned the entire road into a sea of mud. The journey was not only uncomfortable but also unsafe; footpads and highwaymen abounded on the major routes, posing an ever-present threat to wayfarers. A significant breakthrough in terms of speed (though not in price) was achieved at the end of the seventeenth century with the advent of the stagecoach and, towards the end of the eighteenth century, the mailcoach which, through careful organisation and the establishment of suitable staging posts where horses could be changed, reduced the journey to Brighton to a matter of hours. Poor road surfaces continued to make such travel uncomfortable, but at least the discomfort was of shorter duration. Only with the introduction of macadamised surfaces after 1815 was this problem overcome. However within the next two decades the railways arrived, bringing with them the promise of a measure of comfort at an affordable price for the masses.

The development of transport is one side of the coin. The other is the provision of adequate accommodation at the traveller's destination. The traditional hospices for travellers were the monasteries, but these were dissolved during the reign of Henry VIII and the resulting hiatus acted as a further deterrent to travel for all those other than travellers planning to visit their friends or relatives. However, eventually the gradual development of and improvement in lodgings in the ale-houses of the day gave way to inns purpose-built to meet the needs of the mailcoach passengers. Not surprisingly, the inadequacy of accommodation facilities outside the major centres of population led to towns such as London, Exeter and York becoming the first centres to attract visitors for pleasure purposes, although clearly the social life of these cities acted as a magnet for the leisured classes.

There were other constraints for those prepared to overcome these drawbacks. In cities, public health standards were low and travellers risked disease, a risk compounded in the case of foreign travel. Exchange facilities for foreign currency were unreliable and rates of exchange inconsistent, so travellers tended to carry large amounts of money with them, making them attractive victims for the highwaymen. Travel documents were necessary, even in the Middle Ages, and political suspicion frequently made the issue of such documents subject to delay; merchants generally found such documentation easiest to obtain.

Enabling conditions will encourage the growth of travel by motivating the potential tourist extrinsically, but the more powerful motivating factors are intrinsic, that is, they arise out of a felt need or want on the part of the individual himself. The religious travel discussed earlier is an illustration of one such need, but a change of mental attitude towards personal travel had to come about before the secularisation of travel occurred on a wide scale. With this change of attitude, other latent wants and needs became established. These included concern with health, the desire to widen one's education, and curiosity about other cultures and peoples. Historically, as the opportunities for travel have increased, so have the expressed needs for travel expanded, as we shall see.

THE DEVELOPMENT OF THE SPAS

Spas were well established during the time of the Roman Empire, but their popularity, based on the supposed medical benefits of the waters, lapsed in subsequent centuries. They were never entirely out of favour, however; the sick continued to visit Bath throughout the Middle Ages. A regenerated interest in the therapeutic qualities of mineral waters has been ascribed to the influence of the Renaissance in Britain, with a parallel revival of spas on the Continent.

By the middle of the sixteenth century medical writers such as Dr William Turner were again drawing attention to the curative powers of the waters at Bath and at watering places on the Continent. Bath, along with the spa at Buxton, had been showing some return to popularity among those seeking the 'cure', and by the early seventeenth century Scarborough and a number of other resorts were noted as centres for medical treatment. Over the following century, however, the character of these resorts gradually changed as pleasure rather than health became the motivation for visitors. The growth of the stagecoach services to these centres during the

Fig 2.2 The Roman baths at Bath.
(*Courtesy Bath City Council*)

eighteenth century also further enhanced these resorts. Bath in particular became a major centre of social life for high society during the eighteenth and early nineteenth centuries; under the guidance of Beau Nash it became a centre of high fashion for the wealthy, and deliberately set out to create a select and exclusive image.

The commercial possibilities opened up by the concentration of these wealthy visitors were not overlooked; facilities to entertain or otherwise cater for these visitors proliferated, changing the spas into what we would today term holiday resorts rather than mere watering places. Eventually, towards the beginning of the nineteenth century, the common characteristic of almost all resorts to go 'down-market' as they expand led to the centres changing in character, with the aristocracy and landed gentry giving way to wealthy city merchants and professional gentlemen in Bath. By the end of the eighteenth century the heyday of the English spas was already over.

Their decline can be traced to a number of factors. In the case of Bath, a rise in the number of permanent residents (coupled with an increase in the average age of the resident population) led to a change in the character of the town not dissimilar to that occurring in English seaside resorts during the latter half of the twentieth century. Commercial facilities became less popular as private entertaining in the home replaced the former public entertainment. However, it was the rise of the seaside resort which finally led to the demise of the inland spas.

THE GRAND TOUR

A parallel development in travel arose in the early seventeenth century as an outcome of the freedom and quest for learning heralded by the Renaissance. Under Elizabeth I young men seeking positions at court were encouraged to travel to the Continent in order to widen their education. This practice was gradually adopted by others lower in the social scale, and in time it became recognised that the education of a gentleman should be completed by a 'Grand Tour' of the cultural centres of the Continent, often lasting three years or more – the term was in use as early as 1670. While ostensibly educational, as with the spas the appeal soon became social and pleasure-seeking young men of leisure travelled, predominantly through France and Italy, to enjoy the rival cultures and social life of Europe, with Venice, Florence and Paris as the key attractions. Certainly by the end of the eighteenth century the practice had become institutionalised for the gentry.

The result of this process was that European centres were opened up to the British cognoscenti. Aix-en-Provence, Montpellier and Avignon became notable bases for British visitors, especially those using Provence as a staging post in their travels to Italy. When pleasure travel followed in the nineteenth century, eventually to displace educational travel as the motive for continental visits, this was to lead to the development of the Riviera as a major centre of attraction for British tourists, aided by the introduction of regular steamboat services across the Channel from 1820 onwards. However, the advent of the Napoleonic wars early in the nineteenth century inhibited travel within Europe for some thirty years, and at the time of the defeat of Napoleon, the British had become more interested in touring their own country.

THE SEASIDE RESORT

Certainly until the Renaissance sea bathing found little favour in Britain. Although not entirely unknown before then, such bathing as occurred was undertaken unclothed, and this behaviour conflicted with the mores of the day. Only when the sea became associated with certain health benefits did bathing gain any popularity, and this belief in seawater as an aid to health did not find acceptance until the early years of the eighteenth century.

It is perhaps to be expected that health theorists

would eventually recognise that the minerals to be found in spa waters were also present in abundance in seawater. By the early eighteenth century small fishing resorts around the English coast were already beginning to attract visitors seeking 'the cure', both by drinking seawater and by immersing themselves in it. Not surprisingly, Scarborough, as the only spa bordering the sea, was one of the first to exploit this facility for the medical benefits it was believed to offer, and both this town and Brighton were attracting regular visitors by the 1730s. But it was Dr Richard Russell's noted medical treatise *Concerning the Use of Seawater*, published in 1752, that is today generally credited with popularising the custom of sea bathing more widely; soon, Blackpool, Southend, and other English seaside 'resorts' were wooing bathers to their shores.

The growing popularity of 'taking the cure', which resulted from the wealth generated by the expansion of trade and industry in Britain at the time, meant that the inland spas could no longer cater satisfactorily for the influx of visitors that they were attracting. By contrast the new seaside resorts offered almost boundless opportunities for expansion. Moral doubts about sea bathing were overcome by the invention of the bathing machine, and the resorts prospered.

Undoubtedly, the demand for seaside cures could have been even greater in the early years if fast, cheap transport had been developed to cater for this need. In the mid-eighteenth century, however, Londoners still faced two days' hard travel to get as far as Brighton, and the cost of such travel was beyond the reach of all but the well-off. The extension of mailcoach services in the early nineteenth century greatly reduced the time of such travel, if not the cost. As with the inland spas, accommodation was slow to expand to meet the new demand, although as the eighteenth century gave way to the nineteenth, a widening range of entertainment facilities (many associated specifically with the seaside) were developed alongside the new hotels and guest houses that sprang up to cater for the growing demand – a demand, as with the later stages of the life of the inland spas, now generated by pleasure seekers rather than health cranks.

The growth of the seaside resorts was spurred in the early nineteenth century by the introduction of the steamboat services. These were to reduce substantially the cost and time of travel to the resorts. In 1815 a service began operating from London to Gravesend, and five years later to Margate. The popularity of these services was such that similar services were quickly introduced to a number of other, more distant, developing resorts. One effect of this development was the construction in all major resorts of a pier to accommodate the vessels on their arrival. The functional purpose of the seaside pier was soon overtaken by its attraction as a social meeting point and 'place to take the sea air' for the town's visitors.

Thus the first criterion for the growth of tourism was established: a fast, safe, convenient and reasonably priced form of transport made the resorts accessible to a large number of tourists. But a number of other factors closely related to the growth of tourism were also apparent by the early years of the nineteenth century.

One such factor was the rapid urbanisation of the population in Britain. The industrial revolution had led to massive migration of the population away from the villages and countryside and into the industrial cities, where work was plentiful and better paid. This migration was to have two important side effects on the workers themselves. Firstly, and for the first time, workers became conscious of the beauty and attractions of their former rural surroundings. The cities were dark, polluted and treeless. Formerly, workers had little appreciation for their environment – living among the natural beauty of the countryside, they accepted it without question. Now they longed to escape from the cities in the little free time they had – a characteristic still noteworthy among twentieth century city dwellers. Secondly, the type of work available in the cities was physically and psychologically stressful. The comparatively leisurely pace of life of the countryside was replaced by monotonous factory work from which a change of routine and pace was welcome.

The stress was accompanied, however, by a substantial increase in workers' purchasing power as productivity and the insatiable demand for more labour led to higher wages and greater disposable income. Worldwide demand for British goods also led to a rapid increase in business travel at home and abroad, and the greater wealth of the nation stimulated a population explosion, with better paid citizens demanding more goods and services, including travel. Only two factors were lacking for the launch of mass travel: holidays with pay and still faster, cheaper transport. The first was not to arrive on any scale until well into the twentieth century (although a fillip to the development of short-term travel was given by the granting of Bank Holidays in 1871), but the latter arrived in the first half of the nineteenth century in the form of the railways.

THE AGE OF STEAM

Railways

Two technological developments in the early part of the nineteenth century were to have a profound effect on transport and on the growth of travel in general. The first of these was the advent of the railway.

In the decade following the introduction of a rail link between Liverpool and Manchester in 1830, a huge programme of construction took place to provide trunk lines between the major centres of population and industry in Britain. Later, these were to be extended to include the expanding seaside resorts such as Brighton, bringing the resorts within reach of pleasure travellers on a broad scale for the first time. On the whole, however, the railway companies were slow to appreciate the opportunities their services offered for the expansion of pleasure travel, concentrating instead on meeting the demand for business travel generated by the expansion in trade. Competition between the railway companies was initially based on service rather than on price, although from the earliest days of the new railways a new market developed for short day-trips. Before long, however, entrepreneurs began to stimulate rail travel by organising excursions for the public at special fares. In some cases these took place on regular train services, but in others special trains were chartered to take travellers to their destination, setting a precedent for the charter services by air which were to become so significant a feature of tour operating a century later. Thomas Cook was not the first such entrepreneur – Sir Rowland Hill, who became chairman of the Brighton Railway Co, is sometimes credited with this innovation and there were certainly excursion trains in operation by 1840 – but Cook was to have by far the greatest impact on the early travel industry. In 1841, as secretary of the South Midland Temperance Association, he organised an excursion for his members from Leicester to Loughborough, at a fare of one shilling return. The success of this venture – 570 took part – encouraged him to arrange similar excursions using chartered trains and by 1845 he was organising these trips on a fully commercial basis.

The result of these and similar ventures by other entrepreneurs led to a substantial movement of pleasure-bound travellers to the seaside; in 1844 it is recorded that almost 15 000 passengers travelled from London to Brighton on the three Easter holidays alone, while hundreds of thousands travelled to other resorts to escape the smoke and grime of the cities. The enormous growth in this type of traffic can be appreciated when it is revealed that by 1862 Brighton received 132 000 visitors on Easter Monday alone.

Supported by a more sympathetic attitude towards pleasure travel by the public authorities such as the Board of Trade, the railway companies themselves were actively promoting excursions by the 1850s, as well as introducing a range of discounted fares for day trips, weekend trips and longer journeys. By 1855, Cook had extended his field of operations to the Continent, organising the first 'inclusive tours' to the Paris Exhibition of that year. This followed the success of his excursions to the Great Exhibition in London in 1851, which in all had welcomed a total of three million visitors.

Cook was a man of vision in the world of travel. The success of his operations was due to the care he took in organising his programmes to minimise problems; he had close contacts with hotels, shipping companies and railways throughout the world, ensuring that he obtained the best possible service as well as cheap prices for the services he sold. By escorting his clients throughout their journeys abroad he took the worry out of travel for the first-time travellers. He also facilitated the administration of travel by introducing, in 1867, the hotel voucher; and by removing the worry of travel for the Victorian population, he changed their attitudes to travel and opened up the market. The coincidental development of photography acted as a further stimulus for overseas travel, both for prestige and curiosity reasons.

The success of these early forays abroad led the railway companies to recognise the importance of their links with the cross-channel ferry operators. The management of the ferries gradually came under the control of the railways themselves, so that by the 1860s they dominated ferry operations to the Continent and to Ireland.

The expansion of the railways was accompanied by a simultaneous decline of the stagecoaches. Some survived by providing feeder services to the nearest railway stations, but overall road traffic shrank and with it shrank the demand for the staging inns. Those situated in the resorts were quick to adapt to meet the needs of the new railway travellers, but the supply of accommodation in centres served by the railways was totally inadequate to meet the burgeoning demand of rail travellers. A period of hotel construction began, leaders in which were the railways themselves, building the great terminus hotels which came to play such a significant role in the hotel industry over the next hundred years. The high capital investment called for by this construction programme led to the early formation of the hotel chains and corporations in place of the former individual hotel proprietors.

Coincidentally with this technological development, Victorian society was undergoing social changes which were to boost pleasure travel for the masses in Britain and for the better-off minority abroad. The new-found interest in sea bathing meant that the expanding rail routes tended to favour the developing resorts, accelerating their growth. At the same time, Victorian society placed increasing importance on the family as a social unit. This led to emphasis on family holidays for which the seaside resorts were ideally suited, offering as they soon did a range of entertainment for adults and children alike. The foundation of the traditional seaside entertainment was soon laid – German bands, 'nigger minstrels' and pierrots, Punch and Judys, barrel organs, donkey rides, and the seaside pier as the central focus of entertainment. Resorts began to develop different social

Fig 2.3 *Hindostan*, built in 1842, opened P & O's service between Suez and Calcutta in 1843. (*Courtesy the Peninsular and Oriental Steam Navigation Company*)

images, the result in part of their geographical location; those nearer London or other major centres of population developed a substantial market of day trippers, while others deliberately aimed for a more exclusive clientele. These latter generally tended to be situated further afield, but in some cases their exclusivity arose from the desire of prominent residents to resist the encroachment of the railways for as long as possible; Bournemouth, for example, resisted the extension of the railway from Poole until 1870. Some areas of early promise as holiday resorts were quickly destroyed by the growth of industry – Swansea and Hartlepool, for example, and Southampton, where beaches soon gave way to developing docks.

Health continued to play a role in the choice of holiday destination, but emphasis gradually switched from the benefits of sea bathing to those of sea air. Climate became a feature of the resorts' promotion. Sunshine hours were emphasised, or the bracing qualities of the Scarborough air, while the pines at Bournemouth were reputed to help those suffering from lung complaints. Seaside resorts on the Continent also gained in popularity and began to develop their own social images – Scheveningen, Ostend, Biarritz and Deauville became familiar names to British holidaymakers who ventured overseas. Some overseas resorts flourished as a reaction to the middle-class morality of Victorian England; Monte Carlo, with its notorious gambling casino, was a case in point. This desire to escape from one's everyday moral environment was as symptomatic in its way in the nineteenth century as it was to become by the middle of the twentieth.

Other forms of holidaymaking, opened up by the advent of the railways on the Continent, arose from the impact of the 'Romantic Movement' of mid-Victorian England. The Rhine and the French Riviera benefited from their romantic appeal, while the invigorating mountain air of Switzerland offered its own unique appeal which was firmly established by the 1840s. The additional interest in mountaineering, which began as a popular English middle-class activity in the 1860s, secured for Switzerland its role as a major Continental holiday centre for the British, boosted still further when Sir Henry Lunn, the travel entrepreneur, introduced winter ski holidays to that destination in the 1880s. The railways made their own contributions to these developments, but above all they encouraged the desire to travel by removing the hazards of foreign travel that had formerly existed for travellers journeying by road.

Steamships

Just as the technological developments of the early nineteenth century led to the development of the railways on land, so was steam harnessed at sea to drive the new generations of ships. Here, necessity was the mother of invention. Increasing trade worldwide, especially with North America, required Britain to develop faster, more reliable forms of communication by sea with the rest of the world. The first regular commercial cross-channel steamship service was introduced in 1821, on the Dover–Calais route. By 1862, the railway companies had received rights to own and operate steamships, leading to a rapid expansion in cross-channel ferry services. Deep-sea services were introduced on routes to North America and the Far East; the Peninsular and Oriental Steam Navigation Company (later P & O) is credited with the first regular long-distance steamship services, beginning operations to India and the Far East in 1838. They were soon followed by the Cunard Steamship Company which, with a lucrative mail contract, began regular services to the American continent in 1840. Britain, by being first to establish regular deep-sea services of this kind, dominated the world's shipping in the second half of the century, although it was to become challenged increasingly by vessels of the other leading industrial nations, especially across the north Atlantic. This prestigious and highly profitable route prospered not only from mail contracts but also in terms of both passenger and freight traffic as trade expanded. This traffic was boosted later in the century by the advent of substantial emigrant traffic from Europe and the steady growth of American visitors to Europe. Thomas Cook was to do his part in stimulating British tourist traffic to North America, operating the first excursion to the USA as early as 1866.

The Suez Canal, opened in 1869, stimulated demand

for P & O's services to India and beyond, as Britain's empire looked eastwards. The global growth of shipping led, in the latter part of the century, to the formation of shipping conferences which developed cartel-like agreements on fares and conditions applicable to the carriage of traffic to the various territories to which these vessels operated. The aim of these agreements was to ensure year-round profitability in an unstable and seasonal market, but the result was to stifle competition by price and eventually led to excess profits which were enjoyed by most shipping companies until the advent of airline competition in the mid-twentieth century.

LATE NINETEENTH CENTURY DEVELOPMENTS

As the Victorian era drew to a close, other social changes came into play. Continued enthusiasm for the healthy outdoor life coincided with the invention of the bicycle, and cycling holidays, aided by promotion from the Cyclists' Touring Club which was founded in 1878, enjoyed immense popularity. This movement not only paved the way for later interest in outdoor activities on holiday but may well have stimulated the appeal of the suntan as a status symbol of health and wealth, in marked contrast to the earlier association in Victorian minds of a fair complexion with gentility and breeding. The bicycle offered for the first time the opportunity for mobile rather than centred holidays and gave a foretaste of the popularity of motoring holidays in the early years of the twentieth century.

As tourism became organised in the later years of the nineteenth century, so the organisation of travel became an established institution. Thomas Cook and Sir Henry Lunn (who started Lunn Poly) are two of the best known names associated with the development of tours at this time, but many other well-known companies trace their origin to this period. Dean and Dawson appeared in 1871, the Polytechnic Touring Association in the following year and Frames in 1881. In the United States, American Express (founded by, among others, Henry Wells and William Fargo of Wells Fargo fame) initiated money orders and travellers' cheques, although the company did not become involved in booking holiday arrangements until the early twentieth century.

Mention has already been made of the impact of photography on nineteenth century travel. As the nineteenth century drew to a close, the vogue for photography was accompanied by the cult of the guidebook. No British tourist venturing abroad would neglect to take his guidebook, and a huge variety of guidebooks, many superficial and inaccurate, were available on the market, dealing with both Britain and overseas countries. The most popular and enduring of these was Baedeker which, although first published as early as 1839, became established as the leading guide for European countries at the end of the century.

TRAVEL IN THE TWENTIETH CENTURY

The first half of the twentieth century

In the opening years of this century pleasure travel continued to expand, encouraged by the increasing wealth, curiosity and outgoing attitudes of the post-Victorian population and also by the increasing ease of such movement. By now travellers were safer from both disease and physical attack, the Continent was relatively stable politically and documentation for British travellers uncomplicated – since 1860 no passports had been required for any country in Europe.

World War I proved to be only a brief hiatus in the expansion of travel, although it led to the widespread introduction of passports for nationals of most countries. Early post-war prosperity, coupled with large-scale migration, boosted the demand for international travel. Interest in foreign travel was further boosted by the first-hand experience of foreign countries that so many had gained during the war. New forms of mass communication spurred curiosity about other countries; to the influence of posters and the press were added the cinema, then radio and ultimately television, all playing their part in widening knowledge and interest.

After World War I, however, forms of travel began to change radically. The railways went into a period of steady decline with the introduction of the motor car. Motorised public road transport and improved road conditions led to the era of the charabancs, derived from former army surplus lorries which, equipped with benches, provided a rudimentary form of coach. These vehicles achieved great popularity in the 1920s for outings to the seaside, but their poor safety record led to the introduction of licensing regulations for public and motor transport. However, it was the freedom of independent travel offered by the private motor car which destroyed the monopoly of the railways as a means of holiday travel in Britain, although continental rail travel survived and prospered until the coming of the airlines. In an endeavour to stem the regression, rail services were first rationalised in 1921 into four major companies – the LMS, LNER, GWR and SR*– and later nationalised following World War II.

The arrival of the airline industry signalled the beginning of the end, not only for long distance rail services but, more decisively, for the great steamship companies. British shipping lines in particular had been under increasing threat from foreign competition throughout the 1920s – French, German and US liners challenged British supremacy on the north Atlantic routes especially – but before World War II commercial air services did not pose a significant threat to the industry as a whole.

*London, Midland and Scottish Railway, London and North Eastern Railway, Great Western Railway and Southern Railway.

Air services introduced in the 1930s were expensive, unreliable, uncomfortable and necessitated frequent stopovers for distant destinations. Partly for these reasons commercial aviation was more important for its mail-carrying potential in these years than for the carriage of passengers. It was not until the technological breakthroughs in aircraft design achieved during World War II that airlines were to prove a viable alternative to shipping for intercontinental travel.

Among the major travel developments of the 1930s the holiday camp deserves a special mention. Aimed at the growing low-income market for holidays, the camps set new standards of comfort when they were introduced, offering 24-hour entertainment at all-in, reasonable prices, backed by efficiency in operation and including the all-important child-minding services which couples with young families needed so badly. This was in marked contrast to the lack of planned activities and often surly service offered at seaside boarding houses of the day. The origin of these camps goes back to earlier experiments of organisations such as the Co-operative Holidays Association, the Workers' Travel Association and the Holiday Fellowship (although summer camps for boys such as that run by Joseph Cunningham on the Isle of Man have been dated as early as 1887), but their popularity and general acceptance by the public can be ascribed to the efforts and promotional flair of Billy Butlin, who built his first camp at Skegness in 1936, supposedly after talking to a group of disconsolate holidaymakers huddled in a bus shelter to avoid the rain on a wet summer's day. The instant success of the concept led to a spate of similar camps built by Butlin and other entrepreneurs in the pre-war and early post-war years.

It was during the between-wars period, however, that the seaside holiday became securely established as the traditional annual holiday for the mass British public. Blackpool, Scarborough, Southend and Brighton consolidated their positions as leading holiday resorts, while numerous newer resorts – Bournemouth, Broadstairs, Clacton, Skegness, Colwyn Bay – grew annually in terms of residential population as well as in number of annual visitors. Up to the time of the Depression in the early 1930s hotels and guest houses proliferated, both in the seaside resorts and in London. In the latter some of the leading West End hotels were constructed, largely to satisfy demand from overseas tourists.

At this time Britain experienced the first stirrings of government interest in the tourism business as a whole. In this respect Britain was well behind other European countries; Switzerland, for example, had long recognised the importance of its inward tourism and was actively involved in both tourism promotion and the gathering of tourism statistics by this time. The British Travel and Holidays Association was established by the government in 1929, but with the theme 'Travel for Peace' its role was seen as essentially promotional in nature and its impact on the tourism industry was relatively insignificant until its change in status forty years later. By the outbreak of World War II the British government had at least recognised the potential contribution tourism could make to the country's balance of payments; equally, they had recognised the importance of holidays to the health and efficiency of the nation's workforce. The Amulree Report in 1938 led to the first Holidays with Pay Act in the same year, which encouraged voluntary agreements on paid holidays and generated the idea of a two-week paid holiday for all workers. Although this ambition was not realised until several years after the end of World War II, by the outbreak of the war some 11 million of the 19 million workforce were entitled to paid holidays – a key factor in the generation of mass travel.

The second half of the twentieth century

As had occurred after World War I, World War II also led to increased interest in travel partly due to a desire by many people to visit the scenes of such battles as those fought on the Normandy beaches and at St Nazaire. The extensive theatre of war had introduced combatants not only to new countries but to new continents, generating new friendships and an interest in diverse cultures. Another outcome of the war, which was radically to change the travel business, was the advance in aircraft technology which led for the first time to a viable commercial aviation industry. The surplus of aircraft in the immediate post-war years, a benevolent political attitude towards the growth of private sector airlines, and the appearance on the scene of the early air travel entrepreneurs such as Harold Bamberg (of Eagle Airways) and Freddie Laker, aided the rapid expansion of air travel after the war. But more significantly for the potential market, aircraft had become more comfortable, safer, substantially faster and, in spite of relatively high prices in the early 1950s, steadily cheaper by comparison with other forms of transport. Commercial jet services began with the ill-fated Comet aircraft in the early 1950s, but already by then advance piston-engine technology had ensured that air travel prices would fall substantially. With the introduction of the commercially successful Boeing 707 jets in 1958, the age of air travel for the masses arrived, hastening the already apparent demise of the great ocean liners. In terms of numbers carried, air travel overtook sea travel across the north Atlantic in 1957 and although the great liners were to continue Atlantic operations for a further decade, their uncompetitive costs and length of journey time resulted in declining load factors from one year to another.

Fig 2.4 Lockheed L1011 TriStar.
(*Courtesy British Airways plc*)

While the scheduled operations of the state airlines were commercially successful, private airline operators broke new ground with their development of charter services which proved highly profitable. Initally, government policy ensured that these charters were restricted to troop movements, but as official airline policy became more lenient the private operators sought new forms of charter traffic. The package holiday business resulted from co-operation between these carriers and entrepreneurs in the tour operating business. Vladimir Raitz is credited with being in the forefront of this development; in 1950, under the banner of Horizon Holidays, he organised an experimental package holiday programme by air to Corsica. By chartering his aircraft and filling every seat instead of committing himself to a block of seats on scheduled air services, he was able to reduce significantly the unit cost of his air transport and hence the overall price to the public. While carrying only 300 passengers in that first year, he repeated the experiment more successfully the following and succeeding years. The potential profits of this operation soon attracted other travel agents to move into tour operating, and by the early 1960s mass-market package tours were a major phenomenon of the European travel industry, contributing to an escalation in coastal tourism development on the Spanish mainland and the Balearic Islands, as well as in Italy, Greece and other Mediterranean coastal resorts.

Although Britain took the lead in developing package tours to the Mediterranean, other northern European countries soon followed in packaging their own sun, sea and sand holiday programmes, competing with Britain for accommodation in the hotels of the Mediterranean coast. During the 1970s Britain further liberalised its air

traffic regulations and this, coupled with the growth in second holidays resulting from longer paid holidays, led to the development of a new winter package tour market for which both skiing and winter sunshine holidays were provided. By spreading demand more evenly throughout the year in this way tour operators were able to lower their prices still further, increasing the off-season demand.

After the post-war recovery years, standards of living rose sharply in the 1950s and there was a simultaneous increase in private car ownership. Holidaymakers switched to the use of private cars and this change affected both coach and rail services. In 1950 about two out of three domestic holidays in Britain were by rail, but this figure had fallen to about one in seven by 1970. Private car ownership rose during this time from 2 million to over 11 million vehicles. This change in travel behaviour led to the return of the 'transit hotel' or motel, in the tradition of the old staging inns, serving the needs of long-distance motorists. The flexibility of travel arrangements which the private car offers also encouraged the growth of excursions and short-stay holidays, and resorts close to major centres of population benefited considerably. Road improvements, especially the network of fast motorways constructed on the Continent and in Britain following the American pattern, brought other more distant resorts closer in travel time to the major cities, changing in some cases both the nature of the market served and the image of the resort itself. The ever resourceful tour operators met the private car threat to their package holiday programmes by devising flexible packages aimed at the private motorist at home and abroad. Hotels, too, spurred on by their need to fill off-peak rooms, devised their own programmes of short-stay holidays tailored for the private motorist. The demand for hired cars on holidays overseas also increased substantially, producing a major growth in this sector of the travel industry.

In other sectors the shipping lines, hit by air competition and rising prices during the 1960s, were forced to abandon many of the traditional liner routes. Some companies attempted to adapt their vessels for cruising, not entirely successfully; vessels purpose-built for long-distance fast deep-sea voyages are not ideally suited to cruising, either economically or from the standpoint of design. Many were incapable of anchoring alongside docks in the shallow waters of the popular cruise destinations such as the Caribbean. Companies that failed to embark on a programme of building new vessels more suited to the needs of the cruise market, either through lack of foresight or of capital, soon ceased to trade. However, many new purpose-built cruise liners, of Greek, Norwegian and later Russian registry appeared on the market, filling the gaps left by the declining maritime powers, and based predominantly in the popular Caribbean or Mediterranean cruising waters. British shipping was not without its innovations, however; Cunard Line initiated the fly-cruise concept, whereby their vessels were based in the Mediterranean and aircraft were chartered to fly cruise passengers direct to the sun to join their cruise ships.

If the rapid escalation of fuel and other costs during the 1970s placed a question mark over the whole future of deep-sea shipping, ferry services have by contrast been outstandingly successful since the 1950s. Again, this largely resulted from the increased demand of private motorists taking their cars abroad for their holidays, although operational profitability depended also on continuous usage of vessels, fast turn-rounds in port and much lower levels of passenger service than would apply on cruise vessels. Cross-Channel and trans-Mediterranean services in particular have flourished in a pattern of expansion which is likely to continue unabated for the foreseeable future, although those operating from South East England will have to face the challenge of the Channel Tunnel as an alternative connection to the Continent in 1993. Competition has led to larger and more luxurious vessels, but advances in marine technology have been more limited. Both hovercraft and jetfoil craft have been introduced to cross-Channel routes, but have operating limitations that have prevented their posing a serious challenge to the more traditional craft plying the short sea routes.

The growth in private car ownership (there are over 19 million such vehicles now registered in Britain) has given a fillip to camping and caravanning holidays, both within the UK and on the Continent. Ownership of private caravans in Britain has grown to nearly 800 000 (excluding those in caravan parks), and 13 million holidaymakers now make use of caravans for their holidays. This has led to severe congestion on holiday routes during the peak summer months. Visual despoliation of the landscape by touring and static caravans is just one form of tourism pollution about which central and local governments have shown increased concern.

In Britain, the 1970s were marked by a new direction in Government policy towards tourism, with the introduction of the 1969 Development of Tourism Act. This Act, the first in the country specifically and uniquely devoted to tourism, established a new framework for public sector tourism, which took into account the industry's growing importance to the British economy. A greater emphasis was placed on conservation, as the number of foreign tourists leapt. The former largely laissez-faire attitude of successive governments gave way to one of recognising the need for adequate planning and control, to balance supply and demand, to maintain the quality of the tourist product, and to safeguard the consumer's rights. Thus, tour operators became licensed by the Government for the first time in the 1970s, and government incentives were introduced for the construction of hotels and other tourist facilities. The first serious efforts were made to categorise and register the accommodation sector. The failures of public sector planning and control in other countries (notably Spain) where an exceptionally high growth in incoming tourists was registered, added fuel to the British Government's concern. By the 1980s, the Conservative Government's attitude to tourism, while remaining positive, in recognition of the opportunities it provided for employment, supported the concept of partnership between the public and private sectors and widespread aid for tourism initiatives in areas of high tourist potential. The responsibility for tourism within the Government was moved from the Department of Trade and Industry to the Department of Employment, and a greater effort was made to coordinate the various Government departments' interests in tourism through mechanisms such as the Inter-departmental Tourism Coordinating Committee. On the whole, however, the Government adopted a 'market forces' approach to tourism development, and increasingly by the end of the 1980s people looked to the EC for the legislation which is to affect the tourism industry in the 1990s. The European Community introduced plans to liberalise air transport, to ease frontier controls, to seek greater protection for the travel consumer, to harmonise hotel classification within the Community, to harmonise VAT regulations and impose a uniform VAT, which is likely to lead to the imposition of VAT on transport by the early 1990s. This will have the effect of making air travel cheaper to some non-EC countries vis-à-vis adjoining Community nations, and could affect the pattern of mass tourism development.

As Britain's trade prospered, along with that of the developed countries, the 1980s saw a steady expansion of business travel, both on an individual basis and for purposes of conference and incentive travel. As economic power shifted between countries, so emerging nations provided new patterns of tourism generation: in the 1970s, Japan and the oil-rich nations of the Middle East led the growth, while in the 1980s, countries such as Korea and Malaysia showed a rapid escalation in both in-coming and outbound travel.

Changing social patterns have given rise to new patterns in holiday-taking; special interest holidays to cater for the expanding range of interests of a leisure-orientated society, e.g. activity holidays for those whose sedentary occupations encourage more energetic forms of travel experience. As prices soared in the 1970s the keynote in Britain became 'value for money', and millions turned to self-catering holidays. Economy, however, was only part of the reason for this change. Tourists in the free-and-easy 1960s and 1970s rebelled against the constraints imposed by package holidays in general and the accommodation sector in particular. Set meals at set times gave way to 'eat when you please, where you please, what you please'. The package tour industry responded by providing the product to meet the need; self-catering villas and apartments flourished across southern Europe while in the UK resort hotels gave way to self-catering flats. This pattern has continued and grown in the 1980s, while an increased interest in activity and adventure holidays has led to new holiday programmes and new specialist tour operators to provide them. Most noticeably, the market for long-haul holidays grew even faster than that for short-haul, leading to the mass movement of European tourists to the USA, Hong Kong, Bangkok and similar formerly 'exotic' destinations.

The annual overseas holiday is now a habit for millions of Britons, and is seen today by many as a necessity of life rather than a luxury.

QUESTIONS AND DISCUSSION POINTS

1 What factors inhibited travel in the Middle Ages? Are there any similarities you can detect with the factors that still inhibit travel in the latter half of the twentieth century?

2 Could the spas be successfully rejuvenated in Britain? What form of support should Government, local authorities or other bodies offer which would help to regenerate the use of spas? Explain why spas in Britain have generally fallen into disuse, while those on the Continent remain popular.

3 Switzerland is a country which has been a popular tourist destination since the nineteenth century, yet it appears to have suffered few of the problems faced by the growth of tourism to the Mediterranean resorts. Why do you think this is?

4 Long haul travel is expanding at a much faster rate than is short haul travel from Britain. Discuss the possible reasons for this, and its implications for tourism generally.

ASSIGNMENT TOPICS.

1 Prepare a short article for a travel trade newspaper arguing the case for a new Act to supplement the 1969 Development of Tourism Act. In the article, identify your reasons for the need for such an Act, and what you hope it would achieve.

2 You have been asked by a local business club to present a light-hearted after dinner talk to its members, on any subject of your choice involving tourism. You have decided to call your talk, 'Tourism: so what else is new?'

Your aim is to show that tourism and many of its characteristics have been a feature of western society for a very long time. Prepare a set of notes to help you in your talk.

3 The age of mass tourism

Chapter objectives: After studying this chapter, you should be able to:

- outline the growth of mass tourism;
- define different forms of tourism and their motivation;
- describe the origins and development of the package holiday;
- analyse the factors influencing the general demand for tourism;
- identify the main tourist areas and countries;
- analyse the factors influencing individual choice of destination, accommodation and mode of travel;
- identify the main methods by which tourist products may be purchased.

MASS TOURISM AND MODERN TECHNOLOGY

The origins of mass tourism

Although the nineteenth century produced a considerable change in the size and nature of tourism, it was not until well into the twentieth century that 'mass' tourism can truly be said to have come about. There were two main periods of growth.

(a) First between the two World Wars the European countries in particular underwent a period of social upheaval out of which came higher expectations by the masses of holiday entitlement, incomes and material living standards. This led to demands for more and longer holidays. Coupled with this was the development of mass transport by road, whilst railway services were also at the end of their peak. The rate of tourism growth was itself increasing until interrupted in 1939 by World War II.

(b) In the 1950s and 1960s pre-war growth was resumed but spread much more widely so that international tourism began to reach mass markets in many countries. This was stimulated by the development of relatively cheap and fast air transport, and by the application of sophisticated marketing and management techniques by producers in what was now recognised to be the tourism 'industry'.

Mass tourism in the 1930s and early 1950s was largely a domestic business. In Britain, for example, residents took $26\frac{1}{2}$ million long holidays in 1951 of which only $5\frac{1}{2}$ per cent were foreign holidays (by 1987 out of $48\frac{1}{2}$ million long holidays 40 per cent were abroad). The mass destinations were the seaside resorts, using transport by rail, coach or car, and accommodation mostly in guest or boarding houses or staying with relatives. In North America tourists increasingly used private cars for summer camp holidays in national parks and similar destinations.

Holiday camps and holiday villages

During the 1930s there emerged the holiday camp which, while in itself never having been a major form of accommodation, has had a major impact on the way destination facilities for tourists are provided and operated.

The concept of a holiday camp arose in different ways. For example, in Britain Butlin opened his first camp in 1936 to provide cheap purpose-built accommodation with mass catering facilities and a tremendous range of entertainment and amusement all on one site, preferably by the sea. In pre-war Germany the concept of highly organised and often militaristic health and recreation camps provided holidays for many who would otherwise have been unable to afford them. Political and social influences of the time had similar effects, such as the development of villages de vacances in France.

The main attribute of holiday camps to have won widespread adoption is the principle of accommodation

Fig 3.1 One of the indoor activities available in holiday centres
(*Courtesy Warners Holidays*)

Fig 3.2 The Center Parcs' swimming paradise dome by night (*Courtesy Center Parcs Limited*)

and entertainment all in one place. Operators such as Butlin and Warner appreciated early on that in resorts where entertainment was lacking, especially in wet weather, a full programme of activities was a very attractive product. This was particularly true if they were packaged and on-site with accommodation. This idea has spread to some resort hotels, particularly new ones, so that in many destinations it is unusual to find a hotel without games rooms, swimming pool, multi-gym, leisure centre, tennis, dancing and so on.

The concept of the holiday camp or village has changed; it is now less regimented, more flexible, offering mainly self-catering accommodation in tents, caravans or chalets, together with optional catering. One of the most successful operators is Club Méditerranée, a French company whose 'holiday club villages' are spread throughout countries around the world. These are now virtually the 'total resort' where the tourism product is packaged into one place. This theme is taken up in Chapter 7.

Another major development in holiday centres in Britain has been the arrival in 1987 of Center Parcs' holiday village in Sherwood Forest, Nottingham. The Dutch-owned company is responsible for introducing new standards into British holiday centres, and the all weather facilities and wide range of available activities resulted in a sell-out for the company in its first two years of operation. This can perhaps be seen as the first really successful effort to attract the British back to holidaying at home. The company opened a second UK centre in East Anglia in 1989, and is also expanding into other parts of Western Europe.

Movement to the sun

Creating a 'total resort' is symptomatic of the tourism industry's increasing commercial ability during the mid-twentieth century. As mass tourism became established, suppliers of tourism products expanded and developed their marketing expertise. In so doing, increasingly sophisticated market research revealed the motivations of different groups of tourists. One of the most important motivations proved to be the attraction of sunshine and warmth, particularly to the mass of relatively well-off people living in the cool and variable climates of North America and Northern Europe. As time, money and technology have permitted, so the pressure of demand from these markets has moved south, as shown in Fig 3.3.

Major firms in the tourism industry have identified and provided for this demand. For example, large hotel chains such as Sheraton and Hyatt in the USA have built considerable resort properties in Florida, Mexico and the Caribbean; British and German tour operators such as Thomson and TUI have developed bulk inclusive tours to the Mediterranean and north Africa; and charter airlines have opened up increasingly longer-distance routes south.

Expertise in dealing with such mass tourism has spread to other types of tourism where large numbers of people are involved: tours to centres of culture such as London or Rome; winter sports holidays; incentive travel for business people. The mass tourism product has thus become available to many different market sectors.

Jet aircraft

At the core of this longer-distance movement of people to destinations lies the jet aircraft. The first commercial passenger jet services began in the 1950s using Boeing 707 and Comet aircraft. This had two main effects.

(*a*) Average speeds of 800–1000 kph, compared with older propeller driven aircraft travelling at 400 kph, meant that an air traveller could reach a far more distant destination in a given time. This was particularly useful for business journeys where time is valuable.

(*b*) More importantly for mass holiday tourism, airlines scrambled to purchase new jets, leaving a large supply of good, secondhand propeller driven aircraft which were often purchased cheaply by small companies to undertake charter operations. These were able to carry tourists to 'sunshine' destinations faster than trains or coaches. Many of these companies had started operations after 1945 with war surplus aircraft and had developed business during the 1948 Berlin airlift (e.g. Laker).

A second upheaval in air transport occurred after 1970 when the first wide-bodied jets (Boeing 747s), able to carry over 400 passengers appeared in commercial service. The cost of carrying one passenger one kilometre

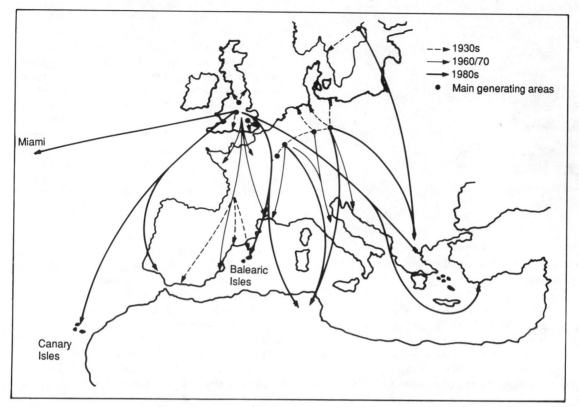

Fig 3.3 Changes in destination trends for mass market holidays, 1930s to 1980s

was considerably reduced and the result was an increased supply of air seats at potentially cheaper prices. At the same time earlier jets were sold to charter operators in the same way that propeller driven aircraft had previously been released.

Aircraft in use by scheduled and charter airlines are now not dissimilar (*see* Chapter 5), and technology has provided a range of relatively cheap, fast and efficient aircraft capable of intensive services on routes of various lengths.

Identikit destinations

The net result of recent developments in tourism for the mass markets has been the establishment of destinations for particular market segments which, in all but their location, are very often remarkably similar. A convention centre, for example, may contain a conference building which may be usable for other purposes, with committee/lecture rooms, modern single- or twin-bedded hotel rooms with private facilities, restaurants with banqueting rooms, bars, exhibition space, indoor and outdoor sports facilities, and good scheduled transport links. The location may be Portsmouth, Basel or Rio – once inside, delegates may not even notice where they are.

The larger the mass market, the less distinctive destinations are likely to be, especially if the destination is small and recently developed. One can find recently built 'marina' type resorts with yachting basins, hotel/apartment/villa accommodation, similar restaurants, cafes and shops, and golf, tennis, watersports, folk singers and barbecue nights in any one of a dozen countries around the Mediterranean, the Caribbean, north Africa and the south Pacific. These 'identikit' destinations are the result of comprehensive market research amongst various generating markets to find products with guaranteed mass demand. They may be compared with the piecemeal development of resorts two or three generations ago which may have had purely local or domestic attractions.

Not all destinations are similar, of course. While many may be 'down-market' in attractiveness, that is they may offer cheap tourism to a large number of people, with the image of great popularity, others may be identikit 'up-market' destinations, allegedly offering higher quality and thus more expensive services to fewer people. So in the former category we may think of Benidorm, Miami or perhaps Niagara Falls, or Seefeld in Austria; in the latter Tahiti, Fiji or Barbados. Many identikit destinations have been developed through the activities of multinational tourism companies such as Sheraton Hotels, Rockresorts, Club Méditerranée, Club Robinson or THF. Within their establishments a tourist will find a comforting degree of uniformity.

Fig 3.4 An identikit destination (*Courtesy Thomson Holidays*)

Mass tourism has therefore demanded and received products designed specifically for its needs as revealed through market research, i.e. products which are *user-orientated* as opposed to *resource-orientated* (that is, based on the resources available at a destination). We must now break down mass tourism into its various forms.

FORMS OF TOURISM

It is important to understand that there are a very large number of reasons why tourism takes place, that is different *purposes* for tourism. Sometimes it is the destination itself that provides the purpose for the visit, sometimes its characteristics and sometimes the destination is merely incidental to the purpose of travel. To simplify the pattern of reasons we can classify tourists into a number of *purpose-of-travel markets* which give rise to different forms of tourism.

Relaxation and physical recreation

Destinations catering for these forms of tourism demand include coasts, countryside and mountainous regions (including so-called 'wilderness regions'). The markets for this form of tourism, however, can be broadly divided between consumers who demand attractive scenery and a sense of 'communing with nature', and those seeking the attractions of sun, sea and sand.

The appeal of countryside and mountains has exercised a strong influence over British tourists for more than a hundred years, as we have seen in the chapter dealing with the history of tourism. Demand for this type of holiday is still substantial, but relatively stable, and is met by the tour operators in the form of 'Lakes and Mountains' package holidays. However, within Europe the major attractions of this kind are situated in countries which have become relatively expensive for the British over the past three decades – Switzerland, Norway, Austria, Southern Germany – and as the currencies of these countries harden against the pound sterling, demand levels off or falls.

By contrast, since sea bathing first became popular during the nineteenth century there has been a consistent demand by tourists for destinations which offer the attractions of the sea with access to a beach – preferably sandy – and hopefully good weather to enjoy it. This demand is common to almost all nations with temperate or cold-temperate climates. The tourist's expectation of a holiday is of clear warm sea, easily accessible, supported by warm sunshine to enhance the pleasure. Sunbathing in itself is a relatively newer objective, and is one that was not common in the last century.

If the above factors provide an indolent person's holiday, then activity is increasingly in demand through a range of entertainment and sports facilities. Destinations which fail to offer sun, sea, sand and these facilities tend to suffer loss of demand. Hence a poor summer in a British seaside resort may drive tourists towards the Mediterranean; pollution in the sea and overcrowded beaches at an Italian resort may drive them to Yugoslavia or north Africa.

The popularity of this kind of holiday seems constant. About 40 per cent of all British tourists in Britain go to the seaside and a majority of those going abroad do so too. However, recent medical evidence linking sunbathing and skin cancer (malignant melanoma) could have a significant impact, if not on travel to the destinations, then on the kinds of activity in which tourists will engage in the future. Increasing focus on this topic by the media, and the fact that it is Anglo-Saxon fair-skinned tourists who are most at risk, has already affected tourist behaviour in Australia and the USA, although it has yet to awaken concern in the UK. The theme 'brown is beautiful' is giving way in some circles to 'pale is interesting', and a growing number of California residents have taken to carrying parasols to protect themselves from the harmful rays of the sun. The so-called 'greenhouse effect' resulting from depletion of the ozone layer is increasing the likelihood of cancer among sunbathers.

Touring, sightseeing and culture

A second major form of tourism is also concerned with leisure. This involves the 'wandering' tourist who, not content to remain on a beach, may travel around sightseeing and possibly stay in a different place each night. He may wish to see as much of a country or area as possible and to visit notable cultural monuments or attractions. In part this may be from a desire for self-education, but may also be for his self-esteem or to be able to show off to his peers that he has visited the places concerned. The camera is the main accessory for this kind of tourist, and the destinations the tourist selects are most commonly urban centres.

An excellent example of this type of tourism is the

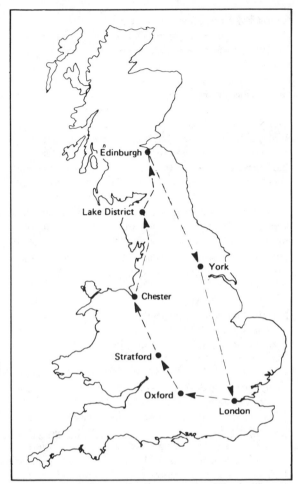

Fig 3.5 The linear tour. An example of the 'milk-run' around Britain

tourist who makes the 'circus' or 'milk-run' around Britain. Typically this may be the trip: London–Oxford–Stratford–Chester – Lake District – Edinburgh – York – London, as shown in Fig 3.5. (Frames Tours and White Horse are two operators who provide this very circuit.)

The destinations visited by sightseeing tourists are likely to be far more widespread than for the sun, sea and sand people. They are likely to need far more transport services in order to travel to a different place each day or two; this is called a 'linear tour', as opposed to a 'nodal tour' where tourists are based in one place, perhaps making excursions from there. Hotels in destinations on these linear tours can have quite a difficult time as they may have to change rooms and receive/bill different guests daily.

There are so many different types of attraction and so many motivations for visiting them that it is difficult to identify a 'mass market' for this type of tourism. Nevertheless the products purchased – the transport, accommodation, tickets to attractions, and so on – are

sufficiently similar to claim that this is an identifiable market segment.

Visiting friends and relatives

It is sometimes claimed that those visiting their friends or relatives (VFR) are not really tourists at all in the conceptual sense. They do not usually purchase accommodation nor much food or drink or other services at the destination, certainly not on their own account. They are therefore seen as of little economic value to the destination (25 per cent of British domestic tourists are VFR).

To the transport operator, however, this is a very important market. One in six of overseas tourists to Britain come for this reason, and from some countries such as Canada and Australia it is more like one in two.

The motivations for VFR are self-evident, but the effects less so. In a way these tourists are like business travellers in that the destinations are not chosen by them but predetermined and they are not often likely to buy holiday attractions. Most of them go to destinations which may not necessarily possess tourist attractions but which are population centres where friends or relatives live. Tourists are therefore visiting 'non-tourist' areas.

Business travel

An area of tourism frequently ignored in planning is travel for business purposes. The business person may travel for a variety of purposes, and in doing so will buy the same, or similar products as do holidaymakers. Business people also spend money on entertainment and recreation while at their destinations, so that it is difficult, if not impossible, to separate the 'business' element of their travel from the 'tourist' element. For this reason, business travel is usually counted along with other forms of tourism in the official statistics for tourism in most countries.

The nature of business travel demand, however, is significantly different in many ways from that of holiday travel demand, and this must be recognised and catered for by suppliers of tourist services. Firstly, business travellers frequently travel to destinations not usually seen as tourist destinations. Cities such as Birmingham, Glasgow, Brussels, Frankfurt and Geneva are important magnets for the business traveller: we can say, therefore, that demand is largely *city-orientated*. Also, demand is not dependent upon seasonal factors such as variation in climate or temperature. It is also less dependent upon economic factors such as a relative decline in the value of the pound sterling against foreign currencies, or the on-set of a recession (indeed, business travel activity may even rise as customer demand falls off, because companies may have to market their products more aggressively abroad).

Business travel is also less seasonal than

holidaymaking. The comparative stability of business travel year-round is a boon to transport services, which can accurately forecast and plan their scheduled services based on known levels of demand.

Business people take relatively short, but frequently occurring, trips, which call for regular and frequent travel connections to the major business destinations. Reservations have often to be made at short notice, and the traveller must be able to obtain confirmation in advance of travel and stay arrangements.

Business travel is relatively price-inelastic; business people cannot be encouraged to travel more frequently by the offer of lower prices, nor will an increase in price dissuade most from travelling. While this general principle holds true, it must be added that during a prolonged depression such as we have recently been experiencing, companies – particularly the self-employed business people – have become more cost-conscious, and the more progressive travel agency chains have responded to this need by identifying discount air travel opportunities for their business house clients.

Within their destinations, business tourists will demand different services. They may require car hire, communications facilities or secretarial services at their hotel; their overall demand for recreational activities may be less than that of holidaymakers, and will focus on evening activities, but it should also be remembered that business travellers are often accompanied by their spouses, who may wish to make use of the tourist attractions of the region.

While seasonality is less apparent in business travel, the problem is replaced by one of *periodicity*. Demand for business flights is particularly high at peak periods of the morning and evening to allow business travellers to optimise their time at their destination. Also, few business travellers wish to remain at their destination over a weekend, posing particular problems of spare weekend capacity for those hotels catering largely for business markets, who must market their rooms to different clients over the weekends.

One important social change affecting the business travel market has been the growth of female business travellers. This calls for special consideration in hotels, such as additional bathroom fittings (make-up mirrors, bidets) and security measures to protect the single woman traveller.

Business travellers expect, and generally receive, a level of *status handling* less apparent in other forms of travel. Much business travel is first class, with a consequent high level of service from the suppliers of travel, including their intermediaries the travel agents. Senior executives, and frequent travellers, receive VIP treatment ranging from the use of special lounges at airports to the placing of complimentary flowers or fruit in hotel bedrooms.

Special forms of business travel

Two forms of business travel deserve special mention here. The first of these is travel for conferences or special events.

The term 'conference' is often rather loosely applied to describe all forms of formal meetings between groups of people with similar interests. These can in fact range from international congresses (dealing, for example, with subjects such as air pollution or nuclear energy) to association conventions such as those of the American Bar Association, down to individual company meetings. Conferences, or conventions as the Americans usually call them, are an important element in the business and professional world, enabling participants to up-date their knowledge and mix socially with others of like interests. Many are arranged on an annual basis, such as those of political parties, trade unions or professional bodies. Participation is often encouraged by arranging these conferences in an overseas location, and this has been stimulated in recent years by the construction of purpose-built conference centres in many major business or tourist resort centres throughout the world, such as those of Berlin, Copenhagen, Hamburg or Las Vegas. The United States has led the field in the development of conference facilities, and has built some of the biggest conference centres in the world, accommodating up to 10 000 delegates. Major conferences may involve as many as 25 000 delegates, with closed circuit television relaying events in the main hall to other centres. In Britain, a number of large purpose-built conference facilities have been built in London and leading resorts such as Harrogate, Brighton, Bournemouth and Torquay during recent years.

Although attracting large-scale conferences to a resort can be highly profitable (the average spend per day by delegates is substantially higher than that of other forms of tourist), there are relatively few international events of this size, and the scale of competition between centres makes it difficult to ensure year-round usage of such facilities unless they are multi-purpose. Consequently, such centres tend to double as exhibition centres, where fairs, pop concerts and similar mass-appeal functions can be mounted to draw markets year round.

While conference and exhibition travel demand is related to the health of the economy, there has been a steady underlying rise in the number of conferences, due to increasing job specialisation and the need for greater communication on an international scale.

More recently, a second business travel phenomenon has appeared, in the shape of incentive travel. This is travel given by firms to employees, or to dealers and distributors, as a reward for some special endeavour or as a spur to achievement. The scheme originated in the USA during the 1960s, but spread rapidly in the following decade. It is estimated that more than four million business people benefit yearly from incentive offers. A good example is the American car company which flies two planeloads of sales executives and showroom managers to the Caribbean for the launch of their new model (British Leyland went one better, hiring a cruise liner for the launch of their Metro). Travel has been found to have greater motivating power than rewards of cash or other incentives, hence its rapid growth.

Both conference traffic and incentive travel are influenced by government policies on the taxation of income and business expenses. When policies favour conference travel as an allowable expense against corporate taxation, this form of travel will flourish. A short while ago, the United States Government decided to restrict such allowances to conferences taking place in the United States and its immediate neighbours (such as Mexico), causing European conference centres considerable consternation. Fortunately for the development of the international conference market, the policy was soon countermanded.

Reference should also be made here to the development of specialist package tours catering to the needs of the business world. Some specialist operators have chosen to concentrate on arranging highly lucrative industrial tours – such as trips for groups of European farmers to see the latest agricultural technology in operation in the United States. These programmes exercise strong appeal, especially where this becomes an allowable expense in the generating country.

Specialist motives

In addition to the above major forms of tourism, there is a variety of specialist needs giving rise to travel demand. We can take four examples.

(a) Study is an important motive. Students travelling to centres of learning or training for short or vacation courses may be legitimately regarded as tourists. For example, many hotels and operators offer holiday tuition courses in the arts or sports; London, Oxford and Bournemouth are just three destinations which provide English language education.

(b) Many tourists travel for sport. This may be participant sport, such as skiing or mountaineering, or spectator sport, such as attending the Olympics or World Cup series.

(c) Then there is health tourism. Ever since the development of spas in the eighteenth century there have been visitors to centres of medical treatment. The continuing popularity of spas on the Continent, with well-used, up-to-date facilities is evidence of this. This tourism can also be aided by government policy. In West Germany, for example, visits to spas can be treated as legitimate claims against medical insurance (providing

such treatment is carried out at spas within the Federal Republic).

(d) Religion may be a strong motivator. There have been pilgrims as long as there has been religion, so that the tourist demand for destinations such as Lourdes or Mecca is constant.

THE PACKAGE HOLIDAY

What is an inclusive tour?

The term package holiday is a popularly used expression for what the tourism industry technically calls an inclusive tour or IT. In a way an IT is a total tourism product as it generally consists of transport from the generating area to the destination, accommodation at the destination and possibly some other recreational or business tourist services. These products are purchased by a firm called a *tour operator*, combined and sold as a package at a single price to tourists. So in many ways the term package holiday may be a better description than inclusive tour, if technically incorrect.

For many, the IT has become identified particularly with the inclusive holiday by *air*. Because of the geographical position of the UK, a generally greater proportion of tourists going abroad use air travel from the UK than from most other major generators. This has allowed air tour operation to be more swiftly developed from the UK than from elsewhere. However, land- and sea-based packages have an equal right to be recognised as ITs.

The origins of ITs

In a sense the operations of Thomas Cook in the 1850s and 1860s were inclusive tours. Cook put together all the elements of his excursions and sold them as a single package and other 'tour organisers' followed his example. Most of these excursions were linear tours, going from place to place, rather than holidays centred in just one destination.

Tour operation proper got under way after World War II and flourished, particularly in Europe, for several reasons.

(a) Economic and social conditions were conducive to mass tourism generation. In the post-war world of promised social and economic equality, more people wanted to take the kind of holidays that previously only a few had been able to enjoy. However, they were often chary of making their own arrangements, even to places which the men of the family may have visited in wartime.

(b) A surplus of aircraft converted from military to civilian use existed, which created the conditions for air charter services. At the same time, owing to technical and cost/price problems with scheduled transport which

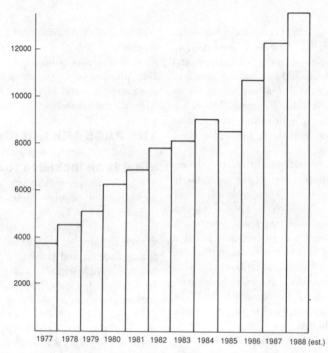

Fig 3.6 The growth of inclusive tours from the UK 1977–1988

will be seen in Chapters 5 and 9, transport operators frequently had surplus seats available on their services which they were willing to sell en bloc at almost any price. A tour operator who could buy cheap transport and also use bulk purchasing power to secure large discounts from hoteliers could put together an IT at a very attractive price.

(c) Conditions were right for marketing ITs. During the 1950s and early 1960s cheap pricing was important to consumers who had been through years of austerity and now wanted to improve their material living without spending too much. Also, American ideas on packaging and advertising had reached Europe, so that consumer acceptability of the packaged IT was high.

(d) Legal and economic controls on tourism were often conducive to IT development, such as the easing of post-war foreign exchange controls and the policy in the UK of restricting private airlines to a virtually all-charter operation.

Figure 3.6 indicates the growth of package holidays from Britain in the period between 1977 and 1988. Forecasts are for continued growth to around 20 million inclusive tours by 1998.

ITXs and ITCs

In air tour operation, two main forms of IT developed, both of which will be investigated more fully in Chapter 9 but which are described briefly here.

Where scheduled services operate with aircraft never fully loaded, airlines may sell blocks of seats to tour operators very cheaply, in fact at any price which more than covers the small extra costs of providing for passengers in seats that would otherwise fly empty. The airlines impose conditions on the tour operator that make it difficult for the operator to resell to travellers who would be using the flight anyway (booked direct with the airline at the normal fare). These seats must be sold on a return or round-trip basis, which in airline terms means an *excursion* ticket for each passenger. The tour operator then builds this into a package called an inclusive tour by excursion or ITX.

Where a tour operator charters a plane, or part of a plane, for a special flight, the resulting package is called an inclusive tour by charter or ITC. In the 1950s and 1960s there were usually two sorts of charter operation: those wholly of charter companies using older secondhand aircraft on a constant basis; and those of scheduled airlines which happened to have expensive aircraft scheduled to do nothing on some days and therefore available for hire. In either case aircraft were often available for the same return flight at the same time each week. This enabled a series of charters to the same destination, where one week's returning flight brings back the previous week's outgoing passengers. This is known as a *back-to-back* operation.

Modern charter operations, which use aircraft identical to those used by scheduled airlines, still fly series returns on the same system.

There is one important distinction which must be made between contracting for seats on chartered and scheduled aircraft. In the case of a scheduled service,

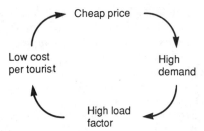

Fig 3.7 The relationship between price, cost and demand

operators do not normally guarantee the sale of seats, and may return unsold seats within an agreed period, without incurring any financial penalties. With the purchase of charter seats, a firm contract is made with the airline at an agreed price, whether or not the operator succeeds in selling the seats.

Selling the IT

One of the great advantages of the IT is the neatness with which it can be sold, particularly in markets which are mass generators of tourists. In the sense that it is almost a complete tourism product, the customer has no problem in putting together elements of a complete cohesive package. It also has a special appeal to those who are rather unsure about travel, especially long-distance travel, in that it offers both ease of booking and a degree of security to the tourist.

Generally, the ITC has tended to be associated with mass-market travel in the cheaper price ranges. This is inevitably because of the circular pattern of price, cost and demand (see Fig 3.7). An efficient charter requires a high load factor, that is aeroplanes and accommodation as full as possible, to keep cost per passenger down. This is passed on as a very cheap price, which in turn assures high demand and therefore a high load factor. This situation is exactly right for the mass-market tourists prepared to go to destinations in large numbers.

The ITX has tended to be identified with slightly more expensive packages, since the air ticket is more expensive and price does not depend so directly on numbers of passengers. As choice with scheduled services is also usually more flexible, tour operators can combine this flexibility with higher-priced accommodation to create a more exclusive IT for smaller numbers of people.

Travel agents like to sell ITs, as they receive commission on single transactions, rather than having to arrange separate services for tourists to make the same total commission. Destination areas that are attempting to develop new resorts or accommodation have also supported tour operators strongly, as they can reach a large market of tourists very quickly.

The IT product therefore has many advantages in selling tourism to mass market generators.

What has happened to tour operators?

We need to paint here a very brief picture of recent tour operators' development in order to review the full scene in Chapter 9. The formative years of air tour operation, and to some extent coach tours, were the 1960s. Firms such as Clarksons, Thomson, Cosmos and Wallace Arnold in the UK, Neckermann and Touropa in Germany or Vingresor in Scandinavia grew fast.

In the early 1970s, four separate but connected series of events took place.

(*a*) Major growth occurred in foreign ITs, particularly by air. This was partly due to reasonable economic growth, partly to the availability of better and more economic aircraft, and partly (from the UK) to the easing of foreign exchange controls (1966–70 £50 per head, 1970–77 £300).

(*b*) Considerable integration took place, both between tour operators (horizontal integration) and where tour operators became involved with other sectors of tourism such as airlines or hotels. This process has continued.

(*c*) There was ruthless competition between the major tour companies, coupled with a four-fold increase in oil prices in 1973, which led to the failure of some companies, notably Court Line (controlling Clarksons Holidays) in 1974.

(*d*) Regulations and controls on the industry were progressively introduced. In the UK, for example, the 1971 Civil Aviation Act provided for a system of licences to control air tour operators, and after the failures of 1974 the current bonding schemes to protect customers were started. In Germany and Switzerland the governments initiated similar controls.

More recently, trends have altered, and new trends emerged. The integration between tour operators and airlines which was a characteristic of the 1970s both in Europe and Japan has continued, and examples of British links between tour operating and airline companies can be found in Chapter 9. European companies in particular have entered international markets, with French companies making their first tentative efforts to establish a base in Britain, while ILG gained a foothold in West Germany, only to be forced to pull out soon after. The giant German operator TUI has a presence in Britain through its Touropa subsidiary. These early efforts are certain to expand when harmonisation within the European Community takes place in 1992.

Anything can be packaged

There has been a steady move away from passive Inclusive Tour programmes towards greater opportunities for activity and adventure holidays which have shown particularly strong growth in recent years. Long-haul holidays have also been expanding at twice the rate of short-haul. At the same time, packaging has become more common for holidays taken within the UK, as the short break holiday has developed. Hotel chains such as THF and Holiday Inns have actively planned and marketed 'theme' weekends and short breaks, backed by local authorities and the Regional Tourist Boards. One noticeable development has been the growth of *heritage tourism*, based on Britain's industrial heritage. Bradford, building on the glory of its Victorian industrial architecture, has successfully marketed itself as a base for day trips to areas such as 'Bronte country', while Wigan, taking advantage of an old music-hall joke, restored its coaling 'pier' to create an unexpectedly successful tourist attraction. Few in the business of tourism could have foreseen success for such unlikely tourist destinations. There is also a growing number of guided tours around work places – not only around potteries and distilleries, etc, but around industrial plants and new civil engineering constructions such as the Channel Tunnel.

Large numbers of tourists can be attracted to special events, and both local authorities and tourist attraction · owners have responded in imaginative ways by creating unique shows or novel events to draw tourists, ranging from more traditional music and arts festivals to Weymouth's highly publicised special event created by blowing up the local bandstand which had become surplus to requirements. In fact the idea of a package can be linked to virtually any theme and any type of tourism. Almost all sectors of the industry contain firms who are prepared to combine their services with others into an inclusive holiday or an inclusive business trip. This may take almost any form and may or may not be theme-based.

Some ITs are designed for particular groups, sometimes known as special-interest or affinity groups (although this title is dropping out of use). Equally, enterprising travel agents can make use of special arrangements to construct a tailor-made individual IT to a customer's specification if he has a special requirement. The IT is therefore capable of being almost a universal tourism product.

DETERMINANTS OF TOURISM DEMAND

So far, this chapter has outlined some of the facts and structures of tourism generation. For a fuller understanding of how and why tourism originates it is necessary to examine some of the theory underlying tourism demand. In this section we shall look only at factors affecting *total* demand, while in Chapter 4 we look at the allocation of that demand.

Psychological/social factors

Is tourism a Good Thing for the tourist? Is it a desirable product that consumers may wish to have, either as an end in itself or as a means to an end (as in business travel)? Most research assumes that tourism is such a product or group of products but often ignores the psychological and social motivations of tourists. Marketing textbooks examine this area but usually only in terms of consumer choice.

Some psychological determinants are obvious. For example, the social need to visit one's friends or family living in another place dominates the VFR market, although for some tourists VFR may only be ancillary to another motive. More complex are the psychological determinants of holiday demand. The psychological and physiological need for a break from work is recognised, almost as a medical need, on a par with the first reasons for visiting spas and the seaside. This implies relaxation and often an environment completely different from that of the tourist's home surroundings. The social pressures towards tourism, however, are far greater than this. A consumer, or consuming family, is likely to be influenced by many different sources, for example work colleagues, neighbours and friends. If such people take a holiday, there may be strong social pressure on the individual consumer to conform also.

Fashion also plays a major role. It may become fashionable to take a holiday at a certain time of year or to take a certain type of holiday; equally it may become fashionable business practice to reward employees by incentive travel. Many people are influenced by fashion in tourism just as they are by fashion in clothing, and resorts have in turns benefited and suffered from a sequential rise and decline of their appeal to trend-setting holidaymakers and later to the mass markets.

The desire for a sun-tan is a relatively recent example of the pull of fashion in tourism. In Victorian times, a white skin reflected high status associated with the leisure classes who were able to stay at home while labourers working out of doors accumulated an unfashionable tan. As the leisure classes took to travel abroad, fashion turned about face, with the wealthy cultivating sun-tans as evidence of their exotic travels, and this was in turn emulated by other travellers. Increasing concern over the rise in skin cancer, as we have seen, is likely to portend another change in fashion, already evident in the USA.

Finally, psychology also influences tourism through habit. People frequently stick to habitual activities through a preference for security and no desire for change. In leisure time use this means they may simply become accustomed to taking a holiday or business trip at a fixed time and maybe always to the same place. Tourism buying can easily become as habitual as always buying the same make of car or brand of coffee. Many seaside resorts in Britain depend heavily on the traditional demand for their attractions by holidaymakers whose parents and grandparents visited the same resort.

Choice is also influenced by the social background of the tourists concerned. Marketers measure social class largely in terms of the occupation of the main breadwinner in the family, and the most commonly used categories for this purpose are those employed by the National Readership Survey and the Institute of Practitioners in Advertising:

A Higher managerial, administrative or professional
B Middle managerial, administrative or professional
C1 Supervisory or clerical, junior managerial
C2 Skilled manual workers
D Semi- and unskilled manual workers
E Pensioners, unemployed, casual or lowest grade workers

It would be a mistake to consider these categories only in terms of income and the ability to pay for more expensive holidays. Indeed, it has been shown that the C2 category of tourist will often spend more than higher categories on their holidays. The significance between the groups is in the different *wants and needs* each seek in their leisure spending. Categories A and B, for instance, are far more likely to select travel which involves visits to cultural and heritage sites, and of those taking short break holidays in the UK, more than 40 per cent fall into these two categories. The distinctions are therefore helpful for those whose role is to market tourist attractions or destinations.

Sociopolitical factors

Tourism demand is also influenced by the society and the political system in which the tourist lives. Many societies actively encourage tourism, mostly as a break from work to provide physical and mental relief and as a reward for effort. In the countries of Eastern Europe, for example, there are policies on *social tourism* where tourism entitlement is deliberately rationed out by the state for everybody, almost regardless of means. The Soviet worker therefore knows exactly when and what his or her holiday entitlement will be. In West Germany, as we have seen, medical insurance schemes often allow the jaded worker to take a long break in a spa resort, ostensibly for medical treatment but in practice also as a holiday. In any event the worker can be regarded as a tourist since the spa resorts are normally residential and well away from the generating areas.

Most countries have a system of public holidays for all. In Britain the first bank holiday (August) was introduced in 1871, and gradually the number of holidays has grown to the current eight days a year (in England). Many other countries have more public holidays, such as twelve in Japan and thirteen in Spain. Pressure to have these holidays may come from various parts of society, such as governments, religious groups or trades unions. The holidays may be patriotic, religious or ceremonial, yet almost invariably become part of popular holiday expectations.

In general, sociopolitical systems influence more especially the choice of tourism destinations, and this will therefore be discussed more fully in the next chapter.

Economic money-related factors

Undoubtedly the main factor governing tourism demand is the constraint of money. The psychological and social pressures discussed above tend to make tourism a desirable product which will satisfy consumer or business needs; thus we may see the purchase of tourism products as a consumer *objective* (some economists may refer to this as providing the maximum *utility* for the consumer). In most countries products are allocated in exchange for money, and so the possession of money can be seen as a *constraint* on achieving the consumer's objective.

Since most individuals make purchases out of their incomes, the size of those incomes is likely to be very important for tourism demand. In fact there has been much research which shows that, typically, when a person's income rises one per cent he or she is likely to spend about $1\frac{1}{2}$ per cent more on tourism (this is called an income elasticity of $+1\frac{1}{2}$). So, for a country which is developing fast and increasing its income, the effect on tourism generation is likely to be great. West Germany and Japan, for example, have generated very large numbers of tourists since the war as their economies redeveloped.

It is important to qualify this by adding that the distribution of incomes within a country is also important. If higher incomes are concentrated in the hands of a few people, as in some Middle Eastern countries, certainly the 'haves' will travel, but with so many 'have-nots' there will be no mass tourism generation.

Business tourism is also constrained by cash. While the income elasticity is likely to be less strong, much business tourism spending such as incentive travel and conference attendance depends on the business having sufficient cash income from its operations. This usually depends on the state of the economy, so buoyant economies generate business tourism.

Tax policy is important here. If governments permit all business tourism spending to be allowed as a business expense, companies may be equally willing to spend on tourism as on stationery and communications. Sometimes governments wish to curtail such spending and place limits on tax deductibility, so forcing businesses to spend out of profits – not a pleasing prospect. Over the last few years US government tax policy has fluctuated with their presidents, and business travel there has changed accordingly.

Equally significant with income is price; and clearly, the relative price of a tourist product against other similar products will be a key factor in tourism demand. Most tourists seek sun, sea and sand and this, as we have seen, has led to the development of 'identikit' destinations. Choice between these destinations is dependent very largely on the relative value for money which each is seen to offer. Two factors are at work here in deciding price: the relative exchange rates between the generating country's currency and that of the destination country, and the inflation rates in these countries. Thus if a country such as Spain, which is heavily dependent upon the tourist trade, suffers inflation at a higher level than that of its leading competitors, or higher than the rate of inflation in its main generating countries, tourists will switch to countries such as Greece or Yugoslavia. The high inflation country may eventually be forced to devalue its currency in order to attract back its tourists.

Sometimes, however, inflation rates may be so low in a destination country compared with the generating country that even unfavourable exchange rates will not discourage travel. Such has been the case in recent times with Switzerland, which, with inflation rates typically averaging less than three per cent per annum, has been able to attract British tourists experiencing up to four times this level of inflation.

Relative prices of overseas and domestic holidays are also key pointers to tourism demand, and will be monitored closely by governments seeking favourable tourism balance of payments. The English Tourist Board, concerned about the image of cheap holidays abroad which is generated by tour operators, has taken steps to promote England as a country offering prices comparable with, or cheaper than, holidays in leading Mediterranean destinations.

Finally, the price of tourism relative to other products must be considered. For an individual, tourism competes with other items such as a car or home improvements for a share of the budget. Thus if someone is debating whether to take a holiday or buy a new car, a special offer on cars coupled with a threat of later price rises will probably stop them from being a tourist. If this price relationship is widespread within a country there could be many car buyers and few tourists!

Economic time-related factors

Especially for people at work or in education, time may be as great a constraint on tourism as money. Whereas buying, say, furniture is only limited by cash, buying tourism involves both cash *and* time, both of which may have limited availability. Holiday entitlement at work or school can then have a spectacular effect on tourism. Over the last few years many schools in Britain have

introduced one-week half-terms, rather than two or three days, and families increasingly use these periods to take a second holiday.

Whilst the timing of holidays may not affect the overall demand it does have an influence via prices. Holiday timing is not simply governed by the weather but is also controlled by public holidays, factory closure and school/college vacations. These often combine to build a peak season where demand often exceeds tourism supply so that prices are high. This problem, known as *seasonality*, leads suppliers such as hotels and airlines to influence demand through adjustment of price during different seasons.

Higher level of demand for domestic holidays during July and August is balanced to some extent by a more even flow of tourists into Britain throughout the year (particularly to London, where theatre and other attractions are less weather-dependent for their success), and by the growing tendency of many Britons themselves to travel abroad in the peak months (*see* Fig 3.8).

Holiday entitlement at work has greatly increased over the past few years – four weeks is now the norm in Britain, with most manual workers now enjoying the four weeks' annual holiday which was formerly the prerogative of their white collar colleagues – and many developed countries have established legal minima for entitlement to holidays with pay. Once the average annual holiday entitlement exceeds three weeks, there is a noted rise in demand for second holidays, and in Britain one person in five now takes two or more main holidays away from home each year.

However, the Government is currently examining the possibility of adding an extra term in the school/college year, which would have a marked effect on when many Britons take their annual holiday.

Technical factors

There are a number of other, largely technical, influences on tourism demand. The needs of businesses affect business tourism, such as the necessity of maintaining business contacts, attending exhibitions or important conferences. Demand in the VFR market is affected by the need for family reunions, for example at weddings and funerals, or simply for a get-together for a group of old friends. Students may need to travel for foreign language education, while pilgrims may need to visit a holy centre at least once in their lives. All of these are examples of factors which stimulate a constant demand for tourism services.

THE MAIN GENERATORS

Which countries generate tourism?

Over a third of the world's international tourism spending is by West Germans or Americans. The factors

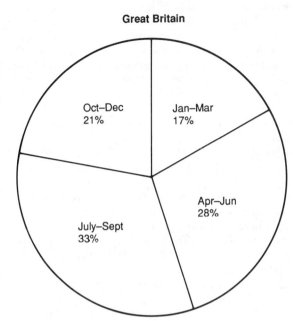

Percentage of trips

Great Britain

Jan–Mar 17%
Apr–Jun 28%
July–Sept 33%
Oct–Dec 21%

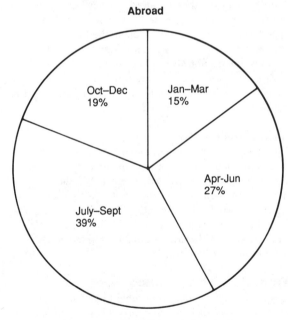

Abroad

Jan–Mar 15%
Apr-Jun 27%
July–Sept 39%
Oct–Dec 19%

Fig 3.8 Seasonality in holidays taken in Great Britain and Abroad (1987)
Source: IPS and British Tourism Survey (m)

discussed above have combined in these two countries to produce large numbers of tourists every year. Germans particularly place a high value on tourism as part of their pattern of living. Major generating countries are shown in Table II.

Table II Main tourism generating countries by Tourism Expenditure (1986)

Country	Expenditure (US$ Billions)
West Germany	20.67
USA	17.63
Gt Britain	8.92
Japan	7.14
France	6.38
Holland	4.43
Canada	4.30
Austria	4.22
Switzerland	3.38
Belgium	2.88

Source: OECD

Domestic tourism is greatest in the United States as it has easily the largest population of the above countries and, with its large land area, can be considered in travelling terms as the equivalent of several European countries. It is estimated by the US Travel Data Centre that about 480 million domestic visits are made by Americans each year. In Britain for comparison the figure is about 131 million visits of which 48 million are major holiday trips of four or more nights.

Domestic tourism is also high in the Soviet Union and other countries where the political system discourages outgoing foreign tourism. Reliable statistics of travel in these countries are rarely available.

Which areas of countries generate tourism?

Urban centres and conurbations are the obvious main generators of tourism, but for more reasons than may be readily apparent.

(*a*) In most developed and industrialised countries the bulk of the population lives in urban areas. In the UK, for example, 90 per cent of people live in large towns and conurbations. Pressures of urban living may also act to make travel a more necessary and desirable purchase for the town dweller than for the countryman.

(*b*) In many countries incomes in urban areas, from industry and commerce, are higher than those in rural areas, from agriculture and other primary production. We must qualify this by adding that incomes will be especially favourable for tourism in newer urban areas rather than in older ones more dependent on declining industries where there may be lower wages and higher unemployment.

(*c*) The country dweller, perhaps engaged in agriculture or fishing where machines cannot be stopped or offices closed at will, may find it more difficult to travel than the town dweller. Thus, for example, farmers are amongst the groups of people least likely to be holidaymakers and have far less need to travel on business than say sales people.

To the urban pattern of population must be added the effects of factors already discussed, principally the regional distribution of income and wealth. A country dweller in northern Italy for example is more likely to be a tourist than a town dweller from southern Italy because income differences are so marked. Social and psychosocial patterns also differ from one part of a country to another.

In the UK the result of the above factors is that the prime tourist-generating area is London and the South East. Then, in order of importance, come the mainly urban areas of the West Midlands, Yorkshire-Lancashire, south Wales and lowland Scotland, followed by the prosperous but less urban areas of southern and central England. A good guide to the relative importance of these markets is the location of travel agents, of which close to one third are in the London area.

Changing patterns of generation

Within the UK the pattern of tourism generation has changed only slowly as some areas become more prosperous and tourism-oriented, such as many new town areas, and others decline, such as inner cities.

Internationally, however, West Germany has again become the leader in expenditure on tourism abroad, displacing the USA, while Japan has risen to fourth place, partially as a result of the encouragement given by the Japanese Government to its citizens to travel abroad, in order to reduce the huge balance of payments surplus the country experiences in its trade in goods. Countries fast developing an industrial base, such as South Korea, Taiwan, Thailand and Singapore, have all experienced a rapid increase in demand for foreign travel by their citizens. While political disturbance has reduced tourism from countries such as Iran and Lebanon, changing political views in the Soviet Union and its satellites could eventually lead to increasing international tourism from, as well as to, those countries. Oil-rich countries such as the Middle East nations, Algeria, Nigeria and even Mexico have all shown growth in tourism demand. Those nations which combine newly industrialised economies, evenly distributed wealth and stable political systems are those most likely to experience growth in the future.

INDIVIDUAL CHOICE IN TOURISM

Up to this point we have looked at the overall or aggregate picture of tourism demand which reveals how and why tourism is generated in certain places and by certain groups of people. We can now go on to look at how decisions are made by individual tourists, whether consciously or unconsciously, on where to go, where to stay, what mode of travel to use and where they will purchase their product. In short, we are looking at the factors leading to individual choice in tourist behaviour.

In many instances choice may be limited or even non-existent. The British business people wishing to conclude a contract this evening in New York for example have no choice of destination and little choice of transport – they must use a British Airways Concorde flight. Their choice is therefore limited to various accommodations and booking methods. Soviet workers may not even have that flexibility – their holiday may be fixed entirely by the state.

Choice is influenced by many factors, but as we shall see there are the recurring ones of money, time and what may loosely be termed fashion. As already seen in connection with overall demand, some factors may make a particular tourism product a desirable consumer objective, whereas others may act as constraints on consumers trying to reach their objective. The constraining factors such as time and money may limit the consumer to a less desirable objective, perhaps one that is less fashionable.

All the time it is important to remember the tourist's overall objective, i.e. for the businessman the contribution to the business's policy and for the holidaymaker the purchase of a (hopefully) satisfying experience. These objectives colour the tourist's view of choices available. It is also important to bear in mind that tourists do not always have full information about choices available, so that they may make a selection which the better-informed employee in the tourism industry would regard as silly.

DESTINATIONS

It is possible to define destinations in different ways. A destination may simply be a resort or a business centre which the tourist visits and where he or she stays. It may be an area or even a country within which he travels. It may be a cruise ship which visits several ports. It is therefore useful to define a destination as *a place or set of places to which tourists go, and in which they may stay, as a prime objective of their visit*.

Tourists with no choice

Sometimes, as seen above, consumers may have no choice in determining their destination. This is especially true with business travel and with the VFR market, where to stay with friends or relatives means going to where they live. In this latter case it is possible that there *is* a choice, between a holiday elsewhere using paid-for accommodation and staying free with family or friends. The choice is therefore partly controlled by money constraints, although this may be unimportant compared with the desire or need to renew acquaintances.

Low-income groups may also have relatively little

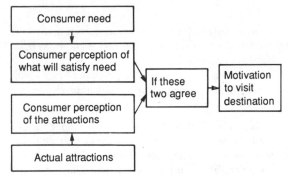

Fig 3.9 The motivation process for a destination

choice of destination in that money and/or time limit the range of alternatives. Thus the excursionist from London with limited means and only public transport available may want to go to the seaside and be limited to reaching either Southend or Brighton. Whilst both are excellent resorts, in many ways superior to others farther afield and more expensive to reach, the excursionist has no opportunity to choose elsewhere.

Attractions

The main reason for choosing a destination must be its attractions. The effect of the attractions on tourists is psychologically complex and is depicted in Fig 3.9.

In Chapter 1 we explored the importance of attractions at a destination which, in aggregate, will act as a magnet for mass tourism. We will now explore this further. The attractions must be things which provide positive benefits or characteristics to the tourist. They might be such things as proximity to seas or lakes, mountain views, safari parks, interesting historical monuments or cultural events, sports events or pleasant and comfortable conference surroundings. The list of possible motivational attractions is very large, but there are many pitfalls in the motivation process.

(a) Intending tourists need to be *aware* of all the attractions. If they are not the process cannot begin.

(b) They may *perceive* the attractions in different ways. One person may perceive the bingo halls in Blackpool as escapist fun which give hours of pleasure, while to another they may be a boring waste of time and money. Perceptions are coloured by experience and attitudes, which are different for everybody.

(c) Intending tourists may not *know or recognise* their needs very well. If they do know them, they may not correctly diagnose the benefits which could satisfy their needs. For example, Mr A at home in New York wants to sample everyday British culture, but books a holiday in London in high summer. He probably finds no-one who speaks English and certainly little typical British culture!

(d) The perceptions of need and attraction must correspond for there to be motivation to visit a destination.

Overcoming these pitfalls is the job of advertising. A good advertising programme makes consumers aware of destinations, allows for the different factors affecting their perceptions and tries to relate benefits to needs in consumers' minds.

Distractions

One can argue that just as important as the positive attractions of a destination are the negative effects of distractions; that is, there are some factors which do not positively motivate tourists to visit a destination, but where they are absent tourists will be put off. A good example is sewage facilities. Tourists are unlikely to visit a destination because it has good clean sewage treatment, but if that treatment is not there then tourists will vanish. This is exactly what happened along the Neapolitan Riviera coast in Italy, where the sea became badly polluted.

Other factors might include good transport links and car parking, good shopping and ancillary services, good weather and good relations with the resident 'host' population. The absence of these has inhibited tourism in many places ranging from wet, cold northern English seaside resorts to some Spanish destinations with accusations of unfriendliness.

It is not always possible to divide clearly attractions from distractions. For example, the existence of good accommodation and food might, for a British family visiting America, be only incidental to choice but for an American family visiting France it might be a major motivating attraction. Similarly, 'fashionable' resorts such as St Tropez or the Costa Smeralda of Sardinia may be primary attractions to some tourists but only secondary to others.

Money and time

If asked to solve a problem, a computer may frequently act by working out an 'ideal' solution, but then have constraints imposed on it that force it to seek a next best, or third or fourth best alternative. The same is often true for tourists. The major constraints as we have begun to see already are likely to be time and money. Ideally, a very long holiday in an exotic destination might satisfy tourists' needs, but they are severely constrained by income or wealth and by their holiday entitlement from work or school.

Obviously these constraints act in different ways for different people. Many old-age pensioners may have no time constraint whatever but be restricted by having only a small pension which limits them to a cheap holiday. A senior company executive or a busy successful farmer may have plenty of money to spend but very little time available. For most of us a combination of time and money dictates the 'optimum' destinations available. Of course, as incomes rise and holiday

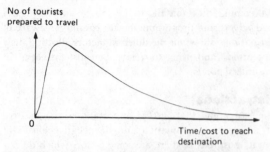

Fig 3.10 How far tourists go to reach destinations

entitlements increase, then the constraints are progressively relaxed. Equally, if prices in a destination rise or the foreign exchange rate for it becomes more expensive, then the constraints on that destination become tighter.

The main control exercised by these constraints is on the distance a tourist travels. Distance in this sense is a combination of time and cost rather than actual kilometres. For example, London to Bath, London to Boulogne and Glasgow to Skye are all similar point-to-point distances, but the long time necessary for the latter two, and particularly the extra cost associated with crossing water, would make them less popular for a day's excursion. This is where new direct or cheaper transport links could bring destinations within constraints, as when motorway links are opened or as when Miami became a cheap destination for British tourists in 1979–81. In this respect, the Channel Tunnel will make a major impact in generating day trips and short breaks between South East England and North West France/Belgium.

There is an interesting relationship between distance to destinations, measured by time/cost, and the number of tourists to travel for a visit of given length. This is shown in Fig 3.10. As one might expect, in general the more time and money it takes, the less people are prepared to travel. There is however a form of *minimum* distance, below which people do not think they are getting away from home and are therefore not very likely to travel. So there tends to be an 'average' travel time (represented by the peak in Fig 3.10) which is related to the total length of time/money available. Excursionists spend on average about 1½–2 hours travelling to a destination, one-week tourists about 4–6 hours, and two-week tourists about 8–12 hours.

These constraints, then, directly relate likely destinations for particular groups of tourists to the generating areas in which they live.

Repeat visiting

For many products, purchasers frequently continue to buy the same type. This is often true for example with instant coffee, where a consumer may always buy the same brand (brand loyalty). In many cases it is also true for tourism destinations. This situation is known as *repeat purchasing* or *repeat visiting*.

There are varying reasons why purchasers, faced with a choice of destinations, may continue to choose the same one many times.

(*a*) It is possible that the constraints mentioned above continue to operate in the same way so that only one destination is ever attainable. Thus a trade association might invariably choose the same centre for its annual conference because it is the only one which all delegates can easily reach within a reasonable time.

(*b*) The attractions of a particular destination to certain tourists may be so strong that no other is ever considered. This often seems to apply to cruising; P & O has found that for some cruises on the SS Canberra repeat visiting was 90 per cent or more, that is 90 per cent of the passengers took a similar cruise previously.

(*c*) Security and comfort may motivate a tourist to choose the same destination time after time. If a family, once having found a destination, likes its attractions, has an enjoyable time and maybe meets new friends, the chances are high that the visit will be repeated. This may extend to using the same accommodation in the same resort, at the same time each year, and therefore meeting the same like-minded people each year.

Sociologists and psychologists have undertaken research to distinguish between people who like this extreme security and those who prefer adventure, new faces and a new destination each time. Those who prefer security are often older rather than younger, are less well-educated and less well-off.

Destinations compete

Choice is also influenced in psychoeconomic terms by competition between destinations. This may be caused directly by advertising and promotion by the destinations themselves, or indirectly by changes in the attractions and distractions of one destination affecting the popularity of another. We have, for example, already mentioned the influence of prices and fluctuating exchange rates on aggregate demand for destinations. Equally, given two sun, sea and sand destinations with very similar attractions, if political conditions in one of these deteriorate, or if it gets a reputation for lawlessness, overcrowding or pollution, we can expect a proportion of tourists to switch to the other destination in preference. Economists refer to this as a cross or cross-price effect.

Obviously the degree of competition depends on the similarity between destinations, so if a destination wants to avoid losing out on cross effects it may attempt to stress its uniqueness in its publicity. The choice of destinations offering an Eiffel Tower is rather limited!

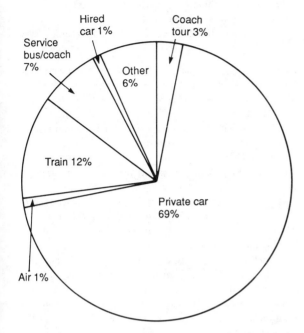

Fig 3.11 Transport modes used by tourists in Britain

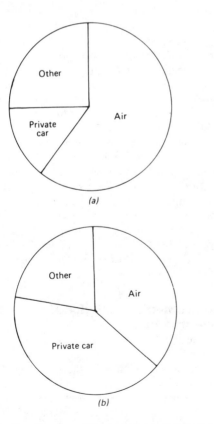

Fig 3.12 Transport modes used by tourists going abroad from **(a)** Great Britain and **(b)** West Germany

MODES OF TRAVEL

For most tourists the choice of travel mode follows on from the choice of destination. Once again there are 'attractions' of particular modes, including convenience, comfort and perhaps speed, as well as 'distractions' such as safety, and the same constraints of time and cost. The resulting pattern of tourist transport within Great Britain is shown in Fig 3.11.

Private or public?

The main choice traditionally has been between private transport (mostly private car) and public transport. In the 1950s public transport by train, bus or coach was predominant, but the 1960s and 1970s produced a major change to private transport. With increased car ownership, tourists have much greater convenience and flexibility with car travel. If a car is owned anyway, the perceived cost of using it for a tourist trip is only the variable cost, mostly petrol, so that for family use in particular it is likely to be considerably cheaper than using public transport. For those who do not have a car, or who decide not to use their own car, the choice may be between public transport and hire cars.

Public transport can be divided into regular service and charter excursion. Most trains are scheduled services, whereas bus and coach travel for tourism within Great Britain is about 50 per cent by charter/excursion. Indeed until deregulation in 1980, long-distance coach services were very largely the province of the National Bus Company exclusively. Since 1980 there has been a much wider choice of coach operators competing with both trains and each other. Competition is fierce and choice mostly dictated by speed, price and comfort.

Although domestic travel by air in Britain is very small in comparison to other modes of travel, it is of growing importance, and of course plays an important role in business travel. Liberalisation of air transport in Britain has led to the formation of a number of small airlines linking airports in major centres of business to provide low capacity flights at comparatively high prices serving the needs of the business community.

For travel abroad the mode is influenced by geography. There is an interesting comparison between travel abroad by the British and the West Germans, shown in Fig 3.12. Because Great Britain is an island, more than half of all outgoing British tourists choose air travel, presumably for speed and convenience. Only one in six take a private car, because of the delay and cost of sea crossings, compared with nearly half of all Germans.

Choosing between airlines or between ferry companies may be related more to the convenience and availability of routes than to comfort or price. It is only when 'price wars' develop, such as on transatlantic air routes between 1977 and 1982, instigated by Laker, or on cross-channel car ferries from 1980, that price seems to become a very significant factor. The likelihood of a cross-channel price war following the opening of the Channel Tunnel will lead to new decision choices between air and various forms of ground transport for travel between Britain and the Continent, both for holidaymakers and business people.

Time, delays and frustration

These are factors often ignored in looking at choice of transport, but which are very important in influencing choice, especially for repeat purchasing. Over the last decade, there has been a very rapid growth in air traffic with the corresponding increase in control mechanisms. Air travellers have frequently complained about delays and overcrowding at London Heathrow, and this has led to attempts by airlines and other airport authorities to develop alternatives. Air UK and Amsterdam Schiphol airport, for example, co-operate to enable travellers from the Midlands and the North of England to avoid London when en route to long-haul destinations. The problems faced by holidaymakers travelling by air during the summer of 1988, affected by go-slows of air traffic controllers in Greece, France and Spain, caused many travellers to reconsider their plans for a foreign holiday. The liberalisation of air routes within Europe will lead to inevitable increases in congestion on the main routes, and unavoidable delays for passengers, notwithstanding improvements planned for air traffic control.

The same applies to virtually all other forms of tourist transport. Users of road bottlenecks for example may choose to visit a different destination or use rail. Ferry companies operating in the western English Channel benefit when there are queues and delays on Dover and Folkestone routes. Strikes or undue red tape at some African gateway airports sometimes cause holiday tourists to change destinations next time. These may all be seen as further constraints on travel mode choice which can only be altered by the competent authorities. In the case of air transport within Europe, the problem can only be solved eventually by the establishment of a single 'Eurocontrol' responsible for the coordination of flights within the Community, but this will be difficult to achieve politically.

ACCOMMODATION AND ATTRACTIONS

Switching to self-catering

Thirty or forty years ago the majority of tourists stayed with friends and relatives or in guest-house type accommodation. Hotels were used by business tourists and the better-off holidaymakers, whilst at the other end of the price spectrum holiday camps were developing their popularity. There have been two major movements in consumer demand since then:

(a) the upgrading of standards of serviced accommodation, which will be looked at below; and

(b) the switch to self-catering accommodation.

This switch is common to all the main generating countries. It can be seen as a logical consequence of the use of private cars for travel and the growing desire for freedom of choice during a tourist visit. At the same time labour costs have generally risen faster than other costs in destinations, causing serviced accommodation to become relatively more expensive.

Since choice in accommodation is inevitably bound up with money constraints, and tourism is a large item in many budgets, many tourists have recently sought long-term ways of maintaining the characteristics of their most desired accommodation but reducing the cost. This has led to many people owning caravans/tents, second homes, and to timesharing.

A caravan or tent may be purchased because, although it involves a high initial outlay, in subsequent times the cost of accommodation is very small and the quality known. Also it may be possible to let it when not required and so regain some of the cost. Pioneers in the use of towed caravans, motor homes and so on are the Americans, whose main concern is often freedom of destination choice and flexibility of movement.

Second homes have a further advantage in that they will probably also appreciate in value. A tourist with savings available may therefore be able to have accommodation virtually free if the appreciation of the property covers the costs of services and maintenance. Many German, French and Dutch tourists buy second homes, often in the country or by the sea, and this is reflected in the nature of the newest Spanish or French resorts where 80 per cent or more of the accommodation available is likely to be for outright sale. For those who cannot afford to purchase a second home outright, timeshare makes an attractive alternative. Timeshare and its impact on the tourism industry are discussed in Chapter 7. Its popularity today, with more than three million timeshare owners around the world, will certainly affect the travel industry, by raising demand for seat only flights, at the expense of the more traditional inclusive tour packages.

Requirements in serviced accommodation

As living standards advance, so tourists have raised the requirements necessary to satisfy their consumer objectives in buying accommodation, i.e. they want higher standards of rooms and facilities. This demand has been spearheaded by American tourists who, being used to high living standards, naturally wish these standards to be maintained on a holiday or business trip.

At the same time technology has spread, enabling

better quality accommodation to be provided without a great increase in cost. Perhaps the most notable improvement over the last few decades has been the spread of en suite facilities – rooms with private bath and WC. This change has come about through the experience of British tourists abroad, who have come to expect and demand facilities of equal quality when taking holidays in Britain, and the realisation by suppliers that they must produce accommodation to a recognised standard in an increasingly competitive market.

Demand has also caused hoteliers to install such things as radio and television, central heating and air conditioning, fitted carpets, swimming pools, in-house entertainment, well-equipped meeting rooms and so on. In these respects large modern hotels in business centres or newly developed resort areas such as Hong Kong, Hawaii or the north African coast have a distinct advantage over older hotels in traditional destinations. Many of these older hotels have been forced into expensive re-equipping and modernisation programmes or faced closure.

To be a desirable choice then, the modern business hotel should contain en suite rooms equipped to this year's standards, conference and meeting rooms with up-to-date communications and information systems, and whatever relaxation facilities are in vogue, such as jacuzzi pools or squash courts. A resort hotel is likely to need a full entertainments programme, either in-house or arranged by the hotel, together with the appropriate indoor and outdoor places for it.

Sightseeing and sport

Choice of attractions is closely linked to choice of destination. However, once a destination has been selected, consumers may have a range of amenities and activities open to them during their stay. As with destinations, their selection is likely to be based on motivation caused by positive attractions, tempered by distractions and regulated by constraints, notably time and money.

There may be no choice at all, as where a coach tour runs to a fixed itinerary with no free time, or limited choice, as in a specialist sports or arts weekend. Apart from activities which *must* take place, such as business meetings or visiting mandatory sights, choice is determined by individual and changing requirements. There has been considerable research into what tourists do with their time, showing that frequently major activities include relaxation, sightseeing, sport, shopping and joining in somehow with the local life.

Here, constraints come into play. For example, a tourist staying in Tunisia for a week may want to go sightseeing in the Sahara, but the only available way might be a four-day package trip. The tourist may feel that this does not allow sufficient time for other activities and therefore limits sightseeing to local half-day excursions. A tourist in the Caribbean might like to spend a day big-game fishing or learning to water ski, but if on a limited budget may not be able to afford either. So choice of activity is restricted.

Fashion is a major determinant of demand. During the 1970s and the 1980s some trends in activities undertaken by tourists have emerged. One is the increase in demand for participant sports so that for example many German tourists may be found learning or playing tennis in Mediterranean resorts, while Japanese tourists are increasingly keen to play golf. Another is the growth of general activity holidays based around themes of sport, arts and crafts or hobbies. Followers of these fashions not only choose destinations to suit but select appropriate and complementary attractions at the destinations.

New attractions for the tourist

Britain has seen enormous expansion in its attractions during the past decade, both in quantity and quality. Some 60 million people visit museums in Britain each year, and museums alone now number in excess of 2300. These range from the large national collections such as the Science Museum, Victoria and Albert and Natural History Museum in London, down to small museums which may be either privately owned and operated, or run by local authorities. At the same time, the concept of a museum has changed, in efforts to attract a wider audience. The traditional 'glass case' exhibit is giving way to interactive exhibitions of living history, where visitors participate in the experience. One outstandingly successful example of this is the Jorvik Museum, which displays York's Viking history; visitors are taken on a slow moving vehicle past set pieces showing the sights, sounds and even smells of everyday Viking life. The success of this attraction has led to other Heritage projects at Oxford and at Canterbury (commemorating the Pilgrim's Way).

Many museums and attractions have built on links with the industrial era, with the Ironbridge Gorge Museum ('Birthplace of the Industrial Revolution'), the Black Country Museum, Beamish Museum and Quarry Banks Mill at Styal, Cheshire being notable examples. More modern history has also provided opportunities for tourism development, as British Nuclear Fuels discovered; opening the Sellafield nuclear processing plant to the public, undertaken largely as a public relations exercise to reassure the public about safety, led to the plant attracting over 100 000 visitors in the first year of its opening. The British Government has shown itself eager to see more links between industry and tourism in this way, and has proposed the opening of factories and assembly plants to visitors. Some companies, such as Ford Motors, already arrange visits

Fig 3.13 The Jorvik Viking Centre in York
(*Courtesy The York Archaeological Trust*)

to production lines, and interest has been expressed by other companies, with the support of the CBI.

Meantime, the development of major theme parks such as Thorpe Park, near London, Alton Towers in Staffordshire, Pleasurewood Hills near Lowestoft, the Kingdom of Camelot near Chorley and, biggest of all, the planned Wonderworld Park in the former steel town of Corby, provide scope for a full day's entertainment for tourists, with a substantial proportion of attractions under cover. All-weather facilities plus the thrilling experience of new rides brought about by advances in technology and electronics have proved to be vital to attract large numbers of tourists on a year round basis, and the coach companies have discovered that people are willing to book excursions entailing quite lengthy journeys in order to enjoy the varied facilities of these attractions.

CHOICE IN PURCHASING METHOD

Finally, consumers may exercise choice as to how they buy tourism products. The distribution channels for these products are varied, and will be discussed more fully in Chapter 8, but it is important here to follow briefly through the paths a consumer may use.

Use an agent?

In most countries the majority of tourism products are not sold through travel agents, although some products may be entirely or almost entirely sold this way. International air tickets are mostly sold through agents, with a minority of customers purchasing directly from airline offices. ITs in Britain, for example, are mostly sold through agents. The use of the agent is largely dictated by control exercised by the principals themselves, such as airlines, or by trade organisations, such as the Association of British Travel Agents.

In some cases consumers have a choice between direct booking and using an agent. Since the price is likely to be the same for buying the same product, choice would be determined by convenience, custom and advice.

Most people are of course likely to choose a convenient booking method. If there is a travel agency next door they will use it. They may also be accustomed to buying through an agent, so that is the first place they will call when going out to buy. On the other hand, if they ordinarily buy direct from suppliers such as hotels they may not think of visiting an agent at all. An agent may be used if the consumer requires (hopefully) impartial advice and wants to know about other products available.

This last factor is also important in determining choice between travel agents. Even in a country like Britain with over 7500 travel agents, most people have a feasible choice of no more than three or four agents to approach.

While incentives offered by travel agents have become an important factor in consumer selection, other factors such as quality of service, advice, friendliness, and the wisdom of personal experience of the agents, in addition to convenience, continue to play their part in the decision.

Use a package?

Another question for the consumer is whether or not to buy an IT. Again tradition and convenience are major factors. Of British tourists going abroad, just over 60 per cent use an IT, whereas only 10 per cent of domestic British tourists do so. This is partly because tourists within the country have traditionally booked their accommodation directly and provided their own transport, and partly because an IT is a convenient way of overcoming the unknown problems likely to be encountered on a foreign trip.

The main influence tour operators can bring to bear is price advantage based on buying accommodation and transport cheaply in bulk. This is difficult in domestic tourism, but often valuable in overseas travel.

In choosing between packages offered by different operators, price and the perceived advantages such as better service or closer departure points are determining factors. Most tour operators also try to encourage repeat purchasing and to maintain customer loyalty.

Alternative channels

Apart from using a travel agent or direct booking, there are a number of alternative ways for the tourist to buy tourism products. These include clubs and societies, mail order, electronic booking methods and so on.

Choice between these is largely a matter of convenience, assuming that the distribution channel concerned offers the products required. These again are discussed more fully in Chapter 8.

QUESTIONS AND DISCUSSION POINTS

1 What recent changes have occurred in British holiday camps? What made these changes necessary?

2 Identify the principal reasons for seasonality in tourism. How could the following help to reduce the problem?
  (a) legislation
  (b) marketing

3 As an in-coming tour operator, suggest ways in which you would plan to cater for the particular needs of the American market, as distinct from the British market, travelling in Britain.

ASSIGNMENT TOPICS

1 As Research Officer in the Planning and Development section of a major tour operator, you have been asked by your Head of Section, Lucia Lamamoor, to provide her with a set of statistics looking at trends over time in the flow of British tourists abroad. In particular, she wants to know how the growth of independent holidays compares with that of package holidays.

Write a short report for her, illustrating the main trends in the form of graphs, pie charts, histograms or other means you judge suitable. Your report should include:
  (a) conclusions about the patterns you identify
  (b) forecasts of what you think are likely to be the main trends over the coming decade.
  (c) particular reference to changes you see occurring in the 'packaging' of holidays.

2 Following on from your report (above), your manager has seen a growing number of references in the media to the association between sun-bathing and malignant melanoma (skin cancer). She is interested in knowing whether this factor is likely to affect the market for the company's *Young Folks* holidays in the near future.

Design and undertake a pilot survey of young people which will help to provide the answers to this question. Analyse the responses, and write a short report to your Head of Section giving the main results of your findings, and suggesting what more extensive research could be commissioned to find out the answers to this question.

4 The structure and organisation of the tourism industry

Chapter objectives: After studying this chapter, you should be able to:

- identify the integral and associated sectors of the tourism industry;
- understand the chain of distribution and how this is applied to the tourism industry;

- distinguish between different forms of integration among tourism organisations and analyse the reasons for such integration.

THE CHAIN OF DISTRIBUTION IN THE TOURISM INDUSTRY

Introduction

Tourism demand is met by the concentrated marketing effort of a wide range of tourist services. Together these services form the world's largest and fastest growing industry. Because some of these services are crucial to the generation and satisfaction of tourists' needs, while others play only a peripheral or supportive role, it is not easy to determine what constitutes the 'tourism industry'. Furthermore, some services, such as catering and transport, provide for the needs of others besides tourists. Some simplification is necessary, and Fig 4.1 provides a framework for the analysis of the industry based on a central *chain of distribution* supported by specific public and commercial sector services.

The term 'chain of distribution' is used to describe the methods by which a product or service is distributed from its manufacturing source to its eventual consumers. Traditionally, this is achieved through the intercession

of a number of intermediaries who buy the products and sell them to other links in the chain. The intermediaries may be wholesalers, buying large quantities of the product and selling in smaller quantities to others, or they may be retailers, representing the penultimate link in the chain, buying from the wholesaler and selling to the consumer (*see* Fig 4.2).

Producers, of course, are not obliged to sell their products through the chain. They may choose to sell direct to the consumers or direct to retailers, thus avoiding the wholesalers. Wholesalers in turn sometimes sell products direct to the consumer (as in 'cash and carry' companies), avoiding the use of a formal retailing outlet. These alternatives are illustrated in Fig 4.2, and all these methods are to be found in the tourism industry.

As we have seen earlier, the tourism product consists essentially of transport, accommodation and attractions, both natural and man-made. The producers of these services include air, sea, road and rail carriers, hotels and other forms of tourist accommodation, and the

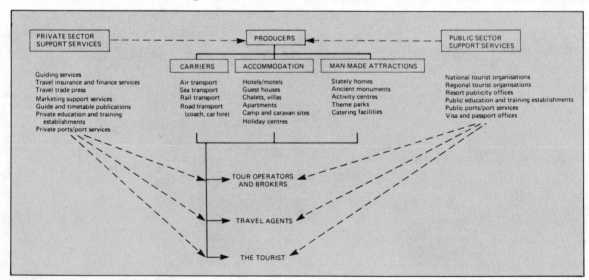

Fig 4.1 The tourism industry

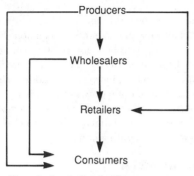

Fig 4.2 The chain of distribution

various man-made facilities designed to attract the tourist, including stately homes and other buildings, catering facilities, amusement parks and activity centres such as skiing resorts. These services may be distributed in a variety of ways to tourists, either direct, through travel agents (the *retailers* of the tourism industry) or through tour operators or brokers.

Brokers are most actively involved in the distribution system in the field of air transport, although they may also bulk-purchase hotel accommodation or certain other services. By purchasing these products in quantity they are able to negotiate lower prices and in turn sell individual air seats or hotel rooms to consumers or travel agents at a mark-up that allows them an acceptable level of profit.

Tour operators buy a range of tourist products in bulk – airline seats, hotel accommodation and coach transfers, for example – and 'package' these for subsequent sale to travel agents or to consumers direct. By buying a number of individual items of tourist services and packaging them into a single product – the 'package holiday' – tour operators are seen by some theorists as *producers* of a new product rather than wholesalers of existing products. This is a fine point, and a debatable one, but in the author's view their role is rather one of 'bulk purchaser' of tourism products and they are better described as intermediaries. (This is especially true as recent developments in the industry have led to tour operators selling 'seat only' aircraft flights to top up their load factors. Here the function of tour operator and broker becomes increasingly indivisible).

Travel agents form the retail sector of the distribution chain, buying travel services at the request of their clients and providing a convenient network of sales outlets catering for the needs of a local catchment area. They do not normally charge for their services, receiving instead a commission from the principals for each sale they negotiate.

A wide variety of support services interact with this central distribution system. For convenience these can be divided between public sector organisations (those directly controlled or operated by national or local government) and private sector organisations. The former include the various public tourism bodies in Britain, government-operated airports and seaports and their support services, passport and visa services, and public authority educational institutions providing courses of education and training for the tourism industry. The private sector includes guiding services, travel insurance and finance services (including foreign exchange and travel credit cards), the travel trade newspapers and journals, institutions providing private courses of education and training for the tourism industry, any private port or port services, travel guide and timetable publishers, and various specialist marketing services such as travel consultants and brochure design agencies. In the following chapters each of these areas will be examined in turn, to explore their role, their functions and the inter-relationships that exist between them and which together create the dynamics of the tourism industry.

Common-interest bodies

A feature of the tourism industry is the extent of association, voluntary or otherwise, that has taken place between businesses that share similar interests or complement one another's interests in some way. Such association can take different forms, but typically three forms can be identified: that based on the interests of a particular sector of the industry (or *link* in the chain of distribution); that based on a concern with specific tourism destinations; and that based on a concern with tourism activity as a whole. These may be referred to in turn as *sectoral*, *destination* and *tourism* organisations, any of which may be regional, national or international in scope.

A further subdivision may be identified between professional and trade bodies. Professional bodies are made up of individuals whose common interest is likely

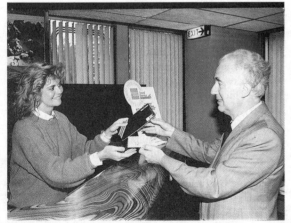

Fig 4.3 Card and travel services provided by American Express

Fig 4.4 ABTA logo

to be based on objectives which include establishing educational qualifications for the industry or sector, devising codes of conduct guiding the standards of behaviour of members, and limiting or controlling entry to the industry or sector. Membership of such bodies is associated with the drive for status and prestige on the part of its members. Trade bodies, by contrast, are groupings of independent firms whose objectives are likely to include the exchange of views, co-operation (especially in the area of marketing), representation and negotiation with other organisations, and the provision of services for members. At times such organisations may also include an interest in activities with which the professional associations are concerned, such as entry to the industry and the provision of appropriate education and training.

Sectoral organisations

Probably the most numerous organisations are those which reflect sectoral interests. As we have seen, there is a wide range of sectors making up the tourism industry and each of these can be expected to have at least one common-interest association. Professional bodies catering for sectoral interests include the Chartered Institute of Transport (CIT), the Hotel Catering and Institutional Management Association (HCIMA), and the Guild of Guide Lecturers (GGL). The Institute of Marketing has a sector devoted to travel industry members, entitled IMTIG (Institute of Marketing Travel Industry Group). The Institute of Travel and Tourism (ITT) and the Tourism Society both aim at a more multi-sectoral membership among those working in the travel and tourism industry, but the ITT's origins as the Institute of Travel Agents is still reflected in the high proportion of travel agents, and to a lesser extent tour operators, among its members, while the Tourism Society's membership draws heavily on those in public sector tourism, tourism attractions, incoming tourism, consultants and tourism educators (the Association of Tourism Teachers and Trainers is an autonomous subdivision of the Society).

Sectoral trade associations include the Association of British Travel Agents (ABTA), which represents both travel agents and tour operators, the Tour Operators' Study Group (TOSG), a consultative body representing the leading tour operators in the UK, and the British Hotels, Restaurants and Caterers' Association (BHRCA).

Similar bodies are to be found in other countries with a developed tourism industry. The American Society of Travel Agents (ASTA), for example, fulfils a similar role to that of ABTA, but also draws on members from other sectors of the industry, and includes members from overseas because of the influence and importance of the USA as a tourist generating nation.

The role of ABTA

The Association of British Travel Agents plays a key role in the British travel industry, and for this reason it is useful to examine the organisation's role here, and to consider its inter-relationship with other elements of the travel and tourism scene.

ABTA was founded in 1950, to represent initially the interests of travel agents, and later, as these developed discretely from the retail sector, of tour operators. It acts as a spokesperson for these sectors of the industry and is consulted by Government and other bodies on issues of national concern and legislation affecting the industry. It administers a system of bonding to protect customers against the failure of any of its members, and imposes Codes of Conduct on its members, which are subject to modification from time to time.

The Association is legally permitted by the Office of Fair Trading to operate a 'closed shop', by which tour operating members are required to sell their products exclusively through member travel agents, who in turn must only sell foreign inclusive tours packaged by tour operating members. This process, known as 'Operation Stabiliser', is likely to be reviewed by the European Commission following the removal of all economic barriers between Community members in 1992.

ABTA is governed by a National Council made up of ten members drawn equally from its two subsidiary Councils, the Tour Operators' Council (TOC) and the Travel Agents' Council (TAC). It operates through Committees which liaise with other sectors of the industry, such as Railways, Airways, Shipping and UK Tourism, together with certain other Committees dealing with issues of current importance such as technology. It also directs the activities of the ABTA National Training Board, which has wide responsibilities for training in the industry, and operates the Youth Training Scheme (YTS) within the industry. The National Training Board also works closely with validating bodies in education such as the City and Guilds of London Institute and the Business and Technician Education Council (BTEC), developing programmes of further education appropriate to industry's needs.

The TOC and TAC each has the responsibility to approve applications from new members in their sector, and to check on their financial standing and competence.

They also have the powers to discipline members who are in breach of the Code of Conduct, by imposing a reprimand, a fine or in extreme circumstances suspension or termination of membership.

ABTA also seeks to protect the interests of the travelling public, through the mechanism of the Codes of Conduct, and through its Conciliation and Arbitration schemes. Where clients of an ABTA member are unable to achieve satisfaction through direct negotiation with the tour operator or travel agency in the event of a complaint, ABTA provides a free conciliation service whereby they will investigate the complaint and attempt to resolve the dispute without recourse to law. If the dispute cannot be resolved in this way, the client may pursue the claim through ABTA's arbitration scheme, in which the dispute is adjudicated by a member of the Chartered Institute of Arbitrators, whose decision becomes legally binding on both sides. Although restricted to cases where claims are limited financially (£1000 per person or £5000 per booking form), it allows the client to avoid high legal costs in processing a claim and the necessity to attend a hearing. There has been a steady increase in the number of complaints dealt with by arbitration since the scheme's introduction in 1975, some 550 being handled this way in 1987. This, however, represents a very small proportion of the millions of package holidays sold each year. Details of ABTA's bonding schemes are provided later in the text.

Destination organisations

A destination organisation is one drawing its membership from public or private sector tourism bodies sharing a common interest in the tourist development or marketing of a specific tourism destination. That destination may be a resort, a state or region, a country, or an area of the globe. Membership of such bodies is open to firms or public sector organisations rather than individuals. These will have two common objectives:

(*a*) to foster co-operation and co-ordination between the various bodies that provide or are responsible for the facilities and amenities making up the tourism product; and

(*b*) to act in concert to promote the destination to the trade and to tourists generally.

These organisations are therefore trade rather than professional bodies by nature, and their structure will range from public sector consortia such as the East Asian Travel Association (EATA) to the Pacific Area Travel Association (PATA) (a mixture of private and public sector bodies), or to the Travel Industry Association of American (TIAA), a wholly privately sponsored body whose aim is to market the United States.

Tourism organisations

The activities of some bodies transcend the sectoral boundaries of the industry. Such organisations may have as their aim the compilation of national or international statistics on tourism or the furtherance of research into the tourism phenomenon as a whole. The World Tourism Organisation (WTO) is perhaps the most significant public body concerned with the collection and collation of statistical data. The organisation represents public sector tourism bodies from most countries of the world, and the publication of its data makes possible comparisons of the flow and growth of the tourism business on an international scale.

Similarly, the Organisation for Economic Co-operation and Development (OECD) has a tourism committee composed of tourism officials drawn from all member countries, and this committee produces regular reports comprising comparative statistical data on tourism development to and within these countries.

INTEGRATION IN THE TOURISM INDUSTRY

The rationale for integration

A notable feature of the industry over recent years has been the process of integration that has taken place within and between the sectors of the industry. If we refer to our model of the chain of distribution, we can identify this integration as being either *horizontal* or *vertical* in character. Horizontal integration is that taking place at any one level in the chain, while vertical integration describes the process of linking together organisations at different levels of the chain.

All business is highly competitive and the tourism industry is no exception to this rule. Such competition, often encouraged by government policy of the day, has been evident in the industry ever since the development of mass market tourism in the 1960s, and the process has accelerated in the 1980s following policies of government deregulation in the airline and coach sectors. Competition forces companies to seek ways to become more efficient and integration offers significant advantages, not least that of benefiting from economies of scale; by producing and selling more of a product the company reduces the unit cost of each product, since the fixed costs incurred are spread over an increasing number of units, whether these be hotel bedrooms, aircraft seats or package holidays. The savings achieved can then be passed on to passengers in the form of lower prices.

Most companies, asked to identify their organisational goals, would cite market expansion as a major objective. Growth in a competitive environment is a means to survival, and history testifies to the fact that few companies survive by standing still. Integration is a means to growth by enabling a company to increase its market share and simultaneously reduce the level of competition it faces.

Greater sales mean more turnover and therefore potentially more reserve funds for reinvestment in the company and thus more profit. This in turn enables the company to employ or expand its specialist personnel. Nowhere is this more true than in companies whose branches are individually quite small. For example a small chain of travel agents or hotels may for the first time, through mergers, be able to employ specialist sales or marketing personnel, or their own legal or financial advisers. More money becomes available too for the marketing effort – a programme of national advertising in the mass media may become a real possibility for the first time.

Perhaps the greatest benefit offered by integration, though, is the negotiating power that the larger company achieves in its dealings with other organisations. By expanding the scope of its operations in this way the tour operator secures purchasing power in negotiating for low prices for hotel rooms or aircraft seats; it ensures that handling companies at the destinations to which its tourists fly are eager for the company's business and will provide attractive quotations in order to secure that business; it reduces the operational risks in its business by ensuring that, where holidaymakers may be at risk in a resort due to the hotels' tendency to overbook its guests, it will be the rival clients rather than its own who are turned away. Similarly, hotels uniting in larger groups will be able to negotiate better deals through their suppliers for the bulk purchase of, for example, food and drink, and airlines will bring more bargaining strength to the negotiating table in their dealings with foreign governments for landing rights or new routes.

In addition to these broad benefits offered by integration generally, there are other advantages specific to horizontal or vertical integration which will now be examined in turn.

Horizontal integration

Horizontal integration can take several forms. One form would be the integration resulting from a merger between two companies offering competitive products. Two hotels may merge, for example, or two airlines competing on similar routes may unite. Such mergers may result from the takeover of one company by another or it may be a voluntary union between two consenting companies. If the association is a voluntary one, however, it need not entail total ownership; arrangements can be made to maintain individual identities while uniting in the form of a consortium – an affiliation of independent companies working together to achieve a common aim. For example, a marketing consortium may be formed to derive the benefits of economies of scale in the marketing effort through, for instance, the publication of a joint sales brochure. Alternatively, a common interest may be the purchase of bulk supplies at discount prices. Both of these advantages are shared by consortia such as Best Western Hotels or the Prestige Hotel chain.

A second form of integration occurs between companies offering complementary rather than competitive products. Tourism, as we have seen, is defined as the travel and stay of people. Close links therefore form between the accommodation and transport sectors, who are interdependent for their customers. Without hotel bedrooms available at their destination airline passengers are unlikely to be prepared to book their airline seats with the air carriers. Recognition of this fact has led many airlines to buy into or form hotel divisions, especially in those regions of high tourist demand where bed shortages are commonly experienced. This trend was given impetus when the 'jumbo jet' era arrived at the beginning of the 1970s and the airlines realised the consequences of operating aircraft with 350 or more passengers aboard, each requiring accommodation over which the airlines had little or no control. This was to lead to the integration of several major airlines and hotel chains; Pan American with Intercontinental Hotels and TWA with Hilton International, and in Europe the formation of the Penta Hotel chain, developed by five European airlines, among them British Airways. Deregulation in the USA later led to the American airlines divesting themselves of their hotel interests in order to raise capital.

For similar reasons airlines may link themselves together. A route operated by one airline company may, for example, provide a logical *feeder* service for another airline's services, and, in the sense that the two services are complementary rather than directly competing, a merger is formed for this reason.

The changing nature of tourism demand may also encourage companies to diversify their interests horizontally. A few years ago shipping companies, faced by a decline in demand for their services as their prices rose and airline prices fell, began buying their way into the airline business, in the short term in order to offer alternative forms of transportation, but ultimately to survive as liner services were phased out. Thus in the early 1960s, Cunard Line first bought British Eagle Airways for the North Atlantic operation and later, as government policy on route operations became more restrictive, a share of BOAC's north Atlantic airline operations, later sold when the capital investment requirements for new aircraft appeared too daunting for the company.

At the retailing level integration also occurs, but because the traditional development of travel agencies has led to regional rather than national strengths, such integration has tended to take the form of regional rather than national expansion. As tourism moved into the 1980s the pattern changed to programmes of national expansion as the large chains bought out smaller ones.

In this decade we have seen Hogg Robinson absorb Wakefield Fortune's travel agency chain and buy out almost 40 shops of the Exchange Travel chain, while Thomas Cook bought out Blue Sky and Frames Travel, American Express bought the P&O retail travel chain, Lunn Poly absorbed Renwicks and Ellermans, and A T Mays, the large Scottish regional chain, took over Hunting Lambert and Grange Travel. Meanwhile, other large chains have been steadily expanding the number of their branches, so that the retail business is now increasingly concentrated among a handful of multi-branch retailers. This so-called 'march of the multiples' is expected to continue, although perhaps not at the same frantic pace as in the 1980s.

Vertical integration

As we have seen, vertical integration is said to take place when an organisation at one level in the chain of distribution merges with that at another level. This integration can be *forward* (or *downward*) where an organisation merges with another lower in the chain than itself (as would be the case where a tour operator buys a group of travel agents), or it is described as *backward* (or *upward*) where the initiating organisation is higher in the chain (e.g. a tour operator buying its own airline or hotel chain). Forward integration is obviously found more commonly since it is more likely that organisations at the production level, rather than the sales level, will have the necessary capital available for such expansion. The higher in the chain the firm being purchased, the greater is the likelihood that high capital investment will be required.

As with horizontal integration, organisations can achieve significant economies of scale through vertical expansion. Where total profits available in each individual sector may be insufficient, taken overall a satisfactory level of profit may be made for the parent organisation to thrive in a strongly competitive environment, while the organisation may also stand to improve its competitive position in the market place.

As with the linking of complementary services in horizontal integration, many companies are concerned to ensure the continuation of their supplies. A tour operator, dependent upon a continuing supply of aircraft seats and hotel beds and facing competition on an international scale for such supplies, can best ensure their provision through direct control, i.e. by 'buying backwards' into the airline sector as did Thomson Holidays with Britannia Airways. It has to be borne in mind, however, that Thomson is in turn a part of a much larger organisation whose interests extend far beyond the tourism industry and whose capital reserves

are substantial for an investment of this kind. Many other tour operators have followed this pattern, either by integrating backwards or by starting their own airline division. Thus we find Cosmos Holidays (itself part of a large Swiss parent company) linked with the charter carrier Monarch Airlines, and Horizon Holidays established Orion Airways, (since absorbed into Britannia Airways, with Thomson's purchase of Horizon), while Intasun set up Air Europe. The major links between tour operators and airlines are shown in Fig 9.4, Chapter 9.

In the same way, many large tour operators have in recent years sought to own and operate their own hotels in key resorts abroad, to ensure availability of rooms at an affordable price. Thomson, Intasun and Horizon all invested in foreign hotel operators, either by direct purchase or by setting up joint venture companies, as between Intasun and Ladbroke. Intasun also formed links with the Ramada Hotel group in the UK to establish an interest in domestic hotels.

Such integration offers the added advantage of improved quality control. Ensuring that standards are uniform, consistent and of the required quality is no easy matter where the product is composed of diverse, disparate services, as in tourism. Clearly, the task is greatly facilitated where such services come under the management of a single parent company.

Equally, the production sector will attempt to exercise control over the merchandising of its product. Airlines, shipping services and hotels represent multi-million pound investments, yet curiously these services rely on fragmented, individual and frequently inexpert retail agencies to sell their products. Travel agents carry no stock and therefore have little brand loyalty to the companies whose products they sell. It is logical for the producers to seek to influence the retail level either by buying into retail agencies (as between Cunard Line and the Cunard Crusader Travel Company) or more commonly, by establishing their own travel shops, as in the case of Horizon Holidays and British Airways. With the merger between Thomson Holidays and Horizon Holidays, the Horizon shops have been integrated into the Thomson-owned Lunn Poly chain, while British Airways has extended its retail travel interests by forming an up-market travel agency chain, Four Corners Travel.

Air carriers can also help to ensure an even flow of demand for their seats by controlling the tour operations. The former BOAC purchased ALTA Holidays (now Speedbird Holidays) and later, as British Airways, bought the direct-sell operator Martin Rooks, as well as forming their own tour operating division under the Sovereign and Enterprise banners (now merged with Sunmed Holidays under the corporate name of Redwing Travel).

There are grounds for believing that vertical

Fig 4.5 The W H Smith Travel Shop in Swindon
(*Courtesy W H Smith Group plc*)

integration of this kind would be less subject to scrutiny by the Monopolies Commission than would horizontal expansion, where a significant sector of the industry may eventually come under the control of a handful of powerful companies. An organisation committed to growth and seeking to expand its operations in the tourism field is likely to see vertical integration as a logical means to its end.

In the long run some danger is posed to the travel agents themselves by the process of vertical integration into the retailing sector. Airlines or tour operators opening their own retail outlets may, by competitive pricing or other marketing strategies, be able to attract the market to these outlets rather than the traditional agencies. A possible counter-move on the part of travel agents would be to form consortia to operate and sell exclusively their own package tours. Numerous efforts have been made since the 1960s to form such a consortium, (most recently with the announcement that NAITA proposes to market tours for its members under the 'Liberty' banner). Although Britain has so far had only limited success in this direction, Continental businesses have been more successful.

Conglomerates

No discussion of integration in the tourism industry would be complete without reference to the role of the conglomerate. A conglomerate is an organisation whose interests extend further than a single industry. By operating in a number of diverse business spheres such a company spreads its business risk; losses in any one year in one industry may be offset against profits in another.

The continuing pattern of growth which the tourism industry has exhibited in the past, and the long-term growth prospects for leisure services, have attracted many businesses outside the tourism field. Thus the breweries have expanded into the hotel operating and holiday camp fields, Thomsons has interests at all levels of the chain of distribution, and even at the retailing level external interest is now apparent, with the development by W H Smith of in-store travel agencies. This pattern is by no means limited to the UK; throughout the world banks, finance houses, department stores and many other organisations are turning to leisure as the demand for consumer durables levels out. Midland Bank's ownership of Thomas Cook and the Royal Bank of Scotland's ownership of A T Mays perhaps mark the start of substantial bank investment in the tourism industry in this country.

QUESTIONS AND DISCUSSION POINTS

1 Operation Stabiliser has been strongly defended by ABTA as the best means of protecting the travelling public. However, European Community legislation threatens the continuation of this protective device. What would be the likely effects of its removal, in the short and long terms, on
   (a) the retail travel agents and tour operators,
   (b) the consumers, and
   (c) ABTA itself?
2 Identify the main patterns of integration that have occurred in the travel and tourism industry in the recent past, both within Britain and internationally, and explain the reasons for this process.
3 Large companies claim benefits of 'economies of scale' in the size of their organisations. Are there also 'diseconomies of scale' which may inhibit their performance and productivity? Where possible, give some examples of situations where massive growth

has led to problems within the organisation.
4 What are the main issues of concern to ABTA in the current year? (A search of reports in the trade press of regional meetings will provide a good basis of data.) Discuss how these issues might best be resolved for the future wellbeing of the trade and its consumers.

ASSIGNMENT TOPICS

1 As a student attending a full-time travel and tourism course, you are undertaking a short period of industrial work experience in a local travel agency, which is a branch of a major chain.

It is clear from the manager's attitude that she feels you are gaining no advantage in spending a long period studying tourism formally. She expresses these views to you while chatting at the end of the day, shortly after you have started your work experience: 'I have usually found it better to take staff on direct from school and train them up in the way we operate here. My staff can learn more in a week here than you will learn about travel in a year at your college'.

Write a set of notes to set out how you would reply to this comment, and identify the benefits of a more formal mode of study of your subject.

2 As a retail agent and member of NAITA, you have been approached by that organisation for help in drafting a letter designed to encourage more companies to join it.

Prepare the draft of a sales letter which is to be sent to the proprietors of small agencies, citing the advantages they might achieve through membership.

You may find it helpful to discuss NAITA membership with a present member before preparing the answer to this assignment.

5 Passenger transport I: the airlines

Chapter objectives: After studying this chapter, you should be able to:

- understand the role that airlines play in the development of tourism, and the effect of government policy on this role;
- understand how air transport is organised and distinguish between different categories of airline operation;
- understand the reasons for air regulation and the systems of regulation in force, both within the UK and internationally;
- appreciate the role and functions of IATA;
- appreciate the role of the air broker as intermediary in the air transport industry.

INTRODUCTION

Tourism is the outcome of the travel and stay of people, and, as we have seen, the development of transport, both private and public, has had a major impact on the growth and direction of tourism development. The provision of adequate, safe, comfortable, fast, convenient and cheap public transport is a prerequisite for mass market tourism. A tourist resort's accessibility is the outcome of, above all else, two factors: price (in absolute terms as well as in comparison with competitive resorts) and time (the actual or perceived time taken to travel from one's originating point to one's destination). Air travel, in particular, over the past 30 years has made medium- and long-range destinations accessible on both these counts, to an extent not previously imaginable. In doing so it has substantially contributed to the phenomenon of mass market international tourism, with its consequent benefits (and drawbacks) for the receiving nations.

Public transport, while an integral sector of the tourism industry, must also provide services which are not dependent upon tourist demand. Road, rail and air services all owe their origin to government mail contracts, and the carriage of freight, whether separate from or together with passengers, provides a significant (and sometimes crucial) contribution to a carrier's revenue. It should also be recognised that many carriers provide a commercial or social service which owes little to tourism demand. Road and rail carriers, for example, provide essential commuter services for workers travelling between their places of residence and work. These carriers (and sometimes airlines, as in the remoter districts of Scotland) provide an essential social and economic service by linking outlying rural areas with centres of industry and commerce, thus ensuring a communications lifeline for residents. The extent to which carriers can or should be commercially orientated while simultaneously being required to provide a network of unprofitable social routes poses a continuing problem for government transport policy.

Most forms of transport are highly capital intensive. The cost of building and maintaining track in the case of railways and of regularly re-equipping airlines with new aircraft embodying the latest advances in technology requires massive investment, available only to the largest corporations, and may call for financial subsidies from the public sector. At the same time transport offers great opportunities for economies of scale, where unit prices can be dramatically reduced. There is a high element of fixed costs, for example, for an airline operating out of a particular airport, whether that airline operates flights four times a day or once a week. If these overheads are distributed over a greater number of flights, individual seat costs per flight will fall.

The question of economies of scale is one for caution, however; there comes a point where the growth of organisations can result in diseconomies of scale which may offset many of the benefits resulting from size. The inability of some major airlines to compete with leaner, more efficient carriers is a case in point. Major airlines, for reasons of prestige, are likely to opt for expensively furnished high-rent city-centre offices, imposing an added burden on overheads.

The air carriers

In Chapter 2 we explored the way in which the development of air transport in the second half of the twentieth century contributed to the growth of tourism, whether for business or for pleasure. Travel by air has become safe, comfortable, rapid and above all cheap for two reasons.

The first reason is the enormous growth of aviation technology, especially since the development of the jet airliner. Since the introduction of the first generation jet (the Comet) in the early 1950s, seat cost per kilometre has fallen in absolute terms and against other forms of travel. Engine and aircraft design has been continuously refined and improved, reducing drag, increasing engine efficiency and lessening fuel consumption. At the same time increases in carrying capacity for passengers and

Fig 5.1   BAe 146-200 landing at London City Airport (Docklands)
(*Courtesy British Aerospace*)

freight have further reduced average unit seat cost. The current third generation, wide-bodied jets, spear-headed by the introduction of the Boeing 747 'jumbo' jet in 1970, reduced seat costs still further (although the sudden escalation of seat availability in such aircraft, from the previous typical 130 seats to a massive 350 seats plus, posed serious marketing problems for the airlines equipping their fleets with jumbos).

Following the huge increases in fuel costs after the oil crisis in 1973/4, research was stepped up to find ways of improving fuel economy. This has been achieved by a combination of improved engine efficiency and reduced weight (even to the extent of cutting down the number of pages in in-flight magazines!). However, the jet engine has now reached a stage of evolutionary sophistication which makes it increasingly difficult (short of a revolutionary breakthrough such as the development of new forms of fuel) to produce further economies, and cost-cutting exercises have largely replaced technological innovation as a means of stabilising prices.

With the pressure of oil prices in the 1980s, technological advances have been in two directions: towards quieter aircraft, and towards aircraft capable of taking off from, and landing on, shorter runways.

The development of quieter engines has been encouraged by the environmental lobby in the USA, where controls on noise pollution have forced airlines either to re-equip with quieter aircraft or to fit expensive 'hush-kits' to existing aircraft. In turn, the airlines have been pressing for a relaxation of controls over night flights, which would enable them to operate more fully around the clock, easing airport congestion and increasing productivity. The British Government, however, has been loathe to permit more than a token increase in night flights.

Short take-off and landing (STOL) aircraft such as the De Havilland Dash-7, Dornier 228 and the BAe 146 jet (*see* Fig 5.1) are revolutionising business travel, allowing the siting of airports much closer to city centres. London City Airport, sited in the docklands, now provides fast business connections to Paris and Brussels on Dash-7s carrying up to 36 passengers.

The second factor in the development of mass travel by air has been the enterprise and creativity demonstrated both by air transport management and by other entrepreneurs in the tourism industry. The introduction of net inclusive tour basing fares for tour operators and variable pricing techniques such as advance purchase excursion (APEX) and 'stand-by' fares have stimulated demand and filled aircraft seats. The key factor though has been the chartering of aircraft by tour operators, first on an *ad hoc* basis for weekly departures and later on a *time series* basis (with the chartered aircraft being placed entirely at the disposal of the tour operator throughout season or year). Chartering in this way, coupled with very high load factors on each aircraft, reduced unit seat cost to a point where low cost package tours (especially to such destinations as the east coast of Spain and Majorca) brought foreign holidays within reach of millions in the UK and Western Europe.

THE ORGANISATION OF AIR TRANSPORT

It is convenient to think of air transport operations under three broad headings:

(a) scheduled air services;
(b) non-scheduled air services (charter services);
(c) air taxi services.

Scheduled services are those which operate on defined routes, whether domestic or international, for which licences have been granted by the government or governments concerned. The airlines are required to operate such services on the basis of published timetables, regardless of passenger load factors (although flights and routes which are not commercially viable throughout the year may be operated during periods of high demand only).

Such services can be further categorised as *public* (state-operated) or *private*. In most countries the public airline will be the national flag-carrier (as with Air France) but the extent of public versus private ownership will vary in air transport according to a country's form of government. In planned economies such as those of the Soviet bloc, all airlines will be run by the state, while in the USA, by contrast, all airlines will be operated by the private sector. Airlines in Europe wholly owned by their governments include Austrian, Air France, Iberia, Air Portugal (TAP), and Olympic, while the carriers Sabena, Swissair and Scandinavian Air Services (SAS) are partially government-owned. All British airlines are privately owned, since British Airways was privatised in 1987.

According to their route network and relative importance within the air transport business, carriers other than the national flag-carrier may be identified as either *second force* or *third force* airlines. Leading airlines providing competitive or complementary services to those of the national flag line on domestic or international routes, or sometimes those providing substantial inter-regional services, are termed second force airlines. Those providing a network of regional or local services are usually termed third force, or *feeder* airlines. There is a growing group of regional and 'commuter' airlines within Europe which are offering important feeder services to the large carriers, such as DLT in West Germany, NLM in Holland, Crossair in Switzerland and Air UK in Britain. Some of these are partially owned by flag carriers; Lufthansa, for instance, has a 40 per cent stake in DLT, and KLM a 15 per cent stake in Air UK. British Airways has a financial interest in Brymon Airways in the UK. The relationship between these levels of carrier and the determination of government policy towards each level (as well as between the public and private sectors) have shaped the present pattern of air transport in Britain.

The economics of scheduled airline operations

The development of an airline route is something of a 'Catch 22' situation. Airlines require some assurance of traffic demand before they are prepared to commit their aircraft to regular service on a new route, while air travellers in their turn require regular and frequent services in order to patronise a route. There is usually an element of risk involved in initiating a new route, especially since seat prices are likely to be high to compensate for low *load factors* (seats sold as a percentage of seats available on an aircraft) and high overheads (in both operational and marketing costs) before traffic builds up. When a route has proved its popularity, however, the pioneer airline is faced with increasing competition (as other airlines are attracted) unless this is strictly controlled by the respective governments. This in turn results in lower load factors and either higher prices or reduced profit margins. Key routes such as those across the north Atlantic attract a level of competition which can make it difficult to operate any services profitably, especially since the deregulating policies of the United States and British governments in the late 1970s, which have supported open competition.

The selection of suitable aircraft for a route is the outcome of the assessment of the relative costs involved, of which there are two kinds, and the characteristics of the aircraft themselves.

(a) *Capital costs.* When supply outstrips demand, as is the case when there are many second-hand aircraft on the market and intense competition for sales between the remaining aircraft manufacturers, airlines can drive very hard bargains in purchasing new equipment. It must be remembered that costs for new aircraft are usually a package embracing not only the sale of the aircraft itself, but the subsequent provision of spares. Loan terms can be a key issue in closing a sale, and some manufacturers are prepared to offer very favourable trade-ins on old aircraft to sell their new models.

(b) *Operating costs.* Aircraft are not easily interchangeable between routes. Broadly speaking, they are designed to operate efficiently on either short-haul (up to 1500 miles), medium-haul (1500–3500 miles) or long-haul (over 3500 miles) routes, but not on any combination of these. Mile for mile, short-haul routes are more expensive to operate than are long-haul, due to two factors. First, short-haul travel requires a greater frequency of take-offs and landings, and in take-offs an aircraft consumes substantially more fuel than it does once it has attained its operational ceiling during flight. Second, short-haul aircraft spend a proportionately greater amount of their time on the ground. Aircraft earn money only while they are in the air, and depreciation of their capital cost can only be written off against their actual flying hours. For this reason it is important that they are scheduled for the maximum number of hours' flying each day. Ground handling charges can be reduced by speeding up the turn-around of an aircraft, and airlines will aim to turn their aircraft around in as little as 50–60 minutes. This time will include off-loading and on-loading passengers and baggage, preparing cabins for the coming flight and refuelling.

Long-haul aircraft usually operate at a ceiling of 30 000–40 000 feet (supersonic flights, between 50 000 and 60 000 feet), while other aircraft operate at lower ceilings. While the cost of getting the long-haul aircraft to their operating ceilings is high due to the length of climb, once at these heights there is little wind resistance and therefore the rate of fuel usage falls considerably.

Direct costs of airline operating include flight expenses (salaries of flight crew, fuel, in-flight catering costs) maintenance, depreciation, aircraft insurance, and airport and en route navigation charges. Airport charges include landing fees, which are based on the weight of the aircraft and the number of passengers carried. Parking and hangar charges may be imposed if the aircraft stays on the ground beyond a given length of time. Navigation charges are also based on the weight of the aircraft, and the distance flown over a particular territory.

Depreciation is the cost of writing off the original purchase price of the aircraft against the number of hours it flies each year (an aircraft may be in the air for something approaching 4000 hours each year). Total depreciation periods vary; in the case of smaller, relatively inexpensive equipment it may be as short as eight to ten years, while in the case of wide bodied jets the depreciation period may be extended to as long as 14 to 16 years. A residual value of about 10 per cent of the original purchase price is normally allowed for. In some cases it might be considered prudent to write off aircraft more quickly because obsolescence can overtake the actual operating life of the aircraft, as technological breakthroughs are introduced, and airlines must keep up with their competitors in re-equipping their fleets. Insurance premiums will range around three per cent per annum of the aircraft purchase price.

Indirect costs include all non-flight expenses such as marketing, reservations, ground handling, administration and other insurances such as passenger liability.

(*c*) *Aircraft characteristics.* These will include the aircraft's cruising speed and 'block speed' (its average overall speed on a trip), its range and field length requirements, its carrying capacity and its customer appeal. In terms of passenger capacities, airline development tends to occur in leaps rather than through slow progression. While the introduction of jumbo jets led to an overnight tripling of seats on jet aircraft, increase in demand was naturally more gradual. While average seat costs fell sharply with the advent of the jumbos, it was to take some time before passenger demand caught up with the new availability.

Carrying capacity, however, is also influenced by the payload which the aircraft is to carry, i.e. the balance between fuel, passengers and freight. An aircraft is authorised to 'take off at MTOW (maximum take off weight)', which is its empty operating weight plus fuel and payload. At maximum payload, the aircraft will be limited to a specific range, but can increase this range by sacrificing part of the payload – i.e. by carrying fewer passengers. Sacrificing both fuel and some passenger capacity may allow aircraft to operate from smaller regional airports with short runways.

Cost savings can be made in a number of ways when using larger aircraft. It is a curious fact that the relative cost of pushing a large aircraft through the air is less, per unit of weight, than a small one (incidentally, this principle also holds true of ship operations, in that large ships are relatively cheaper per unit of weight to push through water). Large aircraft experience proportionately lower drag per unit of weight; we say they are more 'aerodynamic'. They can also use larger, more powerful engines. Equally, maintenance and cleaning costs per seat are less.

Aside from economic considerations, the customer appeal of an aircraft depends upon such factors as seat comfort and pitch, engine quietness and the interior design of cabins. In a product where, generally speaking, there is a great deal of homogeneity, minor differences such as these can greatly affect the marketing of the aircraft to airlines.

Corporate objectives and government policy

Airlines, as are all transport companies, are inevitably faced with conflicting pressures in establishing their objectives. In the case of private airlines, the interests of shareholders may lie in the maximisation of profits, or at the very least in ensuring a reasonable rate of return for their investment. This may be constrained by the need to ensure long-term growth for the airline, and by political or social obligations such as support for the nation's aviation industry, or pressures to reduce noise pollution, or to keep fares down. Public airlines, too, face conflicting pressures in setting objectives. British Airways during the 1970s was paradoxically required to meet target returns on capital invested by the government while simultaneously forced into non-competitive purchasing, and the operation of uneconomic routes as a social service. By the 1980s, however, the British Government's view favoured free market commercial decisions in air transport as in other fields, and with the privatisation of British Airways towards the end of the decade, decisions on route operation and aircraft purchases were taken purely on commercial considerations.

However, in many countries, airlines will often be subject to the dictates of government in the use of their aircraft for defence purposes, or for the operation of air routes seen as politically expedient. Similarly, the development of a new holiday destination may be the outcome of public sector objectives rather than the commercial policy of the airline concerned.

Marketing of air services

It is for marketing to determine the destinations to be served (although, as we have seen, government policies, particularly in the field of regulation, will strongly influence these), flight frequencies and timings (based on traffic potential to the destination, the nature of market demand and current levels of competition). Routes are of course dependent upon freight as well as passenger demand, and a decision must be reached on the appropriate mix between freight and passengers, as well as the mix of passenger markets to be served – business, holiday, VFR, etc.

Flight frequencies and timings may also be subject to government controls. For example, it is common to find countries limiting the number of flights permitted into and out of airports at night. Where long-haul travel, and hence time zone changes, are involved, this can severely curtail services. The congestion of traffic at major international airports will have a further 'rationing' effect on flight operations.

It is particularly important for business travellers that they are able to make satisfactory connections with other flights on comprehensive itineraries. To gain a strategic marketing advantage, an airline will want to coordinate its flights with other complementary carriers, leading to *interline* agreements between carriers (the free interchange of documents and reservations between carriers). In long-haul planning, the carrier must also decide whether the company is likely to maximise its revenue by operating non-stop flights to the destination, or providing intermediate stop-over points to cater for passengers wanting to travel between different legs of the journey (known as 'stage' traffic). This will permit the airline to cater for, or organise, stop-over holiday programmes, with the appeal of duty-free shopping facilities in the stop-over airport.

Following the planning stage, the airline must determine its pricing policy. Fixing the price of airline seats is a complex process, involving consideration of:

(*a*) the size and type of aircraft operating on the route;

(*b*) the route traffic density and level of competition;

(*c*) the regularity of demand flow, and the extent to which this demand is balanced in both directions on the route;

(*d*) the type of demand for air service on the route, determining the mix between first class, economy class, inclusive tour-basing fares and other discounted ticket sales;

(*e*) the estimated break-even load factor (the number of seats which must be sold in order to recover all costs), typically set at somewhere between 50 and 60 per cent of capacity on scheduled routes. The airline's aim is to achieve this level of seat occupancy, on average, throughout the year.

Demand for air travel can change at short notice, depending upon such factors as the state of the economy of the generating country or the political stability of the destination country. This instability can have a serious effect upon the overall viability of airline operations. This uncertainty can be mitigated by leasing aircraft for a route rather than buying. Most airlines will, from time to time, lease out aircraft to unload surplus capacity, and conversely other airlines will take up a lease on an aircraft to cope with sudden increases in demand or to cover a service when their operations are hit by maintenance problems or a crash. Airlines who have specialised in leasing arrangements may well buy new equipment specifically to lease this to other carriers. In most cases such leases are *wet leases*, i.e. they include the lease of the operating crews. Aircraft under lease in this way are painted in the appropriate livery of the carrier for which they are to operate.

Most scheduled services are operated on the basis of an advanced reservations system, with lower (APEX) fares being made available on many routes for bookings taken substantially (2–3 months) in advance and low 'stand-by' fares offered to prospective passengers without reservations who are prepared to take their chance on seats being available an hour or so before flights. An alternative system which has been developed for high density traffic routes is the 'shuttle', for which no advanced reservations are needed and for which all passengers are guaranteed a seat, with an extra flight being added if need be to handle surplus demand. This type of service can only be commercially viable for routes which experience a high level of regular (typically business) demand in both directions. Such services were first operated in the United States in the 1960s, but British Airways introduced a shuttle service in Britain in 1975 between London and Glasgow and has since extended this to other domestic routes in the UK.

Non-scheduled (charter) services

With the gradual liberalisation of air service regulations within Europe, the distinction between scheduled and charter services is blurring; by the late 1980s, scheduled services were seeking routes from the UK to destinations such as Palma, Majorca, which have traditionally been the preserve of the charter carriers, while charter airlines such as Air Europe have sought permission to operate regular scheduled services. One factor in this development has been the steady rise in demand for 'seat only' sales, and the strong demand for independent holidays. Today, we can identify three types of charter operator; those which are wholly independent of other carriers, such as Britannia Airways in Great Britain and LTU in West Germany; those which are charter subsidiaries of scheduled airlines, such as Caledonian in Britain (a subsidiary of British Airways) or Condor in Germany (a subsidiary of Lufthansa); and airlines operating both scheduled and charter services, such as Dan Air in the UK or Aviaco in Spain.

From the 1960s onwards, charter services grew rapidly, at the expense of scheduled operators. Their appeal was essentially one of low price; by setting a very high break-even load factor (typically 85–90 per cent) and by keeping overheads low, prices have been dramatically reduced compared with those of the scheduled services. Charter airlines save on marketing costs (they do not advertise their routes to the public), on operational costs (they provide a less elaborate service, both in the air and on the ground) and on head office costs (being less concerned with status and the need to keep a high profile before the travelling public, they settle for simpler administrative offices away from high-rent central-city areas). But above all they have one great advantage over scheduled airlines in that they are not obliged to operate to a timetable; they can choose to withdraw their less fully booked flights and either transfer their passengers to other charter airlines or *consolidate* their flights with others experiencing similar low loadings. In this way passengers benefit from the lowest possible air fares while sacrificing the guarantee of a specific flight (or even a flight from a specific airport, since a consolidation may involve a switch to a different airport). This sort of 'trade-off' would not suit the business traveller but is acceptable in the holiday market.

Until the mid-1960s the British government permitted charter carriers to operate out of the UK on only a limited scale. Charters were restricted to *closed groups* known as affinity groups, consisting of members of a club or other organisation whose principal purpose was not that of obtaining low-priced air travel. This led to the formation of a large number of bogus 'clubs' and the rules governing the operation of affinity charters were flagrantly ignored. Policing 'bent' charters proved difficult and from the 1960s onwards the government liberalised its policies regarding charter regulations. Tour operators, already experiencing strong growth in demand for the new package tours, were quick to develop the charter market, at first chartering on an *ad hoc* basis but soon turning to time series charters to minimise costs.

The scheduled airlines feared dilution of their traffic by the new charter services, but in fact the charters succeeded in tapping an entirely new market for foreign holidays. Prices tumbled and there was a huge growth in numbers carried, especially from northern Europe to the Mediterranean. On the lucrative north Atlantic services, charters made impressive gains paralleling those of the scheduled services between 1965 and 1977 with the advent of advance booking charters (ABCs), to which the scheduled carriers responded by introducing advance purchase excursion (APEX) fares. However, scheduled airlines had to exercise caution that they did not dilute normal revenue by introducing discounted fares of this kind.

One notable development in the industry has been the tendency for tour operators to form or take over their own charter airlines, predominantly to ensure seat availability for their own passengers. Surplus capacity on these charters is then made available to smaller-scale tour operators mounting their own programmes to the same destination. This development has had the effect of creaming off much of the charter business formerly obtained by the independent airlines, forcing these to seek alternative markets for their aircraft.

While those charter airlines which are subsidiaries of tour operators may have half of their capacity filled with passengers of that tour operator, many charter airlines will also be carrying passengers from a dozen or more different operators on a single flight.

Air taxis

These are private charter aircraft accommodating small groups (typically from four to eighteen persons) and are used particularly by business travellers. They offer advantages of convenience and flexibility; routings can be tailor-made for passengers (for example, a feasible itinerary for a business day using an air taxi might be London–Paris–Brussels–Amsterdam–London, a near impossible programme for a scheduled service), small airfields close to a company's office or factory can be used (there are some 350 of these in the UK alone, with a further 1300 in Western Europe) and flights can be arranged or routings amended at short notice.

Aircraft in use as air taxis range from helicopters seating three or four, with a range of some 400 kilometres, to Bandeirantes flying eighteen passengers within a similar range. Some small aircraft such as HS125-600s can carry ten passengers up to 2500 kilometres but most air taxi work entails journeys of up to 800–1000 kilometres and is therefore an ideal medium of transport for travel between the commercial centres of Europe.

Fig 5.2 Air taxi – Gates Learjet 35A which carries eight passengers
(*Courtesy Northern Executive Aviation Limited, Manchester Airport*)

Some corporations which formerly ran their own fleet of executive aircraft have switched to using air taxis since purchase is difficult to justify unless aircraft have very high usage rates.

Air brokers

One further sector of the airline industry must be mentioned here, that of the air brokers. These are the people who act as intermediaries between aircraft owners and their potential charter market. They act both in an advisory and a sales capacity and their task, which is often overlooked in discussions of the air transport industry, is to find suitable aircraft at the right price, both for *ad hoc* and series charters. To do so they must maintain close contact both with airlines and with the charter market.

They play an important role in securing aircraft seats at times of shortage and in disposing of surplus capacity at times of over-supply, and are also active as intermediaries in tour operators' flight consolidations. The body representing their interests in the industry is the Air Brokers' Association.

Reference should also be made here to the intermediaries, commonly known as 'consolidators', who play an increasingly important role in the industry by purchasing surplus flight seats in bulk from miscellaneous scheduled carriers and disposing of these through non-ABTA non-IATA 'bucket shops' at illegally discounted fares.

THE REGULATION OF AIR TRANSPORT

The need for regulation

With the growth of the industry, regulation, whether of national or international routes, has become necessary for a number of reasons. First and foremost there is the question of passenger safety, which requires that airlines be licensed and supervised. For reasons of public concern other controls will be necessary, such as those designed to reduce noise or pollution.

Since air transport has a profound impact on the economy of a region or a country, governments will take steps to encourage the development of routes which appear to offer prospects of economic benefit and to discourage services on those routes already suffering from over-capacity. While the policy of one government may be to encourage competition or to intervene where a route monopoly is forcing prices up, another government's policy may be directed to rationalising excessive competition in order to save energy waste or to ensure profitability for the national flag-carrier. One characteristic of such involvement is the *pooling* arrangements made between airlines operating on certain international routes whereby all revenue accruing on that route is apportioned equally between the carriers serving the route. This may appear to circumvent competition on a route, but is also one means of safeguarding the viability of the national carrier operating in a strong competitive environment.

Fig 5.3 Loganair's Twin Otter landing on the beach at Barra
(*Courtesy Loganair Limited*)

Pooling agreements are often entered into, where the airlines are not of comparable size, in order to safeguard the smaller carrier's capacity and revenue. By rationalising schedules, pressure is reduced for peak time take-off slots, and costs are reduced. Financial arrangements between the pooled carriers usually limit to a fixed maximum the amount of revenue transferred from one carrier to the other, to reduce what might be judged government support for an inefficient carrier. Pooling agreements, however, are now forbidden in the USA.

In some areas air transport is an essential public utility which, even if commercially non-viable, may be socially desirable to provide communication with a region where geographical terrain may make other forms of transport difficult or impossible (as is the case with some areas of the Hebrides in Scotland). In this case, financial subsidies may be provided to maintain the service. Such services would be required to operate on a regular rather than intermittent basis.

The question of balance between public and private air transport will depend upon the political viewpoint of the party in power, and this will also be reflected in a government's regulatory activities.

Systems of regulation

Broadly speaking, air transport operations are regulated in three ways.

(*a*) Internationally, scheduled air routes are assigned on the basis of agreements between the governments of the countries concerned.

(*b*) Internationally, scheduled air fares are established (for member airlines) by the mutual agreement of the airlines concerned and through the mediation of the traffic conferences of the International Air Transport Association (IATA), a trade body. Agreed tariffs are then subject to ratification by the appropriate governments. Nationally, air fares within the UK are also subject to the formal approval of the Civil Aviation Authority (CAA), acting as the regulatory agent of the government. Similar bodies exist in other countries.

(*c*) National governments will approve and license the carriers which are to operate on scheduled routes, whether domestically or internationally. In the UK the CAA has this responsibility, and is also responsible for the licensing of charter airlines and of tour operators organising package holidays by air abroad.

In North America, Britain, and increasingly, other European countries, government policy is to allow market forces to determine the shape and direction of the airline industry, and regulation is less concerned with routes, frequency, capacity and fares, and more directed to aspects of safety.

Air transport regulations are the result of a number of international agreements between countries dating back over many years. The Warsaw Convention in 1929 first established common agreement on the extent of liability of the airlines in the event of death or injury of passengers or loss of passenger baggage. The limitations on liability soon led to inflation reducing the value of claims, and liability was reassessed by a number of participating airlines as a result of the Montreal Protocol, wherein it was agreed that maximum liability would be revised periodically. Then at the Chicago Convention on Civil Aviation held in 1944, eighty governments were represented in discussions designed to promote world air services and to reach agreement on standard operating procedures for air services between countries. There were two outcomes of this meeting: the founding of the International Civil Aviation Organisation (ICAO), now a specialised agency of the United Nations; and the establishment of the *five freedoms* of the air. These comprised the privileges of:

(*a*) flying across a country without landing;

(*b*) landing in a country for purposes other than the carriage of passengers or freight, e.g. in order to refuel aircraft;

(*c*) off-loading passengers, mail or freight from an aircraft of the country from which those passengers, mail or freight originated;

(*d*) loading passengers, mail or freight on an aircraft of the country to which those passengers, mail or freight are destined;

(*e*) loading passengers, mail or freight on an aircraft not belonging to the country to which those passengers, mail or freight are destined, and off-loading passengers, mail or freight from an aircraft not of the country from which these originated.

These privileges were designed to provide the framework for bilateral agreements between countries and to ensure that carriage of passengers, mail and freight between two countries would normally be restricted to the carriers of those countries. While a handful of countries had expressed a preference for an 'open skies' policy on air traffic regulation, most had demanded controls. An international Air Services Transit Agreement, to which more than 90 countries became signatories, provided for the mutual exchange of the first two 'freedoms of the air', while it was left to individual bilateral negotiations between countries to resolve other issues. The convention agreed not to regulate charter services, allowing countries to impose whatever individual regulations and conditions they chose. Few countries, in fact, were willing to allow a total 'open skies' policy for charters.

The Anglo-American agreement which took place in Bermuda in 1946, following the convention, set the pattern for many of the bilateral agreements which have followed. This *Bermuda Agreement*, while restricting air carriage between the two countries to national carriers, did not in fact impose restrictions on capacity for the airlines concerned, but this was modified when the Bermuda Agreement was renegotiated in 1977 (and ratified in 1980), in line with the tendency of many countries in the intervening years to opt for an agreement which would ensure that a percentage of total traffic on a route was guaranteed for the national carriers of the country concerned. It was Britain's intention, in this renegotiated agreement, to avoid over-capacity on the route by restricting it to two British and two American carriers. A further agreement in 1986 extended the agreed capacities across the Atlantic, following a three year moratorium on new services by the UK and American Governments.

Carriage on routes within the national territory of any one country (known as *Cabotage* routes) is not subject, of course, to international agreement and is normally restricted to the national carriers of the country concerned. In some cases, however, this provides opportunities for a country's national carriers to operate exclusively on international routes in cases where countries have overseas possessions. This is the case, for example, on routes out of the UK to points such as Gibraltar and Hong Kong. More significantly, air fares on such routes are not subject to ratification by IATA. There have been recent calls for cabotage routes to be introduced within the European Community, following harmonisation in 1992, although no decision has yet been taken on this issue.

The role of IATA

For many years effective control over air fares on international scheduled routes has been exercised by the International Air Transport Association, a trade association comprising some 80 per cent of the world's airlines which operate on international routes. The decreed aims of the organisation, which was restructured in its present form in 1945, are to promote safe, regular and economic air transport, to provide the means for collaboration between the air carriers themselves, and to co-operate with the ICAO and other international bodies for the promotion of safety and effective communications. However, it was IATA's fare-fixing role which aroused most controversy since the association has in the past acted in effect as a legalised cartel. Fares had been established at the annual fare-fixing IATA Traffic Conferences by common agreement among the participating airlines; while subject to ratification of the governments concerned, in practice such approval had been largely automatic.

Critics of IATA had argued that fares as a result had been unnecessarily high on most routes and the effect had been to stifle competition. In many cases agreed fares were the outcome of political considerations in which the less efficient national flag-carriers had been able to push for prices unrelated to competitive costs. IATA also controlled many other aspects of airline operation in addition to fares (such as the pitch of passenger seats, which dictates the amount of leg room a passenger may enjoy, and the kind of meals that may be served on board flights), and as a result airlines had to concentrate in their marketing on such ephemeral aspects of the product as service, punctuality or the design of stewardess's uniforms, rather than providing a genuine measure of competition.

It was widely felt that this had led to inertia among the participating carriers, with agreements resulting from a desire to avoid controversy among fellow members. Nor had the cartel ensured profitability for its members, since they faced open competition from non-IATA carriers who successfully competed both on price and added value.

Because of this, and because of governmental commitment to the concept of free competition (especially in recent years in the United States), IATA restructured its organisations in 1979 to provide a two-tier structure: a tariff section to deal with fare-fixing, membership of which is voluntary for member airlines; and a trade section to which all members must belong and participate. A number of airlines, notably US carriers, chose to withdraw from the tariff-fixing section, but continue to gain from the benefits of membership of the trade section. In the intervening years, IATA's role in regulating fares has become relatively unimportant, and airlines have been free to determine their own service and catering arrangements. However, membership still offers benefits, and trade activities now occupy most of IATA's time. Among the achievements of IATA one may cite the provision of a central clearing house system which makes possible quick financial settlements between members; standardised tickets and other documents which are interchangeable between carriers; compatibility on the basis of air fare constructions and changing exchange rates; and the general standardisation of operating procedures (such as the licensing of travel agents). If IATA were to be wound up it would lead to considerable inconvenience for the travelling public; already in the United States the lack of *interlining* facilities (which permit through fares on a single ticket on multi-stop journeys) on non-IATA carriers can be a serious drawback for travellers.

British regulation of air transport

In the UK, the Civil Aviation Act 1971 led to the establishment of the Civil Aviation Authority (CAA), which has five regulatory functions:

1 It is responsible for regulating air navigation services (jointly with the Ministry of Defence), through Britain's Air Traffic Control Services.

2 It has responsibility for the regulation of all British Civil Aviation, including air transport licensing, the award of licences (ATOLs) to air travel organisers, and approval of air fares.

3 It is responsible for the airworthiness and operational safety of British carriers, including certification of airlines, airports, flight crew and engineers.

4 It acts as advisor to the Government in matters concerning domestic and international civil aviation.

5 It has a number of subsidiary functions, including the research and publication of statistics, and the ownership and management of eight airports in the Highlands and islands of Scotland.

Prior to the Civil Aviation Act, no clear long-term government policy had been discernible; as governments came and went, policies with respect to competition or to the balance between public and private carriers changed. With the idea of providing some longer-term direction and stability a committee of enquiry into civil air transport, under the chairmanship of Sir Ronald Edwards, was commissioned by the Government to prepare a report on the future of British air transport. This report, *British Air Transport in the Seventies*, appeared in 1969. The gist of their recommendations was that the Government should periodically promulgate civil aviation policy and objectives; that the long-term aim should be to satisfy air travellers at the lowest economically desirable price; and that a suitable mix should be agreed as between public and private sector airlines. The state corporations (BOAC and BEA) were confirmed in their role as the flag-carriers for the scheduled services, but were recommended to merge and to start charter and inclusive tour operations. The idea of a major *second force* airline in the private sector, to complement and compete with the new public airline, was proposed, as was the suggestion that a more liberal policy be adopted towards the licensing of other private airlines. Finally, the report proposed that the economic, safety and regulatory functions carried out by the previous Air Transport Licensing Board, the Board of Trade and the Air Registration Board should thereafter come under the control of a single Civil Aviation Authority.

The Civil Aviation Act, which followed publication of this report in 1971, accepted most of these proposals. BOAC and BEA were merged into a single corporation, British Airways; British Caledonian was confirmed as the new second force airline, following the merger between Caledonian Airways and British United Airways; and the new Civil Aviation Authority was formed.

The Authority is financed by users of its services, which are mainly the airlines themselves. Any excess profits made are expected to be returned to the users through lower charges for its services. A subsidiary of the CAA is the Air Transport Users' Committee (ATUC), which acts as a watchdog for air transport customers (there is also an international body serving this purpose, known as the International Foundation of Airline Passengers' Associations (AFAPA), based in Geneva).

Government policy since 1971

In introducing the concept of a second force private airline, the Edwards Report had clearly seen this as being designed to compete with the public flag-carrier across the north Atlantic. After the formation of British Caledonian, the Government granted the carrier north Atlantic routes in 1973. Within two years, however, government policy was changing to one of 'spheres of influence', with the second force airline licensed for complementary rather than directly competitive routes. Ignoring British Caledonian's claim that two British carriers on the North Atlantic would have the effect of increasing the British share of the total market by taking away business from the American competition, the CAA redistributed routes, giving British Caledonian South American routes and restricting the north Atlantic largely to British Airways. A White Paper in 1976, *Future Civil Aviation Policy*, indicated the prevailing policy to end dual designation – a policy that has since been eroded by the 1979 Conservative Government in their support for the deregulation of the air transport industry. In the 1980s, increasingly liberal views towards regulation, both in Britain and the USA, led to the 'open skies' policy across the Atlantic and within the UK itself. The privatisation of British Airways in 1987, and the subsequent redistribution and licensing of routes for smaller British carriers, has set the scene for liberalisation throughout Europe.

DEREGULATION IN NORTH AMERICA

Deregulation, or 'liberalisation' as it has come to be known in Europe, is the deliberate government policy to reduce state control over airline operations, and to allow market forces to shape the airline industry. In the 1970s, an increasingly liberal view of regulation by the American Government resulted in the withdrawal of a number of US airlines from IATA's fare fixing agreement. The Carter administration introduced the Airline Deregulation Act in 1978, abolishing collusion in air pricing. The main regulatory body, the Civil Aeronautics Board (CAB) progressively relinquished control over both route allocation and fares within the United States, and was itself disbanded at the end of 1984, the Board's remaining functions such as safety passing to other government agencies (the Federal Aviation Administration, and the Departments of Justice and Transportation). The Act allowed for the continuation of subsidies for services which, linking remote rural airports, were deemed socially essential, although in practice these subsidies have been considerably reduced. In all other respects, market forces would take over, with the expectation that existing inefficient large carriers would be undercut by smaller, highly efficient carriers owing to the latter's low overheads and higher productivity. Choice would be widened, fares reduced and services improved.

In fact, the actual outcome of deregulation in North America has been very different, and has caused advocates of liberalisation to pause in their support for total deregulation. The short-term effects of deregulation are now clear, and longer-term effects are emerging.

In the opening years of deregulation, a rapid expansion of airline operations took place. Airlines that expanded prudently, like Delta Airlines, prospered, while others became over-ambitious, committing themselves to a programme of expansion which, as fares became more competitive, they could not support financially. Some, including mega-carrier Braniff Airways, collapsed (Braniff was to be resurrected on a smaller scale some years later). The first few years of deregulation saw a threefold increase in the number of carriers operating in America. While a few routes saw substantial fare increases initially, especially on long-haul domestic flights, the challenge for market share among carriers new and old held prices down on most routes. New low fares attracted a large number of passengers, and domestic air traffic had increased by nearly 40 per cent by 1985. However, the drive to reduce prices resulted in 90 per cent of all air tickets being sold at discounted fares, with discounts averaging over 60 per cent on published tariffs. Growth was being achieved at the expense of profitability.

Cutting costs to remain competitive forced airlines to abandon union salaries and negotiate new wage agreements and conditions of service. Small, hyper-efficient airlines like People's Express appeared, with aircrew taking turns to shift baggage. Some airlines reverted to propeller aircraft on short haul routes to pare costs, and worries began to emerge about standards of maintenance.

By the second half of the 1980s, the pattern had again changed. More than one hundred US airlines were forced out of business or absorbed in the face of increasingly desperate competition. By 1987, two out of three carriers launched since deregulation had been forced out of business. The uncertainty of jobs among airline personnel led to loss of morale and, in some cases, indifferent service. The drive to make aircraft servicing more 'efficient' was followed by an increase in accidents: air safety violations doubled between 1984 and 1987.

Supplementals, as charter carriers are known in the USA, were particularly badly hit, as scheduled prices dropped to match their own. Charter carriers had neither the public recognition nor the marketing and distribution systems that would have enabled them to expand their operations and capture a share of the growing market. Many charter companies simply ceased operations.

Airline operating in North America had now developed into a 'hub and spoke' system, in which feeder air services from smaller airports provided links to connecting long-haul services out of the major airports. This pattern enabled the airlines to achieve higher load factors and keep prices down. Airports such as New York, Chicago, Atlanta, St Louis and Dallas/Fort Worth became major hubs for international and domestic long-haul flights, with some airports dominated by a single carrier. The airline industry became dominated by six mega-carriers: Texas Air Corporation, American, United, Delta, Northwest and US Air/Piedmont together controlled three quarters of the air travel market in the United States. Two other major carriers, Pan American and TWA, have survived but their long term future remains uncertain at the time of writing.

The six major carriers grew by a process of absorption and merger, and have formed close links with feeder services to control routes. Many small, successful feeder services were also swallowed up in a rash of take-overs.

By 1987, it had become clear that fares were beginning to rise once again, as the large carriers tightened their oligopolistic grip on domestic services. What is now clear is that the original intention of the Airline Deregulation Act has been frustrated; airline services have become more, rather than less, concentrated, choice has been reduced and fares are now being forced up.

While the large carriers owe much of their success to their initial efforts at cost cutting, two other factors have played an important part in this success; the highly creative marketing talent displayed by the new breed of airline management, and the formation of new computer reservations systems (CRS). An example of creative marketing has been the development of 'frequent flyer' programmes, whereby regular airline clients are able to build up 'points' towards free flights for themselves or their spouses, depending upon the mileage travelled with a particular airline during the year. This has enabled airlines to build brand loyalty (for a product noted for its lack of this quality) among frequent business travellers, who can build up sufficient credit for a free flight to Europe based on their regular domestic business flights.

DEREGULATION IN EUROPE

Deregulation in Europe can be traced to the influences of US deregulation in the 1970s, and the termination of fare-fixing across the Atlantic in 1980. Although air fare collusion is forbidden under the free trade clauses in the EEC's Treaty of Rome, efforts by British carriers to end fare fixing on inter-European routes met with strong resistance by some Government-owned carriers, specifically those of France, Italy, Scandinavia, Italy and, to a lesser extent, West Germany. However, the European Commission has determined that liberalisation shall be facilitated by 1990, and it appears inevitable that carriers' efforts to retain fare fixing agreements or restriction on routes within the European Community will be frustrated. In the meantime, more liberal governments within the Community have reached individual agreements for greater or lesser degrees of liberalisation on air travel between their countries. One of the first such agreements, and a far reaching one, was that achieved between the UK and Dutch Governments in 1984, which removed constraints on air fares and capacity between the countries. This led to large increases in demand, and the supply of aircraft seats, with new routes such as that developed to Maastricht by Virgin Airways. In 1988, Britain reached a similar agreement with the Irish Government, involving the complete freedom of routes and a pricing policy which would allow low fares to be disapproved only by both countries (although either nation is permitted to ban a fare which it considers too high). The agreement included fifth freedom rights, making it possible for Irish carriers to pick up passengers in the UK on routes operating between Ireland and the Continent via Britain. The resultant low fares and expansion of traffic between Britain and Ireland has boosted support for liberalisation in Europe.

Within the UK, the CAA freed most routes from regulation in 1985, although certain trunk routes out of London were exempted from this policy due to problems of airport congestion. Again, domestic liberalisation has led to substantial growth both in carriers (some 50 now operate within the UK) and passenger traffic.

Liberalisation tends to lead to more complex fare structures, as each airline determines its own fares and conditions, making it imperative that travel agents have access to up-to-date information through CRSs.

One side effect of deregulation has been the decline of the established 'bucket shops' – non-appointed travel agents who sold off illegally discounted air tickets dumped on the market at short notice by airlines with spare capacity. Discounted tickets are now so freely available through recognised agency outlets that the distinction between the bucket shop and the approved agent has all but disappeared in the past five years.

The growth of passenger traffic resulting from liberalisation in Europe poses problems, however. Europe is rapidly approaching saturation, in terms of the number of air traffic movements it can handle, both as regards runway congestion and terminal congestion. While improvements in air traffic control, additional runways, use of larger aircraft or the easing of restrictions on night flights can help to relieve the situation, the problem is only being postponed, and inevitably other solutions must be found for the movement of passengers within Europe in the longer term.

European carriers now face a new threat, in the shape of US airline competition, under liberalised airline operations. US carriers are now developing their 'hub and spoke' systems within Europe, taking advantage of their rights to carry passengers between European countries. By contrast, European carriers are prevented by US cabotage rights from developing the same 'hub and spoke' systems in the United States. These advantages may lead to US carriers dominating the transatlantic routes, unless some means of regulating them is introduced, such as the concept of a European cabotage for EC carriers.

AIRLINE COMPUTER RESERVATIONS SYSTEMS

Computer reservations systems, known by the initials CRS, have become a major force in marketing airline services, for two reasons. The first is that agents and clients depend upon a fast and accurate indication of flight availability and booking service, together with rapid fare quotations, so that 'best buys' can be quickly identified. The new generation of airline computers provides just this, with most fares now accessible on the system; US CRSs hold some 30 million fares, of which some one million are changed every day.

The second reason is that the system can be, and in the past has been, programmed to display flights in a manner favouring the airline which owns it. Flights are displayed page by page on the screen, and research has shown that 75–80 per cent of all bookings are made on the basis of information displayed on the first page of the screen. Airlines have been able to bias the display of this information by listing their own flights first, both in the

DO YOU KNOW?
THROUGH SABRE WE CAN ARRANGE:

Activities in Australia
  Aussiepass
  Sight-seeing
Bon Voyage Gifts
Business Forms
Chauffeur-driven Limousines
Club Med Vacations
Country, State, City Information
Crewed Yacht Charters
Foreign Exchange Services
  Foreign Currency
  Foreign Drafts
  Travelers Checks
  Foreign Wire Transfers
Hawaiian Activities
  Weddings
  Helicopter Sight-seeing
  Lei Greetings
  Horseback Riding
  Island transfers for events
    and attractions
  Dinner/Cocktail Shows
  Water Sports
  Cruises
  Golf
  Day Tours
Japan Activities
  Sight-seeing
  Transfers
  Special Services

Las Vegas Activities
  Transfers
  Shows, Events, Tickets
Los Angeles Activities
  Airport Transfers for local airports
  Sight-seeing
  Transportation for local attractions
  Luxury Bus Service to Las Vegas
New York Grayline Tours
Passports and Visas
Rail Schedules, Fares, Tickets
Recreational Vehicle Rentals
Telex
  Cable
  Speedmail
Theatre/Event Tickets
  Las Vegas
  New York
  United Kingdom
Travel Insurance
  Flight Insurance
  Accident/Medical/Sickness
  Baggage and Personal Possessions
  Trip Cancellation/Trip Interruption
Travel Merchandise
  Luggage/Luggage Carts
  Hair Dryers
  Travel Irons
  Travel Clocks
  Voltage Converters

Fig 5.4 Services available on the Sabre computer reservation system
(*Courtesy American Airlines*)

case of single flights and for onward flights connecting with other carriers. The result has been a substantial increase in market share for carriers with their own well established CRSs. Governments in the USA and Britain, as a result of the concern expressed by their nations' carriers without such international computer systems, have sought to introduce legislation making it an offence to bias the presentation of displays in this way.

Two US carriers in particular, American Airlines and United Airlines, have developed CRSs with a powerful national following and at the time of writing are poised to expand this system in the European market. Their systems, known as *Sabre* and *Apollo* respectively, together account for four fifths of airline reservations in the USA,

and pose a strong threat to the British Travicom system, which is part owned by British Airways.

The European response to the threat posed by the systems has been for a number of airlines to get together in order to develop their own international CRSs, either building on an existing system or designed to compete with it. Two such systems are currently under development at this time: Galileo and Amadeus. The former is a consortium of airlines (among them British Airways, KLM and Swissair) linked to the United Airlines Apollo system through COVIA, a United subsidiary. Its rival, Amadeus, is under development by a consortium which includes Lufthansa, Air France, SAS and Iberia, linked to PARS, the CRS of TWA,

Northwest Airlines and certain Far East carriers. Both organisations are competing to attract other, smaller carriers into their systems, which are not planned to interface. Consequently, the system with the greatest network of carriers will have the strongest appeal to distributors, and on the principle that success breeds success, will find it progressively easier to attract more carriers and other travel companies' products. CRSs are already expanding beyond airline reservations systems, and include hotel and car hire reservations facilities.

One significant aspect of the new CRSs is their relative user-friendliness. Galileo promises an 'easy' version designed for the less frequent user, and it is a relatively short step, using existing technology, for the systems to become available direct to consumers' homes. The introduction of 'smart cards' (credit cards with built-in micro-chip memories) will enable airlines to direct-debit cardholders for the purchase of airline tickets, posing a further threat to the traditional retailers as the main distributors of airline seats.

QUESTIONS AND DISCUSSION POINTS

1 What were the principal reasons for flight delays in the latter part of the 1980s? Suggest ways by which the problem could have been, or could now be, overcome or reduced.

What 'knock-on' effects would be experienced by tourism businesses in destination resorts as a result of these delays?

2 In the face of increasing deregulation in air transport throughout the world, how important do you feel the role of IATA will be in the future?

3 What is the role of the air broker, and how significant is this function in the air travel business? Would you forecast that this is a role that will continue to grow?

ASSIGNMENT TOPICS

1 As a member of staff with responsibility for route planning at Gemini Airways (a charter carrier considering applying to the CAA for scheduled routes into Europe), you have been asked to assess the impact of deregulation in the United States and to consider how far patterns established there are being repeated in Europe following liberalisation. Produce a report for your Director, Route Planning

and Development, which:

(a) examines the short- and long-term effects of deregulation in North America, and

(b) compares events in Europe resulting from liberalisation within Europe and the European Community's policies concerning air transport.

In particular, you are asked to examine whether the 'hub and spoke' development in North America is likely to be widely repeated in Europe, and if so, to identify likely hubs within the European Community.

Your report should contain suitable illustrations and maps.

2 As a representative of the Air Transport Users' Committee, you have been given the task to investigate air safety and to present a report to the Committee for their consideration at a forthcoming meeting. Your brief is to research civil air mishaps occurring within the space of the last five years, and to identify the causes for these. You should make some attempt in your report to categorise these accidents into suitable groups, such as pilot error, failure in quality control, etc. Suggest some recommendations for action which the ATUC might put to the CAA and/or other interested parties.

6 Passenger transport II: sea, rail and road services

Chapter objectives: After studying this chapter, you should be able to:

- identify the differing categories of water-borne transport, and analyse the reasons for their growth or decline;
- understand the role and scope of public and private railway and coach organisations in Britain;
- understand the importance of marketing and market segmentation for public transport companies;

- understand the consequences of regulation and deregulation of transport, and evaluate the case for or against open competition;
- recognise the impact that private car ownership has had on tourism and the tourist industry, and the role played by car hire companies.

INTRODUCTION

Although air services today play the leading role in providing tourism transport, sea, road and rail services continue to play an important part, both domestically and internationally, in meeting travellers' communication needs. While air transport clearly offers the fastest links over long distances, other methods of travel have their own unique advantages. Coach travel still remains the cheapest means of travel almost universally; the introduction of new technology on the railways has seen the advantage of speed that air services have enjoyed over the railways gradually eroded on short and medium length journeys; and the relaxation and entertainment of a voyage by sea goes a long way towards making up for slower speeds and greater costs. Technology in shipping has enabled new forms of water-borne transport to be developed in recent years – vessels such as the hovercraft (technically an aircraft, since it travels above the surface of the water) and the hydrofoil, with its derivatives the jetfoil and the twin-hulled jet cat. These, too, have provided faster communication over short sea routes and in difficult terrain.

The pleasure that people still enjoy in being afloat has spawned many recent tourist developments, including yacht marinas, self-drive motor craft, dinghy sailing in the Mediterranean and canal barge holidays in Britain. Similarly, the fascination with steam engines has led to the renovation of lake steamers in England and paddle steamers in the USA, as well as the regeneration of private steam railways in Britain and elsewhere. The division is blurred between transport and entertainment, between public and private means of transport; the journey or the vehicle becomes an end in itself for the tourist as much as a means to an end.

WATER-BORNE TRANSPORT

It is convenient to use the generic term 'water-borne transport' in this chapter since this will include not only sea-going vessels, but also river, canal and lake craft, all of which are playing a growing role in tourism. We are faced then with five categories of water-borne transport services:

(a) ocean-going line voyages;
(b) cruises;
(c) short sea voyages (or ferry services);
(d) inland waterway services;
(e) sea-going small pleasure craft.

The history and fortunes of these differing forms of transport reveal strong contrasts, and each will be dealt with separately here.

The ocean liners

Line voyage services are those offering passenger transport on a port-to-port basis. Such services have declined over the past 40 years to a point where today very few exist anywhere in the world, and even these are generally operated on a seasonal basis only. The reasons for this decline are not hard to identify.

From the 1950s onwards, advances in air transport technology, as has been shown, resulted in the price of air transport falling on most routes, and especially across the Atlantic, to a point where it became cheaper to travel by air than by sea. Shipping lines found themselves unable to compete, faced as they were with rising labour costs and a labour-intensive product. Many vessels were old and outdated and the cost of replacing them prohibitive; at the fares passengers would be prepared to pay it would be difficult if not impossible to write off the capital cost of a new vessel during its normal life expectancy of 15–20 years. Other operating costs were also escalating and this, coupled with the advantages of improved speed, safety and comfort standards offered by the airlines, signalled the demise of worldwide shipping. During the 1960s and 1970s the major shipping companies reduced or discontinued their long-established

Fig 6.1 Queen Elizabeth 2
(*Courtesy Cunard Line Limited*)

routes out of the UK – P & O to the Far East and Australia, Union-Castle line to South Africa and Cunard across the Atlantic. The resulting shake-ups in shipping management led to attempts to regenerate traffic or to use existing vessels for cruising, but the large liners' days were numbered. A small but continuing demand for transport by sea remains for those with money and leisure time, or others who suffer from fear of flying or airsickness; and a very limited number of services continue to operate, but on a highly seasonal basis. The *Queen Elizabeth 2* provides a connection between Southampton and New York (via Cherbourg) during the summer months, and cruises for the balance of the year, while *St Helena* carries more than 70 passengers on its year round passenger-cargo service from Avonmouth to South Africa, via Ascension and St Helena islands, and approval has been given for the construction of a new passenger-cargo vessel with twice the present capacity, due to enter service early in the 1990s. These are the only two line voyages operating from the UK on a regular basis. Elsewhere, perhaps no more than a dozen passenger routes can be identified, including such exotic routes as mainland India to the Andaman and Nicobar Islands, Smyril Line's service to Iceland and the Faroes, and Chinese and Norwegian coastal voyages. In addition, some 16 cargo-passenger lines carrying up to 12 passengers each are still operating, although on such vessels passengers are secondary to freight interests, and one way voyages may not be possible.

With hindsight it is easy to pinpoint the inevitability of shipping's decline. However, it must be said that shipping management must bear some of the blame for failing to adapt their product to changing needs. Ships built or operating in the 1950s failed to meet the needs of the post-war market. Insufficient cabins with private bathrooms were available to meet the needs of the American market in particular, and the vessels' specifications and size made them inflexible and unsuitable for routes other than those for which they were built. Because shipping companies did not recognise early enough the threat that the airlines posed for the future of their companies, they did not respond soon enough by moving into that sector of the industry themselves.

For years the shipping business was saddled with a series of cumbersome and bureaucratic 'traffic conferences' whose rules governed the operation of freight and passenger shipping in various geographical regions. Conference membership offered many advantages (as with IATA, members' tickets and other documents were interchangeable), but it also imposed restrictions on operation which tended to inhibit creative marketing by individual members. Prices were strictly controlled and no individual tour-based fares were available; travel agency appointments were limited and sanctions were imposed on agents dealing with non-conference lines.

With the decline of shipping the influence of these conferences waned, and the withdrawal of Cunard from the Trans-Atlantic Passenger Steamship Conference in 1971 signalled their end as an effective power in the regulation of shipping. Shipping associations today are less concerned with regulation and more with co-operation and marketing. In Britain the Passenger Shipping Association concerns itself with marketing and training, but also takes a growing interest in the protection of shipping, whether of line voyages, cruising or ferry operations.

Cruising

Since the late 1950s the passenger shipping industry has steadily shifted its emphasis from line voyages to cruises. Initially this transition proved difficult; vessels in service at the time were for the most part too large, too old and too expensive to operate for cruising purposes. Their size limited them in the number of ports they could visit and they were built for speed rather than leisurely cruising. Some savings in fuel were possible by cruising at reduced speed, but ideally cruise vessels must be purpose-built to maximise their operational efficiency. During the 1960s and 1970s, cost-efficient cruise ships tended to be in the range of 18 000–22 000 tonnes, carrying about 650–850 passengers, but the growth in demand for certain types of cruise, and advances in marine technology have enabled recent cruise ships to be purpose built in a variety of sizes. Many new ships in the range of 50–60 000 tonnes are appearing, while the current contender for the largest ship is Royal Caribbean Cruise Lines' *Sovereign of the Seas*, displacing 74 000 tons and carrying nearly 2300 passengers. Plans have been announced to build ships with a tonnage between 160 000 and 250 000 tons, carrying up to 5000 passengers, although firm orders have yet to be placed for such giants. At the other end of the scale, vessels between 5000 and 10 000 tons carrying as few as 120 passengers have been introduced to provide 'yacht-like' luxury for those willing to pay for the privilege.

Larger ships have been able to pare costs by reducing the ratio of staff to passengers, and providing smaller cabins, with larger areas given over to deck space and public rooms. Further economies on fuel are obtained by spending more time in port and by making a greater number of port calls, which incidentally satisfies cruise clients more.

Cruising was severely hit by the rapid rise in fuel prices during the oil crisis of 1973/4, but the decline in the fleets of the established maritime nations such as Britain was to some extent compensated for by the growth of new maritime powers, most noticeably the Greeks and Russians, whose operating costs are lower.

The world cruise market is currently estimated at between 2.5 and 3 million passengers, of which 75–80 per cent are from North America. Ports such as Miami, Fort Lauderdale and Port Everglades in Florida have become the major home ports for cruise vessels operating to the nearby Bahamas and Caribbean Islands, which offer superb opportunities for island-hopping cruises of between two days and two weeks in duration. In 1987, nearly 120 ships, with some 80 000 berths, were cruising world-wide, and a 20 per cent increase in berths available is forecast by 1991.

The British cruise market, having experienced a slow decline in the popularity of cruising in the late 1970s and early 1980s, reaching a low of 75 000 passengers, has more recently experienced a slow but steady growth in demand, peaking at around 128 000 passengers in 1987 and on target to return to the carryings of 150 000 or more which were the norm in the early 1970s. Over 40 per cent of today's cruise passengers from the UK are *fly-cruise* passengers.

Fly-cruises were developed in Britain in the late 1960s, and have played an important part in the regeneration of interest in cruising in the UK. In this type of cruise, passengers are flown from the UK (or other originating point) to a cruise port in the Mediterranean (or other convenient starting point), and return by air at the end of their cruise, thus avoiding the lengthy period at sea which is necessary before a cruise vessel reaches warmer climes. The shipping companies can offer attractive all-in prices for these packages by chartering aircraft for outbound and return flights. The traditional cruise passengers, who are typically older and more conservative, many of them unprepared to fly, initially resisted this innovation, but the concept has helped to attract a new, younger market.

Broadly, major cruise routes can be categorised as:

- Bahamas and Caribbean Islands, North coast of South America
- West coast of USA/Canada, Alaska, Mexico
- Mediterranean
- Pacific islands, Far East
- Baltic, Northern Capitals, North Cape
- West Africa and Atlantic islands
- Round the World

These routes, and key ports are illustrated in Fig 6.2.

The dominance of the Americans in the world cruising market is accounted for largely by the way in which cruising is sold in the United States. Whereas in Britain cruising is given an expensive, up-market and rather old-fashioned image, in America cruises are tailored to all markets, and at the lower end of the market they are sold very much in the same way as a package tour is sold. As a result, the US market has grown by more than 10 per cent per annum in recent years. This is leading to concern that there is now overcapacity of cruise tonnage, as shipping companies are attracted to the cruise potential in the area. With some 30 000 additional berths coming onto the market in the period 1987–9, and fierce competition among existing cruise operators, discounting is now widespread in the American travel business, and carriers operating out of the USA have turned their attention to European markets in an effort to fill ships. Attractive fly-cruise offers which include free flights across the Atlantic have greatly expanded the European market for Caribbean and other North American based sailings. However, the Mediterranean remains by far the most important area for European clients.

The dominance of the Americans in the world cruising market has resulted in strict standards being imposed on all foreign flag carriers operating out of US ports. All ships sailing ex-USA are subject not only to stringent hygiene and safety inspections, but their companies are required to be bonded against financial collapse. This has had the effect of hastening the demise of older vessels unable to meet these standards.

Innovations in cruising continued during the 1980s with the introduction of new ports of call. More adventurous destinations were introduced (such as cruises to the Antarctic), shipping companies organised cruises with specific themes to appeal to a specialised market, such as archaeological and horticultural cruises, or the 'Jazz' cruises run by Holland–America Line. These cruises were subsequently televised and together with the USA series 'love boat', which popularised the romantic image of cruising, led to heightened interest in cruising for the American market. Companies such as Carnival Cruise Line have changed the traditional concept of cruising as a pastime for older clients, and they have attracted more than half a million clients annually on their three to four day 'fun ship' Caribbean cruises, claiming an average age of 35 years for these passengers. Casinos and non-stop on-board entertainment have also attracted interest from the incentive and conference markets.

While cruises are sold as package holidays in the States, and tour operators there have also played a part as intermediaries to bring the product to the notice of

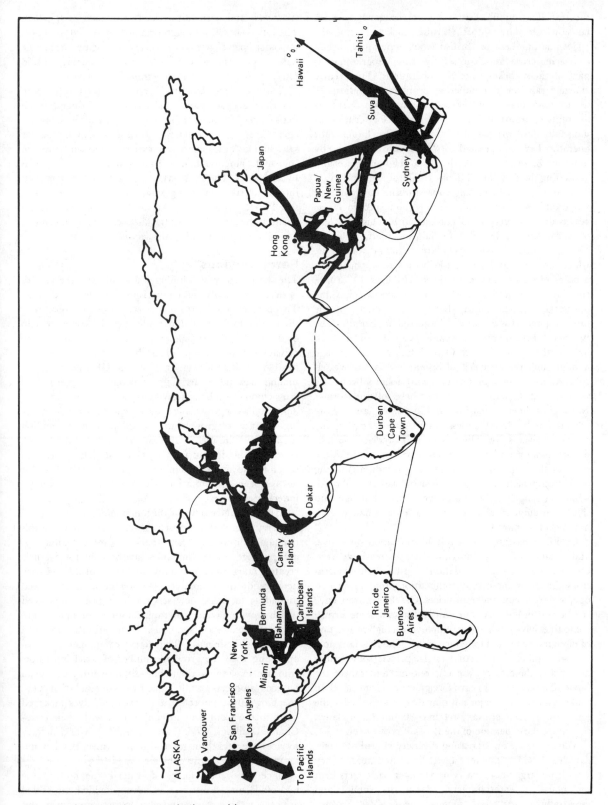

Fig 6.2 Major cruise routes in the world

the travelling public, British tour operators have been far slower to move into the cruise market. During the 1970s a number of British tour operators began chartering cruise vessels to sell fly-cruise programmes as part of their package holiday operations. These early charters ran into a number of problems; standards of service and operation suffered as the tour operators attempted to attract a new market for cruises at unusually low prices. More recently the larger tour operators have co-operated with the cruise companies by bulk-purchasing cruise berths on a regular cruise and marketing these as part of their overall tour programme.

In spite of ever-increasing costs, cruising has remained remarkably resilient. Both cruising and specific cruise vessels draw on very loyal markets with a high pattern of repeat purchasing – P & O claims as many as 60 per cent of *Canberra*'s passengers are regulars. This line, which also owns and operates Princess Cruises, has made a point of segmenting its markets, with P & O Cruises catering for the middle market and Princess Cruises, the up-market clientele. During the 1980s, confidence in the future of the cruise business increased in Britain. The two major British cruise companies, Cunard and P & O, have both expanded: P & O by building new tonnage and through the purchase of Sitmar Line's four vessels (plus a further three on order), giving them a fleet of 13 vessels, and Cunard by its purchase of the former Norwegian liners *Vistafjord* and *Sagafjord* and, more recently, the two 'Sea Goddess' vessels, giving the company a total of seven ships. These latter ships represent a new departure for cruise vessels; a retractable platform at the stern of the ship can be lowered to provide a 'floating deck' from which passengers can swim, sail or surfboard, while the ship is at anchor. Their small tonnage and shallow draught enable the ships to enter smaller ports inaccessible to most cruise vessels.

Cruise vessels are both capital- and labour-intensive, and western shipping companies are increasingly concerned about the rapid escalation of costs in cruise operations. There is increasing competition from lower-cost operators who can undercut prices. Greek operators have the benefit of lower labour costs (although some British companies have retaliated by employing a high proportion of foreign marine staff to reduce costs). The Russians, too, can substantially undercut western prices (some critics argue that these prices are uneconomic and reflect the Soviet Union's desire to earn foreign currency rather than make profits). Two major shipping disasters resulted in the loss of two Russian cruise vessels in 1986, but this has failed to impede the expansion of the Russian cruise fleet.

Today, we see an increasing diversity of cruise vessels, catering to widely different ages, clients and needs. They vary from large vessels carrying younger passengers bent on non-stop entertainment, down to small, and essentially luxury vessels such as the *Lindblad Explorer*,

North Star and even sail assisted ships such as *Windstar*. The latter vessels, although primarily designed to appeal to older passengers, offer cruises ranging from the sedentary to the adventurous, and it can truly be said today that cruising offers something for everyone.

A problem faced by cruise operators in the UK has been that of selling such a sophisticated travel product through mass market retailers. In Britain, less than one in ten travel agents are productive in terms of cruise sales; many counter sales staff lack the expertise or experience to sell cruises, in spite of the potential high levels of commission to be gained by such sales. The PSA has recognised the problem, and introduced special training programmes, under the genetic title PSARA (PSA Retail Agents), to recruit 1000 travel agents in Britain who have the knowledge and expertise to offer a professional cruise sales service to clients.

Ferry services

The success story of shipping is undoubtedly the growth of the short sea voyages within Europe in the last decade. This is attributable to the general growth of tourism in the region, to the growth of trade (especially membership of the EC) and, perhaps most of all, to the increase in private car ownership which has led to demand for flexible mobile holidays. In 1986, the UK saw nearly 28 million passengers arriving or departing by sea, and cross channel traffic is growing by some five per cent per annum. Passengers using cars or coaches represent the highest rates of growth; three million of the 15 million private cars in use in Britain are taken abroad each year, and the decade 1975–85 saw a six-fold increase in coach traffic across the channel. France in particular has always been a destination with a strong attraction for independent British holidaymakers travelling by car.

In the UK and elsewhere the tour operators – and indeed the ferry companies themselves – have responded to this demand by developing and marketing more flexible *self-drive* packages. Ferry companies have been notable for their creative marketing; new ships have been introduced with new standards of comfort, offering faster loading and unloading facilities; new services have been introduced which provide a wider geographical spread of routes to tap regional markets (such as Plymouth–Roscoff and Sheerness–Vlissingen). The ferry companies are co-operating with the growing number of coach operators who are expanding their long-distance intra-European services (a process greatly aided by the deregulation of the coaching industry in 1980), and have themselves packaged tours to the Continent in conjunction with their cross-Channel sailings. Today an extensive network of ferry services operates throughout Europe to meet the demand for intra-European travel by sea (*see* Fig 6.3.)

Since 1968, new forms of water-borne craft – the hydrofoils and hovercraft – have provided an added appeal for those seeking novelty or those in a hurry but

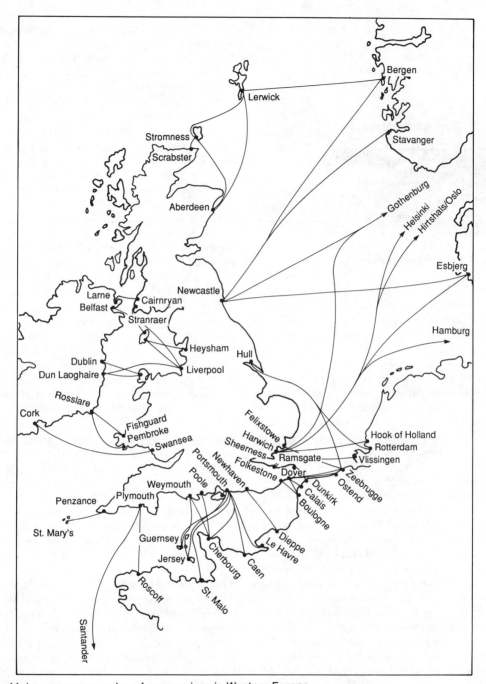

Fig 6.3   Major passenger and car ferry services in Western Europe

disliking to fly. The hovercraft, a vehicle which rides on a cushion of air just above the surface of the water, offers the advantage of speed, and its ability to travel over land as well as water avoids the usual capital costs of dock facilities, since the vessel can be docked on any convenient obstacle-free foreshore. Unfortunately, the vessel was bedevilled by technological problems in its development. It offers its passengers a somewhat bouncy

and noisy ride by comparison with traditional ferries, and cannot operate in high seas.

Some transport economists are doubtful whether the hovercraft offers a viable means of cheap transport in the future, other than over difficult terrain.

The hydrofoil is by contrast thought to offer substantial opportunity for future development, even though it, too, has suffered from technological teething

Fig 6.4 Jetfoil
(*Courtesy P & O European Ferries Ltd*)

problems. This vessel operates with a conventional hull design, but when travelling at speed this hull is raised above the surface of the water on blades, or 'foils'. This enables the vessel to travel at speeds of up to 60 knots. Recent models have been powered by jet engines (jetfoils), and these have been operated experimentally on cross-channel services, but have yet to prove themselves economically viable over routes of this length. They are, however, widely used on shorter crossings in many parts of the world.

Operating short sea services is expensive both in terms of capital investment and direct operating costs. Profitability is achieved through a combination of maximum usage of equipment and sales of on-board duty-free goods. Successful operations require sailings round the clock, a fast turnround at each end of the journey, an even volume of business year-round and, as far as possible, a balanced flow of demand in both directions. This has been easier to achieve out of the UK on the shorter routes to France, Holland and Belgium.

Longer routes, to Scandinavia, Germany and Northern Spain, are less easy to operate profitably as far as passenger revenue is concerned, although marketing the longer (24 hour) crossings as 'mini-cruises' for round trips without stopover has boosted load factors, and the resultant on-board spend has made a useful contribution to profitability. On the northern routes, however it has been difficult to achieve satisfactory load factors in winter, and the routes depend heavily on freight traffic at these times.

Off peak sailings on the short sea routes cross-Channel have been stimulated by low fares, with a wide range of discounted prices aimed at different market segments and travelling at different periods of the year. Quick round-trips on the same vessel or short stopovers of 1–3 days have multiplied with the introduction of judicious low-cost packages of this kind and low budget shopping expeditions to France in the period preceding Christmas have shown great success.

At extreme off-peak periods the ferry companies' aims may be simply to achieve a contribution to fixed costs rather than ensuring a profit with the sale of tickets, particularly when account is taken of the profitability of on-board sales.

The low prices which are the result of open competition across the Channel in recent years reflect a marked change from the previous policy of fixed prices in force until 1979. Prior to 1979 the ferry companies, operating through their membership of the Harmonisation Conference, united to negotiate annual fare agreements, and in some cases 'harmonisation' went as far as revenue pooling on major routes (whereby an equal distribution of all revenue accruing on the route was made to the lines serving the route).

This open cartel was tolerated by the UK government, even after the Monopolies Commission's investigation of the Conference's activities in 1972 which condemned them in principle. However, the system of negotiating tariffs through the Conference broke down in 1979 when a number of carriers decided to opt for an 'open fares' policy. Pooling arrangements were ended on most routes (although they continued in operation on Irish Sea crossings, with revenue pooled between Sealink and B + I Line). A two year price war between the companies led to large losses on operations in 1980 and 1981. This is unlikely to mean a return to the old Harmonisation process – indeed, the Office of Fair Trading has expressly forbidden it – but prices rose significantly in 1982 to offset former losses, and the lesson learned at the time suggests that any widespread cross-Channel price war is unlikely in the near future. Rather, competition is tending to focus on the development of larger and more luxurious vessels. Ships such as the *Konigin Beatrix* on the Harwich-Hook of Holland route, and the North Sea Ferries' new Hull-Rotterdam vessels all exceed 30 000 tons, and in accommodation and public facilities compare favourably with many cruise liners.

The Channel Tunnel

The tragic sinking of the Dover–Zeebrugge ferry *Herald of Free Enterprise* in 1987, with substantial loss of life, temporarily threatened the expansion of cross-Channel passenger traffic, but a more serious threat in the long term is posed by the Channel Tunnel, due to open between Cheriton (Folkestone) and Sangatte (Calais) in 1993. Eurotunnel, a consortium of French and British interests who won the Tunnel contract, estimate that it will attract some 40 per cent of all passenger traffic, and still higher estimates are made for private car and coach traffic. With journey times from London to Paris and Brussels cut to $2\frac{1}{2}$ to 3 hours, the potential increase of visitors to both sides of the Channel is enormous, especially in the short break holiday market. At such short journey times, and at a price below present ferry fares, the threat to ferry companies – especially those operating in the immediate vicinity of the Tunnel – is a very real one. The ferries have accepted the challenge, and claim in turn that, with the cost of their investment in new ferries written off by the time of the Tunnel's opening, they will be in a position to cut fares by up to 40 per cent; a more realistic figure might be in the region of 20 per cent, though this in itself exceeds current profitability on the routes. While the majority of freight traffic will continue to travel by ferry, it seems unlikely that all existing short sea services can continue to operate once the Tunnel is open, and those operating from ports in Kent and Sussex must be under threat. On the Dover–Calais run, new larger (26 000 tons) and faster ferries have been introduced to reduce crossing time from 90 to 75 minutes. However, on this route, the best prospect for survival would appear to be the pooling of existing competitive services. Tentative proposals have been put forward for the formation of a consortium operating a half hourly no reservations service, but any such proposal might be challenged by the Office of Fair Trading as constraint on competition.

Ferries also face the problem common to other sectors of the travel industry, of losing the right to duty-free sales in 1992. The General Council of British Shipping estimates that the loss of duty-free sales revenue alone would require fares to increase by nearly 25 per cent. Should VAT also be imposed on ferry fares by the European Commission, a price rise in the order of 40 per cent would be required merely to retain existing profitability. These cost constraints would make fare cutting to the extent proposed by the ferry companies difficult to implement.

Inland waterways and watersites

The inland waterways of Britain – lakes, rivers and canals – provide exceptional opportunities for water-based recreation and tourism, and the renovation of former canals, derelict docks, and other watersites for leisure use has created new opportunities for boating holidays. Of course, there is a long-standing tradition in Britain of holidays afloat, and the popularity of areas such as the Norfolk Broads stretches back to the early part of the 20th century. However, several factors have contributed to the heightened demand for water-based holidays, and particularly in the UK.

As with other holidays, the growth of disposable incomes has played its part; however, inland cruising is particularly popular among the older segments of the market. These, in addition to having the necessary means, also have sufficient leisure time for leisurely canal and river holiday cruising. The growth of private car ownership has also provided scope to get to sometimes isolated stretches of waterway. But it is undoubtedly the great improvement in the provision of waterways which has aided the growth of this form of leisure most. The

British Waterways Board has encouraged the development and use of waterways for pleasure purposes and, in partnership with private enterprise, has helped to reopen disused canals to provide a network of interconnecting waterways throughout the country. The ability, using these waterways, to follow a *circular* route, has made it possible for boat hire companies to organise packages of one or two week holidays on narrowboats without the need to retrace one's steps. Restoration of key canals such as those of Montgomery, Rochdale or the Kennet and Avon (see Fig 6.6), all recently completed or due for completion, has encouraged the establishment of small boat hire companies and other services catering for the waterborne holidaymaker's needs. Foreign, as well as domestic, tourists are becoming attracted to British waterways, while in turn the British are discovering the attractions of boating on foreign waters, such as the Canal du Midi and the Rhone in France and the Shannon in Ireland. Restoration and landscaping of former commercial canals also leads to the development of other forms of tourism, such as towpath cycling or long distance footpaths along the banks of canals, of appeal to hikers. Pubs, restaurants, hotels and shops along these routes all benefit from the expansion of commercial leisure, while new uses are found for property adjacent to waterways, such as camping and caravan sites, canoe instruction, etc.

It is, however, important to note that, notwithstanding the growth of interest in water-based tourism, the market is competitive and the season comparatively short. Most pleasure boat companies are small, family-run concerns, where return on capital invested is small, and profits only marginal. Some river sites, including the Thames, have seen the decline of boating companies. Effective marketing remains a problem where individual budgets are so small and where the destination sold is *linear* (the Kennet and Avon, for instance, runs through three different Regional Tourist Board areas, making unified marketing with the public sector difficult). In such circumstances, co-operative marketing between the small boat companies themselves, and other private sector interests, may be the best solution.

Turning to other forms of watersite development, the closure and subsequent dereliction of major docklands, and similar commercial waterfronts, has led to massive investment during the 1980s to redevelop them for leisure and residential use. Bristol's floating harbour, Salford Quays, Liverpool's Albert Dock, Southampton's Ocean Village; the planned Brindley Place development on Birmingham's canals; and waterfront restoration in Manchester, Chatham, Glasgow, Gloucester, Dublin and, of course, London all offer opportunities for tourism and leisure development, with construction of marinas, the introduction of waterbuses and ferries, scenic waterway cruises and floating restaurants all playing a part

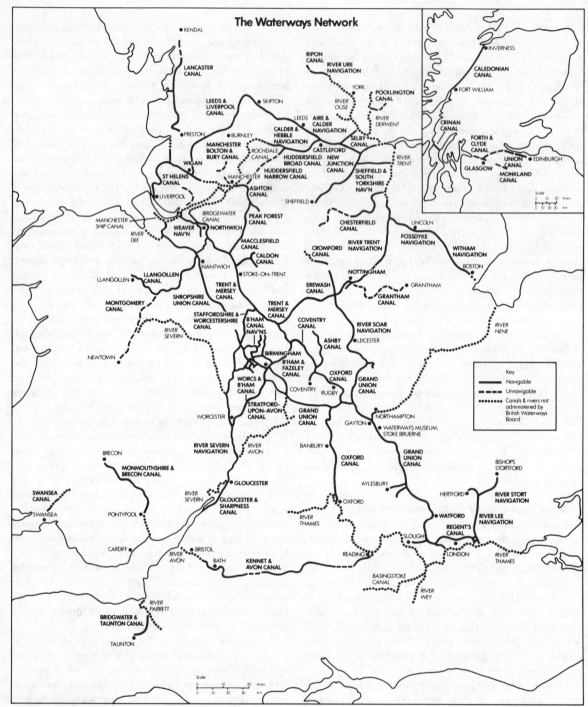

Fig 6.5 Inland Waterways of Britain
(*Courtesy British Waterways Board*)

in regenerating the area's economy. There are currently more than a dozen schemes, under construction or planned, to develop marinas at British coastal sites such as those of Port Solent and Hythe in Hampshire. Abroad, the astonishing success of Baltimore's Harborplace in the USA has sparked off similar schemes in New York, San Francisco and Toronto, while Stockholm and Oslo have both developed their decaying harbours for waterfront recreation. Most of these sites are planned for multiple use, including shops, offices and residential

Fig 6.6 A holiday hire boat on the Trent & Mersey Canal
(*Courtesy British Waterways Board*)

communities, but the leisure theme plays an important part in the redevelopment, in making the sites attractive for visitors, especially those arriving by boat.

Public craft also play an important role in inland waterway tourism, either in the form of day excursions or longer cruises by river or lake steamer. The lake steamer is a familiar sight and an important tourist attraction in such areas as the Scottish lochs, the English Lake District and overseas on the US/Canadian Great Lakes and the Swiss or south German lakes. Mention should also be made of the continuing attraction of excursion boats for day trippers in Britain; boats such as the *Waverley* (the last sea-going paddle steamer) and the *Balmoral* operate summer trips from Scottish ports, South Wales and the West Country, and still have wide appeal among those seeking a pleasant day out in nostalgic surroundings. The great rivers of the world also provide notable cruising services, many of which have been successfully packaged for the international tourist market. These include such diverse services as paddle steamers on the Mississippi, cruises along the Rhine and Danube (which boasts trips on the world's largest river cruiser), China's Yangtse and Li river boats and services up the Amazon, which is navigable to ocean-going vessels as far as Iquitos in Peru.

Many of these services seem to have particular appeal to the British market and the package tour operators, in their search for new attractions overseas, can be expected to incorporate a greater range of inland waterways programmes in their specialist tours of the future. Another noticeable trend is towards greater luxury on board small craft, as boat owners go up-market to beat the competition.

Sea-going pleasure craft

This section would not be complete without some mention of the growing demand for holidays aboard sea-going pleasure craft, a demand which is now being met by the travel industry. It has been estimated that there are more than 400 000 boat owners in Britain, and some two million people sail for pleasure. This is naturally leading to demand for institutionalised sailing holidays, and companies are springing up to cater for these needs. On the one hand, small private companies offer individual holidays for small groups, using small sailing ships or steamboats, with facilities ranging from the luxurious, where passengers are guests, to the more basic, where passengers play an active part in crewing the boat as part of the holiday. On the other hand, tour operating companies have organised flotilla cruising holidays on a massive scale, especially in areas where there are many small islands which provide sheltered anchorage and good weather conditions. The Greek islands, and certain Caribbean islands such as those of the Windward and Leeward groups provide ideal conditions for these types of holiday package, in which individually hired yachts sail together in flotilla formation from island to island. In this manner, tourists have the benefits of the independent use of the yacht while enjoying the social life of the group when together at anchor.

THE RAILWAYS

Public railways

Considering their long lead over other carriers in providing public service transport, it may be considered surprising that the railways in Britain have taken so long to adapt to the needs of mass market tourism in the late twentieth century. Certainly the railways played a major role in providing tourist transport throughout the first half of the century, but as ownership of private cars grew so tourist traffic on the railways fell. This process, which was already notable before World War II, accelerated after 1947 when the railways were nationalised in Britain. The switch to private passenger transport, coupled with the rapid expansion of freight transport by road, meant severe financial difficulty for British Rail in the 1950s and 1960s, which they attempted to solve by a huge reduction in their route operations, especially on unprofitable branch lines. As far as the tourist was concerned this resulted in many smaller resorts and tourist destinations being no longer accessible by rail. The alternative of coach links connecting with the rail termini makes tourist travel inconvenient and time-consuming and this, coupled with continuing fare increases on the railways, has made rail an unattractive contender for tourist transportation to many destinations (although the railways have continued to serve the needs of many major resorts such as Brighton, Bournemouth and Torquay).

In the 1970s and 1980s, however, British Rail became more marketing-orientated in an attempt to win back the tourist traffic, helped by an escalation in petrol prices following the fuel crisis in 1973, which made a major, if temporary, change in patterns of car usage for domestic holidays. Packages using rail transport were introduced to the domestic market on a larger scale than for many years. The packages proved popular for the short break market, but London proved by far the most popular destination of the choice, and with the return to car usage in the 1980s, sales of rail packages to the traditional resorts have declined. British Rail's own 'Golden Rail' holidays, designed to create demand for rail to these resorts, were sold off as 'Gold Star' holidays to the private sector. However, other BR ventures proved more successful, although limited in scale. The 'Merrymakers' programme, launched at the beginning of the 1970s, was a programme aimed at railway enthusiasts, and led to the reintroduction of steam hauled trains for excursion trips, such as the *Shakespeare Ltd* to Warwick and Stratford upon Avon. An upmarket programme of short breaks using Inter City services, entitled 'Interludes', and 'Golden Circle' programmes for the over 55s have been joined by a host of excursion-based fares aimed at the 'away day' traveller, shopper and conference delegate. NAT Holidays, a division of the ILG, chartered entire trains for European holidays in 1987, and companies such as Rainbow Miniholidays have continued to help expand the domestic short break market.

In the field of product innovation, the High Speed 125 train, operating on key InterCity routes, offers a service competitive in time, city centre to city centre, with those of the airlines. However, the Advanced Passenger Train (APT) proved a technical failure, and British Rail technology has fallen behind the high speed developments of foreign railways, such as Japan's Bullet Train and the French TGV (Train à Grande Vitesse). The TGV system is to be extended in France so that all parts of the country are within five hours of Paris by surface transport. Both Germany and Japan are developing Magnetic Levitation (MAGLEV) trains, originally a British invention, and capable of speeds of over 300 mph. These are likely to represent the next generation of high-speed trains. Links are planned between cities such as Paris, Brussels and Cologne, while the Americans are conducting a feasibility study for a MAGLEV service

Fig 6.7 Flotilla sailing in Turkey (*Courtesy Island Sailing*)

between Los Angeles and Las Vegas. Developments such as these will provide strong competition for short haul air services, particularly on major business routes.

The Channel Tunnel and the railways

In the UK, the development of the Channel Tunnel can be expected to lead to increased passenger flows between Southern England and the Continent, especially between London and important business centres such as Brussels and Paris. At the time of writing, Eurotunnel is arguing the case for a new high-speed rail link between London and Folkestone, comparable with the improved French rail connections from Calais to Paris and beyond, using the TGV. Although British Rail has argued that their forecasts suggest that passenger growth will not make this viable until late in the 1990s, Eurotunnel has expressed the view that an additional saving of 15–20 minutes on the journey time in England will be sufficiently attractive to passenger and freight traffic to merit the investment, and the Government is considering offering the opportunity for private enterprise to fund a new railway line to London to meet this need.

This could be the deciding factor for passengers considering whether to travel between the UK and the Continent as rail passengers, or whether to use the rail connection only through the section comprising the

Fig 6.8 Japan's Bullet Train
(*Courtesy Japan Information Centre, London*)

Tunnel itself, travelling by private car or coach. Proposals have been made for British Rail itself to be privatised as part of the Government's policy for privatisation, which will simplify the issue of a private rail link with the Tunnel.

International railways

Although routes and standards of service have declined in many countries, railways still have a useful role to play in the carriage of both passengers and freight, and for the many tourists who are enthusiasts, railways continue to exercise a fascination. Countries in which steam trains still operate, such as India and China, attract both independent travellers and the package tour operator, and luxury rail travel on restored early 20th century rolling stock drawn by steam trains, romanticised by television, continue to attract tourists to Spain and India. Long intercontinental rail journeys reminiscent of an earlier age of travel, such as the Trans-Siberian route, have been exploited by specialist tour operators to provide unusual packages for the rail afficionados.

In North America, rail travel in the 1960s and 1970s declined in the face of lower air fares and poor marketing by the railway companies themselves, who chose to concentrate on freight revenue at the expense of the passenger services. The continuing losses suffered by most US rail companies, and the importance of the rail network in social communications, led the Government to integrate rail services in the country into a centrally funded public corporation known as AMTRAK. This organisation has achieved some success in reversing the decline of passenger traffic, although many of the great names of the past, such as the Santa Fé Superchief and the 20th Century Ltd, have gone for ever; and with them, some of the mystique of North American rail travel. Nonetheless, railways still travel through splendid scenery such as that of the Canadian Rockies and the Western States, providing a base for future regeneration of interest in rail cruises by the European tourist.

The private railways

With the electrification of the railways in Britain, the nostalgia for the steam trains of the pre-war period has led to the re-emergence of many private steam railways. Using obsolete track and former British Rail rolling stock, enthusiasts have painstakingly restored a number of branch lines to provide an alternative system of transport for travellers as well as a new attraction for domestic and overseas tourists. In Britain alone, some forty such lines are in operation (*see* Fig 6.10), with 400 other projects either in hand or under consideration. Some of these depend largely on the tourists' patronage, while others also provide a convenient commuting service for local residents; their profitability however is frequently dependent upon a great deal of voluntary labour, especially in the restoration of track, stations and rolling stock to serviceable condition. Since these services are generally routed through some of the most scenic areas of Britain, they attract both railway buffs and tourists of all kinds, and undoubtedly enhance the attractiveness of a region for tourism generally.

Meantime, the nostalgia boom has supported the resurrection of the old Simplon-Orient Express, extensively renovated and providing a level of luxury and service seldom seen since the heyday of the railways in the period between the wars. Although now operating only as far as Venice, the train has been successfully marketed to the US market and to the British domestic market (nearly half of those booked are from the UK). Carriages used on the London–Folkestone leg of the journey have also been successfully employed for nostalgic day trips to other British resorts like Bath. In Scotland, a second successful venture has been the introduction of the *Royal Scotsman*. Although without benefit of a genuine pedigree, the 1920s style train has been packaged with success in the American market, offering a very up-market tour of the Scottish highlands. These two enterprises have proved that market niches exist for unusual rail programmes, and can undoubtedly be emulated in other tourist regions.

COACH TRAVEL

Coach operators today offer a wide range of tourist services to the public, both directly and through other

Fig 6.9 Royal Scotsman
(*Courtesy Abercrombie & Kent Ltd*)

sectors of the industry. These services can be categorised under the following general headings:

(*a*) express coach routes, both domestic and international;

(*b*) private hire services;

(*c*) tour and excursion operating;

(*d*) transfer services.

Long distance coach services provide a cheap alternative to rail or air travel, and the extension of these both within the UK and from the UK to points in Europe and beyond has drawn an increasing number of tourists

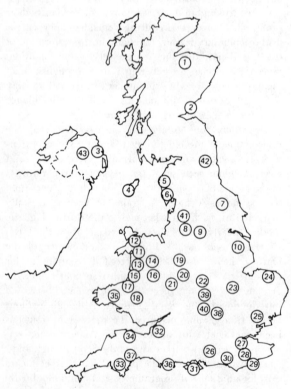

(1) Strathspey Railway; Aviemore to Boat of Garten, 8 km.
(2) Lochty Private Railway; Lochty to Knightsward, 3 km.
(3) Railway Preservation Society of Ireland; Whitehead and special runs. (4) Isle of Man Railway; Douglas to Port Erin, 11 km. (5) Ravenglass and Eskdale Railway; Ravenglass to Dalgarth, 11 km. (6) Lakeside and Haverthwaite Railway; Haverthwaite to Lakeside, $5\frac{1}{2}$ km. (7) North Yorkshire Moors Railways; Pickering to Grosmont Junction, 29 km. (8) Worth Valley Railway; Keighley to Oxenhope, 8 km. (9) Middleton Railway; Turnstall Road to Middleton Park Gates, 3 km.
(10) Lincolnshire Coast Light Railway; Humberstone $1\frac{1}{2}$ km.
(11) Snowdon Mountain Railway; Llanberis to Snowdon, $7\frac{1}{2}$ km. (12) Llanberis Lake Railway; Gilfach Ddu to Penllyn, 3 km. (13) Festiniog Railway; Morthmadog to Tanyfrisiau, 19 km. (14) Bala Lake Railway; Llanuwchllyn to Bala, 7 km.
(15) Fairbourne Railway; Fairbourne to Barmouth, 3 km.
(16) Welshpool and Llanfair Light Railway; Llanfair Caereinion to Sylfaen, 9 km. (17) Talyllyn Railway; Tywyn to Nant Gwernol, $11\frac{1}{2}$ km. (18) Vale of Rheidol Railway; Aberystwyth to Devil's Bridge, 19 km. (19) Foxfield Light Railway; Foxfield to Blyth Bridge, $6\frac{1}{2}$ km. (20) Chasewater Light Railway; Chasewater Lake circuit, 3 km. (21) Severn Valley Railway; Bridgnorth to Bewdley, $20\frac{1}{2}$ km. (22) Great Central Railway; Loughborough to Rothley, 8 km. (23) Nene Valley Railway; Wansford to Orton Mere, 9 km. (24) North Norfolk Railway; Sheringham to Weybourne, $4\frac{1}{2}$ km. (25) Stour Valley Railway; Marks Tey to Sudbury, $18\frac{1}{2}$ km. (26) Mid-Hants Railway (Watercress Line); Alresford to Ropley, 5 km.
(27) Sittingbourne and Kemsley Light Railway; Sittingbourne to Kemsley Down, 3 km. (28) Kent and East Sussex Railway; Tenterden to Wittersham Road, 5 km. (29) Romney, Hythe and Dymchurch Light Railway; Hythe to Dungeness, 22 km.
(30) Bluebell Railway; Sheffield Park to Horsted Keynes, 8 km. (31) Isle of Wight Steam Railway; Haven Street to Wootton, 3 km. (32) East Somerset Railway; Cranmore.
(33) Dart Valley Railway; Buckfastleigh to Staverton Bridge, 11 km. (34) West Somerset Railway; Minehead to Bishops Lydeard, 32 km. (35) Gwili Railway; Carmarthen, 3 km.
(36) Swanage Railway; Swanage to Herston Halt. (37) Torbay and Dartmouth Railway; Paignton to Kingswear, 10 km.
(38) *Leighton Buzzard Narrow Gauge Railway. (39) *Market Bosworth Light Railway. (40) *Cadeby Light Railway.
(41) *Yorkshire Dales Railway. (42) *Bowes Railway, Tyne and Wear. (43) * Shanes Castle Railway.
* All have short track for passenger steam haulage.

Fig 6.10 Britain's private railways

Fig 6.11 Tourism by coach
(*Courtesy Thomas Cook*)

at the cheaper end of the market, particularly among the young (50 per cent of National Bus Company's express service passengers were reported to be under 35 years of age in 1979). Younger passengers in particular have been attracted to the adventurous transcontinental coach packages which provide, for a low price, transport plus minimal food and lodging en route (often under canvas). However, for the most part coach travel remains the medium of transport for the elderly, in spite of efforts by the coach operators to attract a younger market for coach tours and excursions. This is perhaps unsurprising in view of the advantages which coach travel offer to the elderly – not only low prices (which reflect comparatively low operating costs *vis-à-vis* other forms of transport) but the convenience of door-to-door travel when touring, overcoming baggage and transfer problems, and courier assistance, especially in overseas travel, where the elderly avoid problems of documentation and language. One result of this is that coach tour companies have a high level of repeat business. The operation of coach tours is a highly seasonal one, however, and companies, unless able to obtain ad hoc charters or contract work (such as schools bussing), are forced to lay off many drivers and staff out of season.

Most coach companies specialise in certain spheres of activity. While some operate and market their tours nationally, others may specialise in servicing the needs of incoming tourists and tour operators by providing excursion programmes, transfers betwen airport and hotels, or complete coach tours for overseas visitors. These coach companies must build up close relations and work closely with tour operators and intermediaries abroad and in the UK.

Legislation in coaching

Under the terms of the Transport Act 1980, in order to set up or continue to operate a coach service, an operator must apply for a coach operator's licence. This is granted by the Traffic Commissioners, with conditions which

limit the operation to a specified number of coaches. Licences normally run for five years, although under some conditions the term can be shorter. Before granting a licence, the Traffic Commissioners must be satisfied that the applicant has a good financial record and adequate resources to operate the number of coaches for which the licence has been requested. At least one responsible member of the company must hold an individual transport operator's licence, which is essentially a certificate of professional competence based on management experience and appropriate educational qualifications (for example, Membership of the Institute of Transport). The Commissioners must also satisfy themselves that the operator will provide satisfactory maintenance facilities (or in lieu, a contract with a supplier of such facilities), and the operating centre where vehicles are to be garaged must be specified.

Coach operating conditions now fall into line with EC directives, which are designed to ensure adequate safety provisions for passengers. The concern with safety has been highlighted by recent incidents in the coach industry, most noticeably a series of serious accidents on the Continent involving holiday coaches. The EC regulation governing drivers' hours (No. 543/69) dictates the maximum number of hours' driving permitted for each driver per day. These regulations apply automatically to all express journeys by coach with stages over 50 kilometres.

The controversial tachograph, introduced in the EC in 1970 and adopted by Britain in 1981, following the Passenger and Goods Vehicles Recording Equipment Regulations 1979, provides recorded evidence of hours of operation and vehicle speeds by individual drivers. While there can be little doubt that implementation of these regulations has led to higher safety standards in the industry, the effect has also been to increase the cost of long-haul coaching operations, thus making it more difficult to compete with rail and air services. To permit through journeys without expensive stopovers, two drivers must be carried; or increasingly, since rest periods must be taken off the coach, drivers are exchanged at various stages of the journey. With the constraint of a limited number of seats on a coach, this has the effect of pushing up costs per seat by a significant amount.

The financial security of coaching operations has been increased through the Bus and Coach Council, requiring that members be bonded for 10 per cent of their touring turnover, as insurance against the financial collapse of a member (although bonding is not required for domestic coach holidays within the UK).

Deregulation and its aftermath

Recently, substantial changes have occurred in the coaching industry in the UK as a result of the 1980 Transport Act which ended the licensing regulations affecting express coach services on routes of more than

30 miles. Prior to this the licensing system favoured the development of national and regional oligopolies; the trunk routes were effectively controlled by three major carriers, the National Bus Company, Wallace Arnold and Ellerman Bee Line, with National dominating the market. Elsewhere, some 220 licensed coach operators dominated regional routes, the result of historical development of the coach industry. Companies wishing to compete with the established carriers had to apply for a licence to the Traffic Commissioners, who were generally prepared to consider the granting of this only where a new service was to be offered or a new market tapped. Applications could be refused on the strength of existing operators' complaints that their business would suffer. This obviously limited competition and there was little incentive for creative marketing. Similar restrictions applied to all coach tour operations (with the sole exception of tours operated by coach companies on behalf of overseas tour operators on which all passengers had been pre-booked abroad).

With the ending of regulation a spate of new coach services of all types was introduced in 1981. A number of important regional coach companies came together to form British Coachways, a consortium designed to compete with National on their express trunk routes. National responded to this challenge by expanding into the formerly restricted regional territories to compete with the monopolies there. British Rail became the immediate target of the coach operators, who introduced new, low-priced express services between major city centres and initially attracted a considerable amount of traffic away from British Rail, until that organisation introduced its own highly competitive discounted fares.

The chief beneficiary of deregulation appears to have been the National Bus Company, which made substantial gains at the expense of its rivals through its ability to offer greater frequency of service and flexibility. With its huge fleet of coaches and a national network of routes, at short notice it was able to replace a defective vehicle with little inconvenience to its passengers, an advantage denied to its smaller rivals. However, smaller companies operating newer or more 'unusual' vehicles (such as luxurious foreign-built coaches and luxury split level coaches costing £200 000) provided some competition to the larger companies; although many of these companies found they were experiencing severe under-usage of such equipment, as the high capital investment (up to £100 000 a coach), depreciated over a period of five years, drives seat prices out of reach to all except a small, highly selective market. The British Coachways consortium proved unable to challenge National as effectively as they had hoped and, after the withdrawal of some of the founder members, added problems over their terminus location in London led to the collapse of the consortium in October 1982. Fear was also expressed that cut-throat competition could lead to falling maintenance standards and the failure of smaller, less efficient companies without the resources to survive a major price war.

Before deregulation, the market for coach services had been virtually static. The deregulation of the industry led to increased demand, but at the same time increased the capacity available on the market, resulting in lower average load factors for many operators. While the National Bus Company was able to strengthen its market share of coaching operations, the Monopolies and Mergers Commission were disinclined to investigate coach operations since deregulation, working on the premiss that National's major competitor is in fact British Rail, and the competition between these two has held down fares.

A general concern about coach standards and quality control led in 1985 to the formation of the Guild of British Coach Operators, a commercial body whose aim was to promote high standards of service, safety and maintenance, and to reassure the travelling public of the continuing benefits of travel by coach.

Subsequently, the 1985 Transport Act set the scene for almost total deregulation of Britain's bus industry by the end of 1986, opening to competition all local bus routes outside London (provision for later deregulation in London was made in the Act). Passenger Transport Executives and District Councils were required to transfer their bus companies to private companies covered by the Companies Act. The Transport Act had two important implications for the tourist industry. First, it required the break-up and privatisation of the 60 subsidiaries of the National Bus Company, providing small bus operators with greater scope to compete with the former NBC empire. Second, the resulting competition on the short bus routes led to an overall growth in the number of vehicles, for which operators tried to find alternative uses outside of peak travel periods. Equally, of course, the long distance coach operators became free to operate their equipment on bus routes.

While the Act led to random fluctuations in fares, as bus companies competed in the lucrative city commuter routes, no systematic change in pricing policy has become evident.

On the international scene, an interesting development has been the growth of 'shuttle' services between Britain and the Continent. These international stage journeys enjoyed a huge boom between 1981 and 1983, and although profitability went into sharp decline in 1984 (as the differential narrowed between coach and air prices), shuttle profits had recovered well by 1987, partly as a result of a decline in capacity and price increases. Coach tours to the Continent from Britain, on the other hand, suffered as Sterling dropped in value. The relative value of Sterling against Continental currencies, and the relative differential between air and coach fares, are key factors in the success of coach operating to the Continent.

Also on the international scene, mention should be made of the importance of coach operations in North America.

Two powerful coach companies, Greyhound Lines and Continental Trailways, dominated the domestic coach market on that continent, and their low fares had enabled them to compete successfully against both the huge network of domestic air services and the private car. However, in 1982, road passenger transport was also deregulated in the USA, leading to a flood of small low priced coach companies, against which neither of the two giants could compete. Trailways cut services in an effort to remain profitable, but ultimately merged under new management with the Greyhound Corporation in 1987. The restructuring of the company and the introduction of new vehicles, including minibuses, appear to have halted the decline of the company.

In the field of coach excursions, Gray Line, using a franchise system, has built up a network of city-based excursion operators not only within the USA, but also in numerous overseas countries.

THE PRIVATE CAR

Undoubtedly the increase in private car ownership has done more to change travel habits than any other factor in tourism. In Britain this phenomenon occurred after 1950 and had a significant impact on coach and rail load factors. It also gave families a new freedom of movement; not only were costs of motoring falling in relative terms, but car owners tended to perceive only the direct costs of a motoring trip, ignoring the indirect coasts of depreciation and wear and tear. Thus car travel was favoured over public transport. This perception of low cost coupled with greater flexibility led to a great increase in motoring holidays and in particular to day excursions and short-break holidays.

The effect of this on the travel industry has been considerable; the hotel and catering industry has responded by developing motels and transit hotels, roadside cafes and restaurants, geared to the needs of drivers, while hotels and restaurants in more isolated areas away from public transport routes welcomed a growing market of private motorists. Car ferry services throughout Europe expanded and flourished and countries linked by such services experienced a visitor boom (France remains, for the British, the leading independent holiday destination).

Camping and caravan holidays have also grown with car ownership. The tour operators have fought back against this trend to independent holidays by creating flexible self-drive package tours suited to the needs of the private motorist, along with optional car hire packages for tourists on regular package holidays seeking something more adventurous to do abroad than lying on the beach. The car hire companies themselves have developed their services to cater for the needs of business people and other tourists without cars, and rail/drive and fly/drive packages have appeared on the scene. In the United States a market has

been tapped for 'motor homes' or motorised caravans. Even the railways have adapted to motoring needs, providing *Motorail* services for motorists to take their cars by rail with them to their holiday destinations.

In the 1980s the desire for greater freedom and flexibility on holiday suggests that, providing energy costs do not become exorbitant, the demand for private motoring holidays is likely to remain buoyant, at least for family travel. This expansion of motoring has brought, and will amplify, the problem of congestion and pollution. Small holiday resorts and scenic attractions cannot expand sufficiently to meet the demand for access and parking facilities without damaging or destroying the environment which the motorist has come to see. Inevitably, greater controls will be required in the future through action such as 'park and ride' schemes, introduced at Bath, Oxford and St Ives, which require visitors to park their cars outside the resort and travel in on public transport. Extensions of such schemes may ease the problem but will not entirely solve the growing crisis of private car saturation in small countries.

The car hire business

It has been estimated that there are over 1000 car hire companies operating in Britain, with more than 130 000 cars available for hire (many being fleet cars on hire to private companies). The car hire business owes a substantial proportion of its revenue (and in resorts, virtually all its revenue) to the tourist. While in total only 30–40 per cent of car hire is associated with leisure, small companies and local car hire operators get a disproportionate share of this, while the large corporations have the lion's share of the business travel market.

Car hire companies can be divided into two categories:

1 the large international companies, or franchise operators
2 small, local independent hire companies.

The former comprise the market leaders, five of which shared 40 per cent of the UK care hire market in 1985: Hertz (owned by United Airlines), Avis, Europcar (formerly Godfrey Davis in Britain, and market leader with an estimated 11 per cent of the UK market), Budget and Swan National. All charge broadly similar high prices, but offer a choice of cars and hiring locations, and flexibility (for example, the ability to pick up a car at one location and drop it at another). Their flexibility and convenience makes them most attractive to business travellers, who are less sensitive to price, but who insist on speed of service, reliability and a more luxurious standard of car.

On the other hand, there are literally hundreds of small local hirers, who generally offer limited choice but low price and the convenience of a local pick-up –

although perhaps from only one or two locations. Because of their reliance on the leisure market, these operators work in a highly seasonal business, where they may be unable to maximise their opportunities for business in summer because they have insufficient vehicles. In addition, there are a handful of specialist car hire operators such as Guy Salmon (owned by Barclays Bank through Mercantile Credit) who provide very luxurious vehicles to a small up-market leisure or business clientele.

The competitive nature of the industry has once again resulted in good marketing playing a key role in the success of individual car hire companies. The expansion of outlets has been greatly aided by the introduction of franchising – Budget was the first car hire company to franchise in Britain, as long ago as the 1960s, but all the large corporations now do so. Three other factors have been critical:

(a) *contracts with airports and railways*. This allows the car hire company to maintain a desk at the airport or terminal. Opportunities for business which are provided by desk space in these locations make contracts very lucrative, and they are fought for between the major corporations, occasionally changing as competitors offer higher bids at the termination of a contract agreement.

(b) *links with airlines and hotels*. This establishes good relations with, and hence referrals from, hotel chains and larger airlines, generating huge volumes of business, and is critical for maximising sales opportunities for business travel bookings.

(c) *Computer Reservations Systems (CRS)*. The development of a good CRS and accessibility through major airline CRSs such as Sabre or Galileo plays an increasingly important role in the success of the larger car hire companies, who can no longer afford not to be linked to major systems.

Car hire companies also court the travel agents, who can provide a good proportion of advance sales for business and leisure travel. Attractive rates of commission of 15 per cent or more are offered to gain agency support. The growing 'seat only' airline reservations market has helped to expand the demand for car hire overseas, as has the increasing confidence shown by British package tourists abroad in hiring cars at their destination. It is significant that one or two operators, such as Falcon Holidays, have integrated horizontally by establishing car hire companies to handle their clients' needs abroad.

QUESTIONS AND DISCUSSION POINTS

1 Explain why cruising enjoys a higher level of demand in North American markets than in Britain, and suggest what more needs to be done by British shipping companies to increase the attractiveness of cruising to the British market.

2 What role does British Rail play in promoting and satisfying the demand for travel by tourists in the UK? Could BR do more than it is currently doing to increase revenue from (a) overseas visitors to Britain, and (b) British domestic tourists.

3 On express routes from provincial cities into London, a number of small coach operators now offer services which undercut National Express services on price. Consider what other benefits these companies offer to attract passengers, and explain why it is that National is still able to compete at a higher price.

ASSIGNMENT TOPICS

1 As a research assistant for P & O Ferries, you have been asked by the company to make an assessment of the viability of their routes following the opening of the Channel Tunnel. You are required to undertake an assessment of the passenger traffic on these routes, making a case either for:

● withdrawing or reducing one or more services, or
● competing with the Channel Tunnel service.

Present a report to the company on your recommendations. Although concerned mainly with passenger traffic, your report should recognise the importance of freight to the revenue and profitability of these routes.

2 As a result of the European Community's planned programme of harmonisation, a German leisure corporation, Gesellschaft für Internationalen Reiseverkehr, is examining opportunities for expansion into the British market. They already have interests in inland waterways cruising on the continent, and have asked you, as a research officer in a firm of consultants retained by the company, to carry out a study of the opportunities for expansion specifically into this area of tourism in Britain. They are contemplating setting up, or purchasing, a company operating a hire fleet of narrow boats based on a section of Britain's inland waterways network, which would enable holidaymakers to hire vessels for circular trips, avoiding the necessity of retracing their journey over the same route.

In the first instance, you are asked to provide a brief report to the company identifying one or more suitable locations. You should also present evidence of factors favouring growth of this particular form of leisure activity. Your report should be suitably illustrated with maps and graphs.

7 The accommodation sector

Chapter objectives: After studying this chapter, you should be able to:

- explain the structure and nature of the accommodation sector, distinguishing between the various categories of accommodation which a tourist might occupy;
- describe how accommodation is classified and the problems involved in its classification;
- understand the nature of demand for accommodation and how the accommodation sector has responded to changes in demand patterns over time;
- understand how hotels and other accommodation units inter-relate with other sectors of the industry in selling their product and the problems they face in doing so.

INTRODUCTION

In this chapter we are principally concerned with examining the commercial accommodation sector. It must not be forgotten, however, that this sector must compete with a large non-commercial supply of accommodation which is equally important in the tourism business; the VFR (visiting friends and relatives) market is a substantial and growing one in tourism. In addition to this there is a wide variety of other forms of private accommodation used by tourists; that used by campers and caravanners, in privately-owned yachts, in second homes, in the growing market for 'exchange homes' and the swopping of timesharing accommodation. Even a strict distinction between commercial and non-commercial accommodation is difficult to make since the range of accommodation on offer is a continuum between profit- and non-profit-making sectors of the industry. Among the latter, youth hostels and YMCAs may be concerned only with recovering their costs of operation, while the use of educational institutions for tourist lodgings during holiday periods is designed chiefly to make a contribution towards the running costs of the institutions. And to what extent should sleeping facilities on board hired yachts or cruise ships in port be counted towards the sum of the stock of commercial accommodation available to tourists? There are even long-distance coaches in operation which provide specially fitted sleeping accommodation, and in certain parts of the world tour operators charter trains for inclusive tours in which the train acts as a hotel throughout.

None of these forms of overnighting can be ignored by those studying the tourism industry. Quite apart from the fact that even tourists staying in private accommodation away from home are nonetheless making a contribution to the tourism revenue of a region (through local travel and entertainment) and must therefore be counted in the tourism statistics of that region, they may also be commercially exploited by other sectors of the industry. Tour operators, for example, have provided flight 'packages' designed to meet the needs of villa and apartment owners on the Continent; the airlines, recognising that home exchanges can represent a healthy source of flight revenue, have developed and commercialised the home exchange business by founding centralised directories; and national tourist offices keep directories of home owners prepared to make exchanges or willing to welcome overseas tourists into their homes for meals (a particular feature of United States hospitality).

THE STRUCTURE OF THE ACCOMMODATION SECTOR

The accommodation sector comprises widely differing forms of sleeping facilities which can be conveniently categorised as either *serviced* (in which catering is provided) or *self-catering*. These are not water-tight categories since forms of accommodation, such as holiday camps or educational institutions, may offer serviced, self-service or self-catering facilities, but they will help in drawing distinctions between the characteristics of the two categories. Figure 7.1 provides an at-a-glance guide to the range of accommodation which a tourist might occupy.

A feature of the industry is that, as mass tourism has developed, so have the large chains and corporations in the accommodation sector. Hotels and motels are reaching a stage of development in which a few major companies have come to dominate the international market. This expansion has been achieved not only through ownership but also through franchising, whereby hotels and motels are operated by individual franchisees paying royalties to the parent company for the privilege of operating under the brand name. This form of expansion has been used with great success around the world by the largest hotel company in the world, Holiday Inns. Since these chains market their products more aggressively, advertising extensively at

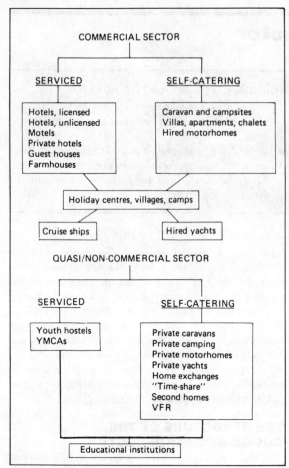

Fig 7.1 The structure of tourist accommodation

home and overseas and establishing links with the tour operators, they tend to play a more significant role in the industry than even their market share might suggest.

In an effort to counteract this influence, a number of independent hotels are now banding together to form marketing consortia to provide a more effective and centralised marketing effort. Consortia such as Best Western Hotels, Inter Hotels and Prestige Hotels provide a strong marketing challenge to the large hotel chains and an attractive alternative to the tour operators.

In recent years a similar pattern of ownership by large corporations is evident in the field of holiday camps and holiday centres, with none of the leading companies in Britain still in private hands (*see* p. 98). Similar trends are beginning to emerge in the caravan and campsite sectors.

CLASSIFYING ACCOMMODATION UNITS

It is no simple matter to differentiate between accommodation units of differing types and standards. The process of classification of the hotel and catering

industry, either for purposes of legislation or for systematic examination of business activity, has been attempted at various times in Britain (for example, under the Standard Industrial Classification system). However, these attempts have concentrated largely on distinguishing hotels and other residential establishments from sundry catering establishments, and statistical or other data based on individual types of residential establishment are less than adequate. The motel or motor hotel is not always clearly distinguished from other forms of hotel in statistical data, and there is a broad spectrum of privately controlled accommodation for tourists ranging from 'private hotels' and boarding houses to guest houses and bed and breakfast accommodation. The terms 'private hotel' and 'boarding house' are virtually interchangeable, no clear distinction being made between them in law. These are distinct from the guest house in that the latter will not have more than four bedrooms or accommodation for a maximum of eight guests. This distinction is important for purposes of legislation but need not concern us further here.

The terms *categorisation*, *classification* and *grading* are also often used interchangeably, and since they describe different characteristics of the accommodation units it will be helpful to adopt here a standard range of definition. The following have been widely accepted.

(a) *Categorisation* refers to the separation of accommodation by type, that is, distinguishing between hotels, motels, boarding houses, guest houses, etc.

(b) *Classification* refers to the separation of accommodation according to certain physical features such as the number of rooms with private bath, etc.

(c) *Grading* refers to the separation of accommodation according to *verifiable objective features of the service offered* such as the number of courses served at meals, availability of night porters, etc.

There is as yet no common agreement within the industry regarding these terms, nor has any term yet been devised which satisfactorily covers the subjective assessment of the accommodation's facilities such as quality of food and service, or atmosphere.

Provision was made under the Development of Tourism Act 1969 for the compulsory classification and grading of the hotel industry in Britain, but this has been widely resisted by the industry itself and the British Tourist Authority has made no attempt to impose it, choosing to rely instead on a system of voluntary registration first introduced in 1975. The separate National Tourist Boards of England, Scotland and Wales have been left to devise their own schemes. Under the Scottish scheme, serviced accommodation is inspected and assigned one of three grades – highly commended, commended or approved – which are shown alongside 'crown' symbols classifying the range of services and

Fig 7.2 Contrasts in accommodation
(a) Luxury hotel in London

(b) Bed & Breakfast in the country
(*Courtesy (a) Holiday Inns International and
(b) Scottish Tourist Board*)

facilities offered by the hotel. The English Tourist Board replaced their former 'rose' grading scheme in 1987 with a 'crown' scheme for hotels, inns, guest houses, bed and breakfast and farmhouse accommodation. The system, which is administered by the Regional Tourist Boards, operates on the basis of six separate grades ranging from 'listed' up to five crowns, depending once again on the services and facilities offered. Annual fees are charged, and annual inspections undertaken, to ensure the accuracy of grading.

While the system is an improvement on the former classification in which the hotels were responsible for the facts provided, it remains a voluntary scheme, and therefore omits a significant proportion of the accommodation sector, for which there remains no composite listing. The Scottish scheme, which includes an assessment of quality, goes further to satisfy the need for qualitative assessment of the levels of service provided, and plans are in hand to revise the ETB

scheme to include these qualitative data in the crown grading by 1989. A compulsory registration scheme, such as those operating in other European countries, is still lacking; but after 1992, EC legislation may bring pressure for a common grading scheme within all member countries.

Of the private classification and grading systems, those operated by the AA and RAC in Britain are probably the best known. These provide for a star-rating of hotel units, the AA's assessment being based on three characteristics:

(*a*) statements of fact on the nature of the premises and the services provided;
(*b*) the number and extent of the premises and services;
(*c*) the subjective assessment of their quality.

Premises are graded from 'approved' through one to five stars, with rosettes being awarded for standards of catering. There are also a number of guides on the market dealing with the subjective assessment of catering in hotels and other establishments, of which Egon Ronay's and the *Good Food Guide* are perhaps the best known.

THE NATURE AND DEMAND FOR ACCOMMODATION FACILITIES

Hotels and other residential establishments share a number of marketing problems. In the first place, what is sold to the tourist is not a single product but the sum of a variety of different products, each of which could be the principal factor accounting for the customer's choice.

First and foremost, a customer's choice is likely to be based on location, a key factor in the profitability of the unit. Location implies both the destination (resort for the holidaymaker, convenient stop-over point for the traveller, city for business people) and the location *within* that destination. Thus the business people will want to be at a hotel close to the company they visit, the seaside holidaymakers will wish to be as close as possible to the seafront, and the travellers will want to be close to the airport from which they are leaving. In economic terms a 'trade-off' will occur between location and price; the tourists unable to afford a seafront property, will opt for the one closest to the front which fits their pocket. Location is, of course, fixed for all time. If the resort loses its attractions for visitors, the hotel will suffer an equivalent decline in its fortunes.

The fact that high fixed costs are incurred in both building and operating hotels compounds the risk of hotel operating. City centre sites are extremely expensive to purchase and run (estimates for central London have ranged as high as £200 000 per room for hotel construction), requiring very high room prices. The market may resist such prices but is nevertheless reluctant to be based at any distance from the centres of activity, even where good transportation is available. This has been evidenced in the problems faced by incoming tour operators to accommodate American visitors in central London at prices competitive with other city centres. The reluctance of many overseas tour operators to base their clients at accommodation on the outskirts of the city has led to loss of business in favour of other European capital cities.

Again, the demand for central London hotels, leading to high capacity and profits, has caused those in the hotel business to maximise profits by up-grading their accommodation and appealing to the business client, rather than cater for the leisure tourist's demand for budget accommodation. The French Novotel chain has been among the first to identify this market gap and has set about catering for the lower price bracket.

The demand for hotel rooms will come from a widely distributed market, nationally or internationally, whereas the market for other facilities which the hotel has to offer will be highly localised. In addition to providing food and drink for its own residents, the hotel will be marketing these services to tourists or residents within only a short distance of the site. Clearly a very different market segment will be involved, calling for different advertising, promotion and distribution strategies.

Another characteristic of the product is that it is seldom uniformly in demand throughout the year. Tourist hotels in particular suffer from levels of very high demand during the summer and negligible demand in the winter months. Even hotels catering chiefly to businesses, while they may experience consistent demand during the year, will find that demand is largely for Monday-Thursday nights and they will have a problem in attracting weekend business, a problem known as *periodicity* as apart from seasonality. This lack of flexibility in room supply and the fact that the product itself is highly perishable (if rooms are unsold there is no opportunity to 'store' them and sell them later) mean that great efforts in marketing must be made to attract off-peak customers, while potential revenue has to be sacrificed during the peak season because demand is greater than supply. Even with creative selling, such as discounted winter-breaks which the hotels have now introduced, many tourist hotels in seasonal locations such as seasides will be lucky to achieve average year-round occupancy of more than 50 per cent. These hotels are then faced with the choice of staying open in winter, with the hope of making sufficient income to cover their direct operating costs for the period, or closing completely for several months of the year. The problem with the latter course of action is that a number of hotel costs, such as rates and depreciation, will continue whether or not the hotel remains open. Temporary closure also has an impact on staff recruitment, with the attendant difficulties of obtaining staff of the right calibre for jobs which are only seasonal. In recent years more and more of the larger hotels have opted to stay open year-round, with special packages designed to attract the off-season market. The increase in second holidays and short breaks off-season in Britain has greatly helped to make hotels viable year round, although room occupancy remains low out of season in many of the traditional holiday destinations.

We have talked chiefly in terms of the physical characteristics of a hotel which attract its market, but no less important are the psychological factors such as service, 'atmosphere', even the other guests with whom the customer will come in contact. Any or all of these factors will be taken into consideration by customers in making their choice of hotel.

Some patterns of demand

Only about 25 per cent of British holidaymakers stay at hotels or guesthouses in the UK, although some 60 per cent will do so when holidaying abroad. This obviously reflects the large VFR market in the UK, as well as the growing camping, caravanning and self-catering market. About a quarter of overseas visitors stay at hotels when in the UK, but the pattern will vary considerably between nationalities, and other socioeconomic variables such as class, age and life-style will also have an influence on choice of sleeping accommodation. In particular, the nature of, and consequent demand for, the large hotel will be quite different from that of the small guest house or bed and breakfast unit. A large hotel may well provide attractions of its own, distinct from the location in which it is situated; indeed in some cases the hotel may be a more significant influence on choice than is the destination. This is often true of the large hotel/leisure complex providing a range of in-house entertainment such as is found in a number of American and, increasingly, European hotels. This type of hotel is still rare in Britain.

One noticeable trend in recent years has been the fall-off among guests staying at non-licensed accommodation in the UK, although licensed hotels have been able to retain their market share.

The provision of a good range of attractions, as well as a drinks licence, can help to off-set the disadvantages created by the unavoidable impersonality of the very large hotels. As the chains increase their hold on the total pool of hotel accommodation, an increase in the average room numbers follows, but outside of London, hotels with over 100 bedrooms remain the exception, and British hoteliers can still emphasise the personal nature of the service provided by them as a feature in their marketing.

Elsewhere, large hotels have been more sensitive to market changes than have smaller units. In the USA, where change and novelty is a feature of market demand, hotels have deliberately 'themed' their architecture and interior decoration to emphasise their uniqueness, and budget for regular redecoration to keep up to date. More traditional hotels, particularly in Britain, have responded by re-emphasising their traditional values and style. There is now some evidence that even in North America the market is moving away from the vast, monolithic 1000-bed hotels to the smaller, more intimate ones.

The point here is to emphasise that in neither case is the product seen by the customer as purely a 'room in which to sleep'. Rather, it is a 'total leisure experience' comprising a range of different services and emotional experiences which together go to make up the holiday or the business stay.

The small guest house, farmhouse or bed and breakfast establishment provides a valuable service to the tourism industry and its consumers. Being largely family-run, it provides a unique, personal service at a low price which is welcomed by a particular segment of the holiday market. It caters effectively for the impulse purchaser in touring holidays and it conveniently expands the supply of tourist accommodation during peak periods of the year in areas which are highly seasonal and where hotels would not be viable.

The traditional domestic holiday in a small seaside guest house or hotel faces competition which threatens the whole future of the smaller accommodation units. First, there is a gradual process of the British market switching from seaside holidays in the UK to overseas package holidays at similar prices and often offering better value for money than the accommodation provided in Britain. The lure of guaranteed sunshine is of course the key factor in this change, but as a result of the experience package holiday tourists have had abroad they have come to demand higher standards on holiday in Britain too – accommodation with swimming pools, private bathroom, better food and wider entertainment. The traditional accommodation sector has not responded to this new demand quickly enough or to the extent necessary. Whatever the reasons for this – margins are often too low to provide for this kind of reinvestment in the property and up to the end of 1982 public sector financial assistance was restricted to the Economic Development Areas now known as Assisted Areas and designated by the Government and EC for grant aid – there is little doubt that a substantial number of small hotels and guest houses are being forced to close their doors, although, as we have noted above, non-licensed properties are being harder hit. Liberalisation of the licensing laws in 1988, permitting alcoholic drinks to be served on weekday afternoons, will no doubt act as a boost for the accommodation sector, and for pubs and inns catering to the tourist, who can now compete more satisfactorily with their European neighbours in this respect.

A second challenge faced by these institutions is the shift towards self-catering. This has come about partly in an effort to hold down holiday prices, but of at least equal importance is the demand from tourists for more flexible types of accommodation and catering than have formerly been available in the smaller British hotels and guest houses. The once-popular fully inclusive holiday comprising three meals a day, taken at fixed times of day in the hotel, no longer meets the needs of the modern tourist who may wish to take day trips by car to the surrounding area and will therefore want to eat irregularly and perhaps omit a midday meal. Self-catering apartments fulfil this need and their popularity abroad with British tourists has led in turn to a fast expansion of similar facilities in the UK, at the expense of the boarding houses. Many smaller hotels have adapted their premises to provide self-catering units in order to survive. The motels have also expanded in number to meet the need for flexibility in touring holidays – it has been estimated that there are some 150 motel units in Britain today – but these units are ideally suited to larger countries where they serve the needs of long-distance motorists travelling on the motorway networks.

Farm holidays have also enjoyed considerable success in recent years, both in the UK and on the Continent. This arises from the recognition by farmers (and the tourist boards) that tourism is a less 'seasonal crop' than are many other more traditional farming activities. Farm-based accommodation is popular, too, among the growing number of holidaymakers whose life-style orientation is towards healthy food and natural outdoor life. Within the Assisted Areas, and

Fig 7.3 A farm holiday
(*Courtesy Irish Tourist Board*)

Fig 7.4 Butlins' three-star country suite accommodation
(*Courtesy Butlins' Holiday Worlds*)

Table III Leading companies in British Holiday Centre Operating, 1987

		Ownership	No of centres	Estimated no of visitors
1	Butlins	Rank	5	770 000
2	Holiday Club Pontins	Scottish and Newcastle Breweries	26	750 000
3	Warners	Mecca	29	750 000
4	Haven Leisure	Rank	30	450 000

particularly in Wales, the tourist boards have provided financial assistance and training for farmers interested in expanding their accommodation for tourists. On the Continent, Denmark in particular has been notably successful in packaging farm holidays for the international market in conjunction with the tour operators and ferry companies.

The market for camping and caravanning remains strong for domestic holidays, with some 21 per cent of holidays in Britain taken in caravans, and a further five per cent in campsites. While many holidays are, of course, taken in private caravans (of which there are over 800 000 in Britain), caravan parks remain popular, and have become an accepted part of the holiday scene. Holiday parks entered the tourist boards' grading schemes in 1987, with the introduction of agreed codes of practice for operators, and quality designated by ticks (a maximum of five ticks can be awarded). Over 800 caravan parks are so graded in the scheme. A trade body, the British Holiday and Home Parks Association (BH&HPA) has been formed to represent the interests of operators.

THE HOLIDAY CENTRES

Holiday camps were very much a British development, introduced on a major scale in the 1930s by three noted entrepreneurs of the day, Billy Butlin, Fred Pontin and Harry Warner, with the aim of providing 'all-in' entertainment for the family at a low price in chalet-style accommodation which would be largely unaffected by inclement weather. The Butlin-Pontin-Warner-style holiday camps were enormously successful before World War II and in the early post-war years, but all three organisations have now been absorbed into large corporations.

The leading companies are shown in Table III.

For the most part, the balance of the market is split between a large number of independent companies operating a small number of sites. The market for holiday centres remains highly seasonal, falling almost entirely between May and September. It had been customary for centres to close during the winter months, but improved marketing, including mini-breaks and themed events, have helped to extend sales into the 'shoulder' months of spring and autumn.

Holiday centres have been affected as much as any other accommodation facilities by changes in public taste for holidays. Before the war they attracted a largely lower-middle class clientele, but in the post-war period their market became significantly more working class and the canteen-style catering service and entertainment provided reflected this market segment's needs. Bookings were made invariably on a Saturday to Saturday basis, with clients booking direct with the companies concerned (each company attracting a high level of repeat business from a loyal market). Guests travelled independently to the camps.

More recently these camps have gone up-market, changing their names to holiday centres, holiday villages, holidays parks or estates. The former working class entertainment orientation has been modified to cater for wider social tastes. Large chalet blocks have given way to smaller units with self-catering facilities. A choice of catering styles has been introduced, ranging from fully serviced, through self-service to self-catering, but the latter form of service reflects the highest growth rate (Butlin's is now 70 per cent self-catering). Butlins in particular have invested huge sums of money to redevelop their remaining five centres and give them a more up-market image, which has been generally successful in winning sales after a decline in trade for holiday centres during the early 1980s.

Perhaps the most interesting development in domestic holiday centres, referred to earlier in this text, has been the introduction into Britain of an up-market holiday village in Sherwood Forest, owned and operated by the Dutch company Center Parcs. Offering a wide choice of all-weather facilities, the village has had an extraordinary measure of success since its inception, leading the company to invest in further sites in Britain.

Billy Butlin's early attempts to introduce his holiday camp concept abroad failed but the holiday village concept has been successful on the continent, with the Club Méditerranée an outstanding example of such success, largely attracting a young market.

Some word is also appropriate here about the growth of second homes ownership, which is influencing the tourism industry. Increasing disposable income, especially among those living in London and the South East, has led to massive growth in second home ownership, both within Britain and in overseas countries such as Spain, France and Greece. There is, however, increasing resentment by the local population against the second-home buyers, for example, in Wales, where in many cases the locals can no longer afford to buy homes in their own area. Where an outright purchase is beyond people's means, the concept of *timeshare*, discussed in the next section of this text, offers an alternative means of taking a holiday in one's second home in the UK or abroad. This major new market has initiated substantial demand for 'seat only' sales on charter aircraft, and poses a new threat to the traditional accommodation sector – indeed, some hotels in Britain have responded to the challenge by converting some or all of their accommodation for timeshare ownership.

The significance of the educational accommodation sector must also be recognised. Universities and other institutions of higher education, seeking to increase the contributions to the revenue through the rental of student accommodation during the academic holidays, have marketed this accommodation for budget holidays to tour operators and others. Often situated in green field sites near major tourist destinations, such as Stirling or York, the Universities have experienced considerable success in this new venture, and have further expanded their involvement with the leisure market by providing other facilities such as activity centres and public rooms for theme holidays. More than $1\frac{1}{2}$ million holidays are now sold each year in the UK using the accommodation of educational institutions.

The development of timeshare accommodation

Timeshare is a scheme whereby an apartment or villa is sold to several co-owners, each of whom purchases the right to use the accommodation for a given period of the year, which may range from a week to several weeks. The initial cost of the accommodation will vary not only according to the length of time for which it is purchased, but also depending on the period of the year, so that a week in July or August, for example, may be three or four times the cost of the same accommodation in winter.

The scheme is reported to have been initiated at a ski resort in the French Alps in 1965, although the Ring Hotel chain in Switzerland were developing along similar lines some years before this. By the early 1970s, timeshare had been introduced in the USA, and arrived in Britain in the mid-1970s. Since then it has enjoyed enormous success, boosted by schemes allowing owners to exchange their properties for others around the world during their period of ownership. A number of timeshare exchange organisations have been established, of which the largest and best-known are RCI and II (Intervac International). These companies keep a register of owners, and for a fee will facilitate home exchanges around the world.

The popularity of timeshare has led to some three million owners around the world, more than 120 000 of whom are British. There are at the time of writing over 2000 timeshare resorts, RCI alone offering exchanges at 1200 of these. Unfortunately, the sheer popularity and profitability of timeshare has led to high pressure salesmanship by less reputable organisations using 'street touts' to approach tourists visiting resorts abroad, and this has drawn some poor publicity for the scheme in the press. The Timeshare Developers' Association has been formed to give the industry credibility, and to draw up a code of conduct for members.

Timeshare is not without its problems. It has been found to be difficult to resell property due to the amount of new timeshare property on the market, and in some cases management and maintenance fees have been high. There can be a problem in getting widely dispersed owners together to take decisions on the management of the property. Notwithstanding these difficulties, timeshare remains popular, and will grow as a threat to the traditional package holiday.

THE DISTRIBUTION OF ACCOMMODATION

Large hotels and hotels chains have considerable advantages in gaining access to their markets. Many international chains have close links, through ownership or financial interest, with the airlines, a situation brought about in the early 1970s when the airlines, introducing their new jumbo jets, hastily set about establishing connections with hotels to accommodate their passengers. This gives hotels access to the airlines' computer reservations systems, important in reaching the international market.

Large hotels depend upon group as well as individual business to fill their rooms, so they must be in a position to maintain contact with tour operators, conference organisers and others bulk-buying accommodation. The tourist boards can play a part in helping such negotiations by organising workshops abroad to which the buyers of accommodation and other tourist facilities will be invited.

Increasingly the larger hotel chains are installing their own computerised reservations systems to cope with worldwide demand for immediate confirmation on availability and reservations. Some chains maintain their own offices in key generating countries (and of course each hotel will recommend business and take reservations for others in the chain), while independent hotels reach the overseas markets through membership of marketing consortia or through representation by a hotel representative agency.

These hotel representatives are not merely booking agents; they are on contract to the hotels they represent and will offer a complete marketing service. Some agencies, such as William R Galley Associates, R M Brooker and Utell International, generalise in their representation, while others specialise, either by representing hotels within a specific geographical area such as the Caribbean or smaller 'character' hotels.

Sales made through hotel representatives are normally commissionable at 10 per cent to the representative. This does not prejudice the commission normally allowable to travel agents, so a hotel being represented abroad may well find that a high proportion of its sales are costing 20 per cent of the room price to obtain. A small hotel must carefully consider whether it can set prices at a level which permits it to pay out commissions of this magnitude.

Sales through travel agents

Patterns of sales through travel agents are inconsistent. Within the UK few agents, other than a handful of specialist business house travel agents, deal regularly with hotel bookings. This is partly the result of the traditional pattern in Britain for tourists to book direct and partly because agents feel that the income accruing in commission for such sales is too small to merit the cost of servicing the business. There is also no common agreement between the hotel associations and ABTA on payment of commissions to agents, so each arrangement must be negotiated individually. Some hotels are prepared to pay a standard commission of 10 per cent on all sales, but these are the exception rather than the rule. Others will set a lower rate of commission or will not pay commission on sales for peak holiday periods.

However, hotels incorporated in domestic package tours, such as Gold Star holidays, or those which have produced a package tour programme which is easy and convenient for agents to sell, such as the weekend bargain break type of programme, do pay commission to domestic agents and sales through this source are increasing, although still relatively small in terms of hotels' overall turnover. Agents do undertake international hotel bookings more readily, especially where the hotel concerned has a UK representative or where the agent is arranging an independent package tour for clients.

The pattern of agency sales for UK holiday centres is similar. Traditionally these have been booked direct, but the leading companies, especially Butlin's, have made a conscious effort to increase their sales through travel agents in recent years, partly as a means of reaching a wider market than the one they have traditionally drawn on in the past. Nearly 60 per cent of Butlin's sales are now made through agents in Britain.

Finally, mention should be made of the sale of accommodation through public sector tourism outlets. This has been undertaken for some years on the continent – in Holland, for example, the Dutch tourist offices (VVVs) provide a reservation service for tourists, charging a fee for doing so – and more recently, the UK tourist offices have come to provide a booking service called 'Book A Bed Ahead' (BABA) for hotels and farmhouse accommodation through their Tourist Information Centres. These Tourist Information Centres could perhaps be called the 'travel agents' of UK destinations as retail agents seem reluctant to market Britain in a major way. One interesting development in this direction, initiated by a local tourist office, was WAVES – a consortium of traditional resorts producing a joint brochure of accommodation bookable through local tourist offices, using a computerised reservations system. Although the scheme suffered some teething problems (mainly due to the failure of its members to accept the need for computerised reservations) and has now passed to the private sector, it offered a foretaste of future co-operative reservations systems between the public and private sectors. WAVES is now expanding to include another 10 resorts. This scheme, which involves very few staff, is a sign of future developments in the tourism market. There has been some initial resistance to this idea from travel agents, but until agents show themselves willing to become more involved in such sales the accommodation sector is bound to seek new outlets for its products as the battle for the accommodation market becomes more acute.

QUESTIONS AND DISCUSSION POINTS

1 Discuss the relative attractiveness of the French 'Gites' to the British market, and the British B&B to foreign visitors. What are the particular features which appeal to the respective markets? How far has Britain attempted to emulate the Gite concept, and the French the B&B concept? Can these efforts expect to have the same degree of success?

2 Argue the case for and against:

(a) the compulsory grading and registration of hotels in Britain; and

(b) formally assessing quality in the hotel industry.

3 Does the concept of timeshare offer opportunities as well as threats to the travel industry? How can the industry best benefit from the growth in timeshare?

4 Why is there an acute shortage of budget-priced hotels in London, and is there a solution to the problem?

ASSIGNMENT TOPICS

1 The Raymonde Hotel is a small county-town property which has recently benefited from a growth in demand for small town tourism, especially short breaks out of season. As a result of three successful seasons, the hotel has now received planning approval for an extension which will bring the total number of rooms to 82.

The result of this growth in capacity is that the General Manager, Mr Jonathan Bromley, is keen to take advantage of sales opportunities wherever they arise. Until now, little active marketing took place, beyond publication of the hotel details in local tourist literature.

Mr Bromley has asked you, as a member of his back office staff, to investigate new ways of increasing sales. He is also interested in computerising the hotel's reservations system for the first time. However, he has doubts that computerisation will provide all the benefits that the computer companies suggest he will gain. He asks you to advise him on the benefits of computerising. Provide him with a report which makes recommendations for a future course of action.

2 Following the report submitted to Mr Bromley, you have been complimented for the detail and care you took in preparing this. One outcome of this is that you have now been appointed as the hotel's first sales representative, with a commensurate increase in salary.

Mr Bromley has read in the trade press of the success enjoyed by certain hotel proprietors, particularly abroad, who have 'themed' their properties to attract more clients. He asks you to suggest a theme which the hotel could adopt, which would help to make it distinctive from other hotels and attract more out-of-season traffic. Provide him with a report suggesting such a theme, how it should be introduced, and the market it should attract.

8 Travel retailing

Chapter objectives: After studying this chapter, you should be able to:

- explain the role of travel agents as a component in the tourism business
- list the functions that a travel agent is expected to perform
- identify the qualities necessary for effective agency management and agency service
- recognise strengths and weaknesses of agents
- be aware of the considerations and requirements in setting up a travel agency, obtaining ABTA membership and obtaining appointments from principals
- understand the threats facing agencies from alternative forms of distribution
- be aware of the key role played by computer technology in retail travel

INTRODUCTION

Most travel principals sell their products to consumers through the medium of travel agents. Such agents have been in existence for over a hundred years (selling mainly shipping and rail services before World War II), but the major growth has coincided with the growth in air travel and package tours. Before these two forms of travel became common, the shipping companies had also provided a reservations and ticketing service in their own offices situated in the leading ports and cities, and likewise the railways and coach companies, with transport terminals close to their markets, could also offer a convenient direct sales service to the public. With the development of air transport, the airlines found that, since the airports were away from market centres and there was already established a satisfactory network of travel agents to handle sales, the additional costs involved in setting up a chain of direct sales offices were not justified. In turn, agents expanded in number, to meet the demand for air tickets.

The origin of package tours can be traced to certain travel agent entrepreneurs who began operating their own programmes of foreign tours (see Chapter 9). Historically, of course, Thomas Cook had originated as a tour operator, and expanded to sell a range of travel services later; the mass market operations by air that we know today owe their origins as much to the handful of travel agents with vision, who recognised the opportunities for mass travel in the 1950s, assuming that air prices could be reduced, and who began putting together their own holidays. These 'packages' were sold in turn through other travel agents, and eventually became the agents' largest source of revenue. Today, the vast majority of airline tickets and eight out of ten package holidays abroad are purchased through travel agents.

There are some 7500 branches of travel agents appointed by the Association of British Travel Agents (ABTA), the major trade association representing both tour operators and agents. In addition, a small number of independent agents operate outside the framework of ABTA. As there has been strong growth in the demand for package tours over the past decade, demand has kept ahead of supply; whereas the average travel agent could expect only some 260 tour bookings per annum in 1977, ten years later the average figure had risen to at least 530. However, a redistribution of bookings has caused a greater proportion to be sold through the larger chains of agencies. Average commission levels would have shown a small increase over this period, but the discount war has held prices below the rate of inflation, so that the average agent's profit on each booking has shown a decrease.

Because of the constraints under which non-ABTA agents operate (as explained later in the chapter), such agents must be content to sell fringe services such as coach trips, or operate as 'bucket shops'. The latter term refers to outlets used by airlines to dump unsold tickets on the market at short notice and at heavily discounted prices. However, with the growth of deregulation in the airline industry, such tickets are now more widely available through ABTA/IATA appointed agencies, and the role of bucket shops has declined sharply in the past few years, although some continue to offer a technically illegal service in 'cross-border ticketing'. This is a scheme whereby the agent issues a ticket for a two-leg or multi-leg journey in which the through cost is lower than the price for a single leg, and discards the first coupon of the ticket. Thus, for example, if the fare between Athens and New York via London is less than the normal London–New York fare, a customer in London might be issued a through ticket with the section Athens–London discarded. This is contrary to IATA regulations, and the agent can be prosecuted for the offence.

THE ROLE OF TRAVEL AGENTS

The travel agent's role is dissimilar to that of most other retailers, in that agents do not purchase travel for resale to their customers. Only when a customer has decided on a travel purchase do agents approach their principal on their customer's behalf to make a purchase. The travel agent does not, therefore, carry 'stock' of travel products. This has two important implications for the business of travel distribution. Firstly, the cost of setting up in business is comparatively small compared to that of other retail businesses, and secondly, agents are not seeking to dispose of products which they have already purchased, and they therefore display less brand loyalty towards a particular product or company.

The latter characteristic can be an advantage to the consumer, since it aids the impartiality of advice that agents give their customers (assuming that commissions on sales are equal). On the other hand, it poses a marketing problem for the principals in their need to count on travel agency support to sell their products.

The main role of agents is to provide a convenient location for the purchase of travel. At these locations they act as booking agents for holidays and travel, as well as a source of information and advice on travel services. Their customers look to them for expert product knowledge and objectivity in the advice offered.

Although the range of products that an agent offers will vary according to the nature of demand in an area, the specialisation of the agency in question and the preferences and marketing policies of the proprietor, these will usually include air, rail, sea and coach transport, car hire, hotel accommodation, and package tours. Ancillary services such as travel insurance, travellers' cheques and foreign exchange may also be offered, and some agents will undertake to arrange travel documentation (such as procuring visas) for their clients.

Travel agents can be classified in a number of ways. In the first place, as we have already noted, a distinction can be made between those who are members of ABTA and those who are not – an important one for purposes of trading, as we shall see shortly. Agents can also be distinguished by the type of business they deal with, which influences, and is influenced by, their location. The significance of this will become apparent in the next section.

Although this text is concerned chiefly with the way in which agencies operate in Britain, mention should also be made of the American Society of Travel Agents (ASTA) whose influence extends far beyond its national borders. Unlike ABTA, ASTA draws its members from all sectors of the travel industry, both within the United States and around the world. This is due to the huge volume of international tourism generated by the American market; and no British agency which depends on the US market for a significant proportion of its business can afford to

ignore the trade body. Many British companies, such as incoming tour operators, will opt to join the Society to develop sources of American business.

SETTING UP A TRAVEL AGENCY

Travel agents are located in major city centres, in the suburbs of large towns, and in smaller towns or villages. To be successful, they need to be sited close to the centre of the shopping district. With other agents, they compete for travel business within a catchment area which, in the case of a large city, may extend only to the surrounding streets, while in the case of an important market town, may draw on residents living within a radius of 30 to 40 miles. Those agents whose location is close to important city centres or centres of business and industry (such as industrial estates) will usually try to take advantage of the opportunity provided by their location to service the business travel requirements of companies in their area. Some agents who specialise in business house travel may go to the extent of providing an implant (or in-plant) office, whereby members of the travel agency staff are based within the business house client's premises to handle the company's travel needs exclusively.

It is also worth noting that agents in city centres will draw clients not only from residents in the area, but also from workers employed in the area, who may find it more convenient to make their travel arrangements close to their place of work rather than nearer to their homes. This is particularly true of central London.

Setting up a travel agency in Britain requires little capital, for reasons already noted, nor are formal qualifications a prerequisite (although ABTA membership will require one member of staff to have a designated period of experience). As yet no licences are required (a situation unlike that of most of our Continental neighbours, and indeed one which may change following the European Community's harmonisation plans in 1992). Consequently, the business is extremely attractive, both to outsiders, who see it as a glamorous occupation with wonderful opportunities for cheap travel, and to senior counter staff in travel agencies seeking to be their own boss and to put their expertise to work for their personal benefit.

Anyone contemplating opening a travel agency will have to consider the merits of buying an existing agency, or forming a new one. There are substantial advantages in taking over an existing agency. To begin with, trading figures for recent years can be examined, and the viability of the agency evaluated, having regard to the asking price. A going concern can be expected to retain its loyal clientele, if service remains comparable, but against this, if there is a strong loyalty in the market, this will affect the price asked for the agency; with little in the way of fixtures and fittings, the purchaser of an agency is paying largely for the 'goodwill' of the business,

Fig 8.1 A typical travel agency
(*Courtesy Lunn Poly*)

that is to say, the ephemeral value of the good name of the business and its loyal customers. In recent years, the eagerness of many multiple agencies to expand quickly by taking over independent local agencies has helped to push up prices beyond what might seem to be economically prudent, were one to judge purely on the company's trading figures. Another significant advantage is that licences and agency appointments, once granted by principals, can generally be retained under new management, and staff, too, will generally stay on, at least until they can judge how the new proprietor will treat them. In the present climate of skilled labour shortages in some towns, qualified and experienced travel agency staff may be difficult to recruit when setting up a new agency.

The attraction of starting from scratch is mainly a financial one; the capital cost is limited to office furnishings, fixtures, computers, phones, perhaps a new external fascia. However, persuading principals to provide you with supplies of brochures, to offer you an appointment and to pay you commission on sales may prove to be difficult, especially if the area concerned is already well served by existing agencies.

A travel agent once declared, 'there are only three things important in setting up an agency: location, location and . . . location'. He was driving home the fundamental point that, to the customer, the convenience of the location is the main criterion in their choice of a travel agent. Any agent choosing a little-used sidestreet away from the main shopping area, merely because rents or rates are lower, can be at a major trading disadvantage. Equally, it can be a mistake to scrimp on floor space and decor. Clients are attracted to roomy shops with plenty of rack space and a bright, cheerful, inviting atmosphere to tempt them in. Increasingly, windows are designed not as settings to display brochures or destination publicity, but as living advertisements for the shop interior. Good lighting, warm colours,

comfortable chairs, desks rather than impersonal counters, all affect the client's perception of the agency and their motivation to enter the shop. Once inside, the good agent takes advantage of the opportunity to make a sale; but enticing the client through the door is the first step to selling. Needless to say, a street-level shop is imperative; only an agency with a well-established clientele and not dependent upon the impulse purchaser (for example, agencies dealing largely with business or group travel) could risk moving to an upper floor.

Sites need to be researched carefully. Existing pedestrian flows should be noted (usually, one side of a major shopping street – often the sunny side – always appears to attract more people than the other) and barriers, whether physical or psychological, taken note of. For instance, shops on traffic 'islands' which involve pedestrians using subways to cross the road will find it more difficult to attract the passing trade. Parking is often difficult in town centres, but if too restrictive, with no nearby car parks, this can be a further major disincentive to the shopper. The local planning office should be consulted for any plans for redevelopment in the area. Residential redevelopment in the immediate area could be an important plus for the site, while commercial redevelopment nearby may pose a threat; another travel agency could well open in competition to you when the site is opened, and if attractive and more accessible, could poach much of your business. It may be better, under such circumstances, to consider delaying your own decision to open until you can rent in the new shopping plaza.

In law, a travel agency is an office, rather than a shop. This is important beyond mere semantics, since in the case of *Ilkeston Cooperative Travel* v. *Erewash Borough Council (1988)*, it was determined that travel agents were exempt from the legal restrictions on Sunday trading applicable to retail shops, and may therefore open to trade. Ilkeston have since announced their intention to open regularly on Sunday, although it remains to be seen whether other agents will be forced to follow suit. In practice it is more likely that Sunday opening will be limited to a few peak weekends during the busy booking season.

Agents earn their revenue in the form of commission on sales. While levels of commission will vary over time and according to the travel product, typical commission rates at the time of writing are as follows:

International IATA airlines	9% (a)
Domestic airlines	7%
British Rail	7% (b)
Tour operators	10% (c)
Cruises	8½–9%
Ferries	9–10%
Insurance	35–40%

Notes:

(a) overriding (incentive) commissions are payable, usually after a minimum target is achieved (£350 000 at the time of writing). The incentive rises by about one per cent on every £100 000 of revenue.

(b) five per cent proposed but not agreed at the time of writing.

(c) up to five per cent extra for overrides. Cosmos pays 11 per cent and some specialist operators up to $12\frac{1}{2}$ per cent.

For most agents, package tour sales represent by far the largest proportion of their sales. Typically, overseas holidays account for 60 per cent of sales, air tickets another 25 per cent and ferry tickets some four per cent. Domestic holidays, a growing area of potential sales, take a further four per cent of sales, with the remaining seven per cent divided between cruises, rail and coach bookings and miscellaneous services.

Value added tax (VAT) is now payable by travel agencies on the 'added value' of package tours (transport alone is still zero-rated); i.e. on the commission earned by the agent. Payment to Customs and Excise can either be undertaken on behalf of the agents by the tour operators, or the agents can deduct the amount due from the settlement they send to the tour operators, making their own returns to Customs and Excise.

e.g. Tour price =   £100
      Agent deducts £10 (commission)
                        £1.50 (VAT due)
                                        ───────
                                        11.50
                                        ───────
      Agent remits to Tour operator   88.50
      Agent remits to C & E   1.50

Most principals today will offer higher rates of commission for agents reaching agreed sales targets, adding up to $2\frac{1}{2}$ per cent or more to the earnings of the agent, particularly for the sale of package tours. However, it is still rare to find an agent averaging more than 10 per cent on the total of revenue achieved during the year.

Out of an average gross profit of between nine and ten per cent, travel agents must pay all the running expenses of their agencies, including their own salary (*see* Fig 8.2). Only after these expenses are deducted can they judge whether they have made a net profit or a loss.

Of increasing importance to the profitability of agents is their status as 'cash' or 'credit' agents. Agents who have credit arrangements with principals have the advantage of simpler recording procedures and improved cash flow, since agents will hold clients' payments for longer before transmitting funds to principals.

Fig 8.2 Operational costs of an independent travel agency. A monthly profit and loss account to show typical expenditure.

Sales	1 060 545	
Gross Profit (Commission deducted @ 9.4% average commission level)	99 691	

Expenditure		% of total costs
Personnel		
Salaries, NHI, pensions, etc	48 140	
Staff travel, training, professional subscriptions	2 250	
	50 390	(52.03%)
Establishment		
Rent, rates, water	14 700	
Light and heat	2 200	
Insurance	1 500	
Cleaning	900	
	19 300	(19.93%)
Administration		
Prestel, telephone	7 608	
Postage	1 700	
Printing and stationery	1 100	
Hire of equipment	3 350	
Advertising and publicity	2 000	
Publications, timetables	1 660	
	17 418	(17.98%)
Financial and Legal		
Credit cards	2 630	
Bank charges	1 060	
Auditing and accounting	1 805	
Legal fees	270	
Bad debts	320	
	6 085	(6.28%)
Depreciation and amortisation	3 655	(3.77%)
Total Operational Costs	96 848	
Net profit before tax (99 691 − 96 848)	2 843	(as % of sales 0.27)

TRAVEL AGENCY SKILLS AND COMPETENCES

It follows that, owing to the extremely competitive nature of the retail travel business, two factors become paramount if the agency is to succeed: good management, and good service. Good management will ensure that costs are kept under control, that staff are kept motivated, and that the agency goes out actively to seek business rather than wait for it to come through the door. Good service will ensure satisfied clients, a build up of regular clientele, and word-of-mouth recommendation which will help to increase the size of the agency's market.

The vast majority of travel agents are small, family-run businesses in which the owner acts as manager, and employs two or three members of staff. In such an agency there is little specialisation in terms of the usual division of labour, and staff will be expected to cope with all the activities normally associated with the booking of travel, which will include:

(a) advising potential travellers on resorts, carriers, travel companies and travel facilities worldwide,

(b) making reservations for all travel requirements,

(c) planning itineraries of all kinds, including complex multi-stopover independent tours,

(d) accurately computing airline and other fares,

(e) issuing travel tickets and vouchers,

(f) corresponding by telephone and letter with travel principals and customers,

(g) maintaining accurate files on reservations,

(h) maintaining and displaying stocks of travel brochures,

(i) interceding with principals in the event of customer complaints.

In addition to product knowledge, therefore, the main skills that counter staff require will include the ability to read timetables and other data sources, to construct airline fares, to write tickets and to have sufficient knowledge of their customers to be able to match customer needs with the products available. There is also today a growing need for staff who can competently operate computers, especially computer reservations systems.

The correct construction of airline fares and issue of airline tickets is a far more complex subject than might be apparent to the uninitiated, and entails a lengthy period of training coupled with continuous exercise of these skills. However, airline computer reservations systems (CRS) increasingly include all the basic point-to-point air fares, and the ticketing function is also widely computerised so that fare quotations and ticketing skills will become significantly less important in the future. An understanding of the principles underlying the construction of fares, however, can be helpful – for example, in explaining complex fares to customers; and of course there will be a continuing need for fares experts in the industry. The large travel agency chains have in some cases centralised this role, so that a handful of experts can quickly determine the lowest fares for a particular journey by air on request from a member of their counter staff at any of the company's branches.

In addition to counter staff functions, agency managers (who frequently spend time at the counter themselves) are required to fulfil a number of administrative functions. On the financial side, these will include:

- maintenance and control of the company's accounts

- invoicing clients
- effecting bank reconciliations
- preparing and controlling budgets
- providing an estimate of the cash flow in the company on a month by month basis, and
- controlling expenditure.

The introduction of VAT has added to their workload, with returns having to be made to the tax authorities. Sales records must be kept, and sales returns completed regularly for travel principals. All these 'back office' jobs can today be computerised, even in the case of the smaller independent agency. Managers also have the task of safeguarding their stock of tickets and other negotiable documents, and in addition have the usual tasks of recruiting, training and supervising office staff, and promoting their business in-shop and externally.

Customer contact skills

The way in which staff communicate with clients is, together with the essential product knowledge they display, the essential ingredient of an agency's success. These communications skills can be divided into three distinct categories:

- language skills
- personal and social skills
- sales skills

Both employers and Government have expressed concern over the lack of basic language skills demonstrated by British workers; and this applies not to a lack of foreign languages, but our poor ability to use our own mother tongue. Written communications to clients which demonstrate poor sentence construction, grammar or spelling reflect not just on the employee, but on the company itself. When such correspondence goes out under the signature of a senior member of staff, the image of the company suffers a still more serious blow.

Personal and social skills are still more important, but fortunately it lies within our own power, to a large extent, to exercise these skills. There is still a tendency to look down upon jobs which involve service in Britain, which is all too often confused with servility. We are gradually learning, as a nation, that if we are to compete with our European colleagues, we must be prepared to offer the same level of 'service' in our service industries as they do. The acceptance of the credo 'the customer is always right' is the first move towards creating the right atmosphere for serving behind a counter, in a travel agency as in any other shop. Customers expect to be received warmly, and with a genuine smile of greeting; staff are expected to be unfailingly cheerful whatever stress they may have experienced during their workday. These qualities need to become second nature to counter staff.

First impressions weigh heavily, and staff will be judged, too, by their dress and appearance. Tourism employees must be prepared to adjust to the constraints that the job imposes, if they wish to succeed in the industry. Employers will insist on neat hairstyles, suitably discreet make-up, overall good grooming and appearance – often to the extent that counter staff in agencies will be required to wear a uniform, and personal hygiene is essential.

Deportment, too, is important. The way we sit, stand or walk says a great deal about us and our attitude towards our customers. Staff who are exposed to clients' view will be expected to look alert and interested when addressing their clients, to avoid slouching when they walk, and to sit upright rather than slumped in their chair.

These 'non-verbal signals' all say a lot about the attitude of the company to its customers. The scene of employees filing their nails and talking to their friends on the telephone, while customers try to attract their attention, is a common one in training videos, but one that encourages us to think about how we present ourselves in public. A warm, welcoming smile and friendly manner in greeting a customer approaching the counter will convey a positive view of the company and make the customer feel at home and in a buying frame of mind. Attentiveness to the customer is not only polite, it ensures that vital client needs are recognised, enabling the employee to match needs with products. When talking to customers, and greeting them, the employee should maintain eye contact and a manner which will breed confidence in the agency and its staff's product knowledge. Even handshakes are important cues to confidence; they should be firm and offered willingly. Use of the client's name enhances the relationship.

Even the way in which we answer the telephone is highly important for generating the right image of the company. Telephones should be answered quickly, and competently. As there are no dress and appearance 'cues' from which the client can make judgements, the voice becomes the sole basis for judgement. If clients are asked to hold on, they should be given the reason, and regularly checked to ensure they are still holding. If the person they are seeking to reach is busy, an offer should be made to call them back, and there should be a follow-up to *ensure* that they have been called back. Similarly, if the employee cannot give an answer immediately to a problem, they should offer to call the client back with the answer in a short while, and *do so*. This failure to call back is one of the most common sources of frustration for clients, leading to loss of business to a competitor.

The sales sequence

Travel agencies are no longer order takers; to compete, they must go out and get the business. Good social skills build the atmosphere which encourages buying, but closing a sale means knowing how to sell. Effective selling is the outcome of four stages in the selling process, which together make up the sales sequence:

- establishing *rapport* with clients
- *investigating* clients' needs
- *presenting* the product to the clients
- getting clients to take action, by *committing* themselves to the purchase

Rapport

To sell products successfully, one must first match them to the customers' needs. If the clients buy a product they do not really want, or which does not provide the satisfaction they expect, they simply do not come back to you. No travel agency can survive without a high level of repeat business, so ensuring that the customer is satisfied is a key objective in the sale. The first aim, therefore, is to establish a rapport, by engaging the client in conversation, gaining their trust, and learning about their needs. This process allows the salesperson to judge how receptive the clients are to new ideas, and how willing to be sold. Some customers prefer to self-select, and should not be badgered into a sale, while others need and seek advice more openly.

To generate a two way conversation, the opening phrase 'Can I help you?' has to be avoided – it simply invites the reply, 'No thanks. I'm just looking'. A more useful way of opening a conversation would be a phrase such as, 'Do you have a particular type of holiday in mind?', or, to a customer who has just picked up a brochure, 'That's a very good programme this year. Were you just looking for sun, sea, sand holidays, or had you something more adventurous in mind?' This forces a reply and encourages the client to open a conversation.

Investigation

Once you have gained the client's trust, the next step is to investigate their needs more thoroughly. Once again, you need to ask open questions, which elicit full answers. The sort of information you need to draw out of your client includes:

- who is travelling, and the number in the group
- when they wish to travel, and for how long
- their preferred mode of travel
- their choice of destination
- what they expect to pay

It must be recognised at the outset that clients will not necessarily have the answer to these questions. They may have only the vaguest idea about where they want to go and what they want to do. Needs must never be assumed, even from a clear statement of intent: a client saying they do not want to take a package holiday may merely be revealing a deep-seated prejudice that such holidays are 'down-market', while on the other hand they may have had a bad experience of earlier such holidays. The salesperson's task is to tease out the real reason so that the appropriate product can be offered – for example, an IIT (independent inclusive tour) where the client would not be one of the crowd. In particular, one should never take for granted that the price the customer states they are willing to pay is the maximum; the industry has encouraged holidaymakers to believe that holidays are invariably cheap, but one is doing the client a disservice not to point out that cheapness is not necessarily value for money, and that by paying a little more one has a better guarantee of satisfaction.

Presentation

Once you are satisfied that you know exactly what the clients need, you may go on to the next stage, that of presenting the products that you feel will suit them. The aim will be to present not only the features of the holiday being offered, but also the benefits:

> 'travelling in the early spring, you have the advantage of lower prices, yet this can be the nicest time of the year in the Austrian valleys, with the blossom out and before the mass of tourists arrive for the height of the season'.

Product knowledge is, of course, critical for the success in gaining your clients' confidence to a point where they are willing to accept your recommendations. Even if you feel that what you are offering is exactly suitable to your clients, it is always a good idea to offer an alternative, so that the client has the opportunity to choose. If you then demonstrate just how one holiday is a better buy than the other, this will make it easier for the clients to decide on the choice you are recommending.

At this stage in the sales sequence, you will often have to handle objections. Sometimes objections are voiced only because the clients need reassurance, or because they have not yet fully understood the benefits you are offering; sometimes objections occur because not all the clients' needs have yet been met, and here a process of patient questioning may be needed once again to draw out the possibly hidden motives for the objections.

Commitment

The final stage is the process leading to closing a sale. This means getting the client to take action – ideally to buy, but of course some clients will need more time to consider the offer. The aim of the counter clerk is then to get the best possible outcome of the sales sequence – taking an option, getting the clients to call back later, or getting them to agree that the salesperson may call them later to follow up the sale. The good salesperson is always looking for the buying signals that herald that the clients are ready to buy; 'Would you like me to take an option on that holiday?' can prompt the clients who are dithering to take action. Care must be taken, however, never to push the clients into a sale before they are ready to buy, or they may be lost for ever.

Finally, having got your deposit for a firm booking, you must remember that the sales job has not finished. You must continue to show interest and concern for the clients, helping to reinforce the sale and their commitment to return. Many agents now send a 'welcome home' card to their clients after their return from holiday, to invite them to come into the shop and talk about their experiences, to ensure they will return for another booking at a later date.

A good selling technique grows with experience, but it takes effort; effort to find out what the clients need, effort to appear constantly friendly and interested, and effort to find the right product to match the needs.

The product portfolio

It is ironic that the travel product requires perhaps greater knowledge on the part of retail staff than does virtually any other product, while travel agents' salaries lag far behind the rest of the retail distributive trade. This makes it particularly hard for agency managers to attract and retain qualified staff. Agents argue that competition and discounted prices make it impossible to pay higher salaries. Principals have come to accept that their retailers cannot be expected to have wide product knowledge of each company's offerings, and concentrate instead on providing agents with easier access to information through computer systems and more informative brochures.

While the apparently unbiased service provided by the independent travel agent appears to be a marketing advantage, it is questionable whether clients themselves actually deal through an agent to gain this benefit, since the proportion of sales through travel agents is highest for the standard package holidays, which could arguably be booked direct with equal simplicity. While 86 per cent of sun/sea/sand holidays are booked through agents, the proportion of lakes and mountains holidays falls to 72 per cent, self-catering holidays to 69 per cent and winter sports (where expertise might be thought of particular value) to only 58 per cent.

The low proportion of bookings achieved by travel agents for domestic holidays owes much to the traditional pattern of booking holidays in the UK. Domestic holidaymakers have tended in the past to contact principals direct to make their holiday bookings, often by writing to resort tourist offices for brochures and details of hotels. Holidays in Britain were neither conveniently packaged, nor seen by travel agents as sufficiently remunerative to justify devoting precious rack space to brochures or training staff in domestic product

Fig 8.3 Domestic holidays marketed by the three National Tourist Boards
(*Courtesy Scottish Tourist Board, English Tourist Board and Wales Tourist Board*)

knowledge. However, two factors have tended to increase sales through agencies. First, UK holidays have risen in price *vis-à-vis* foreign holidays, so that sales of a holiday at home can equal or exceed the 'bargain basement' prices now offered overseas. Secondly, UK holidays have been better packaged by intermediaries in the past few years. This is especially true of the short break holidays, and the three National Tourist Boards for England, Scotland and Wales have encouraged sales through agents by acting as catalysts for the integration of commissionable holidays in their regions into a single brochure, which increasing numbers of agents are finding space for on their racks.

BUSINESS TRAVEL

Agents have made strong efforts in recent years to tap the lucrative 'business house' travel market – bookings for company employees travelling on business. The growth in the economy and in exporting has led to a parallel growth in corporate travel, often seen as highly profitable for the travel agent because capital spent is high and the market relatively price insensitive. However, increasing competitiveness among agents soliciting business travel, coupled with the drive for

greater cost-efficiency in industry, has made this sector of the market more price-sensitive. Business houses now seek, and usually can obtain, 'deals' with travel agents in exchange for agreements to place all their corporate business through the one agency. Agencies in turn attract business houses by providing a standard rate of discount on all travel arrangements – usually in the order of about four per cent – or extended credit terms, whereby companies may not have to settle their accounts until ten to twelve weeks after receiving their tickets.

Businesses are extremely demanding customers. The level of service which an agent must offer to retain their patronage is considerable. Companies often require reservations at very short notice, and will need service outside the normal office hours of the travel agent. They will expect documents to be delivered to their offices, and may also require the agent to obtain visas or other help with documentation. Therefore the additional costs of handling these arrangements must be considered by the agent, particularly where credit is offered to the business house. It is not unusual for companies to delay payments until well beyond the dates due, while the agent himself must still make payments to the principals within the agreed times; thus the agent is helping to fund the company's cash flow at his own expense. However, the attraction of a large account which may in some cases exceed £1 million a year will be sufficient to ensure that agents compete for the business by offering extra levels of service, implants, fares expertise to guarantee lowest prices, and financial incentives.

Since the highest discounts can be offered by agents negotiating the best deals with their principals, this has once again led to the multiple branch agencies dominating the business house market; it is estimated that 30 per cent of all business house earnings are achieved by four major multiples – Thomas Cook, Hogg Robinson, Pickfords and American Express – all of which have chosen to specialise in providing business travel services. Leading agencies dealing with business travel have formed an association – the Guild of Business Travel Agents – to represent their interests. Some of the larger companies have gone further, by joining international consortia of business travel agents, which offer them greater influence and purchasing power with principals. The American consortia, Woodside Management Systems and Travel Trust International, both count large British agencies among their members. However, after 1988, CAA regulations will be relaxed to allow airlines to discount their tickets, by passing back commission to the larger corporations, posing the threat of direct sell on a wide scale. It remains to be seen whether the quality of service that can be offered by the specialist business house agent can continue to attract custom from the large companies. What is certain, however, is that the organisation representing the interests of corporate travel, the Institute of Travel Management, is seeking to use its influence to obtain better deals for its members, while a handful of large corporations have bought into travel agencies in order to retain agency commission within their own organisations. It is interesting to note that the US equivalent of the ITM, the National Passenger Traffic Association, has its own travel agency in New York and is seeking to franchise branches throughout the USA.

TRAVEL AGENCY APPOINTMENTS

ABTA membership
In the UK there are no legal licensing requirements to set up as a travel agent, but in some countries governments do exercise licensing control over agencies, and the EC is currently looking into this issue for its members. However, most principals license the sale of their services through the issue of agency agreements, or contracts. Without such an agreement, the principal will not pay commission on sales, although some companies do dispense with the formal procedures for recognition – it is unusual, for example, for hotels to insist on a formal agreement before they will pay agents' commission on sales.

To sell the services of tour operators who are themselves members of ABTA, the travel agent is required to belong to ABTA as well as entering into a formal agreement with the company concerned. Membership of ABTA is required because of a ruling (upheld by the Restrictive Practices Court in 1982) that only ABTA travel agents may sell the services of ABTA tour operators, and in turn these agents refrain from selling package tours of companies who are not ABTA members. This reciprocal booking agreement, which amounts to a closed shop, is known as *Operation Stabiliser*, and was introduced by ABTA in 1965 as a means of protecting the travelling public. In the event of the collapse of an ABTA member, the Association was able to draw on a *Common Fund* provided from membership subscriptions, which would be used to compensate customers for lost holidays, and ensure that those stranded abroad as a result of the collapse would be repatriated. Later, with the introduction of alternative bonding arrangements for tour operators (*see* Chapter 9), this Common Fund became the Retailers' Fund, and still operates today to protect consumers against the consequences of a retail agent collapsing.

Thus, ABTA membership provides considerable trading advantages, but it also imposes certain obligations on its members. Premises are open to ABTA inspection, agents must abide by a strict Code of Conduct, and at least one qualified member of staff must be employed. 'Qualified' is defined as having two years' experience. Alternatively, an employee can achieve 'qualified' status by obtaining the Certificate of Travel Agency Competence (COTAC) either at level one together with 18 months' work experience, or at level two with one year's experience. However, ABTA's conditions which formerly restrained agents from discounting travel and prevented their selling non-travel products ('mixed selling') have now been overturned by the Restrictive Practices Court. There has, in fact, been a considerable increase in 'mixed business' in travel agencies since restrictions were relaxed, particularly in the sale of complementary products such as luggage and electrical goods. ABTA will investigate the travel agent's financial standing and qualifications for entry prior to admitting the company to membership. This period can take between six and twelve weeks, during which time it is expressly forbidden to deal through existing ABTA agents and split commission (ABTA agents dealing illicitly with non-approved agencies can be subjected to a fine). However, the company concerned may apply for appointment with other principals (domestic air carriers, ferry companies), and sell the services of those principals, although the latter may require agencies to be separately bonded if ABTA approval is not yet confirmed.

Bonding
New agents, during their first year of trading, and agents

judged by ABTA, after inspection of their accounts, to be at risk financially, are required to post a bond which indemnifies them to clients and customers against the risk of their failure. Certain principals may also require the posting of a bond, even if an ABTA bond is held – for example, if the agent plans to hold a principal's ticket stock.

A significantly higher bond will be asked of agents who are without limited liability (i.e. trading as sole traders or partnerships). Additionally, if the retail agents operate tours, whether in the UK or overseas, they will also be required to put up a tour operating bond.

Bonding may be undertaken in one of three ways:

(a) a sum of money equal to the value of the bond can be placed in a trust account. The agent can benefit from the interest accruing on the account, but cannot touch the capital itself. Since this could involve putting up a substantial amount of money, it is rarely chosen except by the largest corporations.

(b) the agent can obtain an insurance policy for the amount required, paying an annual premium (typically at a cost of between £400–£700 per annum).

(c) the agent's bank puts up the bond, against either company assets or, more commonly, the personal guarantees of the directors. A fee is charged which is substantially less than the premium paid for an insurance policy, but the directors become personally liable for the amount of the bond in the event of the company's failure.

As a safeguard, ABTA also has its own annual indemnity insurance policy which can provide additional funds if the bonds posted by an individual member are insufficient to cover the claims against the company in the event of its collapse.

Most contracts with principals are non-exclusive; that is to say, they do not bind the agent from dealing with the principal's competitors. Occasionally, however, a contract may offer the agency the exclusive right to sell the product, and may further restrict the agent's ability to deal with other directly competing companies.

Unless expressly stated in the contract, agents do not have the automatic right to deduct their commission from the monies due to the principal. If bonus commissions are paid for targets achieved, it is generally the case that these additional sums of money are paid to the agent at the end of the season, rather than immediately following the achievement of the target. These facts must be borne in mind by the agent in estimating cash flow.

A licence is required for commission to be payable on the sale of services of members of the International Air Transport Association (with the exception of domestic air services). Since IATA travel makes up a substantial proportion of a typical travel agent's turnover, it is important for travel agents who wish to offer a full range of services (and doubly so for those dealing in business house travel) to obtain the necessary appointment.

Around 2000 agency branches hold IATA appointments in the UK. IATA's Agency Distribution Office deals with applications for a licence, a process which can take up to 45 days. A representative from IATA's Agency Investigation Panel visits the agent to judge whether the site is easily identified as a travel centre and suitable for the sale of tickets (while proof of turnover is no longer required of agents, IATA wishes to satisfy itself that the agency has the scope to generate business). The number and competence of staff will be judged; at least one member of staff will be expected to have COTAC or an equivalent fares and ticketing qualification. The representative must also be satisfied that the agency premises are secure and ticket stock safeguarded.

If approved, a bond is taken out to cover the agency's anticipated monthly IATA turnover. An entrance fee is payable, and a small annual subscription. This approval enables the agent to sell the services of all IATA members. Separate plates are available for every IATA airline, and agents may hold stock of as many as 60 plates if they plan to draw tickets on each airline.

At one time, agents could earn no income on IATA sales until they received IATA approval, and they were not permitted to obtain IATA tickets through recognised agents, splitting commission. This ruling, IATA Resolution 800, was overturned by the CAA in the UK, so that it is now possible for the new agent to trade and earn commission by agreement to split commissions with an established IATA agent.

Other appointments

Approval is also required to make commissionable sales on the services of British Rail, National coaches, domestic airline services and other principals such as shipping and car hire firms. Obtaining approval for most of these is largely a formality, especially for ABTA and IATA appointed agents. Appointments to sell travel insurance, however, will involve closer scrutiny, since the agent will be acting as a broker for the insurance service concerned. Insurance companies are tightening up in the face of evidence that some agents have taken insurance premiums from their clients but have withheld issuing certificates of insurance unless claims were filed.

THE EFFECTIVENESS OF TRAVEL AGENTS

There have been few studies in Britain of travel agency productivity and profitability, although the EIU (Economist Intelligence Unit) report on travel agency profitability (see Bibliography) made an attempt to do so back in 1968. This survey suffered a number of shortcomings in its methodology, but its findings suggested that at that time some two thirds of agents responding to the questionnaire were making profits, while 75 per cent of all agents were generating just 22 per cent of total travel revenue. Clearly, many of these agents were making substantial losses at the time, and conversely a handful of agents were achieving very high revenue figures.

The report recommended that agents should seek to retain at least 20 per cent of the revenue earned (i.e. two per cent out of the 10 per cent commission earned on a booking), but less than a third were actually achieving that figure at the time. ABTA commissioned a study in 1984 which revealed that agents at that time were managing to retain only some 0.7 per cent of turnover.

The report did not make clear that profitability may be as much a factor of location as of efficiency: nor is fast turnover necessarily commensurate with a professional standard of advice and sales assistance. A case may be made for emulating the American approach to retail travel operations, providing a fast and efficient sales service for package tours and simple point to point travel reservations, and at the same time offering a more specialised advisory service for complex travel arrangements through experts in product knowledge (known as Certified Travel Councillors), who may charge fees for their services in addition to earning commission on the products sold.

Another failure of the EIU Report was in not making clear which were the profitable and non-profitable services sold by travel agents. Harry Chandler, of Chandler's World Travel, tried to correct this omission by publishing in 1969 an analysis of his own company records which sought to identify the average costs applicable to each service, in terms of labour units for commission earned. He found at that time that package tours and long haul air travel were subsidising the other travel services sold by agents: a re-evaluation of the records in 1973 found much the same results.

This raises the question of whether agents should continue to provide a full range of travel products for their clients, or concentrate only on those they find profitable. Many adopt the former course, on the grounds that customers buying unprofitable services will be tempted by good service to return to the same agent later to buy more profitable travel arrangements. Nevertheless, a growing number feel that the latter course is the more sensible to adopt. As this approach has become more widespread, it has caused those principals affected to rethink their distribution strategy, either by organising alternative distribution outlets or by improving the efficiency of existing ones, for example by the introduction of cost-effective computer reservations systems.

The system of bonus payments by which principals reward highly productive agents with increased levels of commission is also encouraging agents to become more selective in the products they display and actively sell. This trend is affecting principals' distribution systems to an even greater extent, and is beginning to lead to more specialised travel agents offering a selective range of travel 'brands'; i.e. market nicheing, by the independent agents particularly.

This brings into question the whole role of the agent as provider of information. Evidence points to serious gaps in product knowledge among many agents, particularly in long haul travel, and as agents specialise more, so knowledge becomes narrower. Travel agency work still retains something of a glamour image for many young people, and the prospect of cheap travel is a lure for new staff. However, as we noted earlier, it is not easy to attract the calibre of staff needed to sell such a sophisticated and complex product as tourism. Those staff who do work at the retail level must therefore benefit from the best possible training for their job.

A number of attempts have been made in recent years to compensate for the lack of basic knowledge among young staff. The earlier work of the Institute of Travel and Tourism, and the more recent introduction of the Certificate of Travel Agency Competence validated by the City and Guilds of London Institute have undoubtedly helped to increase travel sales and management skills, and these qualifications have been supported by in-service courses run by the colleges of further and higher education, private training organisations such as Response Tourism Training Services, and the in-service courses offered by ABTA's National Training Board. The Youth Training Scheme (YTS), Government funded through the Training Agency (formerly the Manpower Services Commission), which offers a split between job experience and college based training, has also helped to improve standards at junior counter level, and there can be little doubt that both sales ability and product knowledge have greatly improved throughout the industry. It remains true, however, that low salaries and inadequate promotion opportunities in the independent retail sector depress the quality of intake and lead to high staff turnover, particularly in London and the South East, where salaries fail to keep pace with the rising cost of living. Another worrying trend is the falling number of 16–19 year olds coming onto the labour market; from a high of more than 3.6 million in the early 1980s, the number will fall to less than 2.5 million in the early 1990s, exacerbating the problem of recruiting young staff. Other industries that can afford to pay more will attract potential travel recruits, and the travel business is faced with the need either to pay higher salaries, or to find other means of recruiting staff. ABTA's National

Training Board has responded to the challenge by providing training courses designed to recruit the mature unemployed, under grants awarded by the Government's Employment Training Scheme.

The growth of travel agency multiples is rapidly changing the face of the retail travel business. The large chains, spearheaded by Lunn Poly, Pickfords, Thomas Cook, Hogg Robinson and A T Mays, have expanded the number of their branches rapidly in recent years, as is shown in Table IV:

Table IV The March of the Multiples 1982–8

	Sept 1982	July 1988
Lunn Poly	65	439
Pickfords	186	368
Thomas Cook	186	357
Hogg Robinson	143	247
A T Mays	124	245
W H Smith	88	194
	792	1850
All ABTA agents	4983	7249
% of agencies owned by the multiples	15.9%	25.5%

(*Source: Profit from Travel*)

The expansion has come particularly at the expense of the smaller chains or independents with a handful of branches, who have sold out to, or been taken over by, the larger chains. The result has been a polarisation of travel agencies in terms of size: travel agents with five or fewer branches represented 57 per cent of all outlets at the end of 1987, while the top five agents together represented nearly 22 per cent of outlets.

The chains benefit from a number of advantages over independent agents, favouring their growth. They are able to negotiate more favourable incentive commissions, owing to their strength in the marketplace, and can choose if they wish to discount their prices, by passing on commission to their clients, to an extent greater than a small company will find possible. They have the financial resources to invest heavily in computerisation (and are now using networks to transfer data between their branches); economies of scale can offer increased efficiency in their operations; and they can devote greater resources to staff training.

Faced with declining margins and a continuing expansion in the number of ABTA branches, travel agents have only two choices to remain profitable – either they can cut costs, or they must increase turnover (which will also help their negotiation with principals for higher commission rates). Unfortunately, smaller agencies can do neither as effectively as the large travel chains, and must lose out unless they can find other strategies to retain business, such as racking the less common package tours, or offering some specialist expertise that will attract particular types of client. However, with most agents dependent upon sales of sun, sea, sand holidays, price remains the greatest market incentive and the small agencies lose out.

The seriousness of the agent's predicament is apparent when looking at the margins at which agents operate. ABTA has revealed that in 1986 three per cent of its agents accounted for over 50 per cent of the total revenue, while at the other end of the scale, one quarter of agents had revenue of less than £300 000. If we take 9.7 per cent as the average commission earned by agents on sale of all travel products, net income even at the upper level of this revenue accounts for little more than £29 000 to meet all operating and marketing expenses, and provide a profit.

The polarisation of sales is revealed in evidence that although turnover for all agents increased by 13 per cent over the previous year, that of the smaller agents increased by only four per cent, while largest agents increased by 45 per cent. Profit levels among small agents have fallen, while those of the larger agents have increased.

The decline in profitability has in turn made it more difficult for the small agencies to promote their products; thus they enter a spiral in which low promotion reduces customer awareness, which leads to a decline in custom.

Travel agents are expected to play an active role in promoting travel services – indeed, the retail agents' Code of Conduct requires them to do so – but lack of funds or of enterprise will mean that some agents go no further than to display promotional material provided by their principals in their shops and windows. Others will advertise locally in the press, or run film shows for potential customers. Large multiples, however, can afford extensive advertising on a national scale, and will cooperate with tour operators to run promotional schemes.

Some have questioned whether agency promotion actually increases the propensity to travel, or whether it merely increases the inter-agency competition for a share of the market which is created by principals' own advertising and promotion. There can be little doubt that the huge resources for marketing available to the chains, coupled with their willingness to discount or offer other incentives (low deposit, or even no deposit, offers were widespread during the agents' battle for market share in 1987/8), have helped to divert the lion's share of the travel market into the branches of the large chains.

In retaliation, smaller agents have rationalised the services offered, diversified into new products, or amalgamated with other companies. The National

Association of Independent Travel Agents (NAITA) was formed with the intention of safeguarding its members' interests, and has approached principals (including British Airways) to seek help in developing an 'own label' travel brand, to be sold exclusively through its members' offices. An Alliance of Retail Travel Agents' Consortia (ARTAC) has been established to link the various retail agency consortia that have sprung up, and has plans to develop a closed user group (CUG) computer system as an aid to its members. Whether any of these plans is sufficient in itself to arrest the march of the multiples only time will tell.

DIRECT SELL

Can travel principals sell their products direct to the public at lower cost without losing sales? This is a vital question for both carriers and tour operators. Travel firms which have traditionally sold direct, such as British Rail, and others who are newcomers to the industry and have adopted a policy of selling direct exclusively, do not have to reckon with the retaliatory forces of ABTA members, basing their decision purely on the economics of the trading situation. Selling direct cuts out the high cost of servicing intermediaries and of paying commission on each sale. On the other hand, it involves considerable capital expense in setting up sales offices, and direct marketing costs can be high, especially if a programme of national advertising is thought necessary to reach the travelling public. There will be a need for a large reservations department to deal with enquiries from the public, and a huge telephone system to cope with phone enquiries or bookings.

If principals who presently deal through travel agents decide to sell direct for the first time, or to increase the proportion of direct sales they currently achieve, they stand the risk of antagonising their present distributors. Therefore any effort to increase sales in this way must be handled with extreme discretion, to avoid loss of sales through traditional channels. British Airways was forced to abandon its efforts to expand its own implant offices in the headquarters of large business houses, in the face of strong reaction from ABTA members, who threatened to switch sales to rival airlines. The airline, however, continued to expand its network of city centre sales offices (in order to maintain control over sales, as much as to save on payment of commissions), and has recently announced plans to expand the number of outlets and range of travel services offered under a new name, 'Four Corners Travel'.

Tour operators depend upon agency support for up to 90 per cent of their sales (although most smaller companies licensed to sell less than 10 000 holidays a year cannot afford to distribute through travel agents nationally, and will either develop a policy of selecting a number of key supportive agents or will opt to sell all holidays direct). However, during the 1970s a number of tour operators entered the field with the aim of distributing mass market package tours direct to the public. Foremost among these were Martin Rooks, a medium-sized direct sell operator before its integration with British Airways; Portland Holidays, a direct sell division of the Thomson Travel Group; and Tjaereborg (UK), an off-shoot of a well established direct sell Danish tour operator. To these must be added the well established tour operator specialising in holidays for the elderly, Saga Holidays, a handful of companies formed by diversifying tobacco giants (Peter Stuyvesant, Marlborough, Silk Cut) and a UK division of the Swedish Vingresor. The new companies achieved some initial success by claiming to offer holidays that were substantially cheaper than equivalent packages sold through agents, due to cutting out agency commissions. In some cases this claim could be justified, although a close examination of the companies' pricing structure would suggest that the low prices were highly selective, rather than across-the-board. The market share of direct sell operators reached about 20 per cent in the mid-1980s, but while Portland was able to expand on sales subsequently, the other newly established operators were less successful. Vingresor was soon absorbed into Portland Holidays, while Tjaereborg (UK), after a series of management reshuffles, was put into the hands of the Owners Abroad group in 1988.

It is perhaps significant that none of the principals owning direct sell operations appears to have experienced any antagonistic reaction among travel agents which might have affected sales of their main holiday programmes. After some initial concern in the industry, agents appear to have become reconciled to the fact that direct sell is here to stay, but has stabilised as a proportion of the total holiday market. Concern could be rekindled, however, if advances in computerisation lead to direct access to operators' CRSs by the travelling public.

Perhaps the greatest potential threat to retail agents to emerge in recent years lies with the introduction of direct sell credit card Holiday Clubs, formed by a trading relationship between credit card companies and travel firms which handle the bookings. The scheme was initiated by a link between Page & Moy and Barclaycard, which has since taken over the travel company. Marketing is done by the credit card company through its direct mail contacts with cardholders, who place orders for travel by phone to Page & Moy's office. The travel company provides neither an advice service nor brochures; it acts purely as a booking office, and payment is made, of course, by credit card. The resultant cost savings can be passed back to the customer in the form of a discount on the regular price of the holiday (averaging about six per cent). The huge volume of business this has generated for the company has led to other similar links: Trustcard (TSB) with A T Mays, Access with Thomas Cook, and Girobank with Pickfords.

The extent of success of the various schemes cannot be judged at this point, although Page & Moy estimated their market share at some 50 000 customers in 1988.

Other issues in distribution

In general, it has been tour operating policy to sell products through the entire network of ABTA travel agents. In 1971, however, Cosmos Holidays, among the brand leaders in package tours, adopted a policy of limiting outlets on the basis of their productivity, dropping a large number of their less productive agents. This policy was shortly followed by Global and Thomson Holidays after analysis indicated that 90 per cent of their sales were achieved through some 100 highly productive agents. It is interesting to note that Cosmos later reversed this policy, returning to a pattern of limited support for all agents, with an increased level of support for the more productive, in an effort to increase their overall market share.

In turn, travel agents who do represent a full range of principals' services are in practice fairly selective in the services they recommend, a decision based not only on what they believe to be in their clients' interest, but also on their own self-interest. Rack space being limited, agents are bound to give preferential treatment to best known and best selling tour operators' programmes, particularly where targets have been set by these companies for higher commission. Basic commission rates can be another factor to be taken into account, but of equal importance is the efficiency of the principals' reservations systems. Agents who encounter difficulty making telephone reservations for their clients will be less inclined to favour that principal's services. The personal relationship between travel agency staff and the tour operator or other principal provides another dimension; in this situation, the role of the sales representative can be of immense importance in creating an image for the company, and cultivating the goodwill of the agents concerned.

THE IMPACT OF COMPUTER TECHNOLOGY ON TRAVEL RETAILING

The industry has been profoundly affected by the development of computer technology over the past decade. Since such systems are being constantly modified and improved, there will be little benefit in this text in discussing the relative merits of those systems currently in operation. Suffice to say that today even the smallest travel agents or tour operators can afford to introduce technology for both front office and back office functions – in fact, many would argue that no agent can afford *not* to do so.

The tourism industry is ideally suited for computer technology. It requires a system of registering availability of transport and accommodation at short notice; of making immediate reservations, amendments and cancellations of such facilities; of quoting complex fares and conditions of travel; of rapidly processing documents such as tickets, invoices, vouchers and itineraries; and of providing accounting and management information. All of these functions are available today, to a greater or lesser extent, in agency computer systems which are designed to operate either in isolation or to link with the reservations systems of travel principals.

Computer systems in travel agencies are designed to offer three distinct facilities:

1 Front office 'client relations' systems enabling a counter clerk to access principals' CRSs, check availability and make reservations.
2 Back office systems enabling documents such as invoices, vouchers, tickets and itineraries to be issued, and accounts to be processed with principals.
3 Management systems, producing updated figures on the company's performance to assist managers to guide and control operations.

New computer systems have now been developed which will provide all three facilities for even the independent agent, at prices which continue to fall, but at the time of writing start at around £6000; or equipment can be leased to reduce capital investment and spread costs.

In considering systems which are designed to access travel principals' reservations systems, one can distinguish between those developed by carriers, and those developed by tour operators. In Britain, because of the importance of 'interlining' (common ticket issuing and ability to transfer bookings between carriers) any system used must be capable of booking seats on a large number of different airlines. During the 1980s, the Travicom system, which gave access to more than 30 airlines and their ancillary services such as car hire, came into widespread use in travel agencies, since it interfaced with British Telecom's Prestel as well as other private viewdata systems. Prestel was designed as a computerised information system, for use by both the trade and the public. In the event, consumers were slow to take advantage of computer information systems in the home, but the travel trade became major users, particularly once it became *interactive* through the Prestel Gateway system; that is to say, communications became two-way between the user and the information provider. Travel agents, as members of a Closed User Group (CUG) system, were then able to access the computer reservations systems of the airlines using Travicom 'Skytrack', as well as accessing tour operators' CRSs using private viewdata or Prestel.

In the latter half of the 1980s, airlines have come to

Fig 8.4 The Travicom computer reservation system
(*Courtesy Travicom*)

recognise the power and influence that a CRS exercises in helping to gain market share, and competing systems have battled to become the first choice in travel agencies around the world. US systems such as 'Sabre' and 'Apollo' have penetrated the British market, and European systems 'Galileo' and 'Amadeus' have been developed to combat the American threat. These systems have been detailed in Chapter 5. Although at the time of writing the European systems are only just being introduced into British agencies, there can be little doubt that the focus of the early 1990s will be the need for one's system to be adopted as first choice in the distribution system. Meantime, Travicom in its two forms, 'Skytrack' and the more advanced 'President' system used mainly in business house travel agents, remains the most used system in the UK.

Prestel Gateway as a reservations access system faces competition from two private networks, operated by Istel and Fastrak, which are becoming leading systems for accessing many tour operators' CRSs. While these systems are all capable of interfacing, they are commercially competitive, so that agents cannot go through one network into another without dialling up again. Consequently, as with airline CRSs, these networks are also battling for domination in the travel

distribution systems, although tour operators are finding it increasingly important to be accessible to agents through more than one network. Five of the top six leading operators are accessible at the time of writing through the Istel link, which provides direct connections into their own CRSs, while ILG has developed its own Intalink system separately – although it is unlikely to continue in isolation from the more popular networks. Fastrak offers access to most of the ferry companies' reservations systems, as well as to a number of operators.

Back office systems offer not only faster means of carrying out accounting and documentation procedures, but also the potential to cut costs. Systems such as DPAS (owned by Travicom and available in their President system) have brought computerised accounting procedures within reach of the smaller agents. But perhaps the most significant move has been the introduction of Thomson Holidays' TAB (Thomson Automatic Banking) system, which the company imposed on all its appointed agents in 1988. This system is linked with the Thomson TOP reservations system, and automatically debits travel agency accounts for transactions effected through TOP. Although agents are still given some period of credit, this is the first step towards EFTPOS (Electronic Fund Transfer at Point of Sale) within the travel industry itself. The system can be expected to be adopted widely over the next few years, and will have a marked effect on travel agency cash flows.

Many agents have been slow to come to terms with the computer era, and there is some evidence that their customers also mistrust computer reservations procedures. Other agents, however, have recognised that the technological revolution will affect their business to a greater extent than almost any other industry. One agent, John Neilson, in conjunction with the retail chain 'Next', has established a chain of hi-tech travel shops to take maximum advantage of the benefits computers can bring. More and more information is being made available to the trade electronically (ABC timetables can be accessed through Istel, for example), and agents are beginning to learn that the computer may be the key for survival.

However, just as computers offer great promise for agents, so they also pose a serious threat. Information sources do not have to be restricted to agents: it would be not unreasonable to imagine similar systems in operation in libraries and other public places where travellers may be able to make their reservations direct – or indeed, by selecting from a choice of worldwide flights and hotels, to package their own tours. Nothing in principle prevents the airlines today from establishing computer links with business houses, thus effectively cutting out agents altogether from this lucrative source of revenue. One company, Holiday Designers, has recently installed a CRS which allows agents to buy independent travel services to package tailor-made tours for their clients.

It is but a small step to allowing clients to undertake this themselves – indeed, this is already being introduced in the USA on an experimental basis.

THE FUTURE OF TRAVEL RETAILING

One of the most significant changes to have occurred in recent years in the UK is the entrance of non-travel organisations onto the travel scene. This has affected retailing no less than other sectors of the industry. In the past, ABTA's constraints on mixed business deterred this development, but with this constraint removed by the OFT, the growth prospects for the leisure market have encouraged a number of major companies such as W H Smith to open in-store travel shops, while the travel agency multiples have opened branches within department stores and other shops. Such moves are encouraged by Government support for open competition in the travel industry, although these trends have been carried even further in other countries, where travel is sold in banks, petrol stations and shops, and there is no reason why similar developments should not eventually follow in this country.

Without enormous expansion in travel demand, this will mean a further squeeze on travel agents' turnover, unless the travelling public continues to demand the personal service and sound product knowledge which may be lacking in the 'supermarket' approach to travel sales. This will call for improved standards of training in the small agencies, however.

The multiples have been able to benefit from economies of scale, offering opportunities for specialist management, a hierarchy where job promotion provides real prospects of a retailing career, and the benefits to be gained from large-scale purchasing power, investment in high technology and national promotional campaigns. Small agents continue to survive, but are unable individually to match the price incentives offered by the multiples, as we have seen. The marketing consortium is one possible solution suggested to improve negotiating and bargaining power among the smaller companies. It is significant that tour operators' most productive agents within a district are in many cases independents or small regional chains rather than the offices of the major multiples; yet the national chain can clinch the best deals for overriding commissions. Consortia offer the best opportunities for agents to develop new package tour programmes which can be sold uniquely through consortium members. As long as marketing is based primarily on price advantage, the independents will be forced to find ways to compete in that respect.

With the introduction of harmonisation within the EC by 1992, and the possible end to 'Stabiliser', agents will no longer have the traditional protection of ABTA. There will be new methods of retailing travel products, the possible licensing of agents, and, if the existing ABTA bonding scheme is terminated, principals may well seek individual bonds from their retailers before appointing them.

Large and small agents are looking towards own-brand products, with Pickfords already marketing some of the Lancaster Holidays programmes under their own brand name. New agents have arrived on the retailing scene to develop a 'supermarket' approach to the sale of holidays; one company offers no travel advice, but a fast booking scheme at a discount to generate mass turnover, while another plans to represent only the top twenty tour operators. It has been prophesied by some in the industry that the process of deregulation in the airlines could lead to the introduction of bulk net fares (a concept proposed once before in 1975, but which never became operative). This could radically alter the current trading practice of travel agents, by requiring them to commit themselves in advance to purchasing seats on scheduled or charter services at a net price, to be resold at an appropriate mark-up to the travelling public. Again, larger organisations will benefit from their ability to negotiate lower prices and small agents will be forced to join consortia to compete.

As major tour operators increase their market shares at the expense of smaller companies, it is likely that they, too, will pressure agents to become more productive. Since increasing productivity for one company's products can, in a stable market, only be at the expense of another company's, this will give agents a still greater incentive to specialise in the services they represent, rather than attempting to provide a complete travel service. Some suggest that this will eventually lead to the appointment of agents as General Sales Agents (GSA) for travel principals, marketing brands within a region through other agencies, and receiving an overriding commission from the principal for this additional service.

All of these developments suggest an end to the era of the traditional 'corner-shop' travel agent that we have known in the past. Agents in the future must be flexible, innovative, willing to move with the times and to make use of the new tools of marketing which technology has made available. They can no longer be expected to share the range of product knowledge required by an increasingly sophisticated travelling public, but must find the means to access and make available this information to their clients more effectively, and at the lowest possible cost.

QUESTIONS AND DISCUSSION POINTS

1 Travel agents have taken to stocking travel associated goods in their shops as a means of increasing their profitability. Identify those products currently offered and consider whether the variety of goods could be extended even further. What would be the implications of doing so?

2 Some people believe that retail travel agencies in Britain will eventually segment into three distinct types:

(a) standard agencies offering an extensive information and booking service with limited discounts,

(b) 'supermarket' type agencies offering a booking service for a limited number of leisure products, without an information service, but with greater discounts, and

(c) specialist 'niche' agencies dealing with select products and tailor-made packages, all at regular prices.

Discuss the likelihood of this scenario, or an alternative scenario for the future distribution patterns of tourism. Visit local agencies to see if there is as yet any attempt to move towards the pattern suggested above.

3 Is there a future role for bucket shops? If so, what is their role likely to be? Could they be affected by European Community legislation?

ASSIGNMENT TOPICS

(*Note*: these assignment suggestions are particularly suitable for those engaged in periods of work placement in travel agencies).

1 Assume for the purposes of this assignment that you have been employed by a retail travel agency in your area (you may choose the company.)

You have been asked by your manager, in view of your studies, to produce a study of the agency's brochure racking strategy, to see if this is adequate or could be improved.

Undertake some field research in travel agencies in the area to estimate the typical number of spaces available for racking brochures, and the various strategies adopted to categorise and display the brochures. Taking into account present practice in your own agency, examine alternative solutions in the light of your research, and taking into account the market to which the agency appeals. Make recommendations to your manager in a report which also considers how the agency should deal with 'marginal demand' brochures, for which rack space cannot be found.

Your report should also consider associated racking decisions, such as whether to rack a supply or a file copy only of the brochures. In each case, justify your decisions.

2 Your manager, impressed by your report, now asks you to examine the provision of computers in the agency, in order to judge:

● how well provided the agency is in comparison with others in the area, and

● whether further investment in computers is desirable, or whether better use can be made of the existing equipment.

Conduct research to evaluate the present benefits of the computer systems available, and compare these with those provided by local competitors. Your report should indicate familiarity with systems currently available, and if you plan to recommend additional investment, you should consider the relative merits of buying or leasing.

9 Tour operators

Chapter objectives: After studying this chapter, you should be able to:

- define the role of tour operators;
- understand the reasons for tour operators' activities;
- identify the microeconomic problems of tour

operators;
- distinguish between different operator types;
- understand the structure and control of the industry.

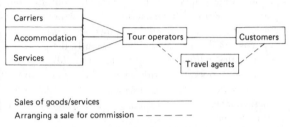

Sales of goods/services   ────────────

Arranging a sale for commission ─ ─ ─ ─ ─

Fig 9.1   Tour operators in the tourism market

THE ROLE OF THE TOUR OPERATOR

Most businesses calling themselves tour operators undertake a distinct function in the tourism industry; they purchase separate elements of transport, accommodation and other services and combine them into a package which they then sell directly or indirectly to consumers. Their position in the market is therefore as demonstrated in Fig 9.1.

Tour operators are sometimes classed as wholesalers, as was discussed in Chapter 4, but this is only partially accurate. A wholesaler generally purchases goods or services on his own account, *breaks bulk*, that is buys in large quantities and resells in smaller quantities as required, and sells very much the same product as he buys without altering it. Tour operators normally perform the first two jobs, but it can be argued that they do change the products sold by *packaging* them. Inclusive tours (ITs) are by their very nature new products, distinct from the elements which constitute them, in the same way that a wardrobe is distinct from a collection of wooden panels and fittings.

Rather than a wholesaler, then, the tour operator may be seen as a light assembly operation, akin to the fitter who puts together a wardrobe. As with the latter, it is quite possible for the customer to be a do-it-yourself assembler by buying accommodation, transport and so on separately. The value of tour operators lies in their ability to secure discounts through bulk purchases and to assemble a very convenient and well-made package.

ECONOMIC ORIGINS OF TOUR OPERATORS

The transport problem

A major problem for many service industries is the balancing of supply and demand. This is especially true for services like transport where the supply is fixed, such as with a scheduled air service – which *must* operate – run by an airline with only one size of plane. Sometimes supply is not entirely fixed but is *lumpy*, that is an operator cannot respond to a small change in demand by making an equally small change in supply; he has to provide a discrete 'lump' of supply. This happens, for example, with walk-on air shuttle services where airlines agree to carry every passenger who turns up at an airport for their service. If one too many passengers turns up for a flight he cannot stand in the aisle, and a second entire plane must be provided.

In these circumstances carriers seek ways to adjust demand to fill all available seats. This is important to keep down costs per passenger (and not to waste resources!). The plane or train or coach costs a certain amount of money to run, regardless of the number of passengers and this fixed cost is likely to be the major part of any transport costs.

From the 1950s onwards tour operators have been very useful to transport carriers, especially airlines. If a carrier knows he will have vacant seats on a journey, rather than leave them empty it is worth offering them at almost any price to someone who can fill them. Let us take an example.

Example

Suppose the fixed cost of flying a 100-seat plane from London to Athens and back is £12 000 (that includes capital costs, fuel, crew's wages and so on). Suppose also the additional, or variable cost per passenger is £15 (to cover writing a ticket, in-flight refreshments, extra fuel, and so on). If the airline wants to budget for a small profit and knows it normally sells sixty seats, then the pricing looks like this:

Fixed cost	£12 000
60 passengers × £15	900
Cost of return flight	£12 900
Sell 60 tickets at £216 each	£12 960
Profit	£60

Of course, if only fifty-nine passengers show up then sales drop by £216, costs by only £15, and the airline loses £141. This is a very risky business!

This is where tour operators prove useful. By agreeing to purchase in bulk, say, twenty-five seats, they can virtually ensure that the airline will fly at a profit. The question arises: What should the ticket price be?

As far as the airline is concerned, anything above £15 a head will be profitable, as the fixed costs are already paid for. Tour operators will want the lowest price possible to ensure they can resell all twenty-five seats. Obviously customers are not willing to pay anything like £216 or else they would already have bought tickets directly from the airline.

Perhaps airline and tour operators negotiate and fix a price of £90 per head. The airline's budget now looks like this:

Fixed cost	£12 000
85 passengers* × £15	£1 275
Cost of return flight	£13 275
Sell 60 tickets at £216 each	£12 960
Sell 25 tickets to tour operator at £90 each	£2 250
Revenue	£15 210
Profit	£1 935

*Assuming tour operators will resell all their twenty-five seats.

The airline should now be very happy; it can lose several standard fare paying passengers and will still be in profit.

Tour operators now have the onus of selling the seats, which may entail heavy selling costs, but as long as they are sensible they should be able to resell at a reasonable and profitable price which will cover the price they pay for the seats plus their overheads, but will still represent a substantial saving to the holidaymaker on the airline's price. A figure of £130 might be considered reasonable.

To ensure that tour operators do not poach carriers' existing passengers, carriers have in the past imposed various conditions on the resale of tickets. The main condition has been that the operator must build the journey in as part of a package or IT. Other conditions from time to time have been:

(a) a fixed or minimum length of stay permitted at the destination;

(b) a minimum (or maximum) advance booking period;

(c) a minimum price at which the IT can be sold;

(d) stipulation of the type of customer (such as a group).

These conditions have all been used to protect carriers' existing business, but have been progressively relaxed as tour operators and carriers have become more interdependent.

From filling empty seats on a particular journey, tour operators progressed to chartering whole planes or other vehicles that were unused for a period of time. The proportion of fixed costs, and consequently the potential saving in ticket price, was rather less, but still provided carriers and operators with exploitable opportunities. Eventually many tour operators came to own their own planes, coaches or railway carriages. The economic value of this lies not in the discount buying as above but in economies of scale, controlling one's own transport and ensuring it is fully and efficiently used.

The accommodation problem

The costs and usage problems of transport are similar for accommodation. Hotels in particular have a high level of fixed cost, so that it is important for them to attract as many guests in as they can while they are open. Many hoteliers, especially in Mediterranean countries such as Spain, were very keen in the 1950s and 1960s to secure contracts with tour operators in order to fill their properties.

The same pricing determinants apply as with transport. Once the fixed costs of a property have been covered from revenue earned by selling accommodation directly to guests, any price which more than pays for the variable cost of accommodating extra guests is straight profit to the hotelier. Tour operators were thus able to secure accommodation at a greatly discounted rate to build into their ITs.

Over a period of time many hotels, holiday villages and self-catering accommodation proprietors have come to depend on tour operators for the bulk or even all of their business. Again, as with transport, some tour operators own their own accommodation in order to secure economies of scale and to ensure sufficient accommodation is available to match the transport they use.

One problem that has arisen from the relationship that has developed between hoteliers and tour operators has been the hoteliers' growing dependence on operators to fill their rooms. Up to 95 per cent of hotel rooms at major resorts are now contracted out to tour operators,

Fig 9.2 Specialist holidays – 'on safari'
(*Courtesy Abercrombie & Kent Travel*)

with the remaining rooms largely bought by passing tourists. Hoteliers have therefore withdrawn from active selling or advertising to the consumer, and are increasingly at the mercy of their main buyers of rooms, who drive hard bargains to secure the lowest possible prices for their clients. The result of this is to drive down the levels of service and maintenance as hoteliers strive to remain in profit as costs rise. By the late 1980s, this was resulting in more self-catering or buffet-style meals and little choice in menus, which in turn led to a high proportion of all consumer complaints aimed at the accommodation occupied. The EC's determination to introduce more safeguards for travel consumers, and their proposals for the harmonisation of standards in hotels throughout the Community, may result in improvements, but essentially this will depend upon the willingness of the British tourist to pay higher prices for better value. As consumers become more independent, they will begin to demand a better quality of service from the hoteliers, which will also produce improvements.

VARIETY IN INCLUSIVE TOURS

Tour operators grew and prospered because of their ability to assemble a popular and saleable product. Although the air inclusive tour has become the most popular of these, inclusive tours using land and sea transport also cater for the needs of those tourists who like to buy a fully packaged product. Some ITs such as coach tours have of course existed for a long time, whereas those run by the hotel groups were introduced only about a decade ago, essentially to improve occupancy figures at off-peak weekends for London hotels and later to fill off-season beds out of town.

Package tours are by no means only down-market, secure and carefree products; although the mass-market tours have tended to dominate the market, there are

many up-market programmes using high-quality accommodation, as well as a wide range of 'adventure' packages appealing to the young or well-travelled, in which transport may consist of a Land-Rover equipped to cross desert roads in Ethiopia or the Sudan and accommodation no more than a sleeping bag and a 'pup' tent. The important point to make is that packages today are available to meet the needs of a very varied market.

Packages by air may be arranged using either the services of scheduled carriers, or of chartered aircraft. On scheduled airline services a tour-basing fare is available to tour operators for inclusive tour excursions (ITXs), and this is used to form the basis for package holidays which are sold individually to tourists. These ITX fares are discussed more fully in Chapter 10. The ITX tends to be a flexible product in which a few seats are available for the use of operators on a great many different flights. This flexibility, tied with superior hotel accommodation, produces a high-quality tour saleable in relatively small numbers at fairly high prices, suiting the needs of the up-market client. It is particularly suited to long-haul destinations where demand is fairly restricted.

The mass market, however, is better catered for by the tour operators' use of inclusive tours by charter (ITCs), in which the entire aircraft is put at the disposal of the operator. Suited particularly to the mass-market destinations of the Mediterranean and similar short-haul package holiday destinations, they are priced more cheaply than are ITXs and have made it possible for millions of tourists in Europe and elsewhere to have holidays abroad for the first time. Not all countries allow carriers to fly charters into their territories, although carriers and local hoteliers will put pressure on the government to allow them to do so. Arguments over charters took place for many years, for example, in Cyprus, where the government wished to protect its national airline from charter competition, and in the Channel Islands, which wished to preserve its scheduled links with the mainland.

LICENSING AND BONDING OF TOUR OPERATORS

Since 1972, an Air Travel Organiser's Licence (ATOL) must be obtained from the Civil Aviation Authority by any tour operator wishing to operate either scheduled or charter air tours abroad. Licences are still not required for domestic tours, nor are they required for tours operated abroad using sea or land transport.

The collapse of Fiesta Tours in 1964, leaving 5000 tourists stranded, followed by the bankruptcy of a smaller company, Omar Khayyam Tours, in 1965, drew the attention of the industry and its consumers alike to the need for some sort of protection against the financial

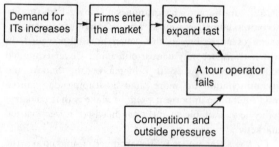

Fig 9.3 Tour operation – market development

failure of tour operators. In 1965 ABTA set up a *Common Fund* for this purpose, assuming at the time that government regulation of tour operators in Britain was imminent. The fund was to consist of 50 per cent of members' subscriptions to be used to protect passengers affected by the collapse of a tour operator. When it became obvious that the government did not intend to act on compulsory registration for operators, ABTA introduced its *Operation Stabiliser* scheme described in Chapter 8, in which Common Fund provisions were to apply only to ABTA members' clients, and reciprocal arrangements were agreed between member tour operators and agents to deal only with fellow members.

However, many agents resented the fact that they were obliged to contribute to a fund to insure tour operators. It also soon became clear that the existing provisions were inadequate. In 1967 the Tour Operators' Study Group (TOSG) held preliminary discussions to consider establishing a bonding scheme for its members. A bond is a guarantee given by a third party (usually a bank or insurance company) to pay a sum of money, up to a specified maximum, in the event that the company becomes insolvent. This money is then used to meet the immediate financial obligations arising from the collapse, such as repatriating tourists stranded at overseas resorts, and reimbursing clients booked to travel later with the company. TOSG's bonding scheme became a reality in 1970, and TOSG itself continues to administer the bonds of its members licensed by the CAA.

Later ABTA itself introduced its own bonding scheme for *all* tour operating members. However, the collapse of Clarksons during the peak holiday period of 1974 revealed that the existing bonding scheme was inadequate to protect clients against major failures, and this led the government, under the terms of the Air Travel Reserve Fund Act 1975, to impose a temporary levy of two per cent on the operating turnover of all tour operators between 1975 and 1977.

In 1986, the ATRF became known as the Air Travel Trust, and although no levy has been imposed since, the funds have continued to grow through payment of interest on the account; at the time of writing, the fund exceeds £23 million. Between the period October 1985

and March 1987, nine of the 22 tour operators who failed had insufficient bonds to cover their obligations, and the Air Travel Trust stepped in to top up the funds required. Today, ABTA administers the bonding system on behalf of the CAA for all tour operating members, other than those who are also TOSG members, while non-ABTA operators must take out bonds payable to CAA direct. The CAA determines the levels of bonding required for ATOLs, which vary in amount over time.

Coach companies operating package tours may sell their programmes through ABTA agents providing they hold either an ABTA bond or are bonded by the Bus and Coach Council, which has received dispensation from ABTA for members to sell their tours through the ABTA network.

ABTA has also introduced a bonding scheme for its members' tour operations which are not under CAA control, in 1982 broadening the scope of protection to include both domestic tours and foreign package holidays using surface carriers.

MARKET DEVELOPMENT

Tour operation has by no means had a straightforward development. It has been marked by periods of expansion and resulting competition, often leading to business failures. In this it is typical of any young industry where businesses are often run by spirited entrepreneurs who do not possess many fixed assets. The cycle of development can be illustrated by Fig 9.3.

In Britain demand for ITs grew fast in the early 1960s and around 1970. In Western Europe, North America and Japan major growth was in the early 1970s and around 1980. During these times tour operators also tended to expand very fast, but some failed, usually for one or more of these reasons:

(*a*) they may have grown too fast, borrowed too much money and have had insufficient management expertise:

(*b*) they may have made almost no profit per tourist in an effort to compete through low prices, in a vicious market.

(*c*) they may have been hit by external problems such as oil price rises, political problems or economic recession reducing demand.

Some of these failures have been landmarks in the development of tour operation. The collapse of Fiesta Tours in Britain in 1964, as shown earlier, led to the tight controls imposed on members by ABTA. The failure of Court Line and its subsidiary Clarksons Holidays in 1974 stranded 50 000 holidaymakers. This collapse was caused by all three of the reasons above and led to the government introducing the Air Travel Reserve Fund mentioned earlier. At the time Clarksons was the largest British tour operator; in similar fashion Canada's largest tour operators, Sunflight and Skylark collapsed in 1982.

Current Developments

In the 1980s, the nature of the tour operating business changed dramatically, as a handful of major tour operating companies came to dominate the market. By 1987, the share of the market held by the top five companies – Thomson Holidays, International Leisure Group (ILG), Horizon Holidays, British Airtours (Redwing since 1988) and Cosmos – exceeded 65 per cent, and taken together the top 30 operators held some 80 per cent of the IT market. As the proportion of the market held by the 'big five' rose inexorably, so the smaller operators found themselves unable to compete. Eleven of the top 30 returned a loss in 1987, while taken together, the 30 returned losses of 0.9 per cent of turnover. Only once since the start of the 1980s have profits of the top 30 operators exceeded 5 per cent.

With profit squeezes, fundamental restructuring took place in the field, as companies attempted to grow through merger. Sunmed Holidays, an operator specialising in holidays to Greece, joined forces with British Airtours to form Redwing Holidays, and set about axing the less profitable segments of the British Airtours programme. Horizon, the third largest operator, purchased the international tour operating interests of Rank Travel, then the fifth largest operator, absorbing such well established names as Wings, Blue Sky and OSL. In 1988, Horizon were themselves taken over by Thomson Holidays, who also bought the Horizon airline Orion, merging it with Britannia Airways. Since the merger gave Thomson a dominant 40 per cent share of the IT market, it was referred to the Monopolies and Mergers Commission, who after deliberation, ruled that it was not against the public interest.

Factors leading to the current economic situation

The expansion of leisure time and improved standards of discretionary expenditure have given rise to continued demand for overseas holidays throughout the 1980s, and with only one exception (1985), these years have seen a steady growth in IT demand, with twice as many Britons buying package holidays abroad in 1987 as had done so in 1980. Major travel companies, seeing international tourism as a long-term growth trend, determined to increase their market share to reap the anticipated rewards of market dominance in what was heading to be the world's largest industry. They sought at the same time to increase the total size of the market by encouraging those who traditionally took domestic holidays to travel abroad. To achieve this, they slashed prices. Large companies used their purchasing muscle to drive down suppliers' prices (at some cost to quality in many cases, as we have seen); they introduced cheap, 'no frills' holidays through subsidiary companies such as Thomson's Skytours, ILG's Lancaster and Horizon's

Broadway (later Sunflight), which attracted the budget conscious C2D (see page 43) market; and finally, profit margins were trimmed: Thomsons and ILG, determined not to be undersold, engaged in the periodic repricing of their holiday programme during the selling season. Thomson in 1983 introduced the strategy of brochure reissues with cheaper prices, and this became a regular feature of the tour operating price war. Holiday prices during the four-year period in the mid-1980s remained almost stationary as a result, while real buying power greatly increased.

While these moves certainly expanded the market, over-optimistic forecasts of traffic growth also led to huge growth in supply; capacity exceeded demand, and operators were then forced into off-loading seats at bargain basement prices. This factor has been a key one in the growth of late bookings. Traditionally, bookings for package holidays have occurred in the weeks immediately following Christmas, allowing operators more time to balance supply and demand, and aiding their cash flow – deposits paid by clients in January would be invested and earn interest for the company until its bills had to be paid – which in some cases could be as late as September or October. Holidaymakers soon came to realise, however, that if they refrained from booking holidays until much nearer their time of travel, they could snap up late booking bargains. The development of computerised reservations systems allowed operators to up-date their late availability opportunities quickly, putting cheap offers on the market at very short notice, which made late bookings convenient as well as attractively priced. It has been estimated that over 40 per cent of all bookings for summer holidays are now made later than 1 April.

The tendency of all mass market operators to focus on low price rather than quality or value for money led these type of tours to move down-market. As they did so, ABC1 tourists (see page 43) particularly those who had travelled frequently, tended to go independently, and to further destinations. Long haul ITs in 1987 were estimated to be expanding at 28 per cent, far faster than the growth of short haul tours.

Meanwhile, adverse publicity was attached by the media to the 'hooligans' who were attracted in increasing numbers to the better known resorts of Spain and Greece, by promises of sun, cheap drink and new encounters. Tour operators were becoming aware of the dangers of 'playing the numbers game'.

Operators sought new locations to develop where hotel capacity was cheap and readily available; first, the more remote areas of Greece, then Turkey became boom destinations for the British seeking sun at rock bottom prices. European travellers were also attracted to the low prices offered by British tour companies, and tourists from Holland, West Germany and Norway, among

Table V Cost structure of typical ITC

Costs	% of overall cost
Charter air fare	45
Hotel accommodation	37
Other services (transfers, etc)	3
Overheads (administration and marketing)	5
Travel agent's commission	10
	——
	100

others, were drawn to booking summer holidays out of the UK. A package tour costing £674 in Holland could be booked in Britain, using identical facilities, for £408, a bargain even with the added cost of the flight between Holland and England. Still greater savings could be achieved on long haul flights to the Far East or Florida.

Consumer complaints

One inevitable consequence of the process of 'trading down' was the increase in customer complaints. ABTA received well over 12 500 formal complaints in 1986 (complaints not satisfactorily dealt with by the tour operator or travel agent direct); this reflected a 100 per cent increase in five years (however, it must be borne in mind that package tours increased by some 40 per cent during this period and that consumers now have a higher propensity to complain). The EC, in a study published in 1988, found that 37 per cent of British package holidaymakers – the highest of any Community member – experienced problems in their holidays. Other studies reveal that some 40 per cent of complaints arise from the 'bargain basement' holidays; consumers were unwilling to accept the argument that they got what they paid for. Minimum standards were simply not up to expectation. Even more worrying to operators is the fact that only 40 per cent of those dissatisfied were prepared to make an official complaint; others simply refrained from booking with the company again.

A growing source of customer irritation has been the application of surcharges. As will be explained in Chapter 10, operating costs for ITs are affected by changes in the inflation rate, exchange rates or costs of supplies, particularly aviation fuel, which is priced in US dollars on the world market, and is therefore affected by either increased costs or changes in the relative values of the pound and dollar. Tour operators have to estimate their costs for all services up to a year ahead of time. They can anticipate higher costs by raising prices, which may make them uncompetitive, or they can take an optimistic approach and price low, in the expectation of stable or declining costs. Until 1988, the latter was more

attractive, as moderate cost increases could be passed on to customers (within established limits) in the form of surcharges. Such surcharges are resented by travellers, and are in any case not applied to scheduled fares (which can respond to market prices more quickly). It also became apparent that a handful of operators were misusing this facility and adding fuel surcharges in excess of cost increases, or even when actual fuel costs had not increased at all, as a means of raising profits sliced by open competition. Fanned by the media, the issue received Government attention in 1988, and pressure was applied to the industry to resolve the problem. ABTA responded by initiating a scheme whereby operators would absorb the first two per cent of any increase, and give passengers the freedom to cancel without penalty if surcharges exceeded 10 per cent. In the event, ABTA's scheme was presaged by the leading tour operators themselves, who determined to phase out surcharges by guaranteeing prices for the following year. Stability in price can be obtained by 'buying forward' the fuel required for the following year. While there is no formal 'futures' market in aviation fuel, negotiation is possible on future purchases of fuel on an *ad hoc* basis, but clearly at a premium, and purchasing forward will further affect the operators' cash flow.

OPERATING ECONOMICS

Inputs

Assuming an operator is a business separate from a carrier or hotelier, then he has three main inputs he must purchase: transport, accommodation and services. Services can be divided into those at destinations, such as transfers from terminals to accommodation, and representatives, and those which are mainly concerned with the selling operation such as the cost of advertising, brochures, post, credit and travel agents' commission. The tour operator also has his own office costs, including rent and rates, wages of staff, computer or other reservation systems and so on.

A typical ITC from Britain to a Mediterranean destination might have the cost structure outlined in Table V.

By selling directly to the public without using a travel agent, as Tjaereborg and Portland do, the commission may be saved but reservations, brochure and advertising costs will be substantially increased. A major part of a tour operator's overheads will be taken up by production and distribution of the brochure (production costs for a leading company's brochure may be as much as £1 million or more). Other marketing costs such as national television advertising involve budgets of millions of pounds. As we have seen earlier, profits may run to no more than one to three per cent of the total price of the inclusive tour, after payment of marketing and

Table VI Structure of sales revenue of a typical tour operator, 1988

Revenue	% of total revenue
Summer IT programme	52
Winter IT programme	15
Seat only sales	12
Holiday insurance	3
Excursions in destinations	8
Interest on deposits and currency speculation	10
	100

administrative costs, so operators will seek whatever means are open to them to keep costs down, or to develop other revenue-producing sources.

The specifics of negotiations with principals, in which operators attempt to keep their costs as low as possible, will be dealt with in Chapter 10.

Outputs

Major air tour operators normally divide their ITs into three main groups: a summer IT programme; a winter IT programme; and a programme involving transport only, with nominal accommodation (usually known as 'seat only' sales). Some operators sell only one of these groups of products, for example winter sports holidays, while others may also sell coach-based, ferry-based, rail-based or fly-drive ITs. In addition, they will sell, directly or indirectly, products such as holiday insurance, to increase total revenue.

A typical breakdown of revenue achieved by a mass market operator can be seen in Table VI. Figures will vary considerably between operators, but those given will emphasise the importance of ancillary sources of revenue to an operator, apart from the main programme of package tours. This will be further examined in Chapter 10.

While the summer programme continues to provide the main source of revenue, the high levels of competition for this trade, which have resulted in a substantial increase in the number of seats available, has meant that great care must be exercised to get the price right, so that sufficient demand is generated to fill available seats, but not so cheaply as to threaten the operator's profitability. Very low margins take no account of added expenditure incurred by the company during the course of the year, for example, in providing accommodation and meals for clients who suffer delays due to air traffic control strikes. It must always be remembered that, as long as variable costs (catering, additional fuel, etc) of carrying extra passengers are covered, any revenue above this will help to contribute to the operator's fixed costs, so it is better to fill every seat, even at very low prices, than to fly with empty seats. This was the initial thinking behind 'seat only' sales in the industry.

'Seat only' sales

The rise in 'seat only' sales in recent years occurred as a result of the relaxation in 1982 of regulations applying to inclusive tours. Demand for 'seat only' sales arises from growth in second home ownership (including timeshare owners), and from increasing numbers of experienced package holidaymakers choosing to travel independently to resorts, where they select their own accommodation on arrival. Under ITC agreements with the destination countries, accommodation must be provided with transport to create a 'package'. Operators have circumvented regulations by providing a voucher which covers minimum priced accommodation, which the purchaser simply discards. The cost of such accommodation might be as low as £1, and consequently is very primitive; a farmer might be paid a retainer, for example, to set aside a room for the season, in the full knowledge that there was little likelihood it would ever be needed. In other cases, operators provided flights for owners of apartments abroad, who would 'lease' the apartment to the operator for the duration of their holiday, and leased it back for the same period. Policing such infringements of regulations is extremely difficult, although the Greek Government in 1988 threatened to check on accommodation to ensure that it was used. Agreements on the sale of seat onlys are made bilaterally between countries, and while the British Government is willing to see an expansion of such sales, many destination countries are unwilling to accept a greater influx of passengers travelling without accommodation. The CAA has allowed an increase in seat only sales out of the regional airports, but exclude London (owing to congestion problems).

Exact figures for seat only sales are difficult to gauge, but were estimated to run in excess of two million in 1987, which would account for more than 15 per cent of all package holidays sold abroad. Undoubtedly, sales are attracting business away from the regular package tours, and this pattern is likely to continue as independent travellers seek to make their own arrangements abroad. As seat only sales also lend themselves to direct booking in the home through computers, any further development in this direction must be worrying to both agent and operator.

TYPES OF OPERATOR

Mass market operators

In Britain the best known tour operators are those which sell large numbers of inclusive tours by air and/or coach.

Table VII Britain's largest tour operators
(Passenger carryings authorised by the CAA, 1987)

Company	Passengers (000s)
Thomson Holidays (a)	3750
ILG (b)	1814
Horizon (c)	884
BA Holidays (d)	478
Rank Travel (e)	447
Airtours	366
Best Travel	270
Yugotours	250
Cosmos (f)	250

Notes:

(*a*) includes Skytours and Portland Holidays. Thomson alone 2697.

(*b*) includes Intasun, Club 18–30 and Select Holidays, inter alia. ILG bought Global Holidays in 1985.

(*c*) bought by Thomson Holidays 1988.

(*d*) merged with Sunmed Holidays in 1988 to form Redwing.

(*e*) foreign package tour companies Wings, OSL, Blue Sky sold to Horizon Holidays in 1987, now owned by Thomson.

(*f*) Swiss parent company. Also owns incoming operator Globus Gateway.

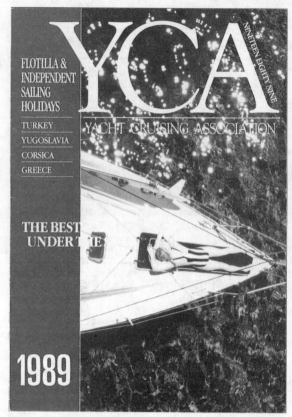

Fig 9.4 A specialist holiday
(*Courtesy Yacht Cruising Association*)

A league table of the largest air tour operators is shown in Table VII.

In 1987, 12 600 000 air inclusive tours were authorised, giving the three leading companies over 50 per cent of the authorised carryings for the year. It should be made clear that these are the authorised number of seats licensed. If sales are poor, tour operators will cut back on their seat numbers. Poor performance may affect medium-sized companies to a greater extent than the largest companies, who have the buying power to increase their promotional budgets or slash prices, to sell seats. Actual market share of the biggest companies is probably underestimated, on the basis of these figures.

The pattern is for greater concentration of sales among the half dozen market leaders, at the expense of 'second force' and small operators.

The twenty or so largest tour operators are members of the Tour Operators' Study Group (TOSG), and are responsible altogether for roughly 80 per cent of all tour operating revenue in the UK. TOSG is a voluntary association, with membership by invitation only, which acts as a forum for discussions on issues of common interest among its members. It has been influential in negotiating with foreign governments and hotel associations and, in addition to being responsible for the introduction of the TOSG trust fund, was also instrumental in ending the 'Provision 1' clause under which the British Government denied tour operators the right to sell their package tours at prices less than the lowest normal scheduled air fares (*see* Chapter 10).

The largest operators concentrate their activities on mass-market sun, sea and sand destinations such as Spain, the Canary and Balearic Islands and Greece. They frequently subdivide their operations to serve different markets and a feature of their structure is that many are linked with their own airlines. This has occurred either by tour operators setting up their own airlines, or by airlines diversifying into tour operating (as in the case of British Airways). The trend to integration has spread to medium-sized operators, with Aspro Holidays and Owners Abroad also establishing airline divisions in recent years (*see* Fig 9.4). This integration of mass tour operators with other travel activity is even more advanced in countries such as West Germany.

Specialist operators

Less well-known than the mass-market operators, but far more numerous, are the specialist operators, who may range from local travel agents organising an *ad hoc* tour for twenty or thirty local passengers up to businesses

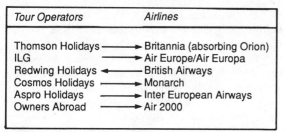

Tour Operators	Airlines
Thomson Holidays ⟶	Britannia (absorbing Orion)
ILG ⟶	Air Europe/Air Europa
Redwing Holidays ⟵	British Airways
Cosmos Holidays ⟶	Monarch
Aspro Holidays ⟶	Inter European Airways
Owners Abroad ⟶	Air 2000

Fig 9.5 Links between airlines and tour operators

offering long-distance inclusive tours to exclusive destinations. It is hard to generalise about such businesses and equally hard to draw a clear distinction between them and the mass-market operators. For example, businesses such as Olympic Holidays, specialising in ITs to Greece, or Intourist, dealing with all forms of travel to the Soviet Union, are large enough to be considered mass-market operators but are specialising in particular geographical regions. Intourist, in fact, is concerned with far more than simply tour operating; it is a complete state-owned tourism industry in its own right.

Specialists may be subsidiaries of carriers or accommodation organisations, existing to provide a sales outlet for the organisation's products.

It is convenient to group specialist operators into five categories:

(*a*) those offering inclusive tours to specific groups of people. Some tour operators follow a policy of *market segmentation*; that is, they choose to cater for one or more groups of clientele, categorised by demographic or other variables. For example, certain operators choose to serve only a market of a particular age group, as in the case of Saga Holidays, serving the elderly, Club 18–30 serving the young adult, PGL Adventure Holidays serving the adolescent, or Solo Holidays serving the 30–55 year old bracket. The latter company also specialises in serving single people of this age bracket, so are segmenting in two ways. Tours are designed to provide a pleasant social environment for developing friendships. Other companies choose to segment *geographically*, dealing with clients in a specific region. Local coach companies or travel agencies often organise special tours aimed at customers in their local catchment area.

(*b*) those offering ITs to specific destinations, such as Yugotours, CIT, or Swiss Travel Service. Often such companies are owned by, or have strong links with, firms or state governments in the destination country.

(*c*) companies using specific forms of accommodation for their ITs, such as camping holidays or holiday villages (e.g. Eurocamp or Haven Leisure).

(*d*) those using specific forms of transport for their ITs. These companies may well be owned by transport businesses, such as the ferry companies, or the Orient Express programme.

(*e*) those offering specialist interest ITs such as Big Game safaris, flotilla cruising, cycling, or hiking holidays (e.g. Rambler Holidays, Anglers World Holidays, MTS Safaris).

Some specialists will clearly fall into several categories.

Over the past 20 or 30 years specialist tour operators have proliferated. Usually they have identified a particular need and sought to cater for it, taking advantage of fashion trends in tourism. While many have only a short business life before collapsing, others have developed over time into mass-market operators. Because many of these companies deal with comparatively small numbers of clients, they may be able to develop a specific expertise which gives them an advantage in the marketplace. Major companies will be unlikely to develop an interest in a highly specialised programme with limited opportunities for sales. One must always be conscious, however, that a category currently attracting a few tourists may have potential to expand substantially, and mass market operators have the ability to set up specialist divisions for that purpose. In this way, specialist operators to Paris were threatened when the giant Thomson Holidays decided to move into that market with an *ad hoc* programme, quickly establishing themselves as market leaders in the field.

Domestic operators

Domestic operators are those who assemble and sell ITs to a destination within the country in which the tourists reside. In general, domestic tour operations have developed after international operations, since the savings consumers can make are not so great; operators also have to overcome the traditional pattern of direct booking of accommodation which is common in Britain.

The oldest domestic ITs in the UK are probably coach tours operated by such companies as Wallace Arnold. Other types of operation have developed more recently in response to the success of the international operators. Customers are getting used to purchasing a package for their foreign trip and the hope is that this will trigger similar purchasing patterns for domestic holidays. Travel agents have been slow to take up domestic tours – perhaps the network of Tourist Information Centres could take on that role.

Domestic tours have been packaged and marketed successfully by leading hotel groups such as Trusthouse Forte, by many leading coach companies, and by Gold Star Holidays (formerly British Rail's Golden Rail). The increase in short break holidays has led several companies to form specialist short break holiday programmes, such as those offered by Rainbow Miniholidays.

The tourist boards have strongly supported the

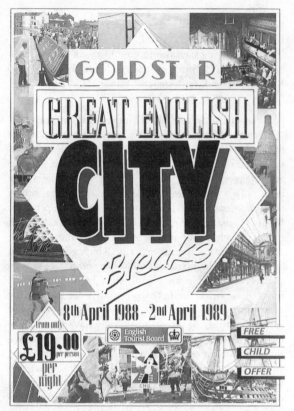

Fig 9.6 Short break promotion
(*Courtesy Gold Star Holidays*)

development of these programmes, and all three boards have co-ordinated programmes of commissionable domestic ITs which can be bought through travel agents in the UK.

Fragmentation in domestic tour operation is reflected in its organisation. In some areas associations have been formed to represent the trade; for example, two dozen or so major operators to the Channel Islands are members of CITOG, the Channel Islands Tour Operators' Group. On the other hand a large number of businesses are not members of any organisation, not even ABTA. Many sell directly to the public and do not need to be involved in the travel agency distribution chain.

Incoming tour operators

Most established tourist-generating countries possess some kind of tour operating industry for outward travel, but for destination countries it may be more important to have incoming operators. These are based in the destination, selling ITs only to that destination, but they may be selling in many different countries.

Many use the airlines or other carriers of the country concerned. Windsor Tours, a division of British Airways specialising in incoming tours to Britain, uses that carrier's services and will put together different types of package according to market demand.

The typical demand for tours to Britain is the 'national heritage' type of programme, or packages arranged for those wishing to study the English language, for which a number of travel/family or hotel accommodation/language school study packages exist. In many countries incoming operators also receive help from the national tourist office of the country concerned, as they may be playing an important role in the development of new tourist facilities in the country.

As with domestic operators, there are several categories of incoming operator. Some are best described as 'handling agents' since their function is to organise tour arrangements for incoming groups on behalf of overseas operators. Some companies go no further than to specialise in meeting incoming passengers and transferring them to their hotels or providing other escort services. Others will offer a comprehensive range of services which include negotiation with coach companies and hotels to secure the best quotations for contracts, organising special interest study tours and providing dining or theatre arrangements. Some companies specialise, for example, by catering for the needs of specific incoming groups such as Japanese or Arab tourists.

In all there are estimated to be over 300 tour companies in Britain which derive a major part of their revenue from handling incoming business. Around 100 of these are members of the British Incoming Tour Operators' Association (BITOA), whose aim is to provide a forum for the exchange of information and ideas among members, to maintain standards of service and to act as a pressure group in dealing with other bodies in the UK who have some responsibility in the field of tourism.

Incoming tour operators' services are marketed exclusively to the trade. Organisations work closely with the British Tourist Authority (through the medium of the BTA Travel Workshops abroad, bringing together the buyers and sellers of tourism and travel services in Britain) and other national and regional tourist boards at home.

QUESTIONS AND DISCUSSION POINTS

1 Is there sufficient protection for the British package holidaymaker abroad, under existing bonding schemes, or is there a need for increased legislation? Should any new legislation be introduced by the British Government, or by the European Community?

2 The Monopolies and Mergers Commission agreed that the purchase of Horizon Holidays by Thomson Holidays in 1988 was not against the public interest. Argue the case for and against this merger, justifying your reasons.

3 In what ways does incoming tour operating differ from outbound operating? Explain why the incoming tour industry tends to be small and fragmented.

4 Find out who are currently the eight largest tour operators in Britain, and their market shares. Give reasons for any changes to the pattern shown in this chapter's figures. You may find it helpful to look at the list of applications for Civil Aviation Authority Licences, published in the CAA's Annual Report, and in the *Travel Trade Gazette*.

ASSIGNMENT TOPICS

1 Industrial Holdings plc is a conglomerate with a rising investment in leisure. They have retained Marketsearch Ltd, a group of consultants with whom you are employed, to weigh up the merits of entering the outbound tour operating business, either by establishing a new company, or by taking over a well-established small to medium-sized company. They have ample financial resources to invest, but have reservations about the wisdom of investing in a field with such low profit levels and high competition.

You are asked to participate in preparing a preliminary report for Industrial Holdings. Your employer has asked you to examine the profitability of this sector of the industry over the past five years, and to evaluate the current market and trends over the next five years. Produce a set of notes which will help you to prepare your section of the report, with statistics that you plan to incorporate into the final report.

2 As a former student of tourism, now employed by a seat broker, you have been invited to address a group of final year students at your old college, on the subject of 'The Current Availability of, and Growth in Demand for, Seat-Only Sales'. Prepare a set of notes for your 40-minute talk, with material to be used on the overhead projector to illustrate your talk.

10 Inclusive tour operations

Chapter objectives: After studying this chapter, you should be able to:

- understand the commercial appeal to the industry of package tours;
- understand how package tours are constructed and operated;
- list the different ways in which package tours can be organised and recognise the appeal of each to different markets;
- be aware of the systems of control over package tour operations in Britain;
- be aware of the role of the brochure as a marketing tool and demonstrate a basic knowledge of brochure production;
- describe reservations systems in operation and be aware of the place of computers in such systems;
- analyse the merits of different forms of tour distribution.

THE NATURE OF TOUR OPERATING

An inclusive tour programme consists of a series of integrated travel services, each of which is purchased by the tour operator in bulk and resold as part of a package at an inclusive price. These integrated services usually consist of an aircraft seat, accommodation at the destination and transfers between hotel and airport. They may also include certain other services such as excursions or car hire. This product is commonly referred to as a 'package tour'. Most package tours are single destination static holidays, but tours comprising two or more destinations are not uncommon, and mobile tours such as coach tours through one or more countries, which until the 1950s were the principal form of packaged holiday, still retain a loyal following.

As we have seen, the success of package tours rests on the fact that the operator, by buying the principals' services in bulk rather than individually, is generally able to negotiate lower prices. Tour operating is a highly competitive business, with success dependent upon the operator maintaining the lowest possible prices while continuing to give 'value for money'. The price factor becomes increasingly important as the package holiday becomes a *standardised* product, differing little between destinations. Most holidaymakers today seek a combination of 'sun, sand and sea'; the particular destination or country no longer plays an important part in the customer's choice, and they will readily substitute an alternative destination for their first choice if the latter becomes in their view overpriced.

The tour operators attempt to keep their prices low both by restraining their profit margins and seeking cost savings. These cost savings originally came about through the chartering of entire aircraft instead of merely purchasing a block of seats on a scheduled flight. Further reductions became possible with *time series* charters, by which aircraft were leased over longer periods of time

rather than for *ad hoc* journeys. Ultimately, larger tour operators, as we have seen, purchased their own aircraft and formed charter airlines to carry their clients – partly as a cost-cutting exercise, but equally to ensure that growing demand for aircraft seats could be matched by supply. If demand outstrips supply, airlines can force up the price of chartering aircraft to operators. Today the emphasis is on productivity achieved through high load factors – the number of seats on each aircraft actually sold as a percentage of total capacity – and maximum utilisation of the aircraft during its period of charter.

Maximum utilisation means keeping the aircraft in the air with its complement of passengers as much as possible during each 24-hour period. While an aircraft is on the tarmac it is failing to earn revenue – in fact it is accumulating airport charges. The aim is therefore to have one's aircraft on the ground as little as possible. This means fast 'turnarounds' (often less than an hour) at airports, involving rapid aircraft cleaning and loading, disembarkation/embarkation and refuelling. Such a policy results in the common 'W' flight pattern of aircraft involved in tour operations (*see* Fig.10.1).

One problem arising from the tight scheduling of W-pattern flights occurs when different operators contract for morning, afternoon and evening flights. If one operator decides to cancel, the airline concerned has to find alternative users for the aircraft, which may mean a longer flight commitment, causing delays, or change of flights, to passengers already booked. The 'knock-on' effect of delays became very apparent during the summer period in 1987, when air traffic controllers in Spain and Greece mounted go-slows. Tight flight scheduling meant that a delay in one flight could have repercussions on flights using the same aircraft for the next two or three days.

High load factors are achieved by setting the *break-even* (number of seats to be sold on each flight to cover

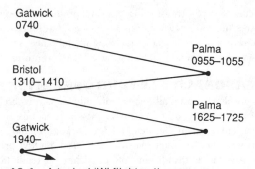

Gatwick
0740

Palma
0955–1055

Bristol
1310–1410

Palma
1625–1725

Gatwick
1940–

Fig 10.1 A typical 'W' flight pattern

all operating, administrative and marketing costs) at a point close to capacity. This brings down the average seat cost to a level which will stimulate market demand. On charter flights today break-even is frequently as high as 90 per cent. Profits are made on the balance of seats sold (and of course on the duty-free sales); since the variable costs of carrying additional passengers are small, tour operators, as we have seen, attempt to fill the entire aircraft by selling *flight only* packages, or offering substantial reductions for last-minute bookings.

Productivity in airline operations can be aided by the procedure of *consolidating* flights. Charter flights with unacceptable load factors can be cancelled, with passengers being transferred to other flights or departures from other airports. This is especially useful on departures towards the end of a season and helps to reduce the element of risk for the operator, who can continue to offer tours at low prices throughout the programme.

In the same way that tour operators have reduced airline seat costs for their passengers, so they have also reduced the prices of hotel accommodation. This was initially achieved by the bulk purchase of blocks of rooms but later this gave way to long-term leasing of entire hotels and, for the largest operators, to eventual ownership of hotels in the most popular overseas tour destinations.

CONTROL OF TOUR OPERATORS

In the initial years of tour operating, until the late 1960s, a government regulation in force in Britain, known as *Provision 1*, made it impossible to price package tours at less than the lowest regular return fares to the destination. The sole exceptions to this rule were in the case of affinity groups. These involved charters arranged for associations whose existence was for a purpose other than that of securing cheap travel; members were required to have belonged to such associations for at least six months before they became eligible for low cost flights.

This rule was designed to protect the scheduled carriers and ensure adequate profit levels for tour operators. However, it severely hindered the expansion

of the package tour business and, furthermore, could be to some extent circumvented by tour operators who used European 'gateways' for tours to more distant destinations (fares to East Africa, for example, were considerably undercut using the Frankfurt gateway, combining package tours from Frankfurt to Kenya with ordinary round-trip flights between London and Frankfurt). There was also widespread abuse of common interest group charters through club secretaries back-dating membership and the formation of spurious associations created primarily for travel benefits.

When the new CAA was established in 1971, restrictions on package tour operations were lifted, initially only in the winter months (leading to a huge increase in off-season travel) but by 1973 for travel at all seasons. The CAA also introduced advance booking charters (ABCs) as a means of widening the availability of charter travel for those then unqualified as affinity group members. ABCs provided similar low prices with the only proviso that seats had to be booked some months in advance of flight dates.

In tandem with the liberalisation of charter flights, control over the tour operators themselves was tightened. For the first time those operating air tours to foreign destinations using chartered aircraft were obliged to hold an Air Travel Organiser's Licence (ATOL) and were closely vetted for financial viability.

Recent concern has arisen over the practice of 'umbrellaing' ATOLs, following the collapse of Michaelangelo Tours in 1987. Umbrellaing allows an unlicensed tour operator to act as an agent of an ATOL operator, with that operator's agreement. While not technically in breach of the law, operators using an umbrella licence are required to specify publicly that they are acting as agents of the licence holders in marketing tours, and are not themselves holders of an ATOL, while licensed operators have the obligation to ensure that their agents comply with this requirement.

Regulation and the EC

In 1992, the single Common Market becomes an economic reality within the European Community, with the harmonisation of regulations. While this will undoubtedly lead to much greater freedom of trade within the Community, allowing travel companies to trade more freely within member states, proposed Community legislation to control the travel industry goes much further than any existing UK legislation.

In 1986, Nouvelles Frontières, a French operator, was taken to court in France for selling air tickets at fares below Government approved levels. Their defence, that the minimum fares set by the Government were in breach of the Treaty of Rome, was upheld by the court, and has become an important factor in the drive to liberalise European air fares. New low-price scheduled air fares into popular European destinations will open up new opportunities for independent package tour arrangements, threatening the traditional charter traffic on some routes.

The Economic Community is anxious to tighten up the responsibilities of tour operators towards their clients, whereas the British Government has in the past been willing to accept the industry's own policy of self-policing. In particular, proposed legislation would make it impossible for tour operators to claim that they act only as agents of their suppliers. Tourists will be able to claim against the tour operator for mishaps (for example, fires) occurring as a result of negligence on the part of the hotel in which they are staying abroad, even if the operator had taken 'due care', as required under British law, to contract with 'safe' hotels. The tour operator would in turn either have to initiate action against the hotel, or to have sufficient indemnity insurance to cover the clients' claims. In the latter case, a substantial rise is forecast in package tour prices to cover the added costs of insurance premiums.

A possible side effect of such legislation would be that tour operators will prefer to contract only with the safest hotels – modern high-rise concrete buildings posing less of a fire hazard than smaller, older, family run hotels built in traditional materials. Not only will this encourage the blight of large-scale development; inclusive tours based on the latter will be far fewer in number, and considerably more expensive.

In a recent court case in West Germany involving the major tour operator NUR, the railing of a hotel balcony gave way, pitching a guest to the ground. The court found against the tour company, charging it to make 'regular checks' of the hotel throughout the season.

The EC's draft directive on package holidays also specifies that passengers who are forced to cancel their bookings before departure for valid reasons may transfer that booking to other passengers without penalty. Such consumer protection may seem only reasonable, but the ability of tour operators to resell a tour in such cases has been a useful source of revenue (although arguably the insurance company owns the package in question, where they have refunded to a claimant).

It is interesting to speculate to what extent the period after 1992 will encourage expansion of British tour operators into other EC member countries, or tour operators from those countries to market their programmes in Britain. Up to now, ventures by the larger British companies into foreign markets have had mixed success. Intasun set up a division in West Germany but was forced to withdraw in 1988; German tourists may have been reluctant to accept the low quality that accompanied low prices vis-à-vis the German operators, and there may also have been some resistance to the idea of sharing hotels with British clients. Simply transferring existing products, however successful, to new markets will not automatically guarantee their success there, and advance market research is needed to make a success of such ventures.

SEASONALITY IN TOUR OPERATIONS

A problem facing all sectors of tourism is the highly seasonal nature of tour traffic. Nowhere is this more apparent than in the demand for package holidays in Europe. This market, however, is also highly price-sensitive and the lifting of Provision 1 regulations demonstrated the potential for off-season package tour growth. This coincided with the development of longer paid holidays in the advanced Western European nations, with four weeks becoming the norm in the 1970s, and five weeks common in the 1980s. The tendency to take a second holiday during the off-season provided a great boost for tour operating, leading to better year-round aircraft and hotel utilisation. Costs could be distributed more evenly throughout the year, reducing average prices.

The policy of marginal costing in the off-season, designed to cover variable costs and make a contribution to fixed costs, led to extremely low prices during the early part of the 1970s, aimed at two distinct markets. Rock-bottom prices for mini-packages of three or four days' duration attracted a new 'experimental' market to the idea of continental holidays, and pensioners were attracted to long-stay holidays of three or four months' duration during the winter months, where hotel prices were so low that packages could be afforded even by those on pensions. This kept the hotels full and provided year-round employment for hotel staff.

OTHER REVENUE-PRODUCING ACTIVITIES

Although direct profits on tour operating may appear to be slim owing to the pressures of competition, in fact operators have at their disposal a number of alternative means of increasing their revenue and profits. By far the most important of these is the result of the time lapse occurring between customers paying for their holiday and the tour operators' obligations to settle their accounts with their principals.

The booking season for summer holidays is under way in the autumn of the preceding year, reaching its peak in the three months following Christmas, so a large proportion of deposits will have been paid by the end of March. Although the tour operators will themselves have had to make deposits for aircraft charters at the beginning of the season, and will often have made some advance to the hoteliers as a sign of good faith, the balance will not fall due until after clients have completed their holiday. Operators will have the use of deposit payments for up to a year in advance and for the balance of holiday payments for two or three months. This money can be invested to earn interest for the operator and profits achieved on these investments are likely to exceed or equal those on the package tour operations themselves. One effect of the growing tendency among British holidaymakers to book their holidays later and pay by credit card in recent years is the consequent reduction in the tour operators' cash flow; if this tendency persists or grows, operators may be obliged to increase package tour prices to compensate for this loss of revenue.

Further profits are achieved through the sale of ancillary services. Of these, the most important are the duty-free goods sold on board flights, the package insurance policies accompanying tour sales and the sale of optional excursions or care hire at the destination.

The European Community's plan to end the sale of duty-free goods within the EC will be a serious blow to revenues and profitability for several sectors of the travel industry, including tour operators. Loss of duty-free profits alone might force up prices for inclusive tours by as much as 20 per cent. Still more significantly, it could affect the future pattern of IT flows, since an undefined proportion of tourists may choose to switch to non-EC countries for their holidays, in order to take advantage of the duty-free benefits. Countries such as Austria, Yugoslavia or Turkey could benefit at the expense of the traditional EC destinations.

A further contribution to operating revenue is achieved by the imposition of cancellation charges. These charges substantially exceed any costs borne by the operators resulting from cancellations (on most ITX packages, for example, hotels will impose no cancellation charges on tour operators for cancelled accommodation), even assuming the operator is unable to resell the cancelled tour booking. On average, some five per cent of tour bookings are cancelled and these, as mentioned earlier, prove highly profitable for the operators.

There is also scope for profit-making through the judicious 'buying forward' of foreign currency at times where exchange rates are favourable. The Spanish peseta and Greek drachma are invariably stronger during the summer at times of tourist demand, so operators are bound to benefit by buying these currencies during the preceding winter. One must caution that forward buying, if ill-judged, can equally lead to substantial losses for operators, but today such risks can be avoided by arrangements with merchant banks by which foreign exchange can be bought forward without the necessity of making actual payment until the foreign currency is required.

Finally, further profits result from selling a proportion of one's package tours direct to the public, avoiding the payment of commission to travel agencies. Typically, 85–90 per cent of an operator's package holidays are sold through agents, so there is scope for considerably increased profits by selling direct. However, as we shall see presently, there is a danger of openly soliciting direct sell business.

NON-CHARTER TOUR OPERATING

The growth of inclusive holidays by air charter caught the scheduled airlines by surprise, but they retaliated by introducing their own tour basing fares, available to operators to put together packages using seats on scheduled flights. As break-even points on scheduled flights are much lower than on charter flights (usually some 50–60 per cent, as opposed to 90 per cent plus), subject to tickets being sold at fares much higher than those available on charter flights, there is scope for considerable profit on the balance of seats sold, even at low prices.

IATA has laid down the regulations which must be adhered to by operators who wish to take advantage of these fares. These include the requirement to print at least 2000 brochures covering the tour (or 200 for tours to a special event within Europe), which in addition to text must include at least one illustration (picture or map) and feature at least one hotel at the destination. The package must include flight, accommodation and one other service (usually this includes transfers between airport and hotel). The tour programme can be organised using one or more IATA carrier, but approval is usually processed through a particular featured carrier who will validate the programme for the use of tour-basing fares by providing an inclusive tour code number which must be quoted on each ticket issued. Tour operators making a forward commitment for a block of seats on scheduled flights will also require to obtain an ATOL. To cater for their clients' individual package holiday needs, many travel companies produce an *umbrella brochure* which is designed to meet the above requirements for a number of destinations and will enable the company to use ITX fares in conjunction with tailor-made packages arranged for individual client needs. In practice, however, these umbrella brochures are falling into disuse, with travel agents increasingly finding that the purchase of 'bucketed' tickets will undercut any tour-basing fares they can obtain through this process.

'PIGGY-BACK' OPERATING

One further option is available to agents who wish to move into tour operating without wholeheartedly committing themselves to the risks involved in running their own programmes. It is possible to negotiate with other tour operators to sell 'blocks' or allocations of their programme at rates of commission higher than the standard 10 per cent payable for retail sales. Agents can go still further by selling these tours under their own trade name and producing their own brochures, i.e. *piggy-backing*. This may involve sharing some of the risks with the other tour operator who has organised the programme.

When agents negotiate such agreements it is important that they fully understand the extent of their commitment, including cancellation dates for unsold tours and any cancellation charges that may be imposed. In the same way, tour operators who wish to mount a programme to a new destination using charter air services, but who do not feel confident of being able to fill all their charter seats, may part-charter aircraft with other operators to the same destination. It should be added that any agent who undertakes to contract for a block of seats on a scheduled aircraft technically becomes a bondable tour operator.

TOUR PLANNING, MARKETING AND OPERATING

Plans for the introduction of a new tour programme or destination have to be drawn up a long way ahead – as much as two years before the first departure takes place. A typical time-scale for a summer programme of tours is shown in Fig 10.2.

Clearly, in planning the time deadlines for the programme one must first establish the launch date and work backwards. The critical problem is the determination of final prices, which have to be established some nine months ahead of the first departures.

MARKET RESEARCH AND TOUR PLANNING

In practice the decision to exploit a destination or region for package tours is as much an act of faith as the outcome of carefully considered research. Forecasting future developments in tourism, which, as a product, is affected by changing circumstances to a greater extent than most other consumer products, has proved to be notably inaccurate. As we have seen, tourist patterns change over time, with a shift from one country to another and from one form of accommodation to another. With the emphasis on price, the mass tour operator's principal concern is to provide the basic sun, sea and sand package in countries providing the best value for money. Transport costs will depend upon charter rights into the country, distance flown and ground handling costs. Accommodation and other costs to be met overseas will be the outcome of exchange rates with sterling and *vis-à-vis* the other currencies of competitive countries, inflation and the competitive environment in which hoteliers find themselves. Tour operators may have to take other factors into account too, such as the extent of support from airlines serving the routes or support

from the national tourist office of the destination, the political stability of the country; attitudes to, and government control over, mass tourism within the country; and the relationship between the host and generating countries (*see* Chapter 1 for a fuller discussion of these issues).

Once tour operators have narrowed the choice to two or three potential destinations, they must produce a realistic appraisal of the potential of these destinations, based on the numbers of tourists which the areas presently attract, growth rates over recent years, present shares held by competing companies and an estimate of the share of the market which their company could expect to gain in the first and subsequent years of operation.

At this point it is important to recognise a fundamental difference between mass-market and specialist tour operating. Small-scale or specialist tour operators can set up a tour programme at short notice and can withdraw from their present commitments equally quickly. Being so flexible, they are less concerned with long-term market trends and respond more quickly to market changes. Mass-market operators, on the other hand, will have a heavy long-term commitment to a destination which may involve them in the purchase of hotels at the resort. With this kind of equity tied up in the resort they must ensure its long-term viability.

Availability of suitable aircraft for the routes must be ascertained. This will in part dictate capacities for the tour operating programme, since aircraft have different configurations and on some routes where aircraft are operating at the limits of their range some passenger seats may have to be sacrificed in order to take on board sufficient fuel to cover the distance. In other cases provincial airport runways may be inadequate for larger aircraft and again fewer passengers than the normal full load may be carried in order that the plane can get airborne.

Planning of course is also dependent upon the availability of adequate finance for marketing and operating the new programme.

NEGOTIATIONS WITH PRINCIPALS

The airline

Once the decision has been made as to destination and numbers of passengers to be carried during the season and the dates of departure have been established, the serious negotiations will get under way with airlines, hotels and other principals, leading to formal contracts. These contracts will spell out the conditions for the release of unsold accommodation or (in the case of block bookings on scheduled services) aircraft seats, or the cancellation of chartered aircraft flights, with any penalties that the tour operator will incur.

RESEARCH/ PLANNING	YEAR1	Summer	First stages of research. Look at economic factors influencing the future development of package tours. Identify likely selection of destinations.
		September/December	Second stages of research. In-depth comparison of alternative destinations.
	YEAR 2	January	Determine destinations, hotels and capacity, duration of tours, departure dates. Make policy decisions on size and design of brochure, number of brochures to print, date for completion of print.
NEGOTIATION		February/March	Tenders put out for design, production and printing of brochures. Negotiate with the airlines for charter flights. Negotiate with hotels, transfer services, optional excursion operators.
		April/May	Typesetting and printing space booked with printer, copy for text commissioned. Illustrations commissioned or borrowed. Early artwork and text under development at design studio, with layout suggestions. Contracts completed with hotels and airlines, transfer services, etc.
		June	Production of brochure starts.
ADMINISTRATION		July	Determine exchange rates. Estimate selling prices based on inflation, etc. Galley proofs from printer, corrections made. Any necessary reservations staff recruited and trained.
		August	Final tour prices to printer. Brochures printed and reservations system established.
MARKETING		September/October	Brochure on market, distribution to agents. Initial agency sales promotion, including launch. First public media advertising, and trade publicity through press, etc.
	YEAR 3	January/March	Peak advertising and promotion to trade and public.
		February/April	Recruitment and training of resort representatives, etc.
		May	First tour departures.

Fig 10.2 Typical time-scale for a summer tour operating programme

Normal terms for aircraft chartering are for a deposit to be paid upon signing the contract (generally 10 per cent of the total cost), with the balance becoming due after each flight. In negotiating with charter services the reputation of tour operators is of paramount importance. If they have worked with that airline, or with similar charters, in previous years, this will be taken into account in determining the terms and price for the contract.

A well-established tour operator does not wish to be at the mercy of market forces in dealing with charter airlines. In any given year the demand for suitable aircraft may exceed the supply, leading the larger tour operators to form or buy their own airline to ensure capacity is available to them.

Part and parcel of these negotiations is the setting up of the tour operating flight plan, with decisions made on the dates and frequency of operations, the airports to be used and times of arrival and departure. All of this information will have to be consolidated into a form suitable for publication and easy comprehension in the tour brochure.

The hotels

Hotel negotiations, other than in the case of large tour operators who negotiate *time* contracts for an entire hotel, are generally far more informal than is the case in airline negotiating. Small and specialist tour operators selling Independent Inclusive Tour (IIT) packages may have no more than a *free-sale* (or *sell-and-report*) agreement with hoteliers, by which the hotel agrees to guarantee accommodation for a specified maximum number of tourists (usually four) merely on receipt of the notification of booking from the tour operator, whether by phone, mail or (customarily) by telex or fax. This arrangement may be quite suitable for small tour programmes, but it suffers from the disadvantage that at times hoteliers will retain the right to *close out* certain dates. As these are likely to be the most popular dates on the calendar, the operator stands to lose both potential business and goodwill. The alternative is for the operator to contract for an allocation of rooms in the hotel, with dates agreed for the release of unsold rooms.

Long-term contracts, either for a block of rooms or for the entire hotel, have the attraction of providing the operator with the lowest possible prices but they carry a higher element of risk. Some contracts will extend for up to five years and while at first glance such long fixed-price contracts can seem attractive, they are seldom realistic and in an inflationary period may well have to be renegotiated to avoid bankrupting the hotelier. This event would obviously not be in the tour operator's interest either.

In addition to operators spelling out their exact requirements in terms of rooms – required numbers of singles, doubles, twins; with or without private facilities;

whether with balconies or seaview; and with what catering provision, e.g. room only, with breakfast, half board or full board – they must also clarify a number of other issues. These include:

(*a*) reservations and registration procedures (including issue of any vouchers);

(*b*) accommodation requirements for any representatives or couriers (usually provided free);

(*c*) handling procedures and fees charged for porterage;

(*d*) special facilities available or needed, such as catering for handicapped customers, or special catering requirements (kosher, vegetarian, etc.);

(*e*) languages spoken by hotel staff;

(*f*) systems of payment by guests for drinks or other extras;

(*g*) reassurance on suitable fire and safety precautions;

(*h*) if appropriate, suitable space for a representative's desk and noticeboard.

It is also as well to check the availability of alternative hotel accommodation of a comparable standard in the event of overbooking. Of course a hotel with a reputation for overbooking is to be avoided, but over the course of time some errors are bound to occur requiring guests to be transferred to other hotels. Tour operators must satisfy themselves that the arrangements made by the hotelier for taking care of clients in these circumstances are adequate.

Ancillary services

Similar negotiations will take place with locally-based incoming operators and coach companies to provide the coach transfers between airport and hotels and any optional excursions. Car hire companies may also be approached to negotiate commission rates on sales to the tour operator's clients.

The reliability and honesty of the local operator is an important issue here. Smaller tour operators in the UK will not be in a position to employ their own resort representatives initially, and hence their image will depend upon the levels of service provided by the local operator's staff.

If the local company is also operating optional sightseeing excursions, procedures for booking these and handling the finances involved must be established and it should be clarified whether qualified guides with a sound knowledge of the English language are to be employed on the excursions. If not, tour operators must reassure themselves that all driver-couriers will be sufficiently fluent in the English language to do their job effectively for the company.

THE OVERSEAS REPRESENTATIVE

Tour operators carrying large numbers of package tourists to a destination are in a position to employ their

Fig 10.3 Overseas representative dealing with clients
(*Courtesy Thomson Holidays*)

own resort representatives. This has obvious advantages in that the company can count on the loyalty and total commitment of their own staff. A decision must be made as to whether to employ a national of the host country or of the generating country. The advantage of a local man or woman as the representative abroad is that these are likely to be better acquainted with local customs and geography, fluent in the language of the country and with good local contacts which will enable them to take care of problems (such as dealing with the police, shopkeepers or hoteliers) more effectively. On the other hand they are likely to be less familiar with the culture, customs or language of their clients, and this can act as a restraining influence on package tourists, especially on first visits abroad. Exceptional local representatives have been able to overcome this problem and if they themselves have some common background with their clients (for example, if they have lived for some years in the incoming tourists' country) they can function as effectively as their British counterparts. However, some countries impose restrictions on the employment of foreign nationals at resorts, so these legal points must be clarified before employing representatives.

The representative's role at the resort is far more demanding than is commonly thought. During the season, he or she can be expected to work a seven-day week and will need to be available on call for 24 hours a day to cope with any emergencies. Resort representatives are usually given a desk in the hotel lobby from which to work, but in cases where tour operators have their own resort representatives. This has obvious advantages own resort representatives. This has obvious advantages clients in two or more hotels in the resort representatives may have to visit each hotel during some part of the day. Their principal functions include:

(*a*) handling general enquiries;
(*b*) advising on currency exchange, shopping, etc.;
(*c*) organising and supervising social activities at the hotels;
(*d*) publicising and booking optional excursions;
(*e*) handling special requirements and complaints and acting as an intermediary for clients, interceding with the hotel proprietor, police or other local authorities.

These routine functions will be supplemented by problems arising from lost baggage, ill-health (referring clients to local English-speaking doctors or dentists) and even occasional deaths, although serious problems such as this are often referred to area managers where these are employed. They will have to supervise the relocation of customers whose accommodation is inadequate or where overbookings occur, and they may also have to rebook flights for their customers whose plans change as a result of emergencies.

The representatives' busiest days occur when groups are arriving or leaving the resort. They will accompany groups returning home on the coach to the airport, ensuring that departure formalities at the hotel have been complied with, arrange to pay any airport or departure taxes due, and then wait to greet incoming clients and accompany them to their hotels on the transfer coaches. They must ensure that check-in procedures operate smoothly, going over rooming lists with hotel managers before the hotel bills the tour operator. Many tour operators provide a welcome party for their clients on the first night of their holiday and it is the representatives' task to organise and host this.

Reps can also expect to spend some time at their resort bases before the start of the season, not only to get to know the site but to report back to their companies on the standards of tourist facilities and to pinpoint any discrepancies between brochure descriptions and reality.

The importance of the representatives' job has been increasingly realised by the larger tour operators, leading to full-time employment and a career structure for this sector of the tour operating business. Larger companies may initially employ staff as children's representatives, responsible for looking after and entertaining children on family holidays. Promotion is to representative, later to head representative (or area manager) based abroad, and ultimately to the job of supervisor of representatives, based at the company's head office, whose task is to recruit and train staff, organise holiday rotas, provide uniforms and handle the administration of the representatives' department. In 1988, the OFT recommended, *inter alia*, improved levels of training for overseas representatives, following a survey which indicated that tour reps were the subject of the second highest levels of complaint by tourists on holiday overseas. Training for this role has in the past been cursory (apart from a handful of the more forward looking companies), since most representatives are employed only for the six months of the summer season; but increasingly, as tour operators come to see that the quality of their representatives is the principal means of differentiating their product from that of their competitors, greater emphasis is being placed on improving the quality of the resort representative.

TOUR PRICING

A key factor in the success of a tour operator's programme is the price at which the package tour is to be marketed. Specialist tour operators whose product is unique may have more flexibility here and may determine prices largely on the basis of the cost of the services purchased, plus a mark-up sufficient to cover overheads and allow a satisfactory level of profit. Mass tour operators, however, must take greater account of their competitors' pricing since the demand for package tours is, as we have seen, extremely price-elastic, especially for off-season or shoulder period departures. The tendency is to follow the market leader's pricing, economies of scale playing a key role in enabling the larger operators to reduce their costs and hence undercut their rivals in tour pricing.

Below are provided two typical examples of cost-orientated tour pricing.

Cost-orientated tour operation pricing (time-series charter)

This first example is based on a series of short-haul charters involving two-week holidays to a destination such as Spain.

	£	£
Flight costs, based on 25 departures (back to back) on Boeing 737 130-seat at £8450 per flight	211 250	
Plus one empty leg each way at beginning and end of the season	8 450	
Total flight costs	219 700	
Cost per flight	8 788	
Cost per seat at 90% occupancy (117 seats) (i.e. £8788 ÷ 117)		75.00
Net hotel cost per person, 14 nights half board		88.00
Resort agents's handling fees and transfers, per person		7.60
Gratuities, porterage, etc.		0.40
Total cost per person		171.00
Add mark-up of approx 30% on cost price to cover agency commission, marketing costs (including brochure, ticket wallet, etc.), Head Office administrative costs and profits		51.00
Selling price:		222.00

A small element of cost arises from VAT imposed on the relevant portion of the ground arrangements. Airport taxes (to include security levies) would be added on a per passenger basis for both the UK departure point and the overseas destination. Many companies would also add a further small fee, say £5, in order to build in a no-surcharge guarantee.

In estimating the seat cost for aircraft, operators must not only calculate the load factor on which this cost is to be based but must also aim to achieve this load factor on average throughout the series of tours they will be operating. This must depend upon their estimates of the market demand for each destination and the current supply of aircraft seats available to their competitors. Since high-season demand will considerably exceed the supply of seats to these destinations, there is scope to increase the above price, and hence profits, for the high-season months of the year, even if this results in the company being uncompetitive with other leading operators. On the other hand, supply may greatly exceed demand at off-peak periods and tour operators may set their prices so low as to aim only to cover their variable costs and make a small contribution towards fixed costs (administrative, marketing, etc.) rather than achieve profits at this time of the year.

They must carefully consider what proportion of overheads are to be allocated to each holiday and destination. As long as these expenses are recovered in full during the term of operation of the programme, the allocation of these costs can be made on the basis of market forces and need not be proportioned equally (as in this example) to each destination. In practice, it is now becoming common for tour operators to recover overhead costs by determining a per capita contribution, based on anticipated corporate costs for the year and anticipated numbers of tourists to be carried. Under this system, of course, each tour carries the same burden of office costs regardless of destination or price. However, there is a case for a more marketing-orientated approach to pricing, based on consideration of market prices and the company's long-term objectives. In entering a new market, for instance, it may be that the principal objective is to penetrate and obtain a targeted share of that market in the first year of operating, and this may be achieved by reducing or even foregoing profits during the first year, and/or by reducing the per capita contribution to corporate costs. Indeed, to some destinations the tour operator may introduce *loss leader* pricing policies, subsidising the cost of this policy from other, profitable routes in order to get a footing in the market to the new destination.

Detailed considerations of value-added tax have not been included here for the sake of simplicity. However, the VAT (Tour Operators) Order 1987 came into force in 1988, and imposes taxation on profit margins (excluding for the present transport costs) for any tours between EC countries. The tour operator will, of course, also be paying VAT costs which are incorporated into the hoteliers' and other services' contractual prices to the tour operator, as noted above.

Most tour operators (but not all) have agreed to pay commission to agents on revenue which includes the VAT costs (which the tour operator can later recover).

Cost-orientated tour operation pricing (specialist ITX scheduled programme)

The second example is of a specialist long-haul tour-operating programme using the services of scheduled carriers to Hong Kong.

	£
Flight cost, based on net group air fare per person, London–Hong Kong, using scheduled flights	470
Price for a twin bed room in medium grade hotel, HK\$600 (at \$13.50 = £1). 7 nights at \$300 per person = \$2100 =	155
Transfers at £3 per person each way	6
	631
Add agent's commission	70
	701
Selling price: 'Lead price' (offered on 2–3 flights off-season)	710
Shoulder season price	750
High-season price (high summer, Christmas or Easter holidays)	820

It will be noted that in the case of this specialist operator, prices reflect market demand at different periods of the year, and there is no equal distribution of office overheads; profits and most overheads are recoverable in the peak prices charged to the market. This is quite a common policy among the smaller specialist operators who may use less sophisticated pricing techniques to

arrive at target profits. Many specialists who operate in a climate where there is no exact competition for their product could be expected to charge a price which would permit them an overall gross profit of up to 25 per cent, while many mass market operators, and some specialists, will be forced by market conditions to settle for a much lower margin.

In developing a pricing strategy for package tours, tour operators must take into account a number of other variables in addition to those shown above. Their overall prices must be right not only in relation to the market and to their competitor's prices but also in relation to the prices of their other tours. This point must also be considered when setting the prices for departures from different regional airports and for operations at different times of the day or night or different days of the week. What special reductions are to be offered to children or for group bookings? Since seat and other costs will be unaffected, whatever reductions are made must be off-set by profits achieved on the sales to other holidaymakers.

As general policy, members of the TOSG standardise the date each year in which rates of exchange are fixed against the pound sterling, usually at the end of June or the beginning of July in the preceding year. This ensures that the public can make meaningful comparisons between the prices of tour programmes to similar destinations. Operators can also *buy forward* in the foreign currency they will require to protect themselves against market fluctuations. If involved in exchanging large sums of money, they can buy *futures* in the international monetary market.

Discounting through the distribution system

Discounts on published tour prices have normally been applied to late bookings, in order to clear unsold seats. There have also been efforts to reduce the late booking trend by offering discounts for early booking. However, in the past, tour operators frowned on any attempt by travel agents to undercut prices published in their brochures, such as by passing on to the client a proportion of their commission, or offering other inducements which would appear to reduce the overall price of the tour. It is illegal to impose resale price maintenance (RPM) on package tours, although it has been the practice of operators to build into their agency agreements the condition that individual agents should not sell their tours at other than brochure prices. However, Ilkeston Co-op's travel agency offered the first significant challenge to this policy in 1987 by offering a voucher scheme, whereby customers buying package holidays in the agency were offered discounts on other goods in the store. In retaliation for what was seen as a breach of contract, some tour operators withdrew their brochures and support for the agency, but Ilkeston's

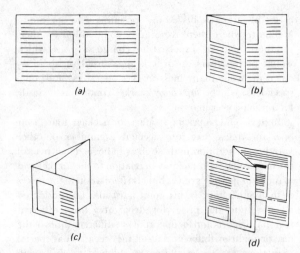

Fig 10.4 Some examples of folders suitable for tour printing: (a) Centrefold, folded to produce simple four-page sheet; (b) Gatefold, an off-centre fold producing a front sheet smaller than the second sheet; (c) A six-page regular fold; (d) A six-page concertina fold

right to negotiate prices on package holidays in this way was upheld.

Travel agents may now offer discounts on any package offered by an ABTA tour operator, and/or other inducements such as free insurance may also be offered. This applies to both conventional ITs and to packages with 'throw-away' accommodation. Technically, discounts should not be offered on air fares, rail tickets or ferry services (although in practice discounts are frequently offered to agency clients offering large volumes of business).

THE TOUR BROCHURE

The tour operator's brochure is a vital marketing tool. Tourism is an intangible product which has to be purchased by customers without inspection and often on the basis of very inadequate knowledge. In these circumstances the brochure becomes the principal means of both informing them about the product and persuading them, by 'purveying dreams', to purchase it.

For this reason the production of the tour brochure represents a major proportion of a tour operator's marketing budget and, with print runs for a typical summer brochure exceeding a million copies in the case of the largest tour operators, it is essential to see that this enormous expenditure achieves the intended results.

Brochure design and format

Larger companies will have their brochures designed and prepared either in their own advertising department or in conjunction with the design studio of their advertising agency, who will negotiate with printers to obtain the best quotation and ensure that print deadlines are met. Other operators may tackle the design of the brochure themselves, but are best advised to undertake this through the medium of an independent design studio who can provide the professional expertise in layout, artwork and copy that are so important in the design of a professional piece of publicity material. Most printers have their own design departments which can undertake this work for their clients, but unless the company has had experience of the standards of work of their printer in the past they are probably better advised to approach an independent studio for this work.

The purposes the brochure serves will dictate its design and format. A single *ad hoc* programme, for example to a foreign exhibition, may be printed on nothing more than a leaflet, or if a limited programme of tours is contemplated these may be laid out in the form of a folder.

Folders can take a number of differing forms, ranging from a simple *centrefold* to more complicated folds (*see* Fig 10.4). Larger brochures (or in printing parlance, *booklets*) consist of eight or more pages printed in units of four sheets which require binding in some way. Smaller brochures are usually machine-bound by *saddle-stitching* (stapling through the spine), while larger brochures may be *side-stitched* with a glue-on cover or bound as a book. It is not the purpose here to discuss printing methods in detail and the reader is referred for further reading in this subject to the many excellent books on the subject of print publicity.

Package tour brochures can be described as falling into three categories; *shell* folders, *umbrella* brochures and regular tour brochures. Use of a shell folder is a convenient way to reduce printing costs and is suitable for limited-capacity tour programmes or *ad hoc* specialist tours. Shells are blank folders interspersed with preprinted photographs and are provided at low cost by airlines or national tourist offices to encourage tour operators to run programmes using these services or destinations. Tour operators can overprint a suitable text describing their tour programme; since only the text needs to be added, a one-colour print run at low cost will meet the requirements of scheduled airlines for inclusive tour basing fares approval.

An umbrella brochure can be produced by a travel agency permitting them to sell IITs to a multitude of destinations overseas. The brochure covers only the basic essentials to satisfy IATA airlines' requirements for inclusive tour approval, and its purpose is to enable agents to produce tailor-made tours for their clients using a net tour-basing (ITX) fare. However, these brochures have largely fallen into disuse, probably because agents can secure 'bucket shop' airline tickets (albeit illicitly) at lower prices than many ITX fares.

The rest of the tour brochures are purpose-designed for operators' regular package tour series. They usually comprise all of an operator's summer or winter holiday tours, and most tour operators have now opted for the annual production of just these two brochures. However, large operators have diversified into a great many different types of holiday – long-haul and short-haul, coach tours as well as air holidays, lakes and mountains resorts as well as seaside resorts, cruises as well as package tours. If all these are to be included in a single comprehensive brochure it will run to hundreds of pages and prove extremely expensive to produce. Equally important, it will weigh a lot and therefore be expensive to deliver to agents or for agents to send to their customers. There will be wastage resulting from clients who know exactly the type of holiday and the destination to which they wish to travel, but who must pick up the complete brochure in order to see the choice of tours to that destination. For these reasons, some tour operators are now producing a variety of specialist brochures to reach different markets.

The first task of a brochure is to attract the attention of the consumer. Most brochures will be seen by consumers in the racks of a travel agency where they will be vying for attention among many competing operators' brochures. To gain attention, operators have developed a 'house style' in which multi-colour covers (usually featuring attractive models in swimwear) combine with an eye-catching symbol and house name across the top of the brochure to obtain maximum impact. While some might contend that there is today a disappointing similarity among leading tour operators' brochure covers, taken individually the quality and professionalism of brochure design is exceptional.

Increasingly, brochures are designed to reinforce an operator's image of quality and reliability. This requires attractive, accurate and easily comprehensible text and layout, high-quality photography and paper of a matching quality.

Obligations affecting tour brochures

As was said earlier, the brochure must both inform and persuade potential tourists. Tour operators are selling dreams and their brochures must allow consumers to fantasise a little about their holiday. But it is also vitally important that consumers are not misled about any aspect of their holidays; the data must be factually accurate. Care must be taken not to infringe the Trades Description Act 1968, section 14 of which deals specifically with the offence of making false statements concerning the provision of services.

In the past, tour operators have also tended to invoke the *law of agency* in claiming that within their booking conditions they act as agents only in representing hotels, transport companies or other principals. However, the provisions of the Unfair Contract Terms Act 1977 could well invalidate such claims, placing a direct responsibility on tour operators for the services they package, even though they themselves may have little control over the management of those services. Disclaiming liability may be interpreted as an unreasonable condition within the meaning of the Act. It has been argued that tour operators will in future need to be less specific about what they are offering in terms of facilities, to protect themselves against claims by their clients.

With the introduction of the Consumer Protection Act 1988, making it illegal to give a misleading indication of the price of goods and services, tour operators are in danger of falling foul of the law if price panels in their brochures do not provide all-inclusive tour costs. However, the industry, following the lead offered by the largest operators, had already been moving in the direction of all-inclusive pricing panels.

Apart from legal liabilities, tour operators have a duty to be fair and reasonable in promoting their services to customers. ABTA's Tour Operators' Code of Conduct imposes specific obligations upon them to provide honest and accurate information and the consumer movement has also made this a central tenet in observing the activities of the travel industry.

To satisfy not only the ITX conditions but also their clients' need for information on regular charter tour programmes, the brochure should contain all of the following information:

(a) the name of the firm responsible for the inclusive tour;

(b) the means of transport used, including, in the case of air carriers, the name of the carrier(s), type and class of aircraft used and whether scheduled or charter aircraft are operated;

(c) full details of destinations, itinerary and times of travel;

(d) the duration of each tour (number of days'/nights' stay);

(e) full description of the location and type of accommodation provided, including meals;

(f) whether services of a representative are available abroad;

(g) a clear indication of the price for each tour, with any extras charged clearly shown (preferably, these extras should be shown on the same page as the basic price of the tour);

(h) exact details of special arrangements, e.g. if there is a games room in the hotel, whether this is available at all times and whether any charges are made for the use of such equipment;

(i) full conditions of booking, including details of cancellation conditions;

(j) details of any optional or compulsory insurance coverage;

(*k*) details of documentation required for travel to the destinations featured and any health hazards or inoculations recommended.

A booking form is usually printed within the brochure for completing a reservation. The terms and conditions of the booking should appear in full in the brochure but should not be printed on the back of the booking form, as they should be retained by the customer.

Negotiating with a printer

Printers will not expect their clients necessarily to be experts in printing methods, but those involved with processing the production of a brochure should be reasonably familiar with current techniques in printing and common terms used. Printers will want to know the following.

(*a*) The number of brochures required.

(*b*) The number of colours to be used in the printing. Full-colour work normally involves four colours, but some savings in cost may be possible if colour photography is not to be included.

(*c*) The paper to be used – size, format, quality and weight. The choice of paper will be influenced by several factors, including the printing process used. Size may be dictated by the industry's requirements; for example, a tour operating brochure needs to fit a standard agency display shelf. Costs can be trimmed by minimising the wastage from 'off-cuts' of each sheet of paper used. Paper quality varies considerably according to the material from which it is made. It may be glossy or matt, but most tour operators select a paper for its whiteness and its opacity. This requires a compromise since very white papers tend to be less opaque, but one must avoid print showing through to the other side of the sheet. The weight of paper will of course depend upon its effect on the overall weight of the brochure if this is to be mailed in quantity.

(*d*) Number and positioning of illustrations to be used (photos, artwork, maps, etc.).

(*e*) Typesetting needs. There are over 6000 typefaces from which to choose and the style of type chosen should reflect the theme of the brochure, its subject and the image of the company.

(*f*) Completion and delivery dates.

When obtaining prices from a printer, several companies should be approached as quotations will vary substantially between printers. Many tour operators choose to have their brochures printed abroad, but today British printers can usually match their continental counterparts both in quality and price. Most importantly, one must avoid attempting to cut corners as an inferior print job can threaten the whole success of the tour programme. The progress of the printing must be supervised throughout, either by the company itself or its advertising agency. Proofs should be submitted at each stage of production to check on accuracy and a final corrected proof should be seen before the actual print run to ensure there are no final errors.

The printer should be asked to quote not only for the basic number of brochures that will be required but also for the *run-on* price of additional copies. Once a brochure is set up for printing, the cost of running off a few thousand extra is very small in relationship to the overall price and it may be better to do this rather than consider reordering another run at a later date.

Brochure distribution and control

As will be discussed later on in this chapter, tour operators must make the decision either to use all ABTA retail agency outlets for the sale of their tours or to select those they feel will be the most productive. Whatever decision is made, operators must also establish a policy for their brochure distribution. If equal supplies of brochures are distributed to all an operator's agencies, many will be wasted in the less productive retailers.

A study carried out by ASTA some years ago in the United States found that about half of all tour brochures produced were eventually thrown away without being seen by the public. While this can partly be ascribed to the American 'shot-gun' approach to distributing brochures, rather than the more selective 'rifle' approach, this does nevertheless bring home the potential for waste if care is not exercised. Wastage can be reduced by establishing standards against which to monitor the performance of travel agents. A key ratio is that of brochures given out to bookings received. 'Average' figures appear to vary a good deal in the experience of different operators. While a major operator would anticipate a booking for every three or four brochures given out (still typically meaning that every booking made carries a burden of about £5 in brochure production costs), a specialist operator (albeit with a much thinner brochure costing a fraction of the largest brochures) might need to give out 20–25 for every booking. However, it should be remembered that a typical booking will average 2.5 to 3 persons. If figures consistently poorer than this are achieved by agents, tour operators should be looking for an explanation. The problem could be accounted for by the agents' lack of control over their own brochure distribution; do they merely stock display racks and allow their clients to collect brochures in whatever numbers they wish or do they make a serious attempt to sell to their 'browsers'? Some agents go even further than this, retaining all stocks of brochures behind the counter with display copies only on the shelves, so that customers have to ask for copies of the brochures they require. This is instrumental in cutting down waste as well as increasing sales.

It is normal practice for the agency sales managers of tour operators to categorise their agents in some suitable manner in terms of their productivity for the company. This could typically take the following form:

		Bookings per year
Category A	Top producing agents	100 +
Category B	Good agents	50–99
Category C	Fair agents	20–49
Category D	Below average agents	6–19
Category E	Poor agents	0–5

A decision will then be made as to what levels of support are to be provided for each category of agent. At the top end of the scale, agents could expect to receive whatever supplies of brochures they feel they could usefully employ, while at the other end perhaps only two or three copies would be sent each year.

THE RESERVATIONS SYSTEM

In order to put a package tour programme into operation, a reservations system must be developed and implemented. The design of the system will depend upon whether reservations are to be handled manually or by computer and on the distribution methods employed, i.e. to what extent tour operators sell direct to their public, use retail travel agents, or sell through a combination of these two systems.

Computer reservation systems

All the bigger tour operators (those carrying 50 000 or more clients) and an increasing number of smaller operators, have computerised reservations systems (CRS), and with the advances in technology and declining costs of such systems which have been experienced in recent years, reliance on a manual system even among operators carrying as few as 5000 clients is becoming the exception rather than the rule. Systems may be shared with other operators to keep down costs, and the need to compete with larger operators, both in terms of rapid response and flexibility, is forcing all operators to introduce CRSs.

The distribution of package tours has been revolutionised by the development of the CRS and its associated computer services. Computers offer substantial advantages in terms of accuracy and speed, and today it is difficult to consider competing in the package holiday business without benefit of a CRS.

Initially, these systems were 'in-house', available to the staff of the operator only. Agents effected a booking by telephoning the reservations staff, who would check availability in their computer and offer a reservation on the phone. It was but a short step to link the agent direct into the CRS, using a VDU in the agent's office.

The use of videotex (viewdata) systems introduced widely in the 1980s has made this possible, and today 80–85 per cent of bookings for major operators' holidays (and over 50 per cent of smaller companies') are made in this way.

The large operators have perfected their own network systems which can be accessed directly, such as Thomson's TOP. So successful has this system been that at the end of 1986 Thomson directed that all bookings for their summer holiday programme would in future be made by computer; telephone sales are no longer handled, making it imperative for the agent to computerise.

For other operators, a number of specialised database network systems have been developed in recent years, through which they may make available their programmes to travel agents. The three leading services are those of BTTS (British Telecom's system, formerly known as Prestel Gateway), Fastrak (formerly known as Travinet, and owned by the Midland Bank), and Istel. Operators, and other travel providers, may choose to join one or more of these systems, which allow travel agents to make late availability reservations and gain access to the electronic ABC or OAG (airline guides), in addition to standard package holiday bookings. A recent advance has been the introduction of *hardwiring*, through which an agent can be permanently connected into a network.

The speed of transition in computer technology development is too rapid to discuss the merits of individual systems in a textbook such as this; students of the industry must keep abreast of developments through the trade press and other media.

Apart from CRSs, computer systems allow for a wide range of management control and accounting information to be made available to a company. One recent development in accounting procedure, certain to become widespread in the industry, is Thomson Holidays' TAB (Thomson Automatic Banking), which enables travel agency bank accounts to be debited electronically. All cash agencies appointed by Thomsons now settle their accounts by the direct transfer of funds from their banks to the Thomson bank account.

Making a reservation

Most tour operators continue to sell their tours through the high street travel agents who are currently responsible for handling 80–90 per cent of bookings made.

If a manual system is provided the operator will deal with these agents' enquiries and bookings by telephone. Reservations enquiries from the public and those from travel agents will be handled on separate lines, and lines may be further distinguished between geographical destinations or between winter and summer holidays or between beach resorts and 'lakes and mountains' holidays. This distinction gives reservations staff the opportunity to specialise in some aspects of the company's products and provide a more personal link with agents, who will come to identify a region with a particular staff member.

All reservations systems suffer from the problem of variable demand over time. In Britain the peak booking period for summer holidays is in the three months immediately following Christmas (although there has been a tendency in recent years for increasing numbers of the public to book later). The operator is therefore faced with the alternative of providing adequate staff and telephone lines to handle all the demand during the peak periods, with consequent under-utilisation of resources at other times, or providing a reduced number of lines year-round, with a delay in service to agents and the public during the peak periods which may cause loss of business.

Travel agents require rapid connections to an operator's reservations system. If lines are engaged or telephones not answered for long periods of time, agents will become frustrated and may prefer to deal with a competitor with whom communications are easier. Installing an automatic call distribution (ACD) system, by which incoming calls are automatically 'queued' until a line becomes free, does not entirely satisfy agents since they are involved in the expense of holding on until the line becomes free.

Once connected to the reservations department agents identify themselves and their company and check on the availability of the tour in which their client is interested. If available, the tour may then be reserved either under option or as a definite booking. Options are usually held by the operator until the end of the following work day, when they will be automatically released unless the agent has telephoned to convert to a definite booking. In both cases, reservations staff provide the agent with a code number to identify the booking. Once a booking is definite the client completes the tour operator's booking form and this is sent together with the appropriate deposit, by the agent to the operator, the booking code being shown on the form. These forms are usually required to arrive in the tour operator's office within five to seven days or again the booking will be automatically released.

The reservations department is situated within the tour operator's chart room. Where a manual system is in operation, the full programme of flights and hotels is posted on the walls of this room and availability can be quickly scanned by the telephone staff. The charts will draw attention to any changes in the programme since the brochure went to press so that the reservations staff can ensure that these changes are brought to the attention of agent and customer.

Actual control of flights and hotel sales can be handled in a variety of different ways. One typical procedure is to use coloured tabs hanging on pegs adjacent to each flight and hotel; as bookings are made, a tab is removed from each and inserted into a booking envelope with the details of the booking shown on the exterior of the envelope, viz. date of booking, 'lead' name of customer, number of seats reserved, agent's identification (ABTA number and personal reference) and sales staff reference. Once all coloured tabs have been removed from a peg this will signify that the flight or hotel is fully booked. When cancellations occur the tabs may be returned to the pegs.

Post-reservations administration

Once the operator receives the booking form in the mail it is processed first by the reservations staff, who mark bookings as 'definite' in the records and arrange for a confirmation to be sent to the agent. Subsequently, booking forms are passed to the accounts section who will raise an invoice and forward this to the agent (it is possible to reduce paperwork by combining the confirmation and invoice). It is the agents' responsibility to ensure that their clients remit the final payment due by the deadline given in the invoice. Upon receipt of the final payment the tour operator issues tickets and itinerary (plus any vouchers that may be necessary) and despatches these to the agent.

Prior to each departure a flight manifest is prepared for the airline, with names of all those booked, and a rooming list is sent to the hotels concerned and to resort representatives where appropriate. The latter should go over the rooming list with the hotelier to ensure that all is in order prior to the clients' arrival.

Larger tour operators can also be expected to have a passenger relations department whose function is to monitor and handle passenger and agency complaints and ensure quality control in the operation of the tour programme.

Late bookings

Tour operators are anxious to fill every seat in their tour programme. The ability to react quickly to deal with last-minute demand for bookings plays a key role in fulfilling this objective. Coupled with late booking discounts, many operators have introduced procedures designed to encourage late bookings, including fast updatings on availability and a telephone booking procedure which merely requires a reference to be given to the agent over the telephone, against which customers can collect their tickets at the airport. Over 40 per cent of all summer holiday bookings were booked late in 1988, i.e. after 1 April, and there is little prospect of this percentage decreasing. A similar pattern is emerging for winter holidays. The computer is playing a major role in the development of late bookings, since availability can be constantly up-dated and agents can provide last minute bargains for their clients.

THE DISTRIBUTION NETWORK

Selection of retailers

Basically tour operators choose between two alternative methods of selling their tours – direct sell or through travel agents. Most choose to sell all, or the bulk, of their tours through the approximately 7500 agents who are members of ABTA; about 90 per cent of their tours are distributed in this way. However, the other 10 per cent of business achieved through direct bookings is highly lucrative for tour operators since it means a further 10 per cent profit for the operator without involving them in additional marketing expense. Most operators are naturally keen to encourage further direct bookings but must not be seen to be doing so by the agents themselves, who may retaliate by withdrawing their support and selling the tours of competitors.

Some operators are more selective in appointing agents to represent them. Like the sale of most consumer goods, some 80 per cent of package tours will be sold through only 20 per cent of retailers, while a large number of agents is likely to produce only the odd booking for the operator. The cost of servicing those less productive agents may be greater than the revenue they produce for the operator – not only must they be supplied with expensive free brochures but they have to receive regular mailings to update their information, be supported with sales material and most will also receive the occasional call from the operator's sales representative.

Principals must therefore decide whether to give varying support to agents dependent upon the latter's productivity (see p. 143), or to dispense with their least productive agents' services.

A number of tour operators have chosen to open their own retail outlets where, like any other agent, they will sell all ABTA tours but will of course prominently feature their parent company's products. Thus Thomson Holidays has a small number of retail shops in key cities, and also owns the Lunn Poly chain of over 250 travel agencies. Where this vertical integration occurs it is the usual policy of the companies concerned each to act as its own profit centre, and the parent organisation will pay commission on sales received through these shops just as it does through any other agent. Thomas Cook is of course best known as a travel retailer, but they also operate a major programme of package tours. The power of Cooks as a retailer is such that they can be highly selective as to which tour operator's services they will handle and can dictate to these operators advantageous terms and conditions, such as extended credit or improved commission rates.

Smaller specialist tour operators are obviously not in a position to support a national network of retailers, carrying as they do perhaps less than 10 000 holidaymakers each year. They will either concentrate entirely upon selling direct or will support a few selected agents in key locations around the country.

Relationships with travel agents

It is customary for tour operators to draw up a formal agreement with the travel agents they appoint to sell their services. These agreements specify the terms and conditions of trading, including such issues as the rate of commission to be paid to agents, whether the travel agent is to be a cash or credit agency, and the dates by which the operator expects settlement of the account. Until recently, agreements required agents not to undercut tour prices, but these conditions have now been relaxed.

An ill-defined area in these agreements is that of the application of the law of agency. A contract is between the principal and the client themself and it is unclear whether the travel agent is to be seen as acting as an agent of the principal (in this case the tour operator) or of the client. Agreements may suggest that the agent is the agent of the principal. However, since the collapse of Clarksons Holidays in 1974, it has generally been assumed that any 'pipeline' money held by agents at the time of a collapse of a principal is rightfully the client's, and some agreements now go so far as to specify this. Legally, however, this remains a grey area.

Under the terms of agency/tour operator agreements, travel agents agree to support and promote the sale of their principals' services. In return, tour operators provide the support and co-operation necessary for the successful merchandising of their products, i.e. provision of adequate brochures, sales promotion material and sometimes finance for co-operative regional advertising or promotional campaigns. Operators will also try to ensure that their agents are knowledgeable about the products they sell. This will be achieved through circulation of sales letters or other mail shots, by invitations to workshops or other forms of presentation, and by inviting selected agents on travel agency educationals.

The travel agency educational

The educational (or 'familiarisation trip' in American parlance) is a study trip organised by principals (whether tour operators, airlines or national tourist offices) for travel agents, with the objective either of rewarding staff for past sales performance or of providing them with new product knowledge of destinations or services. It has the advantage of implanting product knowledge more effectively than any other method while building brand loyalty and improving agency/principal relations,

Fig 10.5 A group of YTS students on a training programme with a retail travel chain (*Courtesy Exchange Travel*)

but the cost of mounting these educationals is high so principals are concerned that they achieve value for money. This has not always been the case in the past where educational visits abroad were often treated as 'jollies', attractive to agents as a social perk rather than an educational experience. The effectiveness of these educationals has been improved by more careful selection of candidates, by providing a more balanced mix of visits, working sessions and social activities, and by imposing a small charge for attendance, so that travel agency managers become more concerned to see that the expense is justified in terms of increased productivity and expertise among their staff.

Careful selection will ensure that all those attending share common objectives and that, for example, senior agency managers and young counter staff do not find themselves on the same educational, to the discomfort of both. Monitoring performance, by soliciting reports from those attending on completion of the educational visit, and by checking sales figures from invited agents will further ensure that the educational study trip is money well spent by the tour operator.

The sales representative

Tour operators, as do most larger travel principals, employ sales representatives to maintain and develop their business through travel agents, as well as to seek other sources of business. The functions of the sales rep are to call on present and potential contacts, advise agents and others of the services offered by their company, and support their retailers by the use of promotional, and sometimes financial, aid.

The reps act as one point of contact between the agent and the operator when problems or complaints are raised, and the often close relationship that develops between the reps and their accounts is valuable in building brand loyalty for the company. This personal contact enables them to obtain feedback from retailers on client and agent attitudes towards the company and its products. The reps are also likely to play a valuable role in categorising agents in terms of their potential and selecting sales staff for invitations to educationals. However, making sales calls in person is expensive and most companies have either reduced the frequency of calls or have switched to telephone sales calls to keep in touch with all but the most productive agents.

Agents themselves have very mixed feelings about the value of sales reps, who are still too often seen as time-wasting socialisers, notably ignorant about their company's and their competitors' products. It goes without saying that if the reps are to do an effective job they must be well trained; reps who are not knowledgeable about their products will carry a very poor image of the company to the retailers.

Direct sell operators

Tour operators that have avoided selling through retail agents and concentrated instead on reaching their public directly are not new to the British travel scene. They have, however, enjoyed a greater measure of success in the last few years, spearheaded by the launch in Britain of the Danish tour-operating giant Tjaereborg in 1978. Working from a base of successful large-scale tour operation in continental Europe, they were able to penetrate the British market with efficient management and low prices which in many cases undercut those of the market leaders who sold through the traditional retail travel agency outlets. Their success soon attracted the Swedish operator Vingresor and subsequently an off-shoot of the Thomson travel empire, Portland Holidays, also entered the direct sell market. Meanwhile, Martin Rooks, an old-established direct sell operator, was absorbed by British Airways and embarked on a programme of expansion. By the end of the 1970s these four companies were carrying almost a quarter of a million passengers on foreign inclusive tours.

However, marketing costs to achieve this level of penetration were high. Unlike sales through travel agencies, direct selling involves a high proportion of fixed costs in advertising, direct mail promotion and similar ventures, and it requires a strong and efficient administrative back-up to deal quickly with telephone enquiries and sales. Marketing costs for a direct sell operator may be three to four times higher than the cost of selling through a retail agency. Such high launch costs in the initial years of operation may be justified if market penetration is achieved.

The total share of the package tour market held by direct sell operators (including the proportion of package tours sold direct by the more traditional operators) is thought to be around 24 per cent, including all sales by direct sell operators and the small proportion of direct purchases made through other tour operators. However, there are interesting variations in the pattern of direct selling: for example, about one in three inclusive tours booked in London are direct bookings, and certain types of package tour, such as ski holidays and coach tours, reflect a much higher proportion of direct bookings. The proportion of bookings for main summer holidays is not expected to increase to any great degree, and the direct sell operators have been engaged in increasingly fierce competition to retain bookings and market share. After two years of operation in Britain, Vingresor was absorbed by its competitor Portland Holidays, while in recent years Tjaereborg has turned in an indifferent performance; Owners Abroad purchased a half share in the UK division of the company in 1987, with the option of purchasing the balance by 1990. There is little doubt that traditional buying patterns die hard in Britain, and many clients still prefer the reassurance of face-to-face contact with the travel agent.

Nonetheless, agents are concerned about the prospect of further encroachment by direct sell operations and particularly by efforts made to sell direct by those tour operators currently supporting agents. While threats have been made that agents will switch their support to loyal tour operators, it is arguable whether this line of attack is practical in the case of the largest companies in the inclusive tour business. An early threat to Thomsons when that organisation launched Portland Holidays had little effect – to refuse sales of the brand leader among tour operators is likely to damage agents as much as the principal. Perhaps a more effective retaliation in the long term is the attempt by travel agents to band together to form a tour operating consortium to compete with the established operators, with tours sold through members of the consortium at cost price to the agent. There is little evidence as yet, though, that this development poses a serious threat to the established operators.

However, agents are moving into marketing operators' tours under their 'own label'; Pickfords and AA Travel have made moves in this direction, while NAITA (the National Association of Independent Travel Agents) has proposed to establish a 'Liberty' own brand programme for sale through its retail members.

QUESTIONS AND DISCUSSION POINTS

1 Is there any action a small tour operator might take in advance of anticipated air traffic delays in the coming year, either to avoid major problems, or to ease the clients' discomfort or dissatisfaction?

2 The number of complaints against tour operators rose sharply in 1987, and ABTA has received a steady increase in the number of complaints against its members for the past decade. Offer reasons which might account for this, and suggest what steps need to be taken to remedy the situation.

3 What are the implications for the larger tour operators of a continuing trend to late bookings?

ASSIGNMENT TOPICS

1 You are a member of the market research team in a major British mass market outbound tour operator. You have been asked by your manager, Sue Grant, to express your opinions on the consequences of the 1992 European Harmonisation Act for British tour operators. Prepare a memorandum outlining your views, to be sent to Sue Grant prior to a meeting she is holding in her office to discuss the issue with senior members of staff.

2 As assistant to the Personnel Officer for Sunwing Holidays, a medium-sized tour operator, you have been advised that the company will be substantially expanding its activities and seeking to recruit a number of key new staff to assist in setting up new tour programmes.

You are required to draft an advertisement for a Contracts Manager, whose role will be to negotiate and contract with suppliers of flights and accommodation; and a Sales Representative, who is to call on travel agents in South West England and South Wales.

You are also asked to draw up a job specification for each of these jobs, suitable for mailing out to people responding to the advertisement.

11 Ancillary tourism services

Chapter objectives: After studying this chapter, you should be able to:

- understand the role of guides, couriers, insurance and financial services in meeting tourists' needs;
- be aware of private and public sector training and educational facilities for those employed in the tourism business;
- understand the role and value of the trade press for the travel industry;
- list the principal guides and timetables in use by travel agents, and their contents;
- be aware of the role of marketing and consultancy services in the industry.

INTRODUCTION

An analysis of the tourism industry leads one to encounter the problem of defining the parameters of the industry. Some services depend entirely upon the movement of tourists but are seldom considered as an element of the industry itself; customs services or visa issuing offices are examples. There are also services which derive much of their revenue from tourism yet are clearly not part of the industry, for example, companies specialising in the design and construction of hotels, and theatres or other entertainment centres.

Having attempted in previous chapters to compartmentalise conveniently the sectors of tourism (as an aid to memory as much as for any other reason), one is left with a number of services and facilities which, while perhaps not meriting lengthy treatment here, nevertheless deserve more than a passing mention. It is convenient to group these miscellaneous services together in this chapter.

Ancillary services can take the form either of services to the tourist themself or of services to the suppliers of tourism, although there may be considerable overlap between these categories. Each will be dealt with in turn.

SERVICES TO THE TOURIST

Guide/courier services

Unfortunately, there is as yet no term which will conveniently embrace all the *mediators* whose function it is to shepherd, guide, inform and interpret for groups of tourists. Nor can one relate these functions to a single sector of the industry; they are employed by carriers and tour operators, while some guide/couriers are self-employed, working freelance for tour operators or for themselves. Resort representatives who are employed by tour operators may also frequently be called upon to take on the rôle of a courier, as discussed in Chapter 10. Here, however, we will describe and differentiate between the role of couriers and of guides.

Couriers are employed by coach companies or tour operators to supervise and shepherd groups of tourists participating in coach tours (either on extended tours or day excursions). As well as couriers, they may be known as tour escorts, tour leaders or even tour managers, although the latter term usually implies a higher level of status and responsibility. As a part of their role they are often called upon to offer a sightseeing commentary on the country or region through which they are travelling and act as a source of information.

Some companies dispense with the separate services of a courier and employ driver-couriers who are responsible both for driving the coach and looking after their groups. Their role of information-giving, however, is restricted both by their limited knowledge and training and by legal constraints in force in most countries which prohibit the use of microphones by drivers while their coaches are in motion (a ruling which in practice is often overlooked).

Courier work offers less job security than is to be found in most other fields of tourism employment, being largely seasonal. However, with the growth of winter holidays resort representatives who also act as couriers are finding it possible to work all year round, some doubling as ski instructors during the winter programmes.

There is as yet no national organisation of couriers in the UK, although the International Association of Tour Managers counts some British members among its largely American membership.

Couriers are still employed largely on the strength of their prior experience. There are as yet no formal qualifications applying to this sector of the industry, although the position is attractive to graduates with relevant qualifications such as languages. Training courses are beginning to make their appearance, but still have to find acceptance among employers, whose criteria for a good courier remain personality, the ability to handle clients with sensitivity and tact, and stamina, both physical and mental. Programmes of induction training, ranging

Fig 11.1 A travellers' cheque

from one day to a week or longer, are beginning to become more common, but many employers pay little more than lip-service to training needs in this area.

Couriers differ from guides in that the latter stress their information-giving role, even though they may also perform other courier functions as part of their job. Guides, or guide-lecturers, are retained by tour operators for their expertise in general or specialist subjects. Their employment is generally freelance and intermittent, being concentrated primarily during the summer months, and outside of London there are comparatively few opportunities for off-season work. In an effort to extend recognition of their services by the tourism industry, guides have formed regional and national bodies to represent their interests. The largest of these is the London-based Guild of Guide-Lecturers, with some 850 members (75 per cent London area members). Their efforts to establish agreed professional fees for members ran counter to OFT rulings on price fixing in the industry, although the Guild continues to encourage the travel industry to employ professional guides with recognised training qualifications.

These qualifications are achieved through formal courses of varying length which are run at colleges of further education (with a handful of private courses offered in parallel), and are validated by the Regional Tourist Boards for guiding within the region. Validation as a registered guide does not, however, offer security of employment and many companies continue to employ unregistered guides who are prepared to accept lower fees for their work. Because the supply of guides outstrips the demand, many undertake guiding as a part-time occupation, while others supplement their general guiding work by working as driver-guides, conducting individual tourists on excursions using their private cars.

Financial services

This section will deal with three financial services for the tourist – the provision of insurance, of foreign exchange and of credit.

Insurance

Insurance is an important and in some cases obligatory aspect of a tourist's travel arrangements, embracing coverage for one or more of the following contingencies:

(*a*) medical care and hospitalisation;
(*b*) personal accident;
(*c*) cancellation or curtailment of holiday;
(*d*) delayed departure;
(*e*) baggage loss or delay;
(*f*) money loss;
(*g*) personal liability.

Tourists may purchase insurance either in the form of a selective policy, covering one or more of the above items, or in the form of a standard 'package' policy in which most or all of these items are included. The latter policy, although inflexible in its coverage, invariably offers the best value if comprehensive coverage is sought. Most tour operators encourage their clients to buy the operators' own comprehensive policies (often by requiring the client to indicate on the booking form if they do *not* require the policy). The operators' own policies, however, may be more expensive to purchase than a comprehensive policy offered by an independent insurance company, and since the travel agent can earn substantially more by selling independent insurance (up to 50 per cent commission, in the case of the largest travel agency chains, compared with the operators' own 10 per cent), agents have considerable incentive to sell insurance and to gain a sufficiently broad knowledge of

Fig 11.2 A Eurocheque card

the subject to be able to match the right policy to their clients' needs.

Insurance remains a lucrative business for both operators and agents, although claims have been rising in recent years (a recent report estimates that one in ten holidaymakers makes a claim against their policy). Free insurance, or a deal involving insurance (such as reduced, or no, deposits for those buying the agent's insurance package) have become a regular form of incentive in recent agency marketing.

Agents are obliged by the ABTA retail agents' code of conduct to draw their clients' attention to insurance facilities and cover (and they are also bound by the codes of conduct of the British Insurance Association or other insurance association whose members they represent) but are faced with a dilemma in deciding whether to sell those policies which are seen as in the customers' best interest or those producing higher revenues for the agents themselves, or some similar benefit (such as extended credit facilities). The decision to sell the policies of one particular company is one to be taken by branch managers of the agency concerned.

ABTA itself, in conjunction with leading travel insurance companies, recommends to its members a specific package, for which it receives an override commission from the company concerned. However, agents who aim to offer objective advice to their clients will have to weigh the benefits offered by the ABTA-recommended package against other insurance policies they represent.

Foreign transactions

Travellers today have an ever-widening choice of ways in which they can pay for services and goods while abroad. These include:

(*a*) taking Sterling or foreign banknotes with them. This can lead to loss or theft, and certain foreign countries have restrictions on the import or export of their currencies.

(*b*) taking travellers' cheques, in Sterling or foreign currency.

(*c*) arranging for the advance transfer of funds to a

specified foreign bank, or for an open credit to be made available through their own bank, at a foreign bank.

(*d*) using National Girobank postcheques.

(*e*) taking Eurocheques.

(*f*) using travel vouchers.

(*g*) using credit cards or charge cards.

Additionally, personal cheques can be cashed against a cashcard, but commission rates for this service can be quite high. Lloyds Bank now has a 'Payment Card' which can be used worldwide to draw out local currency over the counter or from a cash machine in banks where Visa is displayed. The money is drawn direct from the drawer's home town branch.

Travellers' cheques are the most widely used, being readily acceptable throughout the world by banks or commercial institutions, and offering the holder guaranteed security with rapid compensation for theft or loss. For the tourist, this advantage outweighs the standard premium charged of one per cent of face value. The value of the system for suppliers is that there is generally a considerable lapse of time between the tourist purchasing the travellers' cheques and encashing them. The money invested in the interim at market interest rates provides the supplier with substantial profits. Market leaders in travellers' cheque sales in the UK are Thomas Cooks and American Express (the latter being the first to introduce the concept in 1891); but a growing proportion are being issued by the clearing house banks.

Holders of National Girobank accounts can draw postcheques for the equivalent in foreign currency of £100 a day at post offices in most countries around the world (Western Union providing this service in the USA).

The Eurocheque is becoming widely used throughout Europe, especially in West Germany, and it has the advantage of allowing the holder to write a cheque in any local currency, again for the equivalent of approximately £100 a day. As with credit cards and cheque cards, delays occur between the transaction and the debit to the holder's account, and in addition a charge of a few pounds is levied for the cheque card itself, plus a percentage for each cheque drawn abroad. Eurocheques also allow for cash to be drawn from banks abroad.

Travel vouchers such as Barclays' 'Visa' and Citicorp provide for Sterling prepayment for travel services like car hire and hotel accommodation. Although prepaid vouchers of this kind have been in existence in the travel industry for many years, the credit organisations have greatly boosted their use in the 1980s.

Credit cards such as those of Visa and Access (known abroad as Mastercard) can be used to purchase goods and services overseas, or to obtain cash advances. Since transactions can take some time to filter through to one's bank account, users take a chance on the fluctuations of exchange rates. Charge cards such as American Express or Diners Club provide similar advantages and drawbacks. (Charge cards differ from credit cards in that accounts are due for settlement in full after receipt of an invoice from the company. Credit is not extended. However, the limit on charge card transactions is generally much higher than on credit cards – indeed, the company may impose no ceiling on the amount the holder may charge to the account.)

In addition to Visa and Access (Mastercard), there are a large number of other credit cards issued for the purchase of specific goods and services, such as car hire or hotels. Among these, mention should be made of the UATP (Universal Air Travel Plan) card, used for the purchase of IATA tickets throughout the world (although more commonly in use in North America and Europe). However, with the growth in popularity of the two leading credit card organisations, the use of other cards for international credit transactions is likely to decline. Since agents are required to pay a fee to the card companies when accepting credit cards in payment for travel, there has been some reluctance to accept them, but credit card sales are increasing at such a rate that no agent can afford to turn this form of business away.

Some travel agents (most notably Thomas Cooks) provide facilities themselves for the exchange of currency, but travellers more commonly obtain their foreign currency through banks or specialist foreign exchange dealers before their departure. A comparatively small number of travel agents, mainly business house agents, deal with travellers' cheques, Cooks and American Express, with their own cheques, being exceptions.

Mention should also be made here of the Barclay 'Connect' card which brings the reality of EFTPOS (Electronic Funds Transfer at Point of Sale) closer to the industry for the first time. Although operating only on a limited scale at the time of writing, use of 'direct debit' cards of this kind will almost certainly increase substantially over the next few years.

Incentive travel vouchers

Earlier, the role of incentive travel was discussed in generating new forms of tourism. Usually, companies have provided their employees or dealers with a specific travel package as a reward for achievement, the outcome being a form of group affinity travel, with recipients of the reward travelling together. However, an alternative incentive is available in the form of travel vouchers, issued in varying denominations, which can be collected by employees and used towards the cost of individual travel arrangements of the recipients' own choice. This is simply another form of monetary reward for achievement, but the appeal of travel has been proved a stronger motivator than cash or consumer durables. This form of award is also more flexible, and can be given in

small denominations, for example, to reward low absenteeism or for reaching weekly targets. A number of companies currently provide such vouchers. Some are able to be exchanged only against certain travel products or through specific retail travel agencies; others can be used to pay for any holiday arrangements purchased through ABTA agencies.

Duty-free shopping

Under the category of services to tourists, a final mention should be made of duty-free shopping. The purchase of duty-free goods at airports, on board ships and aircraft or at specially designated duty-free ports has always exerted a strong attraction for tourists. Duty-free purchases of spirits and tobacco in particular have been effectively marketed by carriers and the profits on the sale of such items are substantial (on some charter air services they exceed profits accruing on the sale of air tickets). Equally, the sale of duty-free goods at airports provides a substantial proportion of an airport's operating revenue.

This has led in some quarters to criticisms of profiteering, but the principals' reply to such criticism is that without these profits the airports would have to increase their landing charges and the cost of transport for consumers would rise appreciably.

As mentioned previously, with the introduction of tax harmonisation in the European Community by 1992, the purchase of duty-free goods when travelling between member countries is to cease. As we have seen, this may effect the patterns of travel between countries in Europe, as profit declines are compensated for by rises in fares, and travellers re-adjust their holiday arrangements in order to continue to take advantage of duty-free opportunities by travelling outside the Community.

SERVICES TO THE SUPPLIER

Education and training

The approach to training in the tourist industry has been historically a sectoral one. Each sector of the industry has tended to generate its own training courses, which have been largely job-specific. In an industry highly dependent upon entrepreneurially-managed small units there has been little in the way of formal training until recently. Most employees of travel agencies, hotels and tour operators have been trained on the job, often by observation and experience only, although some companies have provided noteworthy in-service training programmes, e.g. those of Thomas Cooks among travel agents. With the growing institutionalisation of sectors, greater emphasis has been placed upon professionalisation, the introduction of national standards of training and more formal training programmes. Professional bodies within the industry introduced their own programmes leading to final membership and offered part-time or full-time courses at colleges of further and higher education. Examples of such courses are those introduced by the Hotel, Catering and Institutional Management Association (HCIMA), the Chartered Institute of Transport (CIT) and the Institute of Travel and Tourism (ITT), the latter embracing principally employees of travel agencies and tour operators. With the rapid expansion of nationally validated tourism courses in colleges of further and higher education during the 1980s, the ITT decided to drop its own courses and to offer approval to those nationally validated courses meeting the Institute's own criteria for membership.

At corporate level in the industry, particularly within the airline sector and among leading tour operators, employers have tended to recruit graduates in appropriate disciplines for their own in-service management training programmes. This has also been true of the public sector in tourism.

In-service training for travel agents has been formalised by the introduction, with ABTA's support, of the Certificate of Travel Agency Competence (COTAC), nationally validated by the City and Guilds and available at two levels. In 1982 the British Government decided to phase out most of the industrial training boards, with the intention that the responsibility for such training should revert to the industries themselves. The Air Transport and Travel Industry Board, which was one of those affected, had successfully operated a number of technician short courses for the travel sectors, and ABTA decided to take over the responsibility for mounting travel agency and tour operating courses themselves, through the ABTA National Training Board. The Board has since widened the scope of its activities to include approval for a number of City and Guilds validated skills courses such as COTOP (Certificate of Tour Operating Practice) and COTICC (Certificate of Tourist Information Centre Competence), and has extended the level of recognition of courses into management with the introduction of COTAM (Certificate of Travel Agency Management). Further courses in management are planned. Coupled with suitable periods of industrial experience, these ABTA approved courses lead to the award of Diploma in Travel Studies or Diploma in Advanced Travel Studies and the Licentiateship of the City and Guilds (LCG).

The difficulty of organising day release courses for those employees of small travel companies has been tackled by the introduction of correspondence courses offered by various public and private sector bodies. In Britain the British Airways Fares and Ticketing courses, which depend largely upon self-study, have found widespread acceptance as a national standard for travel agency employees. Internationally the World Tourism Organisation (WTO) organises an international correspondence course designed to provide a comprehensive knowledge of the industry, and IATA/UFTAA offer self-study courses also covering fares and ticketing.

As we have seen earlier, courses for registered guides are validated within the industry by the regional tourist boards. However, no national standards for these courses have been established and the quality and length of these courses will vary substantially from one region to another.

The question of depth rather than breadth of knowledge has been a point of controversy within the industry, which has generally opted for depth of knowledge within a limited field in formal training courses – hence the sectoral approach to training which has been the norm up to now. However, public sector colleges have for some 20 years (even longer in the case of the hotel and catering industry) been offering courses which combine training for the industry and educational development of the student. These are designed to offer a wider perspective on the tourism business than would normally be available through the sectoral training approach. They range in scope from college diploma courses to the nationally validated courses of BTEC, the Business and Technician Education Council. BTEC First, National and Higher National Diplomas have as their underlying philosophy the aim to provide students with essential business operating skills, with optional modules relating these skills to specific areas of business such as the travel and tourism industry.

For the first time in Britain, 1986 saw the introduction of first degrees in travel and tourism, to join the already well established postgraduate diplomas and masters' degrees in the subject, so that tourism can now be studied formally at all levels of post-school education.

The trade press

In addition to specialised academic and research journals, there is a large selection of weekly and monthly journals serving the needs of those working in the tourism industry. The weekly trade papers, *Travel Trade Gazette* and *Travel News*, provide an invaluable service for the industry, covering news both of social and commercial events.

In an industry as fast-changing as tourism, employees can only update their knowledge of travel products by regularly reading the trade press. The newspapers complement the work of the training bodies in providing up-to-the-minute news, and for untrained travel agency staff they may well be the main source of such knowledge as well as being a forum for trade advertising and job opportunities.

The trade newspapers depend largely upon advertising for their revenue, and in return they support the industry by sponsoring trade fairs, seminars and other events.

Fig 11.3 The weekly trade papers
(*Source: Travel Trade Gazette and Travel News*)

Within the general category of the press one must also include those who are responsible for the publication of travel guides and timetables. The major publications in the field are shown in Table VIII and are those most commonly in use in travel agencies. The task of updating this information is obviously immense, especially in view of the worldwide scope of many of these publications. Since their production becomes more complex each year, this is also a field which lends itself to computerisation. ABC and OAG both now provide access for agents to their air timetables and fares information electronically, and within a few years most of these travel data can be expected to be retrieved electronically by the trade; and perhaps by the general public, too.

Marketing services

A number of services exist either wholly or in part to provide marketing support to members of the travel industry. These include marketing consultants, representative agencies, advertising agencies, brochure design, printing and distribution services, suppliers of travel point-of-sale material, and research and public relations organisations. To this list must now be added the organisations which provide the hardware and software for computerisation of the travel industry.

This book does not propose to discuss in depth the marketing of tourism. The subject is fully covered in a companion text (*Marketing for Tourism*: J C Holloway &

R V Plant, Pitman 1988). Other texts dealing with the topic can be found in the bibliography at the end of this book. The point to be made here is that both large and small companies in the industry can benefit by employing these specialist agencies, while the services of some are indispensable.

General marketing consultants

Management and marketing consultants offer advice to companies in the organisation and operation of their businesses. They bring to the task two valuable attributes, expertise and objectivity. Most tourism consultants have years of experience in the industry on which to draw and have been successful in their own fields before turning to consultancy. Moreover, not being directly involved in the day-to-day running of the company, they can approach their task without preconceived ideas about its operation and thus can offer a wider perspective in seeking solutions to problems.

They may be employed either to advise on the general reorganisation or marketing of a company and its products, or for some *ad hoc* purpose such as undertaking a feasibility study for new tour operating destinations or the introduction of a computerised reservations system.

Representative agencies

For a retainer or payment of royalties on sales these organisations act as general sales agents for a company within a defined territory. This is a valuable service for smaller companies seeking representation abroad. In the travel industry it is found most commonly in the hotel sector, but carriers, excursion operators and public sector tourist offices all make use of this facility in marketing their services abroad.

Advertising and promotional agencies

Many large travel companies, and an increasing number of smaller ones, retain an advertising agent, a number of whom specialise in handling travel accounts. An advertising agent does much more than design advertisements and place them in the media. They will be closely involved in the entire marketing strategy of the company and will be concerned with the design and production of the travel brochures. Many are equipped to carry out marketing research, the production of publicity material and merchandising or public relations activities.

Some larger agencies also produce their own hotel/resort guides, using their own staff's extensive knowledge.

Travel companies may have their brochures designed by the design studios of their advertising agent, they may arrange for them to be produced by an independent design studio, or the work can be undertaken by their printer. Advertising agents can help and advise in the selection of a printer for the production of brochures and other publicity material.

Table VIII. Travel publications

Publication	Details
British publications:	
ABC World Airways Guide (monthly)	Flight and fares information, car hire
ABC Rail Guide (monthly)	Timetables between London and all stations
ABC Shipping Guide (monthly)	Worldwide passenger and cargo/passenger services
ABC Guide to International Travel (Jan/Apr/Jul/Oct)	Passport, visa, health, currency regulations, customs, climate, etc.
Thomas Cook Continental Timetable (monthly)	Rail and shipping services throughout Europe and the Mediterranean
Thomas Cook Overseas Timetable (Jan/Mar/May/Jul/Sep/Nov)	Road, rail and local shipping timetable for America, Africa, Asia, Australia
National Express Coach Guide (Apr/Sep)	Express coach services for British Isles
Travel Trade Directory (Dec)	Directory of travel industry in UK/Eire
IATA Travel Agents' Directory of Europe (annual)	European agents, airlines, hotel groups, car hire, tourist offices
Britain: Hotels and Restaurants (Mar)	BTA official guide
AA Guide to Hotels and Restaurants (Nov)	5000 recommended establishments in British Isles
World Hotel Directory (July)	*Financial Times* guide to business hotels in 150 countries
A–Z Worldwide Hotel Guide (twice yearly)	Comprehensive list of international hotels and reservations offices
Agents' Hotel Gazetteer (annual)	
Resorts of Europe (Mediterranean)	
Apartments Gazetteer	CHG Publications details of resorts and accommodation in Europe and elsewhere
Alpine Resorts Gazetteer	
USA Resorts Gazetteer	
Holiday Guide	
Summer edition (annual)	Identifies tour operators providing package holidays to specific hotels and resorts worldwide
Winter edition (annual)	
Travel Directory (twice yearly)	Directory of the travel industry
Car Ferry Guide (annual)	Index of car ferry routes and operators
American publications:	
OAG Cruise and Shipline Guide (six per annum)	Line voyages, cruises and ferries worldwide
OAG Worldwide Edition (monthly)	Flights outside USA
OAG North American Edition (monthly)	Flights and fares in USA, Canada, Mexico and the Caribbean
OAG Travel Planner and Hotel/Motel Guide (four times per annum)	North American edition and European edition – resort areas and hotels
USA Official Railway Guide (Jun and Nov)	AMTRAK schedules and tariffs for USA, Canada, Mexico and Central America
Russells Official Bus Guide (Jun and Dec)	National guide for USA, Canada, Mexico and Central America
Hotel and Motel Red Book (Aug)	Directory of American Hotel and Motel Association members
Rand-McNally guides for USA	
Campground and Trailer Park Guide (Jun)	20 000 camp sites in USA, Canada and Mexico
Mobil City Guide (annual)	Complete guide to American cities
Mobil Travel Guides (annual)	Seven separate regional guides listing resorts, hotels and facilities in USA
International publications:	
International Hotel Guide (France) (Mar)	Worldwide guide published by International Hotel Association
Michelin Red Guides (France) (annual)	Six separate guides – GB & Ireland, France, Benelux, Spain & Portugal, Italy, Germany
Europa Camping and Caravanning (May)	International guide to campsites
Jaeger's Intertravel (Jun)	Directory of the world's travel agencies

A recent innovation in publicity material for the trade is the use of video cassettes to supplement, and perhaps in time even to replace the travel brochure. They are designed to help customers reach decisions on holiday destinations and services and are already being used experimentally by some agents who loan them to their clients. The cost of the cassette production is borne by the principals whose services are advertised.

In the area of marketing services, mention should also be made of direct mail and distribution services, some of which also specialise in handling travel services. These companies design and organise direct mail promotional literature aimed at specific target markets or at travel retailers. They can also undertake distribution of a company's tour brochures to travel agents in the UK.

Microprocessing organisations

Although carriers have had computerised reservations services for some years, only with the advent of the 1980s has the computer spread rapidly to other sectors of the industry. Virtally all major tour operators today have computerised their reservations services and computers are now being introduced into retail agents, who require *real-time* connections with these reservations systems in order to provide a fast and accurate booking service for their clients.

A number of hardware and software computer companies have been attracted by the growth potential for computers in the travel industry and have designed systems for principals and agencies which combine the three essential functions of information retrieval, reservations and accounting.

QUESTIONS AND DISCUSSION POINTS

1 The Office of Fair Trading has ruled out attempts by the Guild of Guide-Lecturers to establish national fixed charges for their services. Argue the case for and against set fees by guides.

2 Does the concept of target-led commission levels for the sale of insurance policies by travel agencies conflict with the obligation of the agent, as laid down in the ABTA Code of Conduct, to provide 'accurate and impartial information'?

3 Evaluate the two weekly trade newspapers, *Travel Trade Gazette* and *Travel News*. As Manager of a small travel company, where staff are too busy to digest both these, which would you recommend that they read regularly, and why?

4 In the motor trade, if a car owner with comprehensive insurance has an accident that causes the car to be written off, the insurance company, after settling the claim, takes title to the car and may realise any scrap value. In the tour operating business, the operator is free to resell holidays that have been cancelled, in effect selling the same tour twice. Could, or should, the insurance company who has paid out on a cancellation claim, itself retain the right to dispose of this holiday? What would be the implications of such a move?

ASSIGNMENT TOPICS

1 Mrs H, a client of your travel agency who is not well travelled, recently came into a small inheritance, and is proposing to spend it in a way she has always dreamed of – by taking an independent round the world holiday by air. She plans to stop over in Bangkok, Sydney (touring Australia), New Zealand, Rarotonga, Fiji and Tahiti before visiting relatives in Los Angeles and flying home. Her previous trips abroad have been limited to short visits to France and Belgium on prepaid package trips where very little personal spending was necessary, and these costs were met by changing sterling notes into local foreign currency as the need arose.

Her planned tour will cost her between four and five thousand pounds. She is on her way to your shop to ask you about alternative ways of meeting her expenses while abroad. Some of her hotels will be prepaid, but most of her expenses will have to be settled en route.

Prepare a set of notes giving the guidelines on the methods of payment she can choose.

2 As a member of the travel industry of some standing, and a Fellow of both the travel and tourism professional bodies, you have been invited by your local college to talk to their new students of tourism about the two bodies, the Institute of Travel and Tourism and the Tourism Society.

Prepare a set of notes to guide your talk, which discusses the present and future advantages of membership in these organisations. Indicate which of these bodies you would recommend the students to join if they are prepared to join only one.

12 Public sector tourism

Chapter objectives: After studying this chapter, you should be able to:

- understand the part played by local and central governments in the planning and promotion of tourism in a country;
- recognise why governments are becoming increasingly involved in tourism operations;
- understand the meaning of the term 'social tour-

ism' and its importance;
- show how governments in Britain and elsewhere control and supervise tourism in their country;
- explain how public sector tourism is organised in Britain.

INTRODUCTION

As we saw in Chapter 1, tourism plays an important part in a nation's economy by providing the opportunities for regional employment, contributing to the balance of payments and helping economic growth. On the other hand, countries that experience an influx of mass tourism also risk suffering socially from the consequences. For both economic and social reasons, therefore, governments take a direct interest in the development of tourism within their countries and the greater the involvement of tourism in a nation, whether incoming or outgoing, the greater is the likelihood of government intervention in the industry.

GOVERNMENT INVOLVEMENT IN TOURISM

The system of government of a country will of course be reflected in the mode and extent of government intervention. At one end of the scale, centrally planned economies such as those of the Soviet bloc will exercise virtually complete control, from policy-making and planning to the building and operation of tourist facilities, the organisation of tourist movements and the promotion of tourism at home and abroad. Travellers to such countries stay in state-run hotels, travel on state-operated package tours such as those of Intourist, the Soviet travel organisation, and use publicly-owned transport throughout, whether travelling by air, rail or coach within the country. Western nations, however, are by and large mixed economies in which public and private sectors co-exist and co-operate in tourism development. Only the balance of private versus public ownership will vary. The United States' belief in a free enterprise system ensures that government control and ownership is limited to where such involvement is seen as essential for the safety and well-being of its citizens (such as air traffic control), while promotion of the USA as a destination is left to private enterprise to a far greater extent than in any other nation.

The *system* of government is not the only factor

dictating the extent of state intervention. If a country is highly dependent upon tourism for its economic survival its government is likely to become far more involved in the industry. The importance of tourism to Spain is reflected in its political structure, with a minister of state directly responsible for tourism. Tourism also figures prominently in government policy-making and planning directives.

Similarly, countries which have only recently become significant world tourism destinations, and where this sudden growth has become problematic, are likely to adopt a stronger and more centralised role in organising and controlling tourism than will other countries, for example Switzerland, where tourism, although playing an important part in the nation's economy, has developed slowly over a relatively long time.

All countries of course depend upon the provision of a sound tourism infrastructure to encourage and satisfy their tourist markets; adequate public services, roads, railways and airports must be present to generate tourist traffic. But lesser developed nations may have additional incentives for state involvement. Private developers may be reluctant to invest in speculative tourist ventures, preferring to concentrate their resources in countries where demand has already proved itself. In this case it may fall to the government to either aid private developers or to build and operate hotels and other tourist amenities itself in order to attract the initial tourists to the new destination. Where private tourism investment does take place it may be companies from the generating countries who undertake the investment, leading to the danger that profits will be repatriated rather than find their way into the local economy. Private speculators, too, may be overly concerned about achieving a quick return on their investments rather than the slow but secure long-term development that the country is looking for.

The state must also play a co-ordinating role in planning the provision of tourist amenities and attractions. Supply must match demand and the state,

Fig 12.1 Bamburgh Castle, Northumbria
(*Courtesy Northumbria Tourist Board*)

in its supervisory role, can ensure that facilities are available when and where required and that they are of the right standard.

Finally, as tourism grows in the economy so its organisation, if uncontrolled, can result in the domination of the market by a handful of large companies. A mixed economy state has a duty to control the monopolies to protect the consumer against malpractice in the industry.

Apart from economic reasons, there are also social and political reasons for government control or ownership of tourism facilities. In most countries the national airline is state-owned and operated. While of course the income accruing from the operation of this service is important to the government, the national flag-carrier carries with it political prestige. Certain routes that it operates may be unprofitable but important for the social welfare of residents, and the government may see it as its duty to maintain these routes for non-commercial reasons. Governments are also guardians of their nations' heritage. This may be threatened by the uncontrolled expansion of international tourism; beauty spots may be destroyed by over-use or commercial exploitation, for example.

We can sum up by saying that a national government's role in tourism is manifested in four ways:

(*a*) in the planning and facilitating of tourism, including the provision of financial or other aid:

(*b*) in the supervision and control of component sectors of the tourism industry:

(*c*) in direct ownership of components of the industry;

(*d*) in the promotion of the nation and its tourist products to home and overseas markets.

Some of these aspects will now be explored below.

Planning and facilitating tourism

Any country in which tourism plays a prominent role in national income and employment can expect its government to devise policies and plans for the development of tourism. This will include the generation of guidelines and objectives for the growth and management of tourism, both in the short and the long term, and the devising of strategies designed to achieve these objectives. In recent years it has been the policy of the British Government, through the British Tourist Authority, not only to increase the total numbers of tourists visiting Britain but to spread this traffic more evenly through Britain by marketing the off-season months and by encouraging tourists to visit the less familiar regions such as Northumbria. In Spain, since demand has been created for the popular east coast resorts by the private sector, the national tourist office policy has been to promote the less familiar north-west and central regions of the country in advertising aimed directly at the public abroad. Meanwhile, coastal development has become subject to increasing control.

The planning of tourism requires research, first to assess the level of demand or potential demand to the region, and secondly to estimate the resources required in order to cater for that demand and how these resources are best distributed. Demand cannot be generated until an adequate infrastructure and superstructure are available, but it is not enough simply to provide the structures that tourists require. They also need staff to service their needs – hotel workers, travel agents, guides – trained to an acceptable level of performance. Planning therefore implies the provision of training, through hotel, catering and tourism schools, for the skills that the industry requires.

Ease of access to a country or region is, as we have seen, a key factor in the encouragement of tourism, and this depends not only on adequate transport being available but also on the absence of political barriers. If visas are required for entry to a country this will discourage incoming tourism. The degree of difficulty and length of time required to obtain a visa bears a direct relationship to the numbers of tourists visiting that country.

In 1988, the United States finally abandoned the necessity for visas for those arriving from most Western European countries (albeit with some limitations which still hinder the uninterrupted free flow of tourists), having recognised the barrier that such political constraints exercise, at a time when other factors, such as relative exchange rates, favour the rapid expansion of incoming tourism to North America.

The attitude of nationals of the host country to incoming tourists also plays an important role in persuading or dissuading tourists to visit a certain country. Many countries dependent upon tourism have mounted political campaigns aimed at residents, encouraging them to show greater friendliness to foreign tourists. Those residents who most frequently come into contact with tourists, such as customs and immigration officials, shopkeepers and hotel staff, must be trained to be polite and friendly to them. In the past the United States has conducted campaigns to this end directed at customs and immigration officers, and several Caribbean islands have had to mount campaigns to deal with a growing xenophobia among their residents towards foreign tourists.

One difficulty that faces governments in the planning of tourism is the split of responsibility between central and local authorities for issues affecting tourism. In Britain local authorities have direct responsibility for planning permission for all new developments, the provision of parking facilities and a host of other issues directly relevant to the development of tourism projects. Sometimes the views of local authority officials will be at odds with those of the central government. Local authorities, of course, are greatly influenced by the demands and views of local residents, who are often unsympathetic to the expansion of tourism within their area.

The planning and facilitating function of the government may be delegated to the national tourist office of that country and through them to the regional or local tourist bodies, as we shall see shortly.

Financial aid for tourism

Governments also contribute to tourism growth through the provision of financial aid to tourism projects. On a massive scale, the regional development of the Languedoc-Roussillon area in the south of France demonstrates the effective co-operation that can exist between public and private sector investment, with central government providing the funds needed for land acquisition and the basic infrastructure of the region. On a smaller scale, many governments aid the private sector by providing loans at preferential rates of interest, or outright grants, for development schemes which are in keeping with government policy. As an example, a common scheme in operation in several lesser developed countries is for loans to be made on which interest only is paid during the first three or four years, with repayment of capital being postponed until the fourth year or later in order for the project to become viable. Other forms of government aid include subsidies such as tax rebates or relief on operating expenses.

Financial aid for tourist projects comes not only from within a country. International finance is available from a number of sources, particularly for those lesser developed countries where tourism has the potential to make a substantial contribution to the economy. The International Development Association (IDA) – a subsidiary of the World Bank – offers interest free or low rate loans for lesser developed countries, while another Bank subsidiary, the International Bank for Reconstruction and Development (IBRD), offers loans at commercial rates of interest to countries where alternate sources of funding may be difficult or impossible to find.

On a regional scale, within Europe the European Investment Bank (EIB) organises loans (again at commercial rates of interest) of up to £250 000 for smaller companies (normally those employing less than 500 staff). These loans are for up to 50 per cent of fixed asset costs, with repayment terms up to eight years. Interest rates are slightly lower in areas designated 'Assisted Areas' within the EC.

The European Regional Development Fund offers financial assistance (usually up to 30 per cent of the capital costs) for tourism projects generated by public sector bodies in the Assisted Areas. This money can be used not only as pump priming for direct tourist attractions such as museums, but also for infrastructure development supporting tourism, such as airports, or car parking facilities. Northern Ireland in particular has greatly gained from this fund.

Financing available within Great Britain will be dealt with a little later in this chapter.

Social tourism

Reference must also be made here to the government's role in encouraging *social tourism*. This has been defined as the 'furtherance of the economically weak or dependent classes of the population' and is designed to provide aid for low-income families, single parent families, the elderly, handicapped and other deprived minorities in the population. Aid may be offered in the form of finance (grants, low-interest loans or the like) or in direct support through the provision of free coach trips or holiday accommodation. The planned economies of the Soviet bloc have advanced schemes of social tourism, believing that all workers benefit from an annual holiday and as a result will work harder and achieve higher productivity. Workers are helped (and in some cases required) to have a holiday away from their homes at least once a year.

Within Europe, the International Bureau of Social Tourism (BITS), based in Brussels, has been active since 1963 as a base for the study and debate of social tourism, and maintains a databank, issues publications and conducts seminars on the topic. Many European countries have well-established policies of aid for holidays for the handicapped (whether mentally, physically or socially). By contrast, comparatively little support has been shown in Britain for the concept of social tourism. Although many local authorities have budgeted in the past for coach outings for the elderly or other disadvantaged people, cutbacks in recent years have reduced or eradicated most of these facilities. The English Tourist Board in a joint study with the TUC in

Fig 12.2 Downturns in the tourism business seriously affect London's theatres

1975, estimated that some 70 000 people in Britain were then receiving some form of subsidised holiday. (Trade unions often have holiday homes for their members.) Although this report recommended greater public sector spending for the disadvantaged, little has yet been achieved. However, a number of voluntary bodies have developed in recent years to aid or facilitate travel for those with specific impediments (such as the Council for Hearing-impaired Visits and Exchanges, and the British Deaf Tourist Movement). The industry as well has shown an interest in helping the handicapped to take and enjoy their holidays, a notable example being the Holiday Care Service, funded by the tourism industry with the support of the BTA, which provides information on holidays for the handicapped.

Control and supervision in tourism

The state plays an important part in controlling and supervising tourism, as well as faciliating it. This is necessary to restrain undesirable growth, to maintain quality standards, to help match supply and demand

and to protect tourists against industrial malpractice or failure.

A government can act to restrain tourism in a number of ways, whether through central directives or through local authority control. Refusal of planning permission is an obvious example of the exercise of control over tourism development. However, this is seldom totally effective since an area which is a major attraction for tourists will be unlikely to dissuade them from visiting the district simply by, say, refusing planning permission for new hotels; the result may be that overnight visitors are replaced by excursionists or that private bed and breakfast accommodation moves in to fill the gap left by the lack of hotel beds. Cornwall has had control measures on caravan sites in force since 1954 but the local authority has still found it difficult to prevent the growth of unlicensed sites. The option of failing to expand the infrastructure has been taken by some authorities. This can be partially effective, but unfortunately its effects are felt equally by local residents whose frustrations with, say, inadequate road systems may lead to a political backlash.

The price mechanism may also be used to control tourist traffic. This has the added advantage of raising revenue for the government. Selective taxation on hotel accommodation or higher charges for parking can be imposed, but these moves are criticised on the grounds that they are regressive, affecting the less well-off but having little impact on the rich.

Governments will first attempt to control growth by effective marketing, concentrating their publicity on less popular attractions or geographical regions and promoting the off-season. Attempts to do this may be frustrated by private sector promotion. Airlines, for example, will prefer to concentrate on promoting those destinations which attract strong markets. There is always the danger, too, that if the public sector strategy *is* successful, the amenities and attractions at the more popular sites may suffer a serious downturn in business. London has been the great Mecca for the majority of overseas visitors to Britain, but on occasions has experienced downturns in business which have seriously affected the theatres, taxis and other amenities which are heavily dependent upon tourist support. Due to the cost of living in London, hotel accommodation there has tended to move up-market, since the high cost of building and running a hotel can only be viable when high room charges are levied. The result has been a serious dearth of good quality, modern, budget-priced hotels for price-conscious tourists. Some tourist experts have called for a new, Government-sponsored initiative, similar to the 1969 Act, to pump more public funds into the hotel industry, in effect subsidising the capital costs in order to retain this important sector of the tourist market.

To some extent, planning for the more extensive use of existing facilities can delay the need to *de-market* certain attractions or destinations, but it has to be recognised that some tourist destinations are the victims of their own success. As an extreme form of control, limiting or denying access to tourists may become necessary. This can be imposed by a visa system, by some form of rationing or by a total ban on tourist access. In areas where tourist traffic has reached saturation point, it is now common in England to find *park and ride* schemes in force, requiring visitors to leave their cars and proceed into the centre by public transport. The prehistoric cave paintings at Lascaux in France have been so damaged by the effect of countless visitors' breath changing the climate of the caves that the French government has been obliged to introduce a total ban on entry. However an artificial replica of the site has been built and has attracted many visitors.

Sometimes governments will exercise control over tourism flows for economic reasons. As we saw in Chapter 1, governments may attempt to protect their balance of payments by imposing currency restrictions or banning the export of foreign currency in an attempt to reduce the numbers of tourists travelling abroad. The last significant control of this kind in Britain occurred in 1966 when the imposition of a £50 travel allowance severely curtailed foreign travel – although, curiously enough, it proved a boon to some package tour operators who responded to the challenge by creatively packaging tours which maximised value within the scope of the allowance. Nearly 18 per cent more British visitors travelled to the USA in 1967 than in the previous year.

No control over the export of currency from Britain is now exercised, but there have been recent examples of other tourist-generating countries imposing currency restrictions on their residents travelling abroad in an attempt to reduce balance of payments deficits. Notably, France has made several attempts throughout the 1980s to do so, with stringent controls between March and December 1983, when a maximum of Fr 2000 could be taken abroad on any one trip, and credit cards could not be used abroad. France has since progressively relaxed controls (the allowance at the time of writing stands at Fr 50 000 per trip), but there is little evidence to suggest that controls were particularly effective in solving the country's deficit problem. However, the controls did have the side effect of switching travel patterns in favour of French possessions overseas, such as Martinique and Réunion.

Supervision and control is also exercised over the various sectors of the tourism industry. As we have seen in earlier chapters, the need to ensure passenger safety has led not only to licensing of airlines and other forms of public transport but also of tour operators themselves through the ATOL. The government's introduction of the Air Travel Reserve Fund (now the Air Travel Trust) between 1975 and 1977 was designed to protect consumers against the collapse of package holiday companies, the government of the day taking the view that existing bonding safeguards operated by ABTA were insufficient in themselves. There have been occasional calls since on the Air Travel Trust funds, to cope with the collapse of travel firms, but the fund is at a level where it is not considered necessary to impose a topping-up levy. In many countries (although not yet in the UK) travel agencies are licensed to ensure that customers receive professional service as well as to protect them against the collapse of the company. Tourist guides may also be required to have a government licence in order to operate, as in France.

Perhaps the most common form of government supervision of the tourism industry in all countries is in the hotel industry, where compulsory registration and grading is imposed in many countries. Camping and caravan sites are similarly subject to government inspection to ensure consistent standards and acceptable minimum operating requirements.

THE ORGANISATION OF PUBLIC SECTOR TOURISM

For the most part, government policies and objectives for tourism are defined and implemented through national tourist boards (although in many cases other bodies directly concerned with recreation or environmental planning will also have a hand in the development of tourism). The functional responsibilities of a national board are likely to include all or most of the following.

(*a*) *Planning and control functions:*
    (*i*)   product research and planning for tourism plant or facilities;
    (*ii*) protection or restoration of tourism assets;
    (*iii*) manpower planning and training;
    (*iv*) licensing and supervision of sectors of the tourism industry;
    (*v*) implementation of pricing or other regulations affecting tourism.
(*b*) *Marketing functions:*
    (*i*)   representing the nation as a tourism destination;
    (*ii*) undertaking market research and forecasting studies;
    (*iii*) producing and distributing tourism literature;
    (*iv*) providing and staffing tourism information centres;
    (*v*) advertising, sales promotion and public relations activities directed at home and overseas markets.

(c) *Financial functions:*
   (i)   advising industry on capital development;
   (ii) directing, approving and controlling programmes of government aid for tourist projects.
(d) *Co-ordinating functions:*
   (i)   linking with trade or professional bodies, government and regional or local tourist organisations;
   (ii) undertaking co-ordinated marketing activities with private tourist enterprises;
   (iii) organising 'workshops' or similar opportunities for buyers and sellers of travel and tourism to meet and do business.

Some of these activities may be delegated to regional tourist offices, with the national board co-ordinating or overseeing activities.

PUBLIC SECTOR TOURISM IN BRITAIN

Britain has long been in the forefront of international tourism, both as a destination and as a generating country. However, before 1969 governments had largely ignored tourism in their policy-making. Forty years earlier the government of the day had provided the first finance for tourism marketing in funding (£5000) the Travel Association of Great Britain and Northern Ireland, with the aim of encouraging travel to Britain from overseas. During the inter-war years this evolved into the British Travel Association, who were given the responsibility for promoting holidays in Britain domestically as well as abroad. No clear policies were laid down for its activities, however, and its powers were severely limited.

Voluntary tourist boards were established in Scotland in 1930, and in Wales in 1948, the same year in which a board was first established in Northern Ireland. It was to be more than 20 years, however, before a co-ordinated framework for public sector tourism was to be established in the United Kingdom as a whole.

The Development of Tourism Act

By the late 1960s, following the rapid growth in popularity of Britain as a tourist destination in the 1950s and 1960s, it was clear that a new framework for tourism was needed. This was manifested in the Development of Tourism Act 1969, the first statutory legislation in the country specifically concerned with tourism.

The Act, in three parts, dealt with the organisation of public sector tourism, with the provision of financial assistance for much-needed hotel development, and also provided for a system of compulsory registration of tourist accommodation. The last part of the Act, which was designed to include rights of inspection by

government officials, has never been fully implemented although the compulsory display of prices has since been introduced. The industry has preferred to follow a system of voluntary classification and grading of tourist accommodation, with mixed success; however, the implementation of the first two parts of the Act were to have far-reaching consequences for tourism in the country.

That part of the Act dealing with financial assistance for the hotel industry was designed in short term to improve the stock and quality of hotel bedrooms in order to meet changing demand and overcome scarcity. Grants and loans, administered by the three new national tourist boards, were to be made available for hotel construction and improvement until 1973 (during which time some 55 000 bedrooms were added to the stock). Unfortunately, because the Act failed to specify the location in which new hotels were to be built, much of the increased stock was located in London, leading to temporary over-capacity in the city while areas where hotel construction was seen as a greater risk, such as Scotland and the north of England, did not benefit to anything like the extent necessary.

The first part of the Act called for the establishment of four national boards to become responsible for tourism and defined the structure and responsibilities of each of these. At the apex, the British Tourist Authority, to replace the old British Travel Association, was to be the sole body responsible overseas for the marketing of tourism to Britain and would also advise ministers on tourism matters in general. Tourism issues that concerned Britain as a whole were to be dealt with by the BTA while three further boards – the English Tourist Board, Scottish Tourist Board and Wales Tourist Board – were to become concerned with tourism development within their own regions and for the marketing of those regions within the UK. Scotland was later given the freedom to undertake overseas marketing itself, under the terms of the Tourism (Overseas Promotion) (Scotland) Act, 1984. Both the British Tourism Authority and the English Tourist Board were to be responsible to the Board of Trade (now the Department of Trade and Industry), while the Scottish and Wales Tourist Boards were responsible to their respective Secretaries of State. After 1985, the BTA and ETB became responsible to the Department of Employment, indicating the significance attached by the Government to tourism as a factor in economic recovery, particularly in the inner cities. At the same time, a number of services common to the BTA and ETB were merged, in a cost-cutting exercise designed to improve efficiency.

All four bodies, funded by central government, were empowered to provide financial assistance for tourism projects.

In addition to this national structure set up by the Act, other British territories have independently approved legislation governing public sector tourism organisation, and the four British boards act alongside the Northern Ireland Tourist Board, the Isle of Man Tourist Board and the States of Jersey and Guernsey Tourist Committees.

The Act made no provision for a statutory regional public sector structure for tourism. Before the Act some attempt had been made to establish regional tourist associations, these being more advanced in Scotland and Wales than in England. However, following the formation of the three national boards each set about creating its own regional tourism structure. The result was the establishment of twelve regional tourist boards in England funded by the ETB, the local authorities and private contributions. Wales has formed three tourism councils organised along lines similar to the English regional bodies. In Scotland, area tourism promotion was formerly the responsibility of the eight regional councils, with one separate voluntary association (Dumfries and Galloway) and with tourism in the Highlands and Islands the responsibility of the statutory development board for that region. The latter Board subsequently established fifteen area tourist boards within its jurisdiction.

Under the terms of the Local Government and Planning (Scotland) Act 1982, the District Councils in Scotland were empowered to set up area tourist boards which would become responsible for marketing tourism and running the tourist information centres. The Highlands and Islands scheme has been used as a model for the extension of the scheme throughout Scotland and the new boards have been established as a co-partnership between the Scottish Tourist Board, one or more district councils and the tourist trade, with finance provided by grant aid and private contributions. Thirty-two Area Tourist Boards are now in operation in Scotland, but in three areas (Edinburgh, Kirkcaldy and Moray) the District Councils have exercised their option to retain local authority responsibility for tourism in their regions. Seven Districts are not participating in the restructuring of tourism.

The structure of public sector tourism bodies appears in Fig 12.3 and the regional distribution of tourist boards is illustrated in Fig 12.4 (a) (England and Wales) and Fig 12.4 (b) (Scotland).

Public bodies and tourism

The new structure of public sector tourism in Britain has helped to effect great improvements in the planning and co-ordination of tourism, accompanied gradually by more clearcut policies. Nevertheless the diverse nature of tourism and its impact on so many different facets of British life makes cohesive planning difficult. Many public or quasi-public bodies not within the framework of public sector tourism still exert considerable influence in tourism development. The water authorities are a case in point, since water-based recreation plays an important part in leisure and tourism planning; it is interesting to see the attention that tourism was given in the planning and development of the Kielder reservoir in Northumbria compared with the lack of foresight in the planning of earlier reservoirs. With the privatisation of the water companies in Britain, it can be anticipated that fuller use of reservoirs and other bodies of water will be made for leisure purposes, to maximise the commercial opportunities these present. The Countryside Commission, the Forestry Commission, the Nature Conservancy Council, the Arts Council, Sports Council, and the National Trust all have significant roles to play in planning for leisure activities in Britain, whether for residents or tourists.

At government level, too, many different spheres of government activity overlap tourist interest. While the Department of Employment has responsibility for the functions of the BTA and ETB, the Department of the Environment continues to take an interest in many issues related to tourism, such as heritage sites, the inner city environment, and the funding of bodies like English Heritage and the Countryside Commission. The Department of Transport, in addition to its transport responsibilities which impinge on tourism development and planning, also has responsibilities for certain signposting, a critical factor in the promotion of tourism. The Home Office's responsibilities in areas such as liquor licensing and Sunday trading also affect tourism development, while the Treasury has overall control of funding in the public sector. The Scottish, Welsh and Northern Ireland offices all exercise overall responsibility for tourism within their own regions, while the Ministry of Agriculture has played a role in aiding the development of farm tourism. Effective co-ordination between these bodies for the overall planning of tourism development is still lacking.

In 1985, the House of Commons Trade and Industry Committee submitted a report proposing radical changes to the structure of public sector tourism in Britain. Their recommendations included:

(a) the abolition of the four national boards and the establishment of a British Tourist Board, with overall responsibility for tourism development in England, Scotland and Wales.

(b) the creation of promotional boards in the three regions, who would undertake the domestic marketing of their regions.

(c) retention of the Regional Tourist Boards, with Northern Ireland becoming a Regional Board.

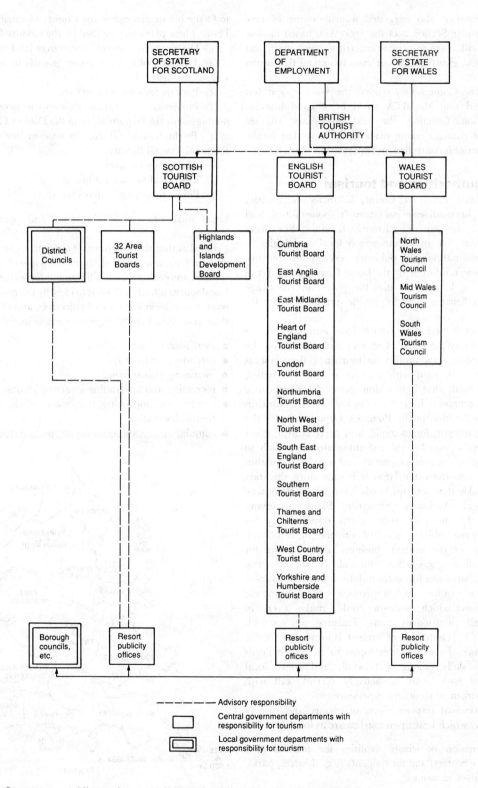

Fig12.3 Structures and lines of responsibility of public sector tourism in Britain

The Committee also suggested a programme of new funding under Section 4 of the 1969 Act, based on low cost, low risk loans to private enterprise companies, and Government grants for labour costs to extend the tourist season.

Since the Committee's report, the Government has also hinted that the BTA could be a candidate for privatisation. Certainly the next few years will see significant changes taking place in the way that public sector tourism is controlled and operated in the UK.

Local authorities and tourism

At local authority level, County Councils and District Councils have diverse statutory responsibilities and interests in the provision of tourist facilities. The Local Government Act 1948 empowered local authorities to set up information and publicity services for tourism, and this was reinforced by the Local Government Act of 1972, giving local authorities the power to encourage visitors to their area and to provide suitable facilities for them.

The organisation of tourism at local authority level is often curiously piecemeal. Counties and districts on the whole relegate responsibility for tourism to departments which are concerned with a range of other activities, with the result that it is seldom given the significance which its economic impact on the area merits. Tourism may be a function of the Planning Department, or the County Surveyor, for example, and there is little effort to develop a co-ordinated and integrated approach to tourism provision, development and marketing within the area – to the extent that it is only since the start of the 1980s that tourism needs have found their way into Local Authority Structure Plans in many counties. In the past, those given responsibility for tourism were seldom recruited on the basis of any knowledge of the tourism business, and training for tourism officers was often minimal. In the last few years, this situation has substantially improved, as local authorities came to appreciate the economic contribution which tourism could make even in traditionally non-tourist areas. Training courses such as COTICC (Certificate of Tourist Information Centre Competence) have been developed to cover the needs for basic skills among TIC staff, and some local authorities have come to actively recruit staff with formal tourism education or experience.

The principal responsibilities of county and district authorities which bear upon tourism are as follows:

(a) Provision of leisure facilities for tourists (e.g. conference centres) and for residents (e.g. theatres, parks, sports centres, museums).

(b) Planning (under town and country planning policies). (Note that District Councils produce local plans to fit the broad strategy of the County Council Structure Plans. These plans are certified by the County Council.)

(c) Development control powers over land use.

(d) Provision of visitor services (usually in conjunction with tourist bodies).

(e) Parking for coaches and cars.

(f) Provision of caravan sites (with licensing and management the responsibility of the District Councils).

(g) Production of statistics on tourism (for use by the Regional Tourist Boards).

(h) Marketing the area.

(i) Upkeep of historic buildings.

(j) Public health and safety control.

Local authorities may also own and operate local airports.

Local authorities who have set out actively to encourage tourism have a number of objectives, some of which may conflict, and each of which will compete for scarce resources. Local tourist officers will need to identify the resources they require to achieve their stated objectives, and to determine their priorities. Typical objectives might include:

- increasing visitor numbers
- extending visitor stays
- increasing visitor spend
- increasing and up-grading local attractions
- creating or improving the image of the area as a tourist destination
- stimulating private sector involvement in tourism

Fig 12.4 (a) Regional tourist board areas in England and Wales

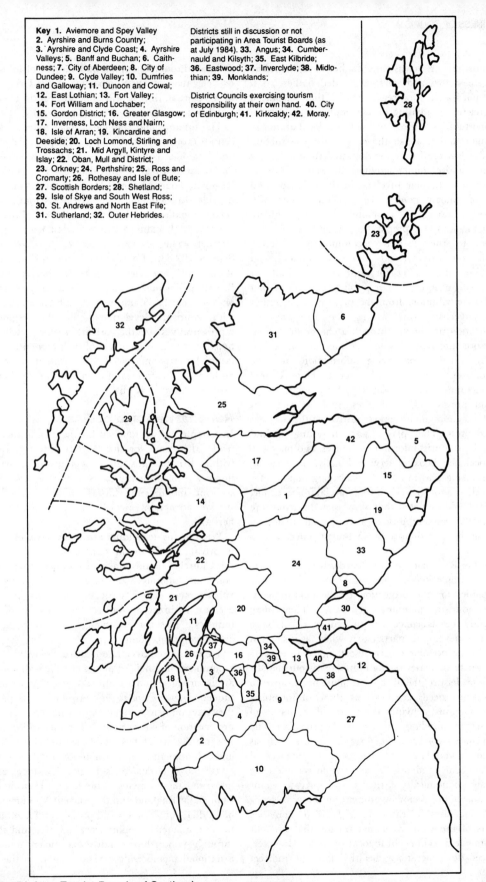

Key 1. Aviemore and Spey Valley 2. Ayrshire and Burns Country; 3. Ayrshire and Clyde Coast; 4. Ayrshire Valleys; 5. Banff and Buchan; 6. Caithness; 7. City of Aberdeen; 8. City of Dundee; 9. Clyde Valley; 10. Dumfries and Galloway; 11. Dunoon and Cowal; 12. East Lothian; 13. Fort Valley; 14. Fort William and Lochaber; 15. Gordon District; 16. Greater Glasgow; 17. Inverness, Loch Ness and Nairn; 18. Isle of Arran; 19. Kincardine and Deeside; 20. Loch Lomond, Stirling and Trossachs; 21. Mid Argyll, Kintyre and Islay; 22. Oban, Mull and District; 23. Orkney; 24. Perthshire; 25. Ross and Cromarty; 26. Rothesay and Isle of Bute; 27. Scottish Borders; 28. Shetland; 29. Isle of Skye and South West Ross; 30. St. Andrews and North East Fife; 31. Sutherland; 32. Outer Hebrides.

Districts still in discussion or not participating in Area Tourist Boards (as at July 1984). 33. Angus; 34. Cumbernauld and Kilsyth; 35. East Kilbride; 36. Eastwood; 37. Inverclyde; 38. Midlothian; 39. Monklands;

District Councils exercising tourism responsibility at their own hand. 40. City of Edinburgh; 41. Kirkcaldy; 42. Moray.

Fig 12.4 (b) Area Tourist Boards of Scotland

Local tourist officers act as catalysts between the public and private sectors and voluntary aided bodies. As a focus for tourism in the area or resort, they become a point of reference, advising on development and grant-aided opportunities. Officers will help the local authority to determine and establish the necessary infrastructure which will allow tourism to develop, and they will carry out research and planning activities themselves. In some areas, they may become involved in the provision and training of tourist guides. In addition, they will undertake a range of promotional and publicity functions, including the preparation of publications such as guides to the district, accommodation guides, information on current events and entertainment, and specialist brochures listing, for example, local walks or pubs. The cost of most of these publications will be met in part by contributions from the private sector, either through advertising or, as in the case of the accommodation brochures, through a charge for listing. Many resorts also now produce a trade manual, aimed at the travel trade and giving information on trade prices, conference facilities and coach parking. Tourist officers organise familiarisation trips for the UK travel trade and press, and, if the resort shows sufficient potential, they may invite representatives of the overseas trade and press. They play a part in setting up and operating local tourist information centres, and may also offer a local bed booking service. Finally, on occasion they even take a part in actively packaging holidays for clients, such as activity weekends or special interest short breaks. It should be noted that all of these functions are frequently the responsibility of a very small team, on occasion no greater than a single tourist officer and a secretary.

Unlike the Regional Tourist Boards, whose aims are essentially promotional, the local authorities bear responsibilities for the protection of the environment, and for tourism planning generally. They may consequently be as concerned to reduce or stabilise tourism as to develop it (particularly when, as is so often the case in the popular tourist resorts, local ratepayers are opposed to increases in the numbers of tourists). In providing for leisure, the authorities must be sensitive to local residents' needs as much as those of incoming tourists. They must convince ratepayers of the merits of public sector funding for tourist projects. The development of conference centres in resorts such as Bournemouth and Harrogate has been a controversial issue with local residents, since very few conference centres are economically attractive for private sector funding, and public sector investment on this scale leads to heavy increases in rates. It is hard to convince ratepayers of the wisdom of investments that are not seen to provide direct benefit to local residents. However, conferences do generate a healthy flow of indirect revenue through shopping and the use of local facilities by delegates and the importance of this form of tourism to a resort is that it will generate tourism outside the usual holiday season.

The funding and staffing of local tourist information centres is often the joint responsibility of local authorities and Regional Tourist Boards (RTB), while the material for these centres is provided by the National and Regional Tourist Boards. Many of these local TICs also provide a booking service for tourists seeking accommodation in the area and they also manage a scheme for booking accommodation from one TIC to another. This is known as the Book-A-Bed-Ahead Scheme (BABA). Local authorities contribute directly to RTB funds, and clearly expect to play a part in the Board's policy making; they will normally be represented on the Board's committees or sub-committees dealing with tourism development in the region. Since representatives of the private sector, such as local hoteliers, are also members of such committees, and the latter's interests may well differ from those of the local authorities, this can lead to conflicts in the policy-making process within the RTBs.

National heritage bodies

In Chapter 1, we touched on the significance of man-made attractions for the tourism industry. In tourism within Britain, this form of tourism is particularly important, as so many overseas tourists visit Britain to see our monuments, historic homes, cathedrals and similar attractions, which are part of our national heritage.

While many individual attractions are, of course, still in private hands, or the responsibility of bodies such as the Church Commissioners, a number of semi-public or voluntary organisations exist for the protection and enhancement of our heritage attractions, and therefore exercise a direct or indirect influence in the tourism industry. The role of these bodies can be usefully examined at this point.

There are well over 12 000 listed ('scheduled') ancient monuments in England alone, of which about a quarter are in private hands. Until recently, major sites such as Stonehenge were under the control of the Department of the Environment, but the growing concern with the preservation of our heritage led to the National Heritage Act in 1983, which has established the Historic Buildings and Monuments Commission for England. This new body, known familiarly as 'English Heritage', and which integrates the functions of the former Historic Buildings Council for England and the Ancient Monuments Board, has a dual conservation and promotion function. It seeks to raise financial support from industry and the public through sponsorship of individual ancient buildings and a national membership scheme similar to the National

Fig 12.5   Stonehenge

Trust. Emphasis is placed on interpretation and visitor management, with Stonehenge designated the first site receiving attention. Initial funding is largely by central government. There is an equivalent organisation, Cadw, in Wales, with similar responsibilities for heritage sites.

Aside from this new organisation, there are a number of bodies with an interest in the protection of British heritage sites. One of the earliest to be founded was the Society for the Protection of Ancient Buildings, which dates back to 1877. Other important bodies include the Ancient Monuments Society, the Georgian Group, The Victorian Society, the National Piers Society and SAVE Britain's Heritage. To these we must add a number of diverse trusts with an interest in the protection of sites of touristic appeal, among which are the Civic Trust, the Landmark Trust, the Pilgrim Trust, the Monument Trust and many others (over one thousand local amenity societies are known to exist in England.) The proliferation of these conservation bodies reflects the changing attitudes towards our architectural heritage.

The new tourism

Success in preserving our industrial heritage is evidenced in such sites as Ironbridge. Few would have believed, a few years ago, that vast numbers of tourists could be attracted to the former 'dark, Satanic mills' of eighteenth and nineteenth century Britain. The success of sites like Coalbrookdale and Blists Mill can be ascribed to a combination of nostalgia for a lost past with which many can still identify, and a growing awareness of our historical heritage in all its forms. It took the public sector to recognise the potential for tourism of this new kind which could be generated in Britain's decaying inner cities; the tourist boards, in partnership with local authorities and private enterprise, successfully established such unlikely places as Bradford ('A Surprising Place'), Glasgow ('Glasgow's Miles Better') and Liverpool's Merseyside ('Full of Magic Memories') as worthy of a

visit and, even better, an overnight stay. The resurrection of Liverpool's Albert Dock has included a new wing of London's Tate Gallery to make it a place of pilgrimage for the culture seeker, and living history museums have been created at Beamish in Northumbria and Quarry Bank Mill, a former cotton mill at Styal, Cheshire.

Not only the inner cities, but derelict waterfront sites, have lent themselves to careful and tasteful restoration to create residential and leisure complexes which also attract tourism. The way in which government policy has shifted from support for traditional tourism towards the encouragement of new forms of tourism in the economically depressed areas is among the most interesting fields of study for the tourism specialist, since it opens up the concept of what we understand tourism to be, and provides almost unlimited new opportunities to generate it.

The origins of this new policy can be traced to public sector policy to establish 'Tourism Growth Points' in the early 1970s, following a review of tourism policy. Areas like the Bude–Wadebridge area of Cornwall were identified as regions for planned tourism growth. While the growth points programme enjoyed mixed success, the development grants it attracted were later directed into Tourism Development Action Plans (TDAP), generally linked to inner cities; Bristol's floating harbour became the first of many such schemes to receive TDAP finance to help resurrect its decaying waterfront areas. The success of similar efforts at restoration in the United States, particularly in Baltimore, San Francisco and Boston, has spurred such programmes in Britain.

The TDAP is a phased programme of planned redevelopment, usually over a period of one to three years, undertaken as a co-operative venture between the English Tourist Board and local authorities.

The 'pump priming' funds which are invested in the schemes by the public sector are designed to act as a spur to additional private investment in the area; small tourist enterprises such as speciality retail shops, excursion boats and eating places are attracted to the site, which then generates its own momentum to become a focal point for the city as an area for leisure and recreation.

Tourism can benefit from the terms of Urban Regeneration Grants, designed to restore life to the decaying inner cities. Where the value of a completed project may be less than the initial cost for its development, government grants can be made available to bridge the gap, making the project possible where a feasibility study might indicate a purely private venture would be uneconomic.

It has been but a short step to the recognition that modern industry, too, offers scope for tourist enterprise. The initiative owes much to British Nuclear Fuels, which opened their Sellafield (formerly Windscale)

Fig 12.6 Glasgow's successful marketing strategy
(*Courtesy Glasgow District Council*)

processing plant to visitors in order to assuage public concern about nuclear energy safety. The success of this venture (more than 100 000 were attracted in the first year) led to the Government holding discussions with the CBI (Confederation of British Industry) with a view to opening factories to tourists, to allow them to observe the processes of manufacture of British products. The public relations value of this exercise has appealed to many firms; Ford Motors has opened its plant, and interest has been expressed by Jaguar Motors and other leading businesses.

The Thames Barrier at Woolwich was recognised as having tourist potential even while under construction,

Fig 12.8 The Sellafield Visitors' Centre opened in June 1988 by His Royal Highness The Prince Philip, Duke of Edinburgh
(*Courtesy British Nuclear Fuels plc*)

Fig 12.7 Fisherman's Wharf, San Francisco

and plans for tourist visits were incorporated into the operating programme.

Authorities in Cheshire have drawn up plans for visits to such 'attractions' as power stations and fire stations, under the 'Insight into Industry' banner. Such initiatives are expected to show considerable growth in the next few years.

Our recent history has also been successfully exploited for tourism, with the public opening in 1984 of Churchill's War Cabinet rooms below the streets of Whitehall, dating to World War II. Such schemes pay tribute to the astuteness of the public sector in recognising and developing the tourism potential of sites in its charge.

Town twinning and tourism

A further boost has been given to international tourism, particularly within Europe, by the town twinning movement. The concept of town twinning developed largely in the aftermath of World War II as a means of forging greater understanding between communities in different countries. Usually the selection of a twin town is based on some common characteristics such as population size, geographical features or commercial similarities. Local authorities and chambers of commerce arrange for the exchange of visits by residents of the twinned towns. Although conceived as a gesture of friendship and goodwill, the outcome has commercial implications for tourism as an increasing number of visitors flows between the two towns. While accommodation is normally provided in private homes, expenditure on transport, shopping and sightseeing can make a significant impact on the inflow of tourist revenue for the towns concerned. Friendships formed through such links result in subsequent independent travel by residents. No accurate studies have yet been made of the financial contribution of such movements to the tourism account.

FUNCTIONS OF THE TOURIST BOARDS

The British Tourist Authority

As we have seen the Development of Tourism Act empowered the BTA to promote tourism to Britain in overseas countries. With the agreement of the respective territories they will also undertake foreign promotion on behalf of the tourist boards of Northern Ireland, the Isle of Man and the Channel Islands. With general responsibility for tourism throughout Great Britain, they act as advisers to the government on tourism issues, and are financed by an annual grant-in-aid from the government channelled through the Department of Employment.

Stated objectives of the BTA marketing policy include extending the tourist season in Britain, promoting areas of high unemployment which can demonstrate tourist potential, and seeking to develop new markets and market segments for tourism to Britain. This has included, in recent years, a focus on business travel and 'adjustment' of established markets. Thus, the fall-off of the US market, which provides the main source of Britain's overseas visitors, will cause the Authority to concentrate on selling the country harder in the USA while seeking to develop alternative markets, such as those within Europe which show promise of substantial growth.

With a staff of nearly 500, the BTA carries out research, liaises with other national tourism bodies in the UK, and, through its overseas offices, encourages organisations abroad to promote tourism to Britain. A notable example of their work entails the mounting of 'travel workshops' which bring together the buyers and sellers of travel services. These workshops, first introduced by the BTA's predecessors in 1966, are held in Britain and in major centres of population in tourism generating countries. They enable coach companies, hotel chains and consortia, tour operators and similar organisations to negotiate face-to-face with foreign tourist organisations who have the responsibility for bringing tourists to Britain. Recent workshops include:

- a European coach and tour operators' workshop
- a youth and special interest travel workshop
- an English language schools workshop

Abroad, the BTA provides an information service through 26 overseas offices throughout the world. They offer marketing advice to UK companies eager to tap foreign markets and will circulate overseas agents and buyers with details of new tour packages to or within the UK. In the past they have also given financial support to commercial enterprises trying to break into overseas markets, providing that these projects meet the Board's own objectives, e.g. helping to generate off-season sales.

At home in London the BTA has a Central Information Department, a tourist information library and a research library available to subscribers. The Authority publishes a large selection of promotional literature in English and major foreign languages, including the well-known publication *In Britain*. Other material includes travel guides, maps, public relations material for the mass media and shell folders for the use of overseas tour operators. Their film and photographic library will also lend out slides and photos for use in tour operators' brochures. The BTA were also instrumental in setting up the British Travel Centre in London for incoming independent travellers. Finally, the Authority can arrange to distribute brochures commercially on behalf of travel companies in the UK.

The English, Wales and Scottish Tourist Boards

The example given here is that of the English Tourist Board, but the other two boards operate along similar lines.

Under the 1969 Act the ETB was given the brief to attract tourists from other parts of Britain and to encourage the growth of domestic tourism within England. The Board also has the responsibility to encourage the provision and improvement of tourism plant in England by advice and, where appropriate, by financial assistance. Until 1982 such financial aid was to be made available only within Economic Development Areas, but government policy has now changed to allow the boards wider scope and assistance can now be offered for the first time in the south of England where seaside resorts in particular are facing strong competition from overseas resorts for a share of the British holiday market.

Like the BTA, the ETB is financed by a grant-in-aid from central government, administered by the Department of Employment (in the case of the Wales and Scottish Tourist Boards, the Welsh and Scottish Offices are responsible for the distribution of these funds). While this funding is still discrete, recent policy has been to integrate wherever possible the offices and administration of the BTA and ETB to avoid duplication and to improve efficiency. In addition to the grant-in-aid, the Department of Employment also provided the Boards with funds to disburse for project development. In 1988, the ETB received a total of £25.7 million, of which more than half was earmarked for development funds.

The grant-in-aid covers the expenditure of the central services of the ETB, and also helps to fund the more than 400 tourist information centres (TICs) in England which are operated in conjunction with the Regional Tourist Boards and, in some cases, the local authorities.

The Board's development service plays an important role as go-between in generating new tourism projects in England. As well as offering advice to local authorities, the Regional Boards and the private sector, it has directly aided the financing of suitable new projects, and facilitated access to tourism investors. It also acts as an agent of the European Investment Bank, which provides medium-term loans for projects in the designated Assisted Areas. The Board offers its services on a consultancy basis, and will aid companies undertaking feasibility studies or seeking planning approval through local authorities (although commercial fees will be charged for such services).

Direct financial aid for tourism projects was first introduced by the Government in 1971. This took the form of loans or, more commonly, grant aid. Initially, funds were restricted to the officially designated 'assisted areas', but since 1982, aid has been available to any project identified as being in an 'area of tourism need'.

There is considerable competition for grant aid, and the Board laid down strict guidelines which typically included the following criteria:

(a) Capital expenditure must be involved.

(b) Approval for aid must be obtained before any work starts on the project.

(c) The project should create employment, and attract more tourists from abroad and from within the UK, while at the same time increasing tourist expenditure.

(d) Facilities to be aided must be accessible to all members of the public.

(e) There must be evidence that the project actually needs tourist board support to get launched.

Aid was typically between 25–30 per cent of the total capital cost of the project, but at no time exceeded 49 per cent. While the ETB relied on the screening process of the regional boards to select suitable applicants, it was keen to support the improvement of existing facilities such as farmhouse accommodation, the addition of bathrooms or central heating to hotels, and similar schemes which would help to extend the tourist season. Museums and art galleries, theatres, wildlife sanctuaries and similar schemes stood good prospects of being approved because they were often unlikely to be economically viable without grant aid of this kind. The Board was also keen to aid support services such as information centres, signposting and car park provision, and recently introduced two new development funds: an innovation fund to back key projects such as year-round holiday villages, marinas, conference facilities and indoor resorts; and a 'small business' fund to help support projects costing in total less than £100 000. However, at the beginning of 1989, development grants for the ETB were frozen (although at the time of writing they continue to be available to the Wales and Scottish Boards).

On the marketing side, the ETB produces its own publications for the trade and public, and engages in promotional activities such as the successful 'Maritime England' theme launched in 1982, national floral schemes, and the 1985 'England Entertains' theme which highlighted the role in tourism played by theatres, concerts and similar attractions. The marketing policy of the Board is directed to spreading the benefits of tourism regionally and extending the tourist season; to raising the standards of the facilities provided for tourists; and to balancing the supply and demand for tourism. The TICs have come to play a greater part in activating reservations, as well as advising on and recommending accommodation. Local bed-booking services have been introduced, enabling visitors to effect reservations at the TICs on payment of a fee or a deposit, while the Book-a-Bed-Ahead (BABA) scheme offers a reservations network for accommodation throughout the country. Co-operation between members of the British Resorts Association

(BRA) and ABTA, supported by the Board, has enabled tourists to make reservations in main generating areas like Leicester and Manchester for accommodation in a number of key seaside resorts, and there are on-going efforts to persuade the travel trade to play a larger role in booking domestic packages. The ETB's policy remains one of identifying and helping to fill any gaps in marketing England as a destination. One means of achieving this has been the ETB's own workshops, known as MOOT (the Scottish Board's Tradefair and Wales Tourist Board's Travelpact have a similar role). The ETB also markets direct to the public through a brochure of organisers' packages brought together under the 'Holiday England' banner.

Information technology initiatives in the public sector

Public sector tourism interests have not been slow to take advantage of the computerised information revolution. At a macro level, the BTA and ETB are together working on the development of a computerised tourism database, TRIPS, part of a five year programme initiated in 1987. UK destination information is also available to travel agents worldwide via British Airways' BABS computer reservations system, while a still more ambitious scheme under development at BTA, known as Access UK, is investigating the potential for a world-wide travel industry-owned commercial computer system which will carry information to the trade on both public and private sector travel products.

At the local level, local authorities and the Regional Tourist Boards have also developed tourism databases and CRSs. The TIC at Bournemouth became the first in Europe to offer a CRS, with its RITA bureau system, allowing reservations to be made through the TIC computer at hotels in the district. The extension of the scheme to other parts of the country has been slow, due in part to the reluctance of the more traditional resorts to become involved in CRSs. However, another initiative inspired by the public sector resulted in a centralised booking system for ten English and Welsh seaside resorts, known as WAVES, control of which has since passed to the private sector.

Few can doubt that the CRS will become common for domestic hotel bookings within the space of the next few years, just as they are today for inclusive tour arrangements. There are present plans for some local authorities, acting as co-ordinators, to allocate rooms within their districts to tour operators for package tour arrangements. Such a centrally controlled allocation of hotel rooms will enable hoteliers to reduce their individual commitments to tour operators, and therefore minimise wastage in the reservations process.

Perhaps one of the more noticeable features of the advance in information technology development within the public sector has been the emergence of Electronic Marketing Units (EMUs) at TICs. These are databases accessible to passers-by outside the TICs, and therefore their use is not limited to the opening times of the TICs themselves. Although the range of information available through these units is still limited, it is expanding fast, and is already equipped to provide the basis for interactive communication between tourists and tourist facilities, which would allow visitors to make reservations for hotels, theatres, and a host of other amenities.

THE REGIONAL TOURIST BOARDS

While the example given here refers to the operation of the 12 Regional Tourist Boards established by the ETB in England, the Area Tourist Boards in Scotland and the three Tourism Councils in Wales operate in a similar fashion. All are financed by their respective National Tourist Boards, with additional funding from local authorities and the commercial sector, although the level of private funding has seldom reached targets originally envisaged by the National Boards.

The objectives of the Regional Tourist Boards are:

(a) to produce a co-ordinated strategy for tourism within their regions in liaison with the local authority;

(b) to represent the interests of the region at national level and the interests of the tourist industry within the region;

(c) to encourage the development of tourist amenities and facilities which meet the changing needs of the market;

(d) to market the region by providing reception and information services (in concert with the ETB), producing and supplying suitable literature and undertaking miscellaneous promotional activities.

Typically, an RTB will work with a very small staff of perhaps ten to fifteen members (an important exception to this guideline is the London Tourist Board which, because of its importance in international tourism and its key information function, will operate with a much larger staff, especially during the summer season). Co-ordination between the RTB, local authorities and the tourist trade will be through policy-making panels, or committees, as exemplified below:

Development panel	Publicity and promotions panel
County Council officers	Resort officers
District Council officers	RTB members
RTB members	Local trade members
Local trade members	

As with the national boards, policies have changed in recent years and now greater emphasis is being laid on commercial activities (such as providing an accommodation booking service for a fee to tourists). Certain of the RTBs have also moved into the field of training by validating tourist guide courses within their regions.

Although the ETB controlled the allocation of funds for financial assistance for tourist projects in England, the task of processing applications was delegated to the regional boards who screened all applications and made their recommendations to the national board. The regional boards have shown themselves to be keen to support smaller tourist ventures which would probably be commercially non-viable without government assistance, e.g. museums, art galleries, theatres, historic buildings, and accommodation facilities in areas where demand is small or the season is short.

The RTBs have a particularly difficult role in their relations with their local authorities. They must work with these authorities and co-operate with them in tourism planning but their aims may be in conflict with those of the local authority, which is often apathetic or negative towards the growth of tourism in their area. Moreover, the local authorities are charged with certain functions which have a direct bearing on tourism, as we have seen. Local authorities can hinder the expansion of tourism by refusing planning permission, although on the other hand they play an important role in preserving the countryside and coastal areas of their regions. Those noted as tourist centres will operate resort publicity bureaux which must co-operate with the RTBs for the successful promotion of their resorts.

Geographically, too, RTB areas are often diverse and cannot be logically promoted as a single destination. The West Country Tourist Board, to take one example, represents counties ranging from Cornwall at its western extremity to Avon on its northern boundary, and parts of west Dorset on its eastern boundary. It is charged with the promotion of all these regions, although Avon County Council makes no financial contribution to the Board's funds, while the promotion of Dorset would arguably be better handled as an integral destination.

To produce a co-ordinated strategy for the promotion of tourism in the face of the diverse interests of the local authorities and the tourist boards is no easy matter.

Co-operative marketing organisations

We have seen how private and public sector interests can differ in tourism, the common lack of co-ordinating tourism policy and the areas of potential conflict which can arise within the public sector. In an attempt to overcome some of the problems arising from this piecemeal approach to tourism development and promotion, several areas have now opted for the formation of a marketing board (or bureau) made up of representatives from both the public and private sector interests. Plymouth was the first city to launch a joint venture of this nature in 1977. The city's marketing bureau is run by six members nominated by the city council, and nine members elected by the private sector. The bureau is financed by a grant-in-aid from the city

council, by membership subscriptions and by commercial activities. Similar ventures have since been established at Chester and Birmingham (Convention and Visitors' Bureau). Bristol briefly introduced a co-operative marketing bureau, but lack of commitment to tourism development by the city council led to its dissolution, following which the marketing of the city as a tourist destination passed to a voluntary organisation funded by the Chamber of Commerce.

The diverse interests of the public and private sector make joint marketing at the local and regional level difficult. However, at national and international levels, good examples can be cited. The BTA itself co-operates in well over 200 joint marketing schemes abroad each year, in association with British and foreign interests in the private sector. The public sector also co-operates to undertake joint overseas promotion, as in the case of that between the BTA and regional tourist organisations. The British Travel Centre in Regent Street, London, is an example of joint funding between the BTA and British Rail.

THE ROLE OF THE EUROPEAN COMMUNITY

Britain has chosen largely to allow the free market economy to operate in the tourism field, with little attempt to centralise policy-making, by contrast with some European Community nations where tourism makes an equally important contribution to the economy. However, as Britain draws closer to the European Community, British travel and tourism interests are increasingly affected by EC legislation. Most importantly, the single Community becomes an economic fact in 1992, when harmonisation will allow unrestricted trade throughout the member nations. British travel firms will be able to compete within the Community on an equal footing and without legal hindrance, and airlines, tour operators and others are already gearing up to prepare for the expansion opportunities this will present. But by the same token, other member nations will have freedom of access to our markets, and British firms can expect a greater measure of competition on their own doorsteps.

As we have seen earlier, harmonisation, which will liberalise air traffic movements and fares in Europe, is to be accompanied by other legislation which is likely to affect travel industry profitability. Notably, tour operators are to be made more responsible to their clients for their suppliers' services, necessitating additional expenditure on quality control and insurance against claims. Almost certainly, with the present low margins on package holidays, this will mean higher package tour prices to compensate. The Community also favours the extension of licensing to travel agencies, Britain being one of the few nations currently allowing agents to trade without any form of government licence. Compulsory licensing is likely to be accompanied by compulsory training to meet the basic standards required for professional practice. Pressure may also lead to the introduction of a common and compulsory grading system for accommodation in Britain. The Commission's policy on open competition is unlikely to endorse ABTA's Operation Stabiliser. This may mean not just open price competition, but a new role for ABTA itself. Finally, we have earlier discussed the likely impact of the Commission's proposals to abandon duty-free shopping between member states. This is expected to substantially increase transport fares between Britain and the Continent, and may lead to some adjustment of demand, as those seeking duty-free opportunities switch their holiday plans to non-EC countries, such as Yugoslavia or Austria.

QUESTIONS AND DISCUSSION POINTS

1 Should Tourist Information Centres be service-orientated or profit-orientated? Can the two objectives co-exist? Discuss the case for and against TICs becoming more commercial in efforts to pay their own way.

2 The US Government in 1988 for the first time waived visa requirements for certain categories of tourists coming from Britain. The initial response was 'disappointing', few of the increasing numbers of British tourists taking advantage of this benefit. Suggest reasons why this may have been the case.

3 Are sources of financial aid for tourism in Britain adequate as they stand? What additional aid needs to be provided to further boost tourism? And why are developers generally reluctant to invest in leisure and tourism enterprises?

4 Discuss the possible consequences for tourism of a change in Government in Britain in the near future. In what ways would tourism benefit or suffer.

ASSIGNMENT TOPICS

1 You have recently been appointed Assistant Tourism Officer in a South Coast resort with a strong traditional market among the C2 D E population. In taking stock of the present patterns of tourism, you are interested in ascertaining whether social tourism plays a significant role in bringing tourists to your resort. As a first step, you need to discover what support social tourism currently has in towns where there are a significant number of deprived or under-privileged people.

Undertake some research within the local authority nearest you with a potential population in this category, to see what their attitudes are towards social tourism, what funds are available, and how support for the concept has changed over recent years. Prepare a short report for your Tourist Officer indicating whether you feel there is any potential in catering for this market.

2 As Tourism Development Officer of a town with tourism potential (decide on a suitable town of your own choice), you have held talks with representatives of your National Tourist Board, who have indicated that there is a possibility of your town benefiting from grant aid under a Tourism Development Action Plan (TDAP).

Draw up a TDAP for the town in preparation for making a bid for grant aid.

13 The impact of tourism

Chapter objectives: After studying this chapter, you should be able to:

- identify and assess tourism's impact on the economy of an area;
- understand the concept of the multiplier and its applications in tourism;
- be aware of the environmental effects of tourism development;
- understand the sociocultural effects created by

mass tourism;
- understand the necessity for planning in tourism and be aware of current moves to conserve the environment;
- analyse the likely effects of change on the future of tourism.

This final chapter will examine the consequences of tourism for an environment and for the people living in that environment. The rapid growth of tourism in the twentieth century has produced both problems and opportunities on a vast scale for societies, and its impact has been economic, sociocultural, environmental and political. Governments have become aware that tourism is not merely a useful means of adding to a nation's wealth but also brings with it serious long-term problems which, without careful control and planning, can escalate to a point where they threaten the society.

The effects of tourism will be examined separately. First we will look at the economic effects and then go on to discuss the social and environmental effects.

THE ECONOMIC EFFECTS OF TOURISM

Like any other industry, tourism affects the economy of those areas in which it takes place and is a drain on the tourist generating areas. Students also need to examine the expenditure that goes out of the areas from which it originated. This effect may be important merely in a single place, such as a resort in a country otherwise untapped for tourism, in a region, or even throughout the entire national economy. Whatever the size of the area affected, we can generally categorise the economic effects of tourism into four groups; the effects on income, on employment, on the area's balance of payments with the outside world, and on investment and development.

Income

The creation of income from tourism is closely bound up with employment. Income in general comes from wages and salaries, interest, rent and profits. In a labour-intensive industry such as tourism the greatest proportion is likely to be in wages and salaries. Income is created most directly in areas with a buoyant level of tourism, labour-intensive accommodation such as hotels, and with a large number of attractions and ground-handling

arrangements available. The higher the amount of labour employed, the greater the income generated.

Income is greatest where wage levels are high, which implies that there are also other high-wage job opportunities and little unemployment in the area. However, tourism may be of *relatively* greater value in areas where there are few other jobs and workers may be otherwise unemployed. In Britain, tourism is significant in many regions where there is little other industry, such as in the Scottish Highlands, western Wales and Cornwall. The tourism industry is often criticised for offering low wages but in these areas there may be no alternative jobs available.

Income is also generated from interest, rent and profits on tourism businesses, which might range from the interest paid on loans to an airline in order to buy aircraft to rent paid to a landowner for a car park or campsite near the sea. We must also include taxation on tourism activities, such as VAT on hotel bills or direct taxation which some countries or regions impose on tourism to raise additional public income. In Austria, for example, there is a *Kurtaxe* imposed on accommodation to raise money for the local authority, while in the United States a *departure tax* is imposed by the federal government on all international travel.

The sum of all incomes in a country is called the national income and the importance of tourism to a country's economy can be measured by looking at the proportion of national income created by tourism. In Britain this is estimated to be about four per cent, including income from accommodation, tourist transport and all kinds of 'extras' for which tourists pay. This may seem small, but even engineering, the country's largest industry, only contributes about eight per cent to the national income. By contrast, tourism in Barbados contributes over 30 per cent to its national income – some would say this denotes a rather unhealthy over-dependence upon one single industry.

Tourism's contribution to the income of an area is in

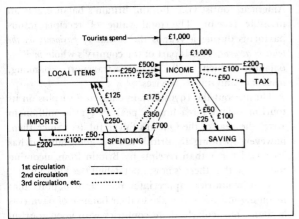

Fig 13.1 The tourism income multiplier at work

fact rather greater than has been so far apparent owing to the phenomenon of the tourism income multiplier (TIM). Multipliers are well-known to economists as a means of estimating how much *extra* income is produced in an economy as a result of the initial spending or *injection* of cash. Let us use an example to illustrate the TIM at work.

Example

Tourists visit area X and spend £1000 in hotels and on amenities there. This is received as income by hoteliers and amenity owners. These then pay tax, save some of their income and spend the rest. Some of what they spend goes to buy items imported into area X but the rest goes to shopkeepers, suppliers and other producers inside area X. These in turn pay taxes, save and spend.

Suppose that the average tax rate is 20p in the £, that people save on average 10p in the £ of their gross income and spend two-sevenths of their spending, or *consumption*, on imports. The £1000 spent by tourists will then circulate as shown in Fig 13.1.

Money is circulating as hoteliers spend on local supplies such as food. The suppliers of this food then pay their workers who in turn shop in local shops. Local shop workers in turn shop at other shops with the money they earn and so the cycle goes on. Some money has, of course, not circulated but has gone to pay tax, has been saved or has paid for imports; these are called *leakages* from the system.

So far, how much income has been created? From Fig 13.1 we can see it is £1000 + £500 + £250 + £125 + ... A progression is developing and by adding up all the figures or by using the appropriate mathematical formula the total will be seen to be £2000. The original *injection* of £1000 by tourists coming into area X has been multiplied by a factor of 2 to produce income of £2000.

It is possible to forecast the value of the multiplier if one knows the proportion of leakages in the economy. In the example above, tax was 20/100ths of original income, savings were 10/100ths of income and imports were 20/100ths of income. Total leakages therefore amount to 50/100ths, or a half of the original income. The multiplier can be found by applying the simple formula:

$$\text{Multiplier} = \frac{1}{\text{Proportion of leakages}}$$

In the example given the multiplier was $1\frac{1}{2}$, or 2.

So in an economy with a high proportion of leakages, such as high tax rates (although we must remember that the government may re-spend this money in the economy) or high import levels, TIM is rather low and tourism does not stimulate the local economy very much. On the other hand, with a low proportion of leakages, TIM will be high and tourism may in total contribute a great deal more income than that originally spent by the tourists themselves.

Many TIM studies have been undertaken, from single resorts such as Edinburgh or Eastbourne to entire countries such as Pakistan or Fiji. In general the value of the TIM has been found to range between about 1 and $2\frac{1}{2}$.

Employment

As well as income, tourism creates employment. Some jobs are found in travel agencies, tour operators and other intermediaries supplying services in the generating areas, but the bulk of jobs are created in the tourist destinations themselves, ranging from hotel staff to deck-chair attendants, from excursion booking clerks to cleaners in the stately homes open to the public.

A very large number of these jobs are seasonal or part-time so that tourism's contribution to full-time employment is considerably less than its contribution to 'job-hours'. Whilst this is a criticism of the industry in economic terms, and one that has resulted in many millions of pounds being spent in an attempt to lengthen the tourist season, once again one must remember that many of these jobs are being created in areas where there would be few alternative employment opportunities. Tourism is therefore relatively beneficial.

The multiplier which works for income also does the same for employment. If tourists stay at a destination, jobs are directly created in the tourism industry there. These workers and their families require their own goods, services, education and so on, giving rise to further indirectly created employment in shops, pubs, schools, hospitals. The value of the employment multiplier is likely to be similar to that of the TIM, assuming that jobs with average wage rates are created.

Recent developments in technology have tended to reduce labour requirements in the tourism generating areas. For example, computer reservations systems

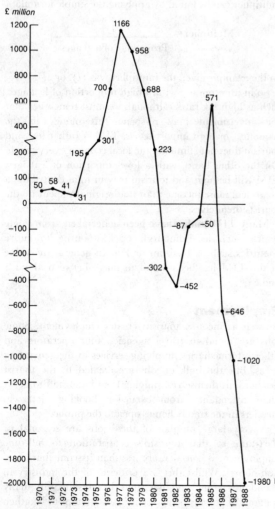

£ million

Fig 13.2 Britain's Balance of Payments on the Tourism account 1970–1988

American tourist visits Britain, Britain's balance gets an invisible receipt. The total value of receipts minus payments during a year is the *balance of payments on the tourism account*. This is part of the country's whole *invisible* balance, which will include transport, banking, insurance and similar services.

Throughout the 1970s Britain enjoyed a surplus on its tourism balance, reaching a peak of £1166 million in 1977, the year of the Queen's Silver Jubilee. Since then, however, spending by British tourists going abroad has increased faster than receipts by Britain from incoming tourists, so that there is now a net deficit (*see* Fig 13.2).

Most countries appreciate the contribution that incoming tourism can make to their balance of payments account, particularly those countries with good tourism facilities but little other industrial or agricultural export potential. They therefore take steps through their national tourist offices to maximise their tourist receipts. The contribution of tourism receipts to total balance of payments receipts in Britain is around six per cent. This may be compared with Spain, where a quarter of total receipts are attributable to tourism, while tourism may account for a third or more of the balance of payments receipts of some countries, such as the Caribbean islands, where economies have shifted away from the traditional agriculture to a major dependence upon tourists.

While incoming tourists in various countries are actively encouraged by the development of new attractions, promotions, specially subsidised exchange rates and other measures, most governments also try to keep their own residents within the country, either by promotions, taxation on outgoing tourists, limitation on foreign exchange availability, or refusal to grant exit permits (as in many Communist countries). These attempts to make tourists buy the domestic product instead of going abroad are a form of import substitution.

Investment and development

Once good business and income levels have been generated in an area, because of its success business people and government agencies may be influenced to invest even more in that area. This is known by economists as an *accelerator* concept. Thus if tourism to area X booms and the value of TIM is high, rapid expansion may lead to yet more investment in both tourism and other industries. Some parts of Spain which started to earn money from tourism during the 1960s have been successful in this way, attracting both new tourism developments and other industries keen to develop in an economically successful area. Other countries have sought to emulate this kind of development by providing the initial boost to tourism. Examples may be seen in Hawaii, Tunisia and the Languedoc-Roussillon area of France.

reduce the need for booking clerks by tour operators, airlines and group hotel owners. In destinations, however, the nature of the industry requires a high degree of personal service, which means that less jobs have been lost through technological change.

Balance of payments

In a national context tourism may have a major influence on a country's balance of payments. International tourists are generally buying services from another country and are therefore paying for 'invisibles'. Thus if a British resident goes on holiday to Spain there is an invisible payment on Britain's balance, and if an

Unfortunately there is no clear link between tourism growth and economic development, owing to many other complicating factors such as inflation, the ability of an area to diversify and the willingness of the local population to work hard. Investment therefore remains as risky as it does in any other industry.

THE SOCIAL AND ENVIRONMENTAL EFFECTS OF TOURISM

Countries subject to rapid growth in tourism, particularly where this is confined to small regions, will experience not just economic change but also social and environmental effects which will have both political and economic consequences. Where the influx of tourists is international in scope these social effects are compounded. This was recognised by the OECD in its report on the impact of tourism on the environment: 'A high quality environment is essential for tourism. On the other hand, the quality of the environment is threatened by tourist development itself which is promoted ... because of its economic importance.' Or, to put it briefly, tourism destroys tourism. In this section we will deal in turn with environmental and social consequences of mass tourism.

The environmental effects of tourism

The technological complexity of twentieth century living has led to various forms of pollution which are both initiated and compounded by tourism development in general and by travel in particular. Any large-scale tourist movement increases air pollution from jet aircraft, car and pleasure-boat exhaust fumes. All three forms of travel can contribute to unacceptable levels of noise in rural surroundings, and the over-use of motor boats in water recreation can damage the environment both by polluting the water and by the effects of constant 'wash' eroding river banks (this is very noticeable on the Norfolk Broads, which have been subject to damage by the many thousands of hire and private craft using the waterways during the summer season).

Perhaps the most immediately apparent form of environmental 'pollution' is aesthetic rather than physical. As an area of scenic beauty attracts greater numbers of tourists, so the natural landscape is lost to tourist development. The scenic countryside retreats before the growth of hotels, restaurants and other amenities catering for tourists' needs, while individual tourist attractions such as stately homes can, without careful control, suffer the consequences of providing for tourists' needs in terms of catering and toilet facilities and parking for coaches or private cars. A proliferation of directional signs or promotional material can reduce the visual appeal of a resort; at its extreme this is exemplified by some of the tourist resorts of the United States (although some might argue that in the case of towns such as Reno or Las Vegas, in Nevada, the forest of illuminated signs dominating the downtown districts at night are an important element of the attraction itself).

Again, lack of foresight in planning leads to a loss of harmony and scale in the construction of new buildings for tourists. The skyscraper hotel syndrome is ubiquitous, from Hawaii to Benidorm, and has led to a conformity of architectural style owing nothing to the culture or traditions of the country concerned.

Thoughtless tourists contribute to visual pollution by littering in areas such as picnic sites and by desecrating monuments with graffiti; Stonehenge is now no longer directly accessible to the public because of vandalism to the stones by scratching and the use of aerosol spray paints.

A further problem of mass tourism is that created by congestion. The subject of congestion can be considered in three ways. There is first the question of the *physical* capacity of an attraction to absorb tourists; car parks, streets, beaches, ski slopes, cathedrals and similar features all have a finite limit to the numbers of tourists that can be accommodated at any given time. However, a second consideration is the *psychological* capacity of a site – the degree of congestion which tourists will tolerate before the site begins to lose its appeal. Quantifying this is no easy matter since perception of capacity will differ, not just according to the nature of the site itself but according to the market which it attracts. A beach in, say, Bermuda will be seen as overcrowded much more readily than in, say, Bournemouth, while in a resort such as Blackpool trippers may tolerate a still higher level of crowding.

In so-called *wilderness* areas, of course, the psychological capacity of the region may be very low. From the viewpoint of hikers, areas such as the Derbyshire Peak District may not support more than a handful of tourists per square kilometre, although the mass influx to its major centres such as Dovedale on August Bank Holiday does not appear to deter the day trippers from the region. Indeed, it has been demonstrated in the case of Cannock Chase, near Birmingham, that this area of natural beauty draws tourists from the Midlands as much for its role as a social meeting place as for its scenic attraction.

The behaviour of tourists at wilderness sites will be a factor in deciding their psychological capacity. Many trippers to an isolated area will tend to stay close to their cars, and hikers who are prepared to walk a few miles from the car parks will soon discover the solitude they seek. This is obviously a key for tourism planners since by restricting car parking and access by vehicle in the more remote areas they can maintain the solitude of a region.

A third capacity is *ecological* in nature – the ability of a region to absorb tourists without destroying the balance

Fig 13.3 Coral reef, Whitsunday Islands, Great Barrier Reef, Australia
(*Courtesy Queensland Tourist and Travel Corporation*)

of nature. Open sites will suffer from the wear and tear of countless feet, particularly in fragile ecosystems such as sand dunes. Many dunes have been destroyed or seriously eroded in the United States by the use of beach buggies and in the UK by motor cycle rallying. Footpaths in areas such as Snowdonia in Wales have been eroded by over-use, soil being loosened by the action of walkers' feet and subsequently lost through wind erosion. In other cases soil has been impacted by walkers, making it difficult for vegetation to grow. Man-made sites have been similarly affected; the Acropolis in Athens has had to be partially closed to tourists to avoid wear and tear on the ancient buildings, while sites like Shakespeare's birthplace at Stratford-upon-Avon or Beaulieu Palace suffer similar wear from the countless footsteps crossing the floors and staircases of the building.

The ecological balance of a region can also be affected by 'souvenir-collecting' by visitors. The removal of plants has given rise to concern in many areas of the world,

and not only where rare plants are concerned. In Arizona visitors taking home cacti are affecting the ecology of the desert regions, while the removal of coral, either for souvenirs collected by the public or for commercial sale by tourist enterprises, threatens some coastal regions of Australia and elsewhere.

The sociocultural effects of tourism

The cultural and social impact on a host country of large numbers of people, sharing different value systems and away from the constraints of their own environment, is a subject being given increasing attention by social scientists and by the planners responsible for tourism development in third world countries. The impact is most noticeable in the lesser developed countries, but is by no means restricted to these; tourism has contributed to an increase in crime and other social problems in New York and London, in Hawaii and Miami, in Florence and on the French Riviera.

Any influx of tourists, however small, will make some

impact on a region, but the extent of the impact is dependent not just upon numbers but on the kind of tourists which a region attracts. The *explorer*, or tourist whose main interest is to meet and to understand people from different cultures and backgrounds, will fully accept and acclimatise to the foreign culture. Such travellers will try to travel independently and be as little *visible* as possible. However, as increasingly remote regions of the world are 'packaged' for wealthy tourists and as ever-larger numbers of tourists travel farther afield to find relaxation or adventure, these tourists bring their own value systems with them, either expecting or demanding the life-style and facilities they are accustomed to in their own countries.

At its simplest and most direct this flow of comparatively wealthy tourists to a region has the effect of attracting petty criminals, as is evidenced by increases in thefts or muggings – a problem that has become serious in some countries of the Mediterranean, Caribbean and Latin America. The tourist may be seen as easy prey to be overcharged for purchases; London has been pinpointed as just such an area, with street vendors exploiting tourists in the sales of ice-cream and other commodities. Where gambling is a corner-stone of tourism growth, prostitution and organised crime often follows.

There are also a number of less direct, and perhaps less visible, effects on the tourist localities. The comparative wealth of tourists may be resented or envied by the locals, particularly where the influx is seen by the latter as a form of neo-colonialism as in the Caribbean islands or East African countries. Locals may come to experience increasing dissatisfaction with their own standards of living or way of life and seek to emulate the tourists. In some cases the effect will be marginal, such as the adoption of the tourists' dress or fashion, but in others the desire to adopt the values of visitors may be sufficiently extreme as to threaten the deep-seated traditions of the community.

Job opportunities and higher salaries attract workers from agricultural and rural communities who, freed from the restriction of their family and the familiarity of their home environment, may abandon their traditional values. One result of this is an increase in the breakdown of marriages and in divorce.

The problem of interaction between hosts and tourists is that any relationships which develop are essentially transitory. A tourist visiting a new country for the first time, and who may be spending not more than a week or two in that country, has to condense their experiences such that these become brief and superficial. Add to this their initial fear of contact with locals and their comparative isolation from them – hotels are often dispersed well away from centres of local activity – and opportunities for meaningful relationships become very limited. Nor

are most such relationships spontaneous; contact is likely to be made largely with locals who work within the tourist industry or else it is mediated by couriers. Language may form an impenetrable barrier to genuine local contact and this limitation may lead to mutual misunderstanding. The relationship is further unbalanced by the inequality of tourist and host, not just in wealth; tourists are on holiday, while most locals they come into contact with will be at work which will often involve the host being paid to serve the needs of the tourist.

One must also remember that while the tourist's contact is fleeting, locals are in continuous contact with them throughout the season, which will affect their attitudes in their dealings with them.

With the constraints of time and place, the tourist demands *instant culture*. The result is what Dean MacCannell (*see* Bibliography) has termed *staged authenticity* in which the search by tourists for authentic experiences of another culture leads to that country either providing those experiences or staging them to make them appear as real as possible. Culture thus becomes commercialised and trivialised, as when 'authentic' folk dances are staged for package tourists as a form of cabaret in hotels or tribal dances are arranged specifically for groups of tourists on an excursion. This trivialisation is exemplified in London by proposals in some quarters that the Changing of the Guard might be mounted more frequently each day to give a greater number of tourists the opportunity of viewing it!

Tourists will seek out local restaurants not frequented by other tourists in order to enjoy the authentic cuisine and environment of the locals, but by the very act of their discovering such restaurants these then become tourist attractions and ultimately 'tourist traps' which cater for an increasing number of tourists, while the locals move on to find somewhere else to eat.

Tourists seek local artefacts as souvenirs or investments. In cases where genuine works are purchased this can lead to the loss of cultural treasures from a country. However, tourists are often satisfied with purchasing what they believe to be an authentic example of typical local art, and this has led to the mass production of poorly crafted works (sometimes referred to as *airport art*), common in the African nations, or to the freezing of art styles in pseudo-traditional forms, as with the 'mediaeval' painted wooden statues to be found in Oberammergau or other German tourist towns.

It is perhaps too easy to take a purist stance in criticising these developments. One must also point to the evident benefits which tourism has brought to the culture of many foreign countries, leading not only to tourists and locals alike widening their horizons but also to a regeneration in awareness and pride in their culture and traditions among the population. But for the advent

Fig 13.4 Ramayana Ballet performing in Bali,
Indonesia
(*Courtesy Garuda Indonesia*)

of tourism many of these traditions would have undoubtedly died out. It is easy to ascribe cultural decline to the impact of tourism, whereas it is likely to be as much a factor of increasing technology and mass communication and the dominant influence of western culture on the third world. In many cases tourism has led to the revival of interest in tribal customs in lesser developed countries (and not just in these lands – the revival of Morris dancing in English rural communities owes much to tourism, as the national tourist boards have been quick to recognise, and the boards have also done much to renew interest in traditional local cuisine with their 'Taste of England', 'Taste of Scotland' and 'Taste of Wales' schemes). Dying local arts and crafts have been regenerated and the growth of cottage industries catering for tourist demand has done much to benefit the economies of depressed regions.

Planning for conservation

The idea of the management of tourist attractions and their protection from the impact of mass tourism is not new; as early as 1872, the United States established the

first of its national parks at Yellowstone, while Europe's Abisco National Park in Sweden was founded as early as 1909. Meanwhile, in Britain growing concern over the possible despoliation of the Lake District led to the formation of a defence society in 1883 to protect the region from commercial exploitation. The National Trust was also founded in the nineteenth century, to safeguard places of 'historic interest and natural beauty'. They promptly bought $4\frac{1}{2}$ acres of clifftop in Cardigan Bay and have added over a half million acres, together with over 150 stately homes, castles, villages, farms, churches and gardens.

There are now ten national parks in Britain (*see* Fig 13.5), established under the National Parks and Access to the Countryside Act 1949. The National Parks are administered by National Park Authorities; either Boards, as in the case of the Peak District and Lake District National Parks, or Committees of County Councils. Central Government provides 75 per cent of the finances needed to run the parks, with the balance contributed by local authorities. This Act also led to the designation of twenty-seven areas (nearly eight per cent of the area of England and Wales) as 'areas of outstanding natural beauty' meriting protection against inconsiderate exploitation. Since then there have been numerous moves by government and private bodies designed to protect features of historical or architectural interest and areas of scenic beauty from over-development, whether from tourism or from other commercial interests. Abroad, too, Mediterranean and third world countries have awoken to the dangers of too rapid or uncontrolled development of tourism.

Planning, whether central or regional, is essential to avoid the inevitable conflicts arising between public and private sectors. Private enterprise, unrestricted, will seek to maximise its profits and this can often best be achieved by catering for high demand where this already exists rather than developing tourism in new regions. Airlines will find it more profitable to fill their services to London rather than encourage traffic to provincial cities, and hotels in a boom resort, seeking fast returns on their capital investment, will build large and comparatively cheap properties rather than concentrate on quality and design which will add to costs. Of course, it would be wrong to suggest that this will always occur – other organisations will see the market gaps left for better quality development – but without some form of central control to ensure good design and careful restoration of old buildings the original attraction of a traditional resort can be lost.

Local authorities can sometimes be a partner in this despoliation too, putting commercial advantage before aesthetic considerations; here central government needs to exercise final control. This can be done through building restrictions in designated areas, and through

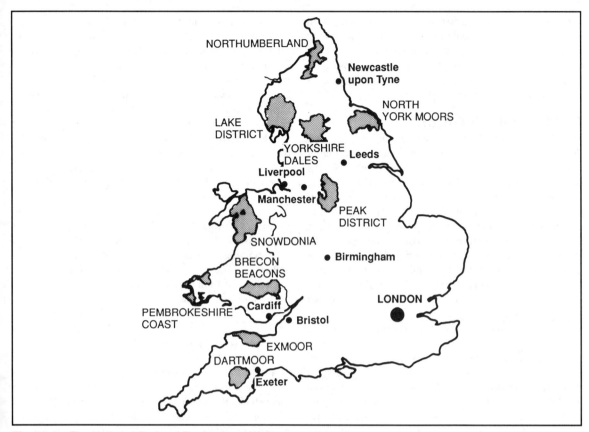

Fig 13.5 The National Parks of England and Wales

positive measures such as grants either to encourage sympathetically designed projects in keeping with the environment or to encourage development in specified areas. Although the original scheme has since been curtailed, Britain had designated certain 'growth points for tourism' which were intended to concentrate future tourism development in areas of potential while relieving the pressure on other rural areas.

Countries with a long history of evolutionary tourism development such as Austria and Switzerland have successfully expanded tourism without destroying their environment, while Spain, whose tourism boom was more recent and sudden, experienced massive over-development along its shorelines on the east coast and in the popular Balearic islands until the government stepped in to arrest this exploitation. Countries on the brink of mass tourism, such as Mauritius and certain Caribbean islands, have adopted a more cautious approach from the outset; close government restrictions on hotel construction in Mauritius, for example, have led to less intrusive developments of single- or two-storey buildings constructed in traditional local materials and in traditional architectural styles.

Government policies to attract larger numbers of tourists have given way to policies designed to attract particular tourist markets. While this has in most cases meant trying to attract wealthy 'high-spend' visitors, in some cases it has led to a move to encourage visits by those who will have least impact upon local populations, i.e. those who will integrate and accept local customs rather than seek to export their own customs.

Lesser developed countries have taken dichotomous approaches in trying to resolve the visitor-host confrontation. In some cases, as in Senegal and Indonesia, positive attempts have been made to avoid the development of tourism 'enclaves', thus ensuring more authentic contact with local inhabitants. Other countries, of which Tunisia is an example, have developed tourism resorts well away from populated areas, thus reducing the impact of tourists on the local population. This 'ghetto' policy of tourist development, while offering advantages in terms of environmental conservation, has the social consequences of alienating the tourist from the culture and life of the community. It also has the incidental effect of increasing the tourist spend within the hotels and other immediate facilities in the ghetto, which, should these be foreign owned, increases the leakage factor and reduces the benefits of tourism to the local shops, restaurants and entertainments. Tourism can also have longer lasting effects for host countries: for example someone who has visited Portugal in the past will often buy Portuguese wine from the supermarket in the future. The need remains for tourists and locals to be educated to understand one another better and tolerate each other's values so that tourists in particular are welcomed as guests in foreign countries rather than being seen as prospects for commercial exploitation.

THE FUTURE OF TOURISM

We have seen over these past chapters how tourism has developed to a level where it has become a major industry and a major influence for social change. We have also indulged in speculation about the future of tourism, with the possible economic and social consequences of international tourists increasing five-fold or ten-fold by the beginning of the twenty-first century. However, an increase in mass tourism on the scale of the expansion during the 1950–80 period is unlikely. The growth in economic wealth of the developed countries has slowed and economists are now uncertain whether a continual improvement in the material wealth of our society is possible, or even desirable.

Nevertheless, the world, and in consequence tourism, is in a period of rapid transition. Some nations are moving from an industrial society to a post-industrial one and life-styles and values are changing. The present desire to accumulate material possessions shows signs of lessening. The big question is will this result in a desire to accumulate experiences as eagerly as we formerly accumulated possessions? And what effect will this have on our desire to travel?

Forms of travel in the future will undoubtedly change greatly, influenced by changes in technology and in available energy sources. Aviation experts agree that the current development of the jet aircraft has reached a point where productivity and efficiency have peaked and the real costs of travel are unlikely to decline until some radical breakthrough in technology is achieved. This is likely to come early in the twenty-first century, with the development of aircraft capable of leaving and re-entering Earth's atmosphere. Plans for British Aerospace's experimental HOTOL (Horizontal Take-off and Landing) craft have been affected by the massive costs of development and the refusal on the part of the Government to commit public funds to the project; but certainly a version of this craft will eventually be built, if not in the UK then in the USA. HOTOL is capable of flights into space, carrying its own supplies of liquid oxygen to burn when beyond Earth's atmosphere, but using oxygen from the air, as does a normal airliner, when flying within the atmosphere. Orbiting the globe up to 185 miles above the Earth's surface, the aircraft is expected to be capable of flying between London and Sydney, Australia, in a little over one hour.

Meanwhile, research continues in other areas of advanced transport. In shipping, work is continuing on designs for more fuel efficient craft. Successful sea trials have taken place with vessels that complement the use of their engines with metal sails, increasing the overall speed while reducing costs. The appeal of cruise ships that resemble floating hotels with a full range of leisure facilities is leading to the construction of ever larger vessels. Proposals have been advanced for much larger catamarans and trimarans (twin hulled and triple hulled vessels) capable of transporting large numbers of passengers at high speed and in far more comfort, without the customary problems of motion sickness experienced in single hull ships. Such vessels might be constructed to cross the Atlantic in under 48 hours.

Japan, too, is working on the use of electromagnetic thrusters for ships. Toshiba has designed a 150 ton vessel which is pushed through water by the effect of counteracting magnets; they claim that the technique will be operational by 1991, and this could again lead to the development of vessels of much larger size.

On land, as we have seen, railway development is making great strides. Japan's Linear Express, capable of cruising at speeds up to 300 mph, has already reached its prototype stage, and may be in service by 1990. This vehicle has the advantage of superspeed and super quietness; the track consists of a metal trough generating a magnetic field which repels magnets in the train, causing the vehicle to ride 10 cms above the track. There is therefore little wear and tear, and in consequence, much reduced maintenance cost. If the technology proves successful, rail services could certainly pose a major threat to air routes of distances overland up to 1000 miles.

Some futurists have prophesied that there will be little need to travel away from home in the twenty-first century. Holographs are capable of reproducing any environment artificially, so that we will be able to recreate in the home any environment of our choosing to 'experience' foreign travel. This could include activity holidays such as simulating white water canoe and raft rides, winter sports or the piloting of an aircraft.

Other forecasters predict that underwater leisure cities will be built on the seabeds adjoining our coasts, where a controlled climate will make the annual exodus to the sun no longer necessary.

Some of these predictions take us into the realms of science-fiction. We can be safer in forecasting those short-term changes which are reinforcements of current trends and which are likely to take place during what is left of the twentieth century.

Holidays abroad have now become a habit for millions in the developed countries. Unless our economies take a marked turn for the worse, many will continue to insist on an annual break in the sun. This tendency spells trouble for the future of British seaside resorts, which have depended to far too great an extent on the habits of an earlier breed of holidaymaker.

Radical innovations to off-set the uncertainties of the British climate, such as indoor leisure complexes on a scale even greater than Center Parc's Sherwood Forest scheme, will be required in the future in our more traditional seaside resorts if they are to retain tourists. Efforts are being made in this direction by the more forward-thinking (and larger) resorts such as Blackpool and Bournemouth, but smaller resorts which depend on outdoor entertainment to attract the tourists could face a bleak future.

Some hope might be held out by the prospect of radical change in our attitude to sunbathing, brought about by the medical evidence linking sunbathing with skin cancer. In the short term, this fear is more likely to affect the older traveller than the young, who have largely chosen to ignore the evidence to date or, as with smoking, to feel that the risk is too remote for it to concern them. In the longer term, the message may get home, but reaction is more likely to be to cover up and to engage in different activities, rather than to shun the traditional sunshine holiday resorts of the Mediterranean.

Significant changes can be expected in the next few years in the field of business tourism. Some see advances in technology dispensing with the need for much of today's business travel, arguing that with closed-circuit television and inter-office computer linkups, personal meetings will not be necessary on present-day scales. The international conference market could well be seriously affected by these developments, but many people believe that business people will continue to need personal and social contact with their colleagues, which will ensure the continuation of much of today's pattern of business traffic. The growth of the travelling business-woman will doubtless continue, and hotels and other suppliers of tourist facilities will need to adapt their products to the special needs of female travellers to gain the support of this market.

Changes in life style will affect the traditional forms of holiday accommodation. The desire for greater flexibility, coupled with advances in 'convenience' food and more adventurous eating habits, suggest that the swing to self-catering, with more meals out for 'special occasions', will continue, at the expense of hotels and guest house accommodation, unless, again, these can be made attractive alternatives by providing a wider range of leisure facilities for their guests at no added expense. Activity and special interest holidays organised by small specialist tour operators will proliferate to cater for a more educated and adventurous tourist market.

As numbers travelling abroad increase, many holidaymakers will seek to move up-market. Value for money will play a more important role, *vis-à-vis* low price. Long haul holidays can be expected to continue to outpace short haul in rate of growth. British tourists will take more frequent holidays (already the number taking at least four holidays of four or more nights is approaching one million), and more short breaks.

Advances in computer reservations will allow individual holidaymakers to select their destinations, accommodation and flights, put together their own packages, book and pay for the booking by direct debit to their bank account, all without leaving their armchair. Already British Telecom has initiated a programme of experimental 'computerised shopping' along these lines. The ability to book from home would suggest a rise in impulse booking, and demand for even more 'late availability' products, coupled with a decline in traditional patterns of advanced booking. Indeed, if the consumer can 'package' their own arrangements at home at the push of a button and can conjure up on their home TV screen all the images of the resorts they wish to choose from, the question must be asked – will this make the tasks of both tour operator and travel agent obsolete by the year 2000?

QUESTIONS AND DISCUSSION TOPICS

1 Should Britain impose a tax on its visitors from overseas as a means of raising revenue to support tourism growth? If so, how should this tax be imposed: on hotel beds, departing tourists, or some other way?

2 Static caravan sites are frequently criticised for the 'visual pollution' they bring to a scenic region. Is present legislation to control caravan sites sufficient, and what more needs to be done?

3 Is there an inevitable conflict between conservation and tourism development? Can any examples be found in Britain where the two are in harmony?

4 Argue the case for and against ghetto development for tourism in lesser developed countries.

ASSIGNMENT TOPICS

1 As a member of your local authority's sub-committee on tourism and leisure, you are constantly frustrated by the apparent failure of your Councillors to understand the benefits which tourism can bring to your area. In Council meetings there are constant references to 'a candy floss industry', 'Mickey Mouse jobs' and the inevitable low-paid seasonal work which Council members believe to be the typical picture of the tourism business.

The Council is now preparing to debate expenditure amounting to some £18 million for a new Conference and Exhibition Centre for the town. This is meeting a lot of resistance, both within the Council and from ratepayers and the local press. You have been invited to address the Council to explain the advantages of the investment.

Prepare a set of notes for your talk, which includes an explanation of the multiplier effect presented in a form which will be easily understood by your audience. Give some examples of how the multiplier could affect the economy of the area.

2 You have been retained as a consultant by the local authority of a town nearby, which attracts tourists, to examine the adequacy of visitor signposting. Prepare a report suggesting how signposting can be improved to help traffic flow and to attract visitors to more sites. You should make reference in your report to the need to avoid damage to the environment, and show how this can be achieved by good design and planning.

Bibliography

Adamson, Simon H, *Seaside Piers*, Batsford 1977

Addison W, *English Spas*, Batsford 1951

Airey D and Bamford R G, *Travel Agents' and Tour Operators' Liability and its Insurance in Great Britain*, University of Surrey 1981

Alderson F, *The Inland Resorts and Spas of Britain*, David and Charles, 1973

American Express, *World Tourism Overview*, American Express Publishing Corp (annual)

Anon, *Careers in the Travel Industry*, Kogan Page, 1985

Archer B H, *Demand Forecasting in Tourism*, University of Wales Press, 1976

Archer B H, *The Impact of Domestic Tourism*, University of Wales Press, 1973

Archer B H, *The Importance of Domestic Tourism as a Development Factor for the Developed and Developing Countries*, Institute of Economic Research, 1975

Archer B H, *Tourism Multipliers: the State of the Art*, University of Wales Press, 1977

Ashworth M and Forsyth P, *Civil Aviation Policy and the Privatisation of British Airways*, Institute for Fiscal Studies, 1984

Association of British Travel Agents, *Annual Report*, ABTA (annual)

Association of British Travel Agents, *Computer Systems for Small Tour Operators*, ABTA 1985

Association of British Travel Agents, *Computer Systems for the Retail Travel Agent*, ABTA 1985

Association of British Travel Agents, *Survey of Attitudes by the British to Holidays in UK and Abroad*, ABTA 1980

Association of District Councils, *Tourism: a Handbook for District Councils*, ADC 1982

Baldwin R, *Regulating the Airlines: Administrative Justice and Agency Discretion*, OUP 1985

Banks R, *New Jobs from Pleasure: a Strategy for Creating New Jobs in the Tourist Industry*, The Bookshop Smith Square 1985

Baron R, *Travel and Tourism Data – a Comprehensive Research Handbook on World Travel*, Euromonitor 1987

Beaver A, *Mind Your Own Travel Business*, Beaver Travel 1979

Benson D and Whitehead G, *Transport and Distribution*, Pitman 1985

Binney M, *Our Vanishing Heritage*, Arlington 1985

Binney M and Hanna M, *Preservation Pays: Tourism and the Economic Benefits of Conserving Historic Buildings*, SAVE Britain's Heritage

Bishop J, *Travel Marketing*, Bailey Bros & Swinfen 1981

Boniface B and Cooper C, *The Geography of Travel and Tourism*, Heinemann 1987

Bosselman F, *In the Wake of the Tourist: Managing Special Places in Eight Countries*, Conservation Foundation 1978

Bouquet M and Winter M, *Who from their Labours Rest? Conflict and Practice in Rural Tourism*, Avebury 1987

British Tourist Authority, *Annual Report*, BTA (annual)

British Tourist Authority, *Britain's Historic Buildings: a Policy for their Future Use*, BTA 1980

British Tourist Authority, *The British Domestic Holiday Market: Prospects for the Future*, BTA 1982

British Tourist Authority, *The Channel Tunnel: an Opportunity and a Challenge for British Tourism*, BTA 1988

British Tourist Authority, *The Future of British Spas and Health and Pleasure Resorts*, BTA 1980

British Tourist Authority, *International Tourism and Strategic Planning*, BTA 1979

British Tourist Authority, *Legislation affecting Tourism in the UK*, BTA 1982

British Tourist Authority, *The Measurement of Tourism*, BTA 1974

British Tourist Authority, *Museums: Lessons from the USA*, BTA

British Tourist Authority, *Promoting Tourism to Britain: How the BTA can Help*, BTA 1977

British Tourist Authority, *Report on Overseas Visitors and Stately Homes*, BTA 1983

British Tourist Authority, *Selling UK Tourism Products through ABTA Agents*, BTA 1982

British Tourist Authority, *Strategy for Growth 1986–1990*, BTA 1986

British Tourist Authority, *Survey of Overseas Visitors to London Museums*, BTA 1983

British Tourist Boards, *Resorts and Spas in Britain*, BTA 1975

British Travel Educational Trust (C Smith), *New to Britain: a Study of Some New Developments in Tourist Attractions*, BTA 1980

Brougham J and Butler R, *The Social and Cultural Impact of Tourism: a Case Study of Sleat, Isle of Skye*, Scottish Tourist Board 1977

Bryden J M, *Tourism Development: a Case Study of the Commonwealth Caribbean*, CUP 1973

Burkart A J and Medlik S, *The Management of Tourism*, Heinemann 1975

Burkart A J and Medlik S, *Tourism: Past, Present and Future*, Heinemann 1981

de Burlo C, *The Geography of Tourism in Developing Countries: an Annotated Bibliography*, Council of Planning Librarians (Chicago) 1980

Burton A and P, *The Green Bag Travellers: Britain's First Tourists*, Deutsch 1978

Butler J, *The Economics of English Country Houses*, Policy Studies Institute 1981

Cabinet Office Enterprise Unit, *Pleasure, Leisure and Jobs: The Business of Tourism (the Young Report)*, HMSO 1985

Cahill W D and Neale C A, *The Economic Impacts of Recreation and Tourism: a Selective Bibliography*, Council of Planning Librarians (Chicago) 1979

COIC (Careers and Occupational Information Centre), *Skills for the Tourist Industry*, COIC 1986

Carpenter S and Jones P, *Recent Advances in Travel Demand Analysis*, Gower Press 1982

Carsberg B and Lumby S (Eds), *Privatising British Airports Authority*, Public Money Publications 1984

Cassee E and Reuland R, *The Management of Hospitality*, Pergamon 1983

Casson L, *Travel in the Ancient World*, George Allen and Unwin 1974

Centre for Urban and Regional Studies (CURS), *The South Wales Valleys: Realising the Tourism Potential*, University of Birmingham 1983

CERT, *The Scope of the Tourism Industry in Ireland*, 1987

Channel Tunnel Joining Consultative Committee (Kent Impact Study), *The Channel Tunnel: a Strategy for Kent*, 1987

Civil Aviation Authority, *Annual Report*, CAA (annual)

Chairman's Policy Group, *Leisure Policy for the Future: a Background Paper for Discussion*, Sports Council 1983

Cleverdon R C, *The USA and UK on Holiday*, EIU 1983

Committee of Enquiry into Civil Air Transport (Edwards Report), HMSO 1969

Coppock J T, *Second Homes: Curse or Blessing?*, Pergamon 1977

Corke J, *Tourism Law*, Elm Publications 1988

Cornforth J, *Country Homes in Britain: Can They Survive?*, Woodcote 1974

Curran P, *Principles and Procedures of Tour Management*, CBI (Boston) 1978

Dann G and Sethna R, *Guide to the Tourist*, Eastern Caribbean Printers (Barbados) 1977

Delgado A, *The Annual Outing and Other Excursions*, George Allen and Unwin 1977

Devas E (Ed), *The European Tourist: a Market Profile*, Tourism Planning and Research Associates 1985

Dilsaver L M, *The Effects of International Tourism: a Bibliography*, Council of Planning Librarians (Chicago) 1977

Doganis R, *Flying off Course: The Economics of International Airlines*, George Allen and Unwin 1985

Doswell R, *Case Studies in Tourism*, Hutchinson 1978

Doswell R et al, *Further Case Studies in Tourism*, Hutchinson 1979

Doswell R and Gamble P, *Marketing and Planning Hotels and Tourism Projects*, Hutchinson 1979

Dower M, *Tourism Enterprise by Local Authorities: a Review of New Developments*, ETB 1982

Drower J, *Good Clean Fun: The Story of Britain's First Holiday Camp*, Arcadia 1982

EIU (Economist Intelligence Unit), *Air Inclusive Tour Marketing: the Retail Distribution Channels in the UK and West Germany*, EIU

EIU, *Choosing Holiday Destinations: the Impact of Exchange Rates and Inflation*, EIU 1987

EIU, *Developing Strategies for the World's Airlines*, EIU 1988

EIU, *The Economic and Social Impact of International Tourism on Developing Countries (Special Report No 60)*, EIU 1979

EIU, *International Business Travel: a New Megamarket*, EIU 1988

EIU, *Seasonality in Tourism*, EIU 1975

Edgerton R, *Alone Together: Social Order on an Urban Beach*, Univ of California Press 1979

Edington J and M A, *Ecology, Recreation and Tourism*, CUP 1986

Employment, Department of, *Action for Jobs in Tourism*, HMSO 1986

Employment, Department of, *Tourism 87: Making the Most of Heritage*, HMSO 1987

English Tourist Board, *Academic Research into Leisure, Recreation and Tourism*, ETB 1982

English Tourist Board, *Annual Report*, ETB (annual)

English Tourist Board, *Aspects of Leisure and Holiday Tourism*, ETB 1981

English Tourist Board, *Curtain up on the Resorts*, ETB 1984

English Tourist Board, *Developing a Touring Caravan or Camping Site*, ETB

English Tourist Board, *English Churches and Visitors*, ETB 1984

English Tourist Board, *English Heritage Monitor*, ETB (annual)

English Tourist Board, *The Facts about the Tourism and Leisure Industries*, ETB 1986

English Tourist Board, *Financing Tourist Projects*, ETB 1983

English Tourist Board, *Future Marketing and Development of English Seaside Tourism*, ETB 1974

English Tourist Board, *Holiday Home Development: Multi-Ownership*, ETB 1981

English Tourist Board, *Holidays on England's Rivers and Canals*, ETB 1979

English Tourist Board, *How to approach a Bank for Finance*, ETB

English Tourist Board, *Jobs in Tourism and Leisure: an Occupational View*, ETB 1986

English Tourist Board, *The Impact on Hotel Pricing Policies of Development and Operating Costs – an International Comparison*, ETB 1982

English Tourist Board, *Letting Holiday Properties*, ETB

English Tourist Board, *Local Government and the Development of Tourism*, ETB 1979

English Tourist Board, *Management of Touring Caravans and Camping*, ETB 1979

English Tourist Board, *Planning for Tourism in England*, ETB 1981

English Tourist Board, *Proposed Major Conference and Exhibition Centres*, (periodically updated)

English Tourist Board, *Prospects for Self-Catering Development*, ETB 1980

English Tourist Board, *The Provincial Theatre and Tourism in England*, ETB 1983

English Tourist Board, *Purpose Built Chalets and Cabins*, ETB

English Tourist Board, *Putting on the Style*, ETB 1981

English Tourist Board, *Raising the Standard*, ETB

English Tourist Board, *Report of the Working Party to Review TIC Services and Support Policies*, ETB 1981

English Tourist Board, *Services of the Clearing Banks for Developers in London*, ETB

English Tourist Board, *Starting a Bed and Breakfast or Guest House Business*, ETB 1981

English Tourist Board, *Surveys on Regional and Resort Brochures: a Practical Guide*, ETB 1975

English Tourist Board, *Tourism and the Inner City*, ETB 1980

English Tourist Board, *Tourism and Urban Regeneration: Some Lessons from American Cities*, ETB 1981

English Tourist Board, *Tourism and Leisure: the New Horizon*, ETB 1983

English Tourist Board, *Tourism Enterprise by Local Authorities: a Review of New Developments*, ETB 1982

English Tourist Board, *Tourism Multipliers in Britain*, ETB 1976

English Tourist Board (S Medlik, Ed), *Trends in Tourism: World Experience and England's Prospects*, ETB 1983

English Tourist Board/Trades Union Congress, *Holidays: the Social Need*, ETB 1976

EEC (European Economic Community), *Tourism and the Economic Community*, EEC 1985

European Travel Commission (ETC), *The Changing Face of European Tourism*, ETC 1984

European Travel Commission, *European Tourism 1980–1990*, ETC 1983

European Travel Commission, *Seasonality in the Transatlantic Vacation Market*, ETC 1983

Finney B R and Watson K A (Eds), *A New Kind of Sugar: Tourism in The Pacific*, Honolulu East-West Centre 1975

Foster D, *Travel and Tourism Management*, Macmillan 1985

Frater J, *Farm Tourism in England and Overseas*, Centre for Urban and Regional Studies (CURS) University of Birmingham 1983

Gamble P, *Small Computers in Hospitality Management*, Hutchinson 1984

Gay J, *Travel and Tourism Bibliography and Resource Handbook*, Travel and Tourism Press (California) 1981

Gearing C et al, *Planning for Tourism Development: Quantitative Approaches*, Praeger 1976

Gee C et al, *The Travel Industry*, AVI (Westport) 1984

Goodall B and Ashworth G, *Marketing in the Tourism Industry: the Promotion of Destination Regions*, Croom Helm 1988

Gordon S, *Holidays*, Batsford 1972

Gorman M et al, *Design for Tourism*, Pergamon 1977

Gray H P, *International Travel, International Trade*, Heath Lexington 1970

GLC (Greater London Council), *Tourism: a Paper for Discussion*, GLC 1978

GLC, *Tourism: a Statement of Policies*, GLC 1980

Greene M, *Marketing Hotels into the 90s*, Heinemann 1981

Gullen H V and Rhodes G E, *Management in the Hotel and Catering Industry*, Batsford 1983

Gunn C, *Tourism Planning*, Crane Russak 1979

Gun C, *Vacationscape: Designing Tourist Regions*, University of Texas 1972

Hanna M and Marris T, *English Cathedrals and Tourism: Problems and Opportunities*, ETB 1979

Haulot A, *Social Tourism: Thought and Action 1963–1980*, Bureau Internationale du Tourisme Sociale (Brussels) 1980

Havins P J N, *The Spas of England*, Robert Hale 1976

Hawkins D E et al (Eds), *Tourism Marketing and Management Issues*, George Washington University 1980

Hawkins D E et al (Eds), *Tourism Planning and Development Issues*, George Washington University 1980

Heeley J, *Regional and Local Planning for Tourism: a Historical Perspective*, University of Strathclyde 1979

Henderson D M et al, *The Economic Impact of Tourism: a Case Study of Greater Tayside*, TRRU, University of Edinburgh 1975

Heneghan P, *Resource Allocation in Tourism Marketing*, TIP 1976

Hern A, *The Seaside Holiday*, Cresset 1967

Hesmondshalgh S (Ed), *Run a Successful Travel Agency*, Which? Business Publications 1984

Hewison R, *The Heritage Industry: Britain in a Climate of Decline*, Methuen 1987

Hibbert C, *The Grand Tour*, Weidenfeld and Nicholson 1969

Hibbs J, *Bus and Coach Management*, Chapman and Hall 1985

Hill J M M, *The Holiday*, Tavistock Institute of Human Relations 1965

Hindley G, *Tourists, Travellers and Pilgrims*, Hutchinson 1983

Hodgson A, *The Travel and Tourism Industry: Strategies for the Future*, Pergamon 1987

Holloway J C and Plant R V, *Marketing for Tourism*, Pitman 1988

Holloway J C, *The Role of the Excursion Guide: an Interactionist Perspective*, University of Surrey (unpublished MSc Thesis) 1979

Horne D, *The Great Museum: the Representation of History*, Pluto Press 1984

Houston L, *Strategy and Opportunities for Tourism Development* (Planning Exchange Occasional Paper), Planning Exchange 1986

Hudman L, *Tourism: a Shrinking World*, Grid (Ohio) 1980

Hudson K, *Air Travel: a Social History*, Adams and Dart 1972

Hudson K and Pettifer J, *Diamonds in the Sky: a Social History of Air Travel*, BBC Publications 1979

Hunziker W, *Social Tourism: its Nature and Problems*, Alliance Internationale de Tourisme 1951

International Air Transport Association (IATA), *World Air Transport Statistics*, IATA (Geneva) (annual)

Jakle J A, *The Tourist: Travel in 20th Century North America*, University of Nebraska Press 1985

James G W, *Airline Economics*, Lexington Books 1982

Jordan and Sons (Surveys) Ltd, *British Travel Agents and Tour Operators*, Jordans (periodic)

de Kadt E, *Tourism – Passport to Development?* OUP 1979

Kaiser C and Helber L E, *Tourism Planning and Development*, Heinemann 1978

Kamp J, *Air Charter Regulation: a Legal, Economic and Consumer Study*, Praeger 1976

Kelly J, *The Recreation Business*, John Wiley 1985

Kent County Council, *The Channel Tunnel and the Future for Kent*, Kent CC 1986

Keynote Publications, *Tourism in the UK*, Keynote 1984

Keynote Publications, *Travel Agents and Overseas Tour Operators*, Keynote 1988

King J R and Brumwell R A, *The Tourism Gap: Can it be Bridged?* Laventhol, Krekstein, Horwath and Horwath 1972

Krippendorf J, *The Holiday Makers: Understanding the Impact of Leisure and Travel*, Heinemann 1987

Lavery P, *Travel and Tourism*, Elm Publications 1987

Lawson F and Baud-Bovy M, *Tourism and Recreation Development: a Handbook of Physical Planning*, Architectural Press 1977

Lea J, *Tourism and Development in the Third World*, Routledge 1988

Leisure Studies Association, *Tourism: a Tool for Regional Development*, LSA/University of Edinburgh 1977

Lewes F and Brady G, *Holidays in Britain*, Ginn and Co 1970

Lewes F et al, *Leisure and Tourism*, Heinemann 1975

London Tourist Board, *Tourism in Greater London: an Assessment of Current Needs*, LTB 1982

Lowe D, *The Bus and Coach Operators' Reference Book*, Cornhill Publications (annual)

Lundberg D and C, *International Travel and Tourism*, John Wiley 1985

Lundberg D, *The Tourism Business*, Cahners (Boston) 1980

Lynch J, *Airline Organisations in the 1980s*, Globe Information Services 1984

MacCannell D, *The Tourist: a New Theory of the Leisure Class*, Schocken (NY) 1976

Mathieson A and Wall G, *Tourism: Economic, Physical and Social Impacts*, Longman 1982

Mayo E J and Jarvis L P, *The Psychology of Leisure Travel*, CBI (Boston) 1981

McIntosh R and Goeldner C, *Tourism: Principles, Practices and Philosophies*, John Wiley 1984

Medlik S, *The Business of Hotels*, Heinemann 1980

Medlik S and Airey D, *Profile of the Hotel and Catering Industry*, Heinemann 1978

Metelka C J (Ed), *The Dictionary of Tourism*, Merton House 1981

Middleton V, *International Tourism Reports: England and Wales*, Economist Publications 1986

Middleton V, *Marketing in Travel and Tourism*, Heinemann 1988

Middleton V, *Tourism in Wales: an Overview*, Wales Tourist Board 1980

Middleton V, *Tourism Policy in Britain: a Case for a Radical Reappraisal*, EIU 1974

Mill R C and Morrison A, *The Tourism System: An Introductory Text*, Prentice Hall 1985

Mills E, *Design for Holidays and Tourism*, Butterworth 1983

Moir E, *The Discovery of Britain: the English Tourists 1540–1840*, Routledge and Kegan Paul 1964

Monopolies and Mergers Commission, *Foreign Package Holidays*, HMSO 1986

Morell J, *Employment in Tourism*, BTA 1985

Moynahan B, *The Tourist Trap*, Pan 1985

Murphy P E, *Tourism: a Community Approach*, Methuen 1985

National Consumer Council, *Air Transport and the Consumer: a Need for Change?* NCC 1986

National Consumer Council, *Freedom of the Air: Competition and the Domestic Airlines – a Consumer View*, NCC 1983

National Consumer Council, *Package Holidays: Dreams, Nightmares and Consumer Redress*, NCC 1988

Nelson Jones J and Stewart P, *A Practical Guide to Package Holiday Law and Contracts*, Fourmat 1985

North R, *The Butlin Story*, Jarrolds 1962

O'Connor W E, *Economic Regulation of the World's Airlines*, Praeger 1971

Organisation for Economic Cooperation and Development (OECD), *The Impact of Tourism on the Environment*, OECD 1980

Organisation for Economic Cooperation and Development, *International Tourism and Tourism Policy in OECD Member Countries*, OECD (annual)

Pape R, '*Touristry – a Type of Occupational Mobility*', Social Problems 2/4 Spring 1964

Patmore J A, *Land and Leisure*, David and Charles 1980

Patmore J A, *Recreation and Resources: Leisure Patterns and Leisure Places*, Blackwell 1983

Pearce D, *Tourism Today: a Geographical Analysis*, Longman 1986

Pearce D, *Tourist Development*, Longman 1981

Pearce P, *The Social Psychology of Tourist Behaviour*, Pergamon 1982

Peters M, *International Tourism*, Hutchinson 1969

Pimlott J A R, *The Englishman's Holiday*, Harvester Press 1977

PTRC Education and Research Services, *Planning for Tourism in Developing Countries*, PTRC 1986

Reilly R, *Travel and Tourism Marketing Techniques*, Delmar 1980

Rosenow J et al, *Tourism: the Good, the Bad and the Ugly*, Century Three Press 1979

Sampson A, *Empires of the Sky: the Politics, Contests and Cartels of World Airlines*, Hodder and Stoughton 1984

Schmoll G A, *Tourism Promotion*, TIP 1977

Scottish Tourist Board, *Annual Report* (annual)

Scottish Tourist Board, *Planning for Tourism in Scotland*, STB 1977

Sealey N, *Tourism in the Caribbean*, Hodder and Stoughton 1983

Senior R, *The Travel and Tourism Industry*, Euromonitor 1983

Senior R, *The World Travel Market*, Euromonitor 1982

Seward S and Spinrad B, *Tourism in the Caribbean: the Economic Impact*, International Development Research Centre (Ottawa) 1982

Shaw S, *Air Transport: a Marketing Perspective*, Pitman 1981

Shepherd J, *Marketing Practice in the Hotel and Catering Industry*, Batsford 1982

Shivji I G (Ed), *Tourism and Socialist Development*, Tanzania Publishing 1975

Sigaux G, *History of Tourism*, Leisure Arts 1966

Smith S L J, *Tourism Analysis: a Practical Handbook for Students*, Longman 1988

Smith V (Ed), *Hosts and Guests: an Anthropology of Tourism*, Blackwell 1978

Swinglehurst E, *Cook's Tours: the Story of Popular Travel*, Blandford Press 1982

Swinglehurst E, *The Romantic Journey: the Story of Thomas Cook and Victorian Travel*, Blandford 1974

Taneja N K, *Airline Planning: Corporate, Financial and Marketing*, Lexington Books 1982

Taneja N K, *Airlines in Transition*, Lexington Books 1981

Taneja N K, *Airline Traffic Forecasting*, Lexington Books 1978

Taneja N K, *The Commercial Airline Industry*, Lexington Books 1976

Taneja N K, *US International Aviation Policy*, Lexington Books 1980

Taylor D, *Fortune, Fame and Folly: British Hotels and Catering from 1878 to 1978*, Caterer and Hotelkeeper 1977

Tiltscher R, *An Investment Review of the UK Hotel Industry*, Sector Investments 1983

Tourism and Recreation Research Unit (TRRU), *Recreation Site Survey Manual: Methods and Techniques for Conducting Visitor Surveys*, C and F N Spon 1982

Tourism Planning Research Associates, *A Profile of European Holidaymakers*, TPRA 1985

Trade, Department of, *Court Line Ltd: Final Report*, HMSO 1978

Transport, Department of, *Airline Competition Policy*, HMSO 1984

Transport, Department of, *Airports Policy*, HMSO 1985

Transport, Department of, *Fixed Channel Link Report of UK French Study Group*, HMSO 1982

Transport, Department of, *Review of Arrangements for Protecting the Clients of Air Travel Organisers (Lane Report)*, HMSO 1984

Travel Association's Consultative Council, *The Anatomy of UK Tourism*, TACC 1982

Travis A S et al, *The Role of Central Government in Relation to the Provision of Leisure Services in England and Wales*, CURS, University of Birmingham 1981

Turner L and Ash J, *The Golden Hordes: International Tourism and the Pleasure Periphery*, Constable 1975

Wahab S, *Tourism Management*, TIP 1975

Wahab S, *Tourism Marketing*, TIP 1977

Wales Tourist Board, *Annual Report*, WTB (annual)

Wales Tourist Board, *More Money from Tourism: a Practical Guide for Welsh Farmers*, WTB 1974

Wales Tourist Board, *A Survey of Community Attitudes towards Tourism in Wales*, WTB 1981

Wales Tourist Board, *Tourism in Wales: a Strategy for Growth*, WTB 1983

Walvin J, *Beside the Seaside: a Social History of the Popular Seaside Holiday*, Allen Lane 1978

Ward C and Hardy D, *Goodnight Campers! The History of the British Holiday Camps*, Mansell 1986

White J, *A Review of Tourism in Structure Plans in England*, CURS, University of Birmingham 1981

Williams A and Shaw G, *Tourism and Economic Development*, Belhaven Press 1988

Wood M, *Tourism Marketing for the Small Business*, ETB 1980

World Tourism Organisation (WTO), *World Tourism Statistics*, WTO (Madrid) (annual)

Young G, *Tourism: Blessing or Blight?* Pelican 1973

KEY TRADE, PROFESSIONAL AND ACADEMIC MAGAZINES AND JOURNALS OF RELEVANCE TO TRAVEL AND TOURISM

ABTA News	monthly
AIEST Tourist Review (Revue de Tourisme) (Switzerland)	quarterly
Airline World	weekly
Annals of Tourism Research (USA)	quarterly
ASTA Travel News (USA)	monthly
British Travel Brief (BTA)	quarterly
British Traveller	monthly
Buses	monthly
Business Traveller	10 p a
Business Travel World	monthly
Coaching Journal and Bus Review	monthly
Countryside Commission News	monthly
Executive Travel	monthly
Executive World (British Airways)	monthly
Flight International	weekly
Holiday Which? (Consumers Association)	quarterly
ICAO Bulletin	monthly
In Britain (BTA)	monthly
International Tourism Quarterly (EIU)	quarterly
Journal of the ITT	quarterly
Journal of Leisure Research	quarterly
Journal of Transport Economics and Policy	Jan/May/Sep
Leisure Management	monthly
Leisure Studies (Leisure Studies Association)	quarterly
Motor Transport Weekly	weekly
Revue de l'Academie Internationale du Tourisme	quarterly
Service Industries Journal	Mar/Jul/Nov
Tourism (Bulletin of the Tourism Society)	quarterly
Tourism in Action (ETB)	monthly
Tourism Intelligence Quarterly (BTA)	quarterly
Tourism Management	quarterly
Transport (CIT)	bi-monthly
Transport Management (ITA)	quarterly
Transport Reviews	quarterly
Travel Agency	bi-monthly
Travel Business Analyst	10 p a
Travel GBI	monthly
Travel News	weekly
Travel Research Journal	quarterly
Travel Trade Gazette	weekly
Travel Trade Gazette Europa (Continental edition)	weekly
World Travel (*Tourisme Mondiale*) (WTO)	bi-monthly

Index

Also available from Pitman Publishing

Travel and Tourism Assignments

Produced by the Travel and Tourism Programme for the new GCSE in Travel and Tourism. Founder Business Partners for the Programme are the American Express Foundation, the British Tourist Authority/English Tourist Board, Crest International Leisure Group, Hotels International and Trusthouse Forte Hotels.

Travel and Tourism Assignments Pack 1

1989 / 224 pages A4 Ringbinder / ISBN 0 273 03078 7

Travel and Tourism Assignments Pack 2

Following the same lively format as Pack 1, this pack concentrates on travel and tourism and technology, design aspects of travel and tourism, leisure time activities, food service and communication strategies for working with visitors from abroad.

1990 / 224 pages A4 Ringbinder / ISBN 0 273 03079 5

LISA
YORK